Lacan in the German-Speaking World

Lacan in the German-Speaking World

Edited by
Elizabeth Stewart
Maire Jaanus
and
Richard Feldstein

Translated by
Elizabeth Stewart

State University of New York Press

Cover image: Caspar David Friedrich, Wanderer above the Sea of Fog, 1818; Oil on canvas, 94 x 74.8 cm; Kunsthalle, Hamburg. Courtesy of Bildarchiv Preußischer Kulturbesitz, Berlin.

Published by
State University of New York Press, Albany

© 2004 State University of New York

For information, address State University of New York Press,
90 State Street, Suite 700, Albany, NY 12207

Production by Judith Block
Marketing by Susan Petrie

Library of Congress Cataloging-in-Publication Data

Lacan in the German-speaking world / edited by Elizabeth Stewart, Maire Jaanus, and
    Richard Feldstein ; translated by Elizabeth Stewart.
        p. cm. — (SUNY series in psychoanalysis and culture)
    Includes bibliographical references and index.
    ISBN 0-7914-6087-8 (alk. paper) — ISBN 0-7914-6088-6 (pbk. : alk paper)
        1. Psychoanalysis—Europe, German-speaking. 2. Lacan, Jacques, 1901– I. Stewart,
Elizabeth. II. Jaanus, Maire. III. Feldstein, Richard. IV. Series.

BF173.L135 2004
150.19'5'092—dc22   2004042989

10 9 8 7 6 5 4 3 2 1

Contents

Part III   Clinical

Part IV   Philosophical

Acknowledgments

We wish to thank Cary Plotkin for his help with translations from Latin and French, Richard G. Klein for his help in finding references, and especially Peter Widmer for help with everything and for steadfast support, faith, and friendship throughout. At State University of New York Press we wish to give special thanks to Henry Sussman and James Peltz for their interest, ever ready assistance, and guidance.

General Introduction

MAIRE JAANUS AND ELIZABETH STEWART

Beyond the United States there is a growing global—one could perhaps say "intercivilizational"—community of interest in the Lacanian legacy. Various cultures are in the process of developing interpretations of Lacan and, in many instances, appear engaged in the adaptation of Lacan's ideas to their own specific historical, cultural, and geographic-linguistic experiences, and their own traumas. The German-speaking domain is no exception.

Lacan in the German-Speaking World is a first collection of its kind and contains some of the best essays that have appeared on Lacan in Germany, Austria, and Switzerland. All were originally published in *RISS*, the Swiss journal founded in 1986 by Peter Widmer that has done the most to promote Lacanian studies in the German-speaking world. *RISS* also published certain translations from the French that it considered particularly pertinent to its interests and of these we have included five (the essays by Bernard Baas, Monique David-Ménard, Alain Juranville, Anne Juranville, and André Michels.) *RISS* is an abbreviation for the Real, Imaginary, and Symbolic (and echoes the seminar entitled "R.S.I."). The second S stands for Subject and *Schrift* (meaning "writing" or "letter"). *RISS* also resonates with the Freudian terms *Abriß* (as in *Abriß der Psychoanalyse—An Outline of Psycho-Analysis*); *Abriß* also means "hasty sketch" or "draft," a "summary"—that is, something abbreviated, perhaps torn off; it also resonates with *Grundriß* (outline), similar in meaning to *Abriß*, but with the additional semantic element of "foundation" *(Grund)*; in any case, both carry within them the meaning of something "torn off" from a whole or outlined on a "ground." *Riß* itself means "tear," "rent," "laceration," "fissure," "gap," "break," or "flaw," as well as "plan," "design," "schism," and "breach"; all these meanings relate to the symptom, the inevitable concomitant of flawed human nature, or, one can perhaps say, the defective "design" with which it sutures its sufferings. The symptom forms where the fundamental break occurs between body and language.

These associations are fundamental to all of the articles translated here, as is the even more central one of the traumatic nature of the tear, of "being torn into" or "rent apart," "slit," "dragged," or "seized," which are the various meanings of the verb *reißen* (to tear). On the whole, it is possible to generalize about these articles by saying that they circle around the hole of the Real, trauma, and a psychotic form of melancholia, while addressing this hole from the perspectives of the fantasm, castration, and sacrifice (both in its historically ominous and in its restitutional or subliminatory sense). The authors frequently refer to the cultural, historical, and sociopolitical ramifications of their psychoanalytic investigations, and, in addition, to modernist and avant-garde art and literature, thus centering the birth of psychoanalysis where it belongs—that is, in early-twentieth-century Europe and its historical catastrophes and consequent psychic devastation. The historical disasters these authors retain as their background and the political and social "dangers" they keep in the foreground, together with their rigorous deconstructive impulse and their abiding interest in the centrality of trauma, anxiety, and constructedness in Freud's and Lacan's theories—all this is profoundly instructive and may become more so as we enter a new historical period of increasingly possible ecological and nuclear emergencies, intercivilizational conflict, and outbursts of genocide.

Lacan lectured in Zurich in 1949, in Vienna in 1955, and in Munich in 1959. His work, however, began to be known more widely in these countries only gradually after the publication of the French *Écrits* in 1966. Recognized at this time primarily as a central author of Structuralism, he was often taken to task for his supposed indifference to history. This "misreception" began to be corrected after 1973, a turning point in the reception of Lacan in Germany when the first volume of his collected work appeared in German. Subsequently, work groups formed, especially in Strasbourg, Heidelberg, and Karlsruhe, and the Sigmund Freud Schule was founded in Berlin but subsequently dissolved in 1987. Various journals with a Lacanian orientation appeared: *Wunderblock* in 1978 in Berlin; *frag-mente* in 1981 in Kassel; *RISS*, *Wo Es War*, and *Arbeitshefte*, *Kinder-Psychoanalyse* in 1986. However, Slavoj Žižek's *Wo Es War* put out only a few issues; *Wunderblock* also disappeared, and *frag-mente* was never exclusively Lacanian. *RISS* alone continued to appear regularly and to put out a wide-ranging and intensive series of special issues on focused topics: *Interpretation* 1988; *Identification* 1989; *Oedipus?* 1990; *the Mother* 1991/92; *Music* 1992/94; *Psychoses* 1993; *Kleist* 1993; *Perversion* 1994; *Phallus* 1994; *Democracy* 1995; *Psychosomatik* 1995; *Semiotic* 1995; *Derrida/Lacan* 1996; *Obsession* 1996; *Object* 1996; *Philosophy* 1997; and *Film* 1997. A similar range of interests is reflected in nearly every essay we have included.

Because there have been almost no translations hitherto of the work on Lacan in the German language, our collection is a translation in a double sense:

a literal translation and a transference, an effort to introduce to America something of the interpretive work on Lacan in Germany. Although a German Lacan (in contrast to the French Lacan) can in some sense perhaps never exist any more than can a truly German Aristotle or Homer, yet the better known American, British, and Spanish acquisitions of Lacan do differ from each other and from the German interpretations, which are rooted in the philosophers close to Lacan: Kant, Hegel, Husserl, and Heidegger—and the deconstruction of these philosophers. Also extraordinary here is the attention given to the exegesis, language, and precise translation of Freud by Lacan. A further interesting commonality in this German-speaking reception of Lacan, aside from the centrality of historical trauma, anxiety, and the deconstruction of metaphysics, is their focus on the order of the Real and their often brilliantly detailed elaboration of the operations of the *object a*, the concept Lacan particularly claimed as his original invention. In addition, because of their specific vantage point, nearly all authors foreground the body in various and fascinating ways.

The essays presented in this volume overlap in significant ways: they are modernist in conception and orientation, are linked to a specific historical sense, and, in a more muted form, are postmodernist in their adherence to Lacan's reading of Freud. Many of them make reference to modernist art as a traumatic art form that can throw light on the structure of psychic trauma. With the birth of psychoanalysis as a modernist phenomenon itself, these essays not only illuminate the common frame of reference of psychoanalysis, Surrealism, Dada, Expressionism, and high modernism, but also treat Lacan's philosophical frame of reference in modernist and postmodernist fashion. In all cases we see the recognition of trauma, anxiety, vertigo, and the illusoriness of stable meaning as the proffered paradigm for human experience. Lacan's roots in surrealism are continuously highlighted, implicitly and explicitly. There is emphasis on sacrifice, sublimation, and mourning, and on the threat of fascism, murder, and collective psychosis. The essays are also highly relevant to theorizations of the legacy of European fascism, to the problem of memory and amnesia, and to the scars of historical trauma. Finally, basic to all of the authors represented here is a powerful sense of the historical significance of psychoanalysis, often together with an acute awareness of the historical and political task of psychoanalysis, and, even more importantly, of psychoanalytic discourse.

Because of the far-reaching spectrum of interests, perspectives, and themes dealt with by nearly all these authors, we have organized our selection of nineteen articles from *RISS* into the broad encompassing categories of cultural, sexual, clinical, and philosophical, and our attempt to give synopses of what is offered under each of these catgories will be found at the beginning of each section.

Part I
Cultural

Introduction

Maire Jaanus and Elizabeth Stewart

With Sebastian Leikert's essay, "The Object of *Jouissance* in Music," we turn to the frequent cultural association of Germany with music and to writing on the body, a topic picked up later by André Michels. Both phenomena stand in a close relationship to the breaching of the limits of the pleasure principle and therefore to *jouissance* and perversion. Music and bodily scars are mediated by the figure of the castrato, who performs the dramatic opposition of the "cry of the angel," inundated as it is with *jouissance,* on one side, and on the other, a mutilated body carrying marks and scars. Leikert argues that the seduction exerted on most everyone by the "uncut," full voice of the castrato is that of the *objet a* as voice, liberated from the musical signifier and from its binary logic and meaning. The castrato's "absolute" voice, unmarked by castration, becomes a sublime fetish, and its "cry," the sound of the cadenza that transgresses the borders of tonal articulation, culminates in *jouissance.* The castrato presents himself as the fetish, the impossible gateway to absolute enjoyment. But this blissful musical moment, in which "the cry manages to trace the impossible," while still covering the Real, depends on a temporal cut with symbolic musical notation and a surgical cut on the body. In the figure of Michael Jackson, the castrato of our time, the Other's law of castration is inscribed into the bodily Real—in the shape of the cuts and scars incurred by his many plastic surgeries— even as his voice continues to be the object of fascination.

By way of shifting the focus away from the son's murderous feelings directed at the father and towards the murderousness of the father (or parents) directed at the child, Peter Widmer, in his essay, "On Murder, or: Tell's Projectile," examines an aspect of the Oedipus complex that is most often shrouded in silence: parents' hatred for their children, and thus also the subversive real and imaginary elements at work within the symbolic order. The focus here is on

5

the possibility of infanticide rather than patricide. This essay is the first of several in this collection that deal with the question of sacrifice within the constellations of the Real, the Imaginary, and the Symbolic. Widmer asks: which order sacrifices which other order and when does it do so? If the Symbolic "murders" the Real, the Real and the Imaginary also repeatedly "murder" the Symbolic, and so on. Widmer's key question is: are oedipal and family relations just a reflection of the "splitness and nonidentity of the registers" or even of the registers' mutual "hatred"? In the saga of Wilhelm Tell, particularly as taken up by Schiller, the motivation for the (more or less repressed) murderous hatred of Tell for his son, at whom he aims his weapon, is largely imaginary in origin: Tell may be motivated by a jealous desire to separate mother and son, but he is no Chronos, as part of his motivation is to separate them in order to initiate the son into the Symbolic. As Widmer points out, "This apple-shooting scene stages the crucifixion as negation." The conflictedness of the orders and their inter-relationship with the subject therefore avoid the murder that would introduce the Real. On the other hand, the *akeda* (Abraham's almost-sacrifice of his son Isaac) may be the counterparable to Tell's shot insofar as the latter is moti-vated by Tell's imaginary possessiveness. In this case, symbolic unpredictability (the child's move toward independence) would appear to the father as a murderous attitude on the part of the child vis-à-vis the parents' control, which, in turn, unleashes murderous anxiety. Widmer ends the essay with a curt, fascinating epilogue on Dali's painting, *The Enigma of Wilhelm Tell* (a work he created in the same year Hitler came to power). Here Tell becomes the representative of what Dali perceived to be his father's cannibalistic authoritarianism, and with that Widmer sets the tone for many of the essays that follow.

Borens's essay, "Perversion: Tragedy or Guilt?" turns to the world of trag-edy and the correlations between tragedy and perversion. The world of tragedy is marked by rigid repetition and a lack of mediation in its emphasis on un-changeable fate. It is a world of natural laws, unchangeable and absolute, which has more to do with need than with desire, and with the maternal symbolic rather than the paternal. It was superseded by our world of guilt, duty, and contracts. The world of the pervert is tragic and fated to repeat its own pure lack, hence static and rigid. Nature, as the inexorable and implacable, is tragic and disjunct from culture. It is the realm of the mother, a natural world of all-compelling needs, seductions, and arbitrary coincidences that lies apart from the father's world of cultural law, of crime and punishment. This natural world is the excuse and explanation for the pervert's actions. The pervert is aware of the domain of the father (as the psychotic is not), but unwilling to recognize it. The father's world is ridiculed as powerless and meaningless. The pervert belongs fundamentally to a world of nature as the neurotic does to that of culture. Borens's essay is one of a number of essays in this collection that interpret the differential uses of metaphors by patients representing the various neurotic and psychotic structures. The pervert, Borens claims, tends to use metaphors of flora, fauna, and minerals—the unchangeable world. The pervert is incapable of joining the world of guilt, which is also the world of recognition, and remains stuck in the world of tragedy, marked by a sense of unchangeable fate, powerlessness, dependency, submissiveness, and of being delivered over to arbitrariness. Don Juan, the archetypal pervert, remains situated in the tragic and preethical world of the maternal, forever repetitiously staging his drama of seduction and of being seduced, the scenario of the tragic pleasure of mother and child that the father has no power to neutralize. It is fruitful to link this essay to the one by Rudolf Bernet in chapter 6 on the rigid repetition typical of pornography and its lack of mediation, recognition, and symbolic play, all of which constitute sexuality. Both make the final disquieting suggestion that our contemporary world seems to be reentering the world of tragedy, closer to the Real, to woman, to *jouissance,* and also to perversity, rigidity, and fetishism.

Saalfrank's essay, "Identification in the Name of Lolita," strengthens this suggestion. Saalfrank's focus in his examination of the structure of perversion is on identification. Identification, he points out, cannot be fusionary unification, but is instead "the realization of a split"—say, the split or cut between the character on stage with whom the spectator identifies, and the body of the spectator sitting in the audience. Both, the desire for identification and the desire of the identified with object, enter into this split. Identificatory desire, in order to maintain itself, is aimed at lack itself, pure desire, the Real, and possessing the abyss. While a neurotic like Odysseus both encounters and avoids this abyss by listening to the Sirens' song tied to the mast, the pervert seeks to possess his object—the "abyss"—from as many perspectives as possible. Identification is a basic topic in almost all of these essays, as in its pathological variant it constitutes the gateway to the seduction by the Real, to melancholia, psychosis, and the perversions. Saalfrank is interested in it here as the pervert's demand for a transcendental object: desire, in the pervert, is for "desire-become-figure," that is, the demand that the variability, the play, of the symbolic cease and crystallize itself. (This is an ominous demand as it links up with the group identificatory processes described by Freud in *Group Psychology and Analysis of the Ego,* often read as a sort of blueprint for the structure of fascism, the love for a leader born of a spell of fascination.) The most extreme scenario of identificatory perversion would be necrophilia, in which the demand for the rigid embodiment of desire "is met." These three essays end, then, with the image of a corpse as the product of the disavowal of absence.

The role of rhetoric and aesthetics in Lacanian psychoanalysis is central to August Ruhs's essay, "The beauty Behind the Window Shutters," the last one in this Cultural section. In his presentation of truth in psychoanalysis—that is, the unconscious—the unfillable hole and inaccessible good, as the "Beauty,"

Ruhs is not only making reference to the Kantian elements in Lacan, but even more so to Lacan's lifelong affiliation with surrealism. Thinking of the unconscious not only in terms of negation, but also as a poetic and rhetorical whirlpool, makes clear the place of aesthetics in Lacan's discourse, as well as his surrealist stance of rejecting common sense. Ruhs discusses Lacan in relation to Nietzsche and Freud. All three recognized the truth of the unconscious as Baubo, but due to their different cultural-historical conditioning, each reacted differently to the discovery. Nietzsche wanted at first a rebirth of tragic art but later an art that valued appearances—"another kind of art, mocking, light, fleeting, divinely untroubled, divinely artificial." Freud sought refuge in a chemical formula, in a return to biological language and the kind of definition and closure that also defined the novelistic style of his time, and Lacan reacted in an art-for-art's-sake way, in the style of surrealism, playfully yet seriously attempting to match the uncertain, accidental style of the unconscious itself as it revealed itself primarily in and between words and images. Ruhs argues that Lacan was more capable than Freud of facing, with laughter, the truth of the unconscious as Baubo, as an anxiety-producing, irrational uncertainty. Psychoanalysis for Ruhs is as well an art of interpretation that is fundamentally aesthetic in that it constructs, reconstructs, or perceives behind the analysand's language the objects and references of his words, which are sensual and carnal. Thus, psychoanalytic interpretation is not for the sake of meaning, as was classical hermeneutics; rather, it is an interpretation for the sake of the "history of the conditions of love." With Lacan it becomes necessary to think of truth together with the senses and to shut out understanding because in the imaginary perspective the unconscious appears as sensuousness.

1

The Object of *Jouissance* in Music

Sebastian Leikert

> Denn das Schöne ist nichts
> als des Schrecklichen Anfang, den wir noch gerade ertragen,
> und wir bewundern es so, weil es gelassen verschmäht,
> uns zu zerstören.
>
> For beauty is nothing
> but the beginning of terror, which we are just able to bear,
> and we admire it so because it serenely disdains
> to destroy us.
>
> —Rainer Maria Rilke, *Duineser Elegien*, "Erste Elegie"

I

The brilliant labyrinth of music is one of the last psychic strongholds that have remained closed off to us and that have evaded the comprehensive grasp of psychoanalysis. Despite a tradition of psychoanalytic texts attempting to do so, not one of them has yet managed to reveal the concealed meaning of music. Is it not possible that the reason for this is that it is fundamentally wrongheaded to attempt to approach the discourse of music from the vantage point of meaning—that is, the register of neurosis? Isn't the single and most penetrating aim of music to produce *jouissance*—which belongs to the register of perversion whose polymorphously oscillating willfulness refuses to let itself be bound to the imaginary destination of univocal meaning?

The concept of perversion does not, in this context, imply an obscure erogenous zone in the eardrum; it refers, instead, to a use of the signifier, which, sublimated to a greater or lesser degree,[1] leads into a praxis of pleasure.

Conceiving of music as perversion enables one to avoid the pitfall of attempting to assign to it a meaning it does not possess, while it still forces one to accept the challenge to reveal within it those structures that mark the vicissitudes of the drive uncovered by Freud in 1915. In his commentary on this text Lacan accentuates the role of the object: the signifier in this context is a mere "envelope . . . something other than what it dresses in. What is fundamental at the level of each drive is the movement outwards and back in which it is structured."[2] The drive cycle enfolds an object; for this reason it is easy to understand why the object lies at the center of interest of those Lacanian texts that treat the problem of music and that are of interest to us here.

<h1 style="text-align:center">II</h1>

This essay will carry a similar accent, and we will, therefore, confine ourselves to just a minimal definition as far as the musical signifier is concerned. We are in this context only interested in the fact that the musical signifier articulates; how it does so, or in what way this articulation is different from the articulation of speech, will not concern us. Somewhat reductively, perhaps, we presuppose the identity of the signifier in music and musical notation, that is, the actual musical score.

Well, now one could ask, what could there possibly be aside from the score? After all, the score is everything; we have nothing but the score. The entire (musical) "canon," music historical literature—the symphonies of Beethoven, the operas of Mozart, and so forth—has been handed down to us solely in the form of scores, and it would be impossible to claim that in themselves these scores are in any way lacking. And, in fact, they are lacking in nothing—nothing except *jouissance*, that is: as long as the Real of the notation is not infected with the other Real, the bodily Real of the voice, music remains dead as far as the subject's enjoyment is concerned.

Music produces *jouissance* only when it sounds.[3] Only when a singer lends it his voice, or when a musician lends it the voice of his instrument, is it actualized. Only when the musician *sacrifices* his body to the musical signifier, only by *losing* his body to it, does music become real. And it makes no difference whether one actively plays it oneself or just listens to it; the voice is the object of the signifier in the sense that the former is articulated by the latter. The voice is the signifier's material, is subjugated to it; as soon as music sounds, the voice disappears under the despotism of the signifier.

This fundamental opposition between the musical signifier, which can be recorded simply and unambiguously, and its material aspect—the sound, the timbre, the "life" of music—requires no further elaboration. What *is* surprising is that the latter is referred to as the "object" of music even as it evades, in its vagueness and amorphousness, all objectlike consistency. And yet it is this *objet sonore*[4] that the French authors always come back to when discussing that element in music that is of interest to psychoanalysis.

This seeming contradiction is resolved, however, when one remembers that the object in psychoanalysis is always thought of as a *lost* object. Only as a lost object does it become the object of the drive. It is unnecessary to trace again the conceptual paradigm *[das Denkbild]* of the lost object—primary experience of satisfaction, secondary tension produced by the pressure of the drive, cathexis of the memory trace, and so on; rather, let us point out that Lacan adds two more objects to Freud's original list of the objects of the drive: to the "classics"—*the breast, the faeces,* and *the phallus*—Lacan adds *the gaze* and *the voice.* In Lacanian terminology these objects—with the exception of the phallus, which, after all, for Lacan, has the status of an imaginary signifier—are referred to as *objet a.*

J.-A. Miller[5] points out that the last two objects owe their discovery to Lacan's psychiatric practice and, in fact, it is almost incomprehensible—when one recalls that the psychotic subject, for example, is confronted by "the voices" as object in the course of an "episode"—how this particular object could have evaded the attention of other psychoanalysts.

In relation to music, now, it will be propitious to clear up two potential fallacies concerning the voice as object. It is surely incorrect to bring this object into too close a proximity with the psychoses; this object plays a role in neurosis as well—for example, in the "voice of conscience" of the superego. But the "historical fallacy" must be avoided as well: the voice as object is not the voice of a historical person in the subject's life, as, for example, the voice of the father, which the subject then looks for again in music. To approach our subject matter, it is necessary to review the general concept of the *objet a* in order then to analyze methodically the concrete condition of music.

The *objet a* is the object of *jouissance,* the object of the "primary experience of satisfaction," where the word "primary" must be understood in its logical, not in its historical, sense. This object is then, in Freud's terminology, represented by a memory trace, that is, it is symbolized, recorded into the register of signifiers. This representation, however, does not take place without a loss of some kind. The signifier, which is supposed to bind the experience of *jouissance,* covers it up, makes it disappear. Precisely by re-presenting it, the signifier leaves it behind; the prefix *re* is clear on this always unsuccessful attempt to repeat the original *jouissance*—the result is always a merely dull imitation, an insipid substitute.

Within this relation between *jouissance* as the full presence of the Real and the representation of pleasure through the agency of the signifier we can already see the foundations for the structure of the oedipal complex: the prohibition of pleasure by the law of the signifier; "Mommy and Daddy" are, from this point of view, merely the contingent figures of a necessary structure.

This prohibition modifies the subject's relation to *jouissance* in a fundamental way: the *objet a* is no longer the *object of jouissance,* but becomes, as a lost object, *the origin of desire*. The *objet a* becomes the aim of a search which from the start has been condemned to failure insofar as the subject has been surrendered to the law of the signifier.

III

The figure of the castrato is surely an example of how far this search for the lost object can go in music. The tradition of the castrato, which became extinct only in the middle of the last century, exemplifies this mission with irreproachable clarity: what is at stake is the *jouissance* of the absolute voice. Between the worship and the horrified revulsion that the voice of the castrato has aroused, it is clear that, as a phenomenon, it has not left anyone cold; it has prompted that split in the listener that is characteristic of the encounter with the object of *jouissance*.

Apparently, no sacrifice is too great in this search for the voice as such in music: before his voice breaks, the singer's scrotal genital glands are split apart in order to retain the high vocal register; consequently, the secondary marks of sexual identity, and, of course, male potency as well, are completely lacking. Because of a fuller resonance within the chest as well as greater technical and expressive maturity, the voice of this "adult child" then develops that characteristic power and suppleness the fascination with which is obvious in all its historical descriptions.

The logic of this sacrifice must, however, not be understood as a logic of oppression or degradation, but rather, as G. Wajeman[6] shows in his brilliant historical study of the Neapolitan opera in the sixteenth century, as a necessary evil to endure within the context of a much greater gain. After all, the astonishing thing about the castrato is not that he is castrated, but rather that he has chosen castration as actual castration.[7]

The gain of this choice is easy to understand considering the condition of things we sketched out above: the castrato reverses the loss which the signifier causes the [ordinary, that is, noncastrated] subject; *he does not constitute himself as the subject of the signifier, but rather identifies himself with the object of jouissance.* "The castrato," says Wajeman, "demonstrates the truth of the object which is at stake in the opera; as he alternately conceals and reveals it, the object exhibits the opera's sublime fetish around which every singer—be it man, woman or castrato—circulates. In this sense, the opera was not made for the castrato, but rather he himself is the opera."[8] "The castrato presents himself as the exact formula of the fetish, as the object of *jouissance*, which can establish itself only on the basis of lack."[9]

To recognize the castrato as the *fetish* of music means to inscribe music into the register of *perversion*, in other words, into that register, among the three possible existential structures as they have been outlined by Freud, which has a direct relation to *jouissance*. While *jouissance* is prohibited in neurosis (which exhibits no structural difference with "normality"), in psychosis it enforces itself delusionally and in paranoid fashion as the *jouissance* of the absolute Other— in Schreber's central delusional idea, for example, of being the woman or wife of God *[das Weib Gottes]*. But even perversion, even though it denies the fact of castration, stands in a given relationship to castration; the figure of the castrato provides almost comically concrete evidence for this.

This relationship transcends the historical and the anatomical; even though the castrato tradition no longer in fact exists, it continues to exist virtually, in structure, and the position of the castrato is even today still attractive. It is surely no accident that the fetish of today's music industry—Michael Jackson, the best-paid singer worldwide—situates the image of himself on the far side of sexual difference, on the other side of castration. In addition, Jackson's cut-up face demonstrates how here, too, in a manner that coincides uncannily with the castrato, the fantasm of the Other's law of castration is inscribed into the bodily Real. The surgeons' knives, which have continually and over years transformed Jackson's own features into their pale angelic monstrance that today adorns the music industry's storehouse of images, have left scars which can be concealed only by heavy layers of make-up.

This is the price of beauty, of prestige, of being the cause and object of desire. The absolute prestige of this position, which in the case of Michael Jackson translates literally into ready money, can be found also, in a slightly different form, in Neapolitan opera, where paradoxically precisely the roles of the holders of unlimited power, the roles of the sovereign, of the emperor, were played by castrati. "The only form of agreement that played a role here was that between the power of the role and the power that the voice exerted over the audience's desire,"[10] says M. Poizat in this connection in his book on opera.

IV

The figure of the castrato leads us into the structure of music without allowing us to refer to its concrete and material elements. This figure offers us something like a condensed, summary image of one aspect of music. The subjective position which the castrato realizes in his very being also appears at a certain point in the development *[Ablauf]* of a piece of music. Two other authors, who support our thesis, share this point of view: in his book, *L'opéra ou le cri de l'ange*, Poizat interprets the history of opera within this perspective. According to Poizat, both the development of the genre as such and the development of each individual opera is geared towards isolating this "object of *jouissance*."[11] This "cry of the angel" is the culmination of what drives, obsesses even, the lover of opera; this moment, in which the voice as such peels away, detaches itself, and with the cry almost frees itself from the chain of signifiers, is the point of extreme *jouissance*

for which the opera goer pays his money. It is this culture of the voice that
drives him to follow his operatic star in the star's travels.

It is not possible, in the context of this short article, to gloss one or the
other of the works Poizat discusses; we will attempt to show below, in terms of
another musical form, where this object inscribes itself. Important for us is that,
according to Poizat, it is in this cry that the opera reaches its goal.

Let us for a moment examine this cry from a theoretical viewpoint: we
have been prepared for its structure by the figure of the castrato. It is the
attempt to bind *jouissance* beyond the signifier by giving the Real—what has
been covered up and excluded by the signifier—a graspable presence. And it is
precisely the difference with the articulating function of the signifier that this
"moment of the voice" throws into relief: this cry consists of a single held note,
usually in a high register. Poizat speaks in this context of "the other silence, that
which results from destruction, petrifying silence, absolute presence, unbroken
by the pulsation of the rhythm of presence and absence."[12] The beat of the
signifier is abandoned here; the object voice, which in itself is not binarily
organized, contradicts the articulative logic of the signifier, opposes it with the
pure presence of sound.

That this is a general phenomenon is made clear by the fact that in his
text, "De quatre temps subjectivants dans la musique,"[13] Didier-Weill offers a
completely parallel analysis of the execution of a jazz improvisation. He applies
to the object voice the term that Chopin gave it; he speaks of the "blue note":
"Should you hear, for example, a truly inspired jazz improvisation, you will
surely be astonished by the fact that the web of notes, by which you will allow
yourself to be carried, will unfailingly lead you to a certain point of which one
can certainly say that it—the blue note and its concomitant explosion of sense,
where a temporal rupture takes place—already announces itself in the preceding
notes. . . . In this sense it is the fulfillment of a promise, the vehicle of which
had been the preceding musical discourse."[14]

The temporal rupture of which Didier-Weill speaks is yet another sign for
the opposition between object and signifier: the order of time which, as a
relational construction of presence and absence, is the work of the signifier, goes
out of service at the moment of *jouissance*. Just as in delirium—which, of course,
is also a breaking-in of *jouissance*—the coordinates of time and space get lost,
so here, too, the order of the signifier is momentarily suspended.

Again it is the binary logic of the signifier, that is, a logic that constantly
refers to an Other—in this case it refers to and thereby articulates another
moment in time—that the object contradicts. The unmodulated roughness of
the *objet sonore*, which seems to stretch out into the limitlessness of silence
without referring to anything else, precludes the dismembering cuts and splits
of the signifier.

V

The battle carried out in musical works consists in bringing the contradiction between the signifier and the object of music into an appreciable form. The central European tradition of instrumental concerts since the Baroque has found an especially clear way of retrieving from the ornament of the signifying web the object voice: namely, in the cadenza. In the classical violin concerto the virtuoso is here given a space in which he can drive the work to its climax. Simply the circumstance that here the only sounding voice is the violin allows the object to separate off from the other voices in brilliance and prestige. Originally this part of the work had been improvised; that is, it had situated itself, in a sense, outside of the sphere of the signifier of the Other, whose "slave"[15] the soloist had been up until this moment. The relationship to time changes as well, and does so doubly: on the one hand, the cadenza, insofar as it is improvised, is produced directly by this moment, and is not bound in duty to the fixed letter of the score; on the other hand, it is played as a rubato—the ordering time of the signifier is loosened towards the reality that lies on the other side of it.

At first, it is true, it is the soloist's virtuosity, his mastery over the musical signifier, that stands in the foreground; but the space given to sonorous materiality increases in size during the course of the cadenza, until, finally, a single, stretched-out trill in an extremely high register concludes the cadenza in a condensed climax before the orchestra joins in again. Here all the features that play a role in the moment of the voice converge: the showing, the exhibiting of the object of pleasure beyond the signifying articulation, the accentuation of its material character in the flickering of the trill and the rupture of the temporal flow at the culminating point of the work.

VI

The instant of the voice is situated, as the moment of pure *jouissance*, outside of the signifier and is in that sense to be understood as the latter's central lack *[vide]*. In his Seminar on *The Ethics of Psychoanalysis*, Lacan writes, "*Tout l'art se caractérise par un certain mode d'organisation antour de ce vide*" [All art is characterized by a certain mode of organization around this emptiness].[16] Music corresponds to this program insofar as it deploys its art in order to close in on this instant and to frame it. In the same Seminar Lacan applies to the encounter with this lack the term "the beautiful," the function of which is—and this corresponds entirely to the quotation from Rilke above—to bind and cover up the horror of castration, which is coterminous with the encounter with the unbearable.

This is a paraphrase of the comprehensive topological schema which Lacan outlines in "The Subversion of the Subject and the Dialectic of Desire in the Freudian Unconscious."[17] The central lack corresponds to $S(\cancel{A})$, the signifier of the lack of the Other which he identifies with *jouissance*. From there we move into the formula for the fantasm—($\cancel{\$} \diamond a$)—where the split subject determines its place in reference to the object, which covers up the lack of the Other. This manner of notation accentuates the split subject by putting the element $\cancel{\$}$ in first position. It describes thereby the neurotic subject which evades *jouissance*, bars itself against it. Since we understand music from the viewpoint of perversion, we suggest now to lay the accent on the object, that is, to reverse the formula of fantasy: $S(\cancel{A}) \rightarrow (a \diamond \cancel{\$})$. This manner of notation is accountable to the fact that in music the subject does not understand itself merely as the subject of the signifier, as $\cancel{\$}$, but that it subjugates itself to the signifier only to the extent that it itself—$S(\cancel{A})$—closes in on its own lack. *At the instant of jouissance the subject separates itself off from the order of the signifier in order to become itself the object of jouissance of the Other.*

VII

In conclusion, a question we sidestepped earlier needs to be addressed: that is, the question concerning the nature of the *objet a*. At first we set it up in opposition to the signifier insofar as the latter articulates, and later on we added that this articulation is binary in nature. This structure corresponds essentially to the signifying pair operative in music: the elementary opposition of note and pause. In opposition to this signifier, which is always articulated in dialectical oppositions, we submit the Real of sound which is essentially limitless and therefore lacks all objectlike consistency. The Real, however, is not simply the formless and chaotic; for the subject, the Real is always the unbearable. This becomes clear in the context of delirium in which the psychotic subject loses its status as subject. The destructive force of *jouissance* robs the subject of all splitting, that is, all relationship to the encounterable; no delirious subject is in the position to doubt his or her delusional experiences—their power is completely real.

In order to be bearable, the Real has to be bound, represented, and dialecticized; the terms Lacan has introduced into psychoanalysis—the Real, the Symbolic and the Imaginary—are capable of representing the different constellations of this knot. The *objet a*, as an element of the fantasm, is an imaginary moment. In terms of enjoyment, it is that element which, as one last screen before the unbearable, binds the Real and disguises it. What is at stake, then, in the moment we have described in which the *objet a* frees itself and for an instant lends presence and form to destructive and overflowing *jouissance*, is by no means the presence of the Real. On the contrary, exactly where it could emerge, the voice as object closes off the passageway. And still: within that monolithic opacity of the cry lies a liminal act of binding which allows for the Real to shine forth in its fascinating force; in this way, the cry manages to trace the impossible.

Notes

1. Jacques Lacan, *Le seminaire VII: L'ethique de la psychanalyse* (Paris, 1986), 131. In his "Seminar on the Ethics of Psychoanalysis" Lacan points out that perversion and sublimation are identical insofar as both go beyond the pleasure principle's relationship to the object.

2. Jacques Lacan, *The Four Fundamental Concepts of Psycho-Analysis*, ed. Jacques-Alain Miller, trans. Alan Sheridan (New York: W. W. Norton, 1981), 177.

3. The special case of Beethoven's deafness, or of the pianist who studies the score on the train, does not really work as a counterargument, as music is represented corporeally even in these cases: here, too, music is experienced only insofar as it reaches into the bodily Real.

4. Anonymous, "De l'objet musical dans le champ de la psychanalyse," *Scilicet* 6/7 (1974), 330ff.

5. Jacques-Alain Miller, "Lacan et la voix," in *Colloques d'Yvry* (Paris: Lysiaques, 1989), 180.

6. G. Wajeman, *Voix-le, face à la chute des sons mus* (Lausanne: Argo, 1979).

7. Of course, one could argue that this has nothing to do with an "actual" choice; the poor singer was surely "too young" [to make an informed decision], or "society" forced him to make this choice. . . . While these arguments are valid, they can, however, be applied to any and every choice; never is a subject aware—when making any sort of decision—of all conditions or consequences. In terms of our argument, there really is no logical difference between the decision at stake here and other potential decisions.

8. Wajeman, 17.

9. Ibid., 16.

10. A Poizat, *L'opéra ou le cri de l'ange. Essay sur la jouissance de l'amateur de l'opéra* (Paris: Bétaillé, 1986), 57.

11. We should note here, by the way, that personally we stand critically opposed to this conception of development—or even, progress—and agree, rather, with Wajeman, according to whom the bourgeois opera of the nineteenth

century tends to stand in a regressive position in terms of *jouissance* vis-à-vis Neapolitan opera, because of its exclusion of the castrato and its glorification of the Enlightenment.

12. Poizat, 247.

13. A. Didier-Weill, in *Ornicar?* 41: 42–55.

14. Ibid., 43.

15. We understand "slave" here in the sense of Roman Antiquity, where the actor was designated a slave because he was not master of what he said; he was a slave insofar as he was subjugated to the text of the Other.

16. Jacques Lacan, *Seminar VII: The Ethics of Psychoanalysis*, ed. Jacques-Alain Miller, trans. Dennis Porter (New York: W. W. Norton, 1992), 130.

17. Jacques Lacan, *Écrits: A Selection* (New York: W. W. Norton, 1977), 315.

2

On Murder, or: Tell's Projectile

Peter Widmer

ith Freud and against Freud I attempt to put the Oedipus complex into question. Death wishes are directed less at the father than they are at "primary narcissism" (Leclaire). Neither primary narcissism nor death wishes are generation or gender specific. Only by way [of these insights] does it become possible to examine the dimension over which silence has reigned much more than it has over the already well-known Oedipus complex: the dimension of the parents' hatred for "their" children. Can't the Symbolic be identified with the dead child as much as it can with the dead father? Whatever the case may be: it all depends on whether murder occurs in the Real, or, as the Ethics of Psycho-analysis has it, in the Symbolic. I will concretize these questions by way of the myth of Wilhelm Tell.

In my paper I would like to attempt to lend a voice to the question mark that is included in the title of our conference[1]—it looks like the mirror image of an S, which could stand for the "subject"—and question the Oedipus complex, or at least its dominant position as the paradigm of psychoanalysis as such.

In the end Freud regarded the oedipal conflict as being anchored in phylogenesis; he thought that it established itself even where actual conditions gave no occasion for hostile feelings towards the father. In order to support this thesis of universality, Freud wrote *Totem and Taboo*, a myth of the origin of history in which the highest significance is ascribed to the incest prohibition. In this light the drama of Oedipus plays the role of the repetition of history's origin as much as do the murder of Moses, which Freud postulated, Hamlet's strange behavior concerning the issue of avenging his father's death, and the history of each and every one of us.

Freud assumes that the murder of the primal father and the subsequent cannibalistic act had led to the establishment of the incest prohibition, to the belated [*nachträglich*] obedience to the primal father. Thereby the incest prohibition too is established as having a phylogenetic basis, though, according to Freud, it is weaker than drive-backed desire and therefore in need of cultural reinforcement. Consequently, drive-backed desire and incest prohibition constitute a split within the subject whose incestuous aims are to be repressed—or, even better, to be overcome—by the work of culture, and drive-backed desires are to be directed at objects other than the mother. Under pressure from castration anxiety the desire for union with the mother is transformed into defense; for narcissistic reasons hatred of the father is transformed into love of him. The line of conflict is drawn by the younger generation against the older one. In this representation the starting point of the conflict is to be found in the younger generation and it is directed at the older generation.

The critique of the Oedipus complex and the work *Totem and Taboo*, which provides the complex with a foundation, comes from many quarters, and I propose to summarize it in five points. I will confine myself here to criticizing Freud's exposition and exclude those voices which have attempted to read a totally different dimension into the oedipal drama.

The first critique traces the events in Freud's exposition of *Totem and Taboo*—at the center of which lies a deed, a real murder—back to structural conditions and not to a historical event. What appears to be a personal drama and an actual event is in fact and in reality the effect of the three registers—the Imaginary, the Symbolic, and the Real. According to this critique Freud attempted to trace the origins of the law historically, and to find the origins of the incest prohibition in the dead and devoured father. But in actual fact the law precedes every human being. For this reason the figure of the lawless primal father is not grounded in actual fact but is rather a heuristic necessity: if everyone is subject to the law, then it is necessary to assume the existence of the exception that proves the rule. Since the law, which is ultimately the law of language, precedes all human existence, its internalization is not a question of cannibalism but rather of identification; not of a real murder, but rather of a symbolic murder. If there is such a thing as an oedipal wish, then it must consist in transgressing the law, the incest prohibition, in order to (re)constitute an imaginary wholeness with the mother, in not accepting and maybe even foreclosing the severing instance of the Symbolic and its representative, the father. From the perspective of this particular critique the oedipal wish appears as an attempt to overcome the split which is effected by the three registers which constitute subjectivity: the conflict is then the nonaffirmation of the conditions which are laid out for every human being.

The second critique regards the Oedipus complex less as an unsurpassable psychic reality than as a constructed perverse structure. The incest prohibition becomes the center of observation and critique: it is invented in order to prop up and maintain the belief that what is desired is not something impossible but rather something complete and existing—the prohibited mother. But desire has no full object, and this fact is masked by the rivalry with a father who is presumed to be prohibitive.

The third form of critique, which is easily brought into connection with the second, questions the assumption that hatred for the father and love for the mother constitute the last fundamental instance. Doesn't clinical experience demonstrate that there can be love for the father which is fed neither by the fear of castration nor by a complete turning away from heterosexuality? And don't these same experiences also sometimes show a terrible hatred of the mother—even if it is not possible here either to speak of actual homosexuality—a hatred of the mother which threatens to tear the affected subject to pieces?

The fourth type of critique bemoans the dominance of the masculine in the Oedipus complex and in addition throws doubt on the idea that the female Oedipus complex develops in the same way as the masculine up until the phallic phase. Put differently, it questions the assumption that, at least in the first phase, the Oedipus complex is not sexualized.

Finally, the fifth argumentation questions whether the oedipal conflict originates in the descendent generation, or whether it is not, in fact, the parents and their desires that play a central role in the oedipal conflict. This particular critique sometimes bases itself on some of Freud's works—"On Narcissism: An Introduction," or the late writings on female sexuality, in which Freud assigns a central role to the maternal desire for the phallus, that is, the child-phallus.

Elsewhere I have attempted to trace the consequences that Lacan's reading of Freud, including his application of his three registers, has had for Freud's deductions regarding the Oedipus complex. I have also concerned myself with the critique that regards the Oedipus complex as something conditional rather than unsurpassable. Here I wish to question the validity of Freud's conception that the generational conflict always moves from the descendants to the parents.

In my investigation of this fundamental component of the oedipal conflict I am influenced not only by Lacan's reading of Freud and my own experiences but also by Freud himself—I have already mentioned "On Narcissism: An Introduction" and the late writings on female sexuality—as well as by the works of Serge Leclaire (*On tue un enfant*), Alain Juranville (*Psychanalyse et religion*), Marie Balmary (*Le sacrifice interdit*) and Jacques Bril (*Le meurtre du fils*).

When talking about the story of Oedipus, one usually thinks of incest and patricide and forgets that this has a prehistory: Laius, Oedipus's father, wanted to have his son killed as soon as he was born. So the first one to commit an unnatural act is Laius. One could argue, of course, that he (Laius) was subject to the influence of the prophecy that his son would one day kill him and marry his wife. Even if one grants validity to the prophecy as it is represented in the tragedy, that is, if one does not read it as a rationalization for some sort of dark motive (Laius's envy and rivalry), Oedipus is merely the agent of the conflict, the agent of a fate which is playing a cruel game with him—and not only with him, but also with Jocasta, and later even with Antigone, Polyneices, and Eteocles. The puppeteers of the conflict are then to be sought among the gods, among those figures who predict the roads of human beings and their wrong turns even before they are born.

So once again our observations lead us away from the generation of the descendants, away from Oedipus, and in the direction of the dark gods whose power embraces the virtually differentiating and liberating Symbolic and reduces it to the status of mere mask.

We can oppose to this Greek story a Jewish one, which has a much happier ending: the story of Abraham and Isaac. Here too we have a son, Isaac (the name means "laughter"), and here too a dark God seems to be holding the strings in this inducement of the father to sacrifice his own son. The knife is already drawn when God's voice is heard commanding Abraham to stop. The planned murder turns out to be—I am here following Marie Balmary's interpretation—a misinterpretation of God's word on the part of Abraham: it is not the sacrifice of the son's body and life that is being demanded of Abraham, but rather the affirmation of a *symbolic belonging to* God, a belonging via the Symbolic covenant. The divine, the Symbolic, announces a division, a severance, which lies at the origin of subjectivity, which begins with speaking in one's own name, where one's own name is the name of the Other.

The two stories stand for two types of death. In Sophocles' tragedy the real murder, real death, is at the center, and one could say that Oedipus's murder of Laius perpetuates and confirms the violence that has been staged by the gods. The story was already written before it even began; like a script, it precedes time; even one who knows how to read it is incapable of changing it. Acting human beings are in reality the pawns of divine providence; wanting to escape destiny leads one into it just as much as affirming it does. Do we not see here the powers of the Imaginary at play, which also haunt human beings? They oppose historicity, openness, unpredictability. The future has long belonged to the past by the time it is realized. The powers of the Imaginary are operative in Abraham's story as well: in the imaginary demand attributed to God, in Abraham's deadly obedience [*Kadavergehorsam*], especially in his homicidal intentions vis-à-vis his son, and finally in Sarah's desire to possess Isaac. Following Freud one could say that Sarah cathects Isaac as her phallus. But this aspect of not-letting-go, this desire to arrange, the consequence of which is the extermination of all historicity—life ends when the descendants are dead—is traversed by the symbolic power of the unpredicted, the unpredictable, the Symbolic, the pacifying. This Other power, which does not submit to the Imaginary but rather itself kills the Imaginary, is missing in Oedipus's story, in which the Symbolic is instead the powerless witness of destiny. Symbolic death, on the other hand, means the letting-go of Isaac on the part of Abraham and by Sarah as well. It also means the end of physical belonging, the becoming-symbolic of the subject as it moves out of the conditions of infancy. One must point out here, following Marie Balmary, that the biblical story is located in the context of weaning the child from the breast, a point in time that requires a letting-go, a freeing, on the part of the parents.

This indicates that the Symbolic and the Imaginary are not simply objective powers that unfold their effectiveness outside of human subjects. Rather, they are realized only through subjects. Objectivity and subjectivity are mutually dependent. What is interesting about this is less the subjective/objective dialectic than the question to which power the parents have pledged allegiance. In his book *On tue un enfant* Leclaire mentions the case of a patient he calls Pierre-Marie. The analysis shows that this subject has been woven into the mother's desire to have a comforter who will help her leave behind the emptiness of her being. Could such a condition of being bound to the maternal fantasm, which makes a mockery of the process of affirming the child's belonging to the Symbolic, really be the essence of the infantile subject's desire? Abraham and Sarah see their child as a possession as well; the child is being denied recognition as a subject: Sarah speaks of *her* son, and Abraham wants to sacrifice Isaac to God. But the subject can be constituted only when it is surrendered to the Other, which requires some work of mourning on the part of the parents. So often analysis leads to confronting not only the analysands but even more so their parents with a work of mourning which they had been able to ward off as long as they had been able to retain the docility of "their" child.

Of course what we are concerned with here is not some sort of sterile accusation of the parents but the question about to what extent children who are woven into the discourse of others, to use one of Lacan's formulae for the unconscious, have allowed themselves to be woven in. But it does make a difference—something analysands feel keenly—whether their conflicts are confined to their own fantasms or whether these fantasms are propped up by others as well. In the latter case everyone can feel what symbolic death is, what sort of drama and affect are inherent in it.

In reference to the Oedipus complex some cases show that a profound hatred for the mother, directed at the possessive mother, is held together by the fantasy of union, which is shared with the mother. The breaking up of this repressed or denied hatred must not be confused with homosexuality. The analysand searches for support in the struggle against the mother's power in the father, and uses this support for however long it takes for the raging elements to calm themselves. It is possible that afterwards a differently constituted desire will come into being, which is again directed at the mother, but which is invested with more traits belonging to the subject. Thus one must differentiate between a desire that is directed at the mother and that veils a deep hatred for her, as in the case of Pierre-Marie, and a desire that has resulted from the experience of lack and that is merely searching for an object.

Is it not necessary to conclude, along with Alain Juranville, that Freud idealized the mother-son relation a little too much and that, by and large, he neglected hatred? There is an infantile dream of Freud's which he calls the dream of the "bird-beaked figures." In it he sees "my beloved mother, with a peculiarly peaceful, sleeping expression on her features, being carried into the room by two (or three) people with birds' beaks and laid upon the bed."[2] Freud's interpretation hinges on his fear that his mother may die, but then ultimately comes to settle on a sexual motive of his, "that had found appropriate expression in the visual content of the dream." No thought here that perhaps Freud may have become frightened by another wish, a less loving one—a death wish.

But let us stay with that critique of the Oedipus complex that I set up at the beginning, which puts into question the assumption that the motive for murder should be sought primarily in the son, the descendants. Is it possible simply to reverse this assumption? Can one attribute the guilt to the parents? But the parents were children once, too, and perhaps their conflicts began where they—once again—came into contact with the conflicts of the older generation. So it makes little sense to simply reverse the direction of the conflict. At stake is not the conflict between the generations, but rather the conflict that concerns every generation: the conflict between the three registers of the Symbolic, the Imaginary, and the Real.

Much more crucial than the question concerning the origin of the conflict is the question about what it is that is being murdered: the Real or corporeal, the Symbolic, or the Imaginary?

We recognize the difference in the story of Abraham and Isaac: Abraham almost sacrificed his son's life, almost carried out the real murder, before he learned that, yes, a sacrifice was necessary, but not the sacrifice of a life; rather, what was to be sacrificed was the desire to possess the life of another. The murder of this demand for possession does not destroy the imaginary dimension but transforms it, subjects the Imaginary to the Symbolic and opens up, to begin with, the possibility of recognizing a son, a recognition that is possible only on the basis of the Symbolic. Without this dimension of the Symbolic there is nothing to laugh about. This also goes for every analysis in which the transference points to what again and again lies adjacent: better to make oneself an object than to forge out into new territory.

But there is not only the kind of murderousness that is directed at the Real, the corporeal, and symbolic murder, which dissolves the imaginary and totalitarian demand to dominate the lives of others; there is also the murderousness directed at the Symbolic which works on behalf of either the Imaginary or the Real. In face of this wish to lift all contracts, to annul all laws, one immediately thinks of Sade's program for a new republic, which follows the laws of nature. From the perspective of psychoanalysis the oedipal conflict must be thematized once again in this context. Insofar as it belongs to *childhood*, isn't it directed at the father whose function it is to separate from the mother, the father, in other words, who embodies the Symbolic? This is an open question, as far as I am concerned, precisely because maternal desire is involved here as well. To formulate this tentatively, I suspect, as does Juranville, that the hatred for the father who represents the Symbolic corresponds to a fantasm of the mother who searches for the Other, which she has been able to discover in neither her father nor her husband, in the child. On the other hand, I suspect, as does Leclaire, that the death wishes that are articulated by *analysands* are directed not so much at the father who represents the Symbolic, but at the infantile, narcissistic, and imaginary aspects of him, which precisely do not belong to the symbolic dimension.

Conversely, one must also ask what the motives could be for the murderous feelings which fathers develop vis-à-vis their children. Are they directed at their imaginary totality, at "his majesty the baby," or at the child as the representative of a future that confronts the father with his own finitude, his own mortality? Any answer to this question would have to assume that there is such a thing as *the* father. But there is the real, the symbolic and the imaginary father, and this "there is" points to a distinction which is not empirical. It seems, then, that it is all a matter of the registers and their compatibility. Do the Imaginary, the Real, and the Symbolic hate each other? Is each striving to become dominant and to keep the others as small as possible or to do away with them completely? What is it that holds them together?

How big a leap is it if I now move from the registers to the family? To me it appears to be a dangerous leap. Because the Real, the Symbolic, and the Imaginary are irretrievably interconnected; the family, on the other hand, can and is supposed to dissolve once the child leaves. It is apparent that the three registers are present in each and every subject. Nevertheless, there is a tendency to assign the three registers to people and to genders, to deny everyone's belonging to all three of the registers. The mother, then, simply turns into the force which holds the family together and which struggles against its dissolution; the father turns into the one who works for its material survival; and the child turns into the instance that holds the parents together. And as the representative of the future, of the not-yet-symbolized, it attracts the hatred and the envy of its parents. The mother protects it against life, protects it from incurring its own experiences, and the father is jealous of this conspiracy. The more this sort of thing occurs, the less one lives in the splitness and nonidentity of the registers, the more dramas there will be, dramas whose presence one can always sense in the life of the family.

There is a legend in which all of these motifs—real as well as symbolic murder, imaginary demands for possession, and the demand to be subservient to no one; oedipal motifs such as the motif of sacrifice as well as the motif of the overcoming of sacrifice—are bound up with each other in an exemplary fashion:

the legend of Wilhelm Tell. Friedrich Schiller adapted it into a play. I would like to place the apple-shooting scene at the center of my observations.

After he has failed to salute the hat on the pole and thereby insulted the governor of the district who has just arrived on the scene, Tell can avoid a prison sentence only if he is capable of hitting an apple on his son Walter's head with an arrow shot from his crossbow. I am not interested here in whether or not the story ever actually took place—earlier Nordic legends seem to make that unlikely—nor do we have to concern ourselves with attempting to strip away the mythological layers of the story by revealing Tell to be a fearful lingerer. Only the apparently symbolic content of this story, which has left its traces all over Switzerland, is of interest here. It is impossible to overlook these traces: in our immediate vicinity we have the Stauffacher Square and Stauffacher Street, and it is not so long ago that the Psychoanalytic Seminar of Zurich was located in Tell Street, from where everyone was busy shooting arrows aimed at all types of repression. The only thing missing was seeing Freud as a governor from Austria!

What is immediately striking about this apple-shooting scene is its, so to speak, oedipal moment: Tell/Son/Oedipus does not submit to Gessler/Father/ Laius. "Clear the path"—the wish is the same for Oedipus and Tell; it makes their blood boil and intensifies their rage to the point of murder. In this oedipal moment it becomes apparent that it is not only a paternal instance that is the addressee of the slaying, but also an instance which demands submission, an instance which does not recognize the subjectivity and the otherness of the other. Its law, even though it is juridically legal, stands in the service of a master-slave relationship, of the nonrecognition of the other subject. The first aggressor is not Tell but rather the Governor—that is, his law; this gives Tell the moral, not the juridical, right to do away with the tyrant.

Let us now look at the second moment in this apple-shooting scene: the relationship between Tell and his son Walter. There is no trace here of oedipal rivalry, neither in the scene of the action, nor at home with his mother. And yet there is this extremely dangerous action on Tell's part aimed at his son. If he hadn't been ordered to carry it out one would be reminded of a number of infanticide stories: Moses in the basket among the reeds, the quasi-sacrifice of Isaac, Oedipus's banishment, Herod's massacre of children, the struggle between Hildebrand and Hadubrand as it has been handed down in the *Hildebrandlied*, the myth of Kronos who devours his children, Prometheus who is mistreated by Zeus, and so on. (These stories can also be read differently: as the symbolization of symbolic murder, the murder of primary narcissism, as Leclaire would say.)

Detached from a possible real, historical background and from the context of Gessler's orders, the apple-shooting looks like an initiation of Walter into which are also channeled Tell's countercurrent motives: the moment of separation which is connected to a test of courage for Walter, but also an aggressive moment which is perhaps fed by Tell's jealousy vis-à-vis the boy. Evidence for this would seem to lie in the fact that a scene preceding the apple-shooting throws light on the relationship between Hedwig, Tell's wife, and her children: in this scene she appears as a totally devoted mother who likes nothing better than to press her two sons up against her bosom and to protect them from the crude extrafamilial world. Accordingly, she opposes the child's wish to go away together with the father for a long time. She finds comfort by keeping the other boy, whose first name is the same as his father's, at home with her.

Later, when she is told about the apple-shooting scene, she doesn't even listen to the end of the story, but immediately asks what happened to the child and assumes that Tell shot at Walter intentionally: "Where is my child? Let me . . . I must see him. . . . My little Walter! Oh. he's alive! . . . Is it true, though? Are you unharmed? Is it possible? How could he aim at you? How could he? Oh, he is heartless—he was capable of shooting an arrow at his own child."

Later, under pressure to make amends, she accuses her husband of having been in collusion with Gessler's orders: "Oh, had he the heart of a father, he would have died a thousand times before having done it!" Apparently her desire is directed more at Walter, her child, her suckling baby, than at her husband.

Let us note also that it is Hedwig's father, Walter Fürst, who tells his daughter about the apple-shooting scene. Her son, in other words, the one she had allowed to leave with her husband, has the same name as her father. One can see in this constellation how Tell's wife attempts to fill her lack with the child-phallus-Walter. This fits in with the fact that she puts herself in his place: "I see the boy standing there, eternally tied up, I see his father aiming at him, and forever the arrow pierces my heart." "Eternally" [*ewig*]—this is almost an anagram for "Hedwig," who in this statement denies her own finitude and (re)incarnates herself in child-father-Walter. One can interpret Tell's deed as providing a countercurrent to this, as lying at the point of intersection of two motives: one that separates and initiates, and another—insofar as what is at stake here is not just a symbolic castration but a symbolically real castration— that is aggressive and vengeful. Walter does not become a real sacrifice to the extent that his father's action is motivated more by his desire for a separation of mother and child to occur than it is by revenge or jealousy. This second motive is well rationalized in the play, and this is expressed in a series of negations: it is not Tell who wanted the apple-shooting, but Gessler; in addition, had Tell refused to shoot, the son himself would have encouraged him to do so. It is only Tell's wife who expresses the idea that the father's action was cruel. Thereby she can simultaneously give motivations for her provident caring as a mother and feed her husband's feelings of revenge. Of course, the drama's tension is based entirely on this possibility of infanticide, and the successful shot repeatedly produces feelings of relief from this undesirable thought. Even thinking of the possibility that the father might miss the mark and hit his son's head still covers up the most horrific motive of all: intentional murder of the son. But never fear—this never happens. It is as if this apple-shooting scene staged the crucifixion as negation. We are touching here upon motives that go way beyond what I can say for now. At any rate, it seems noteworthy that there are historians who accept the possibility of the story of Wilhelm Tell having been introduced [into Switzerland] by pilgrims to Rome arriving from the North.

Epilogue

Following my presentation, a person in the audience asked me whether I had seen the Dalí exhibit which had just opened in Zurich at the time, since it included a large painting by Dalí of Wilhelm Tell. I was very astonished when I went to stand before the larger-than-life painting, *The Enigma of Wilhelm Tell*. At first I only noticed Tell's importuning phallicism. Then I realized that Dalí had given Tell the face of Lenin and the peaked cap typical of the workers' movement. Lenin's picture had actually been hanging in the lecture hall where the RISS Convention where I had spoken about Tell had taken place; the lecture hall belongs to the *Volkshaus* [People's House], an abode of the workers' movement which commemorates Lenin not only out of political conviction, but also because Lenin had spent time in Switzerland, including Zurich, before the October Revolution, before he traveled to Russia in his lead-encased railroad car.

My astonishment intensified when I read Dalí's own commentary on his painting in the exhibit catalog: "*The Enigma of Wilhelm Tell* is probably one of those paintings which represent one of the most dangerous moments in my life. Wilhelm Tell is my father; I am the small child he holds in his arms and which has a raw cutlet on its head instead of an apple. This signifies that Wilhelm Tell has cannibalistic intentions: he wants to devour me." The catalog's author adds, "What fascinated him (Dalí) about this was the fact that Tell, as the epitome of the tyrannical person of authority, was apparently ready to kill his son; he saw in this a parallel to his father. The version we have here, which was created the same year Hitler came to power, is the largest version of this motif, which fuses autobiographical elements with political allusions."

Notes

1. Widmer's reference is to the conference entitled "Oedipus?" that took place in Zurich, September 23–24, 1989, in commemoration of Freud's fiftieth date of death. A special issue of *RISS*, also entitled *Oedipus?* 13/14 (spring 1990) published the papers delivered at this event.

2. Sigmund Freud, *The Interpretation of Dreams. The Standard Edition, Volume 5*, trans. James Strachey (London: The Hogarth Press), 583.

3

Perversion: Tragedy or Guilt?

RAYMOND BORENS

Fearing legal complications, two pedophiles came to see me during my office hours—or rather, they had been sent to me by their families. Their discourses were marked by two particularities: on the one hand, at least at first sight, there was a total lack of guilt feelings and, on the other, they were under the impression that they themselves were passive and were being delivered up to their sexual objects. "What I'm doing is surely not ideal," one of them said. "That's just the way things are," said the other, who told me about his incapacity to resist, to not fall prey to, the "perverse play of seduction" (these were his own words) of the little girls he tutored. "They look at me so strangely, they kiss me in a special way—it just kills me, paralyzes me; I just have to react, have to take some initiative." The first one emphasized his total yielding to, his powerlessness vis-à-vis, what he considered to be seductive, or at least, ambiguous, behavior on the part of the boys he took care of at holiday camp.

One may think that these statements have the function of preventing guilt and guilt feelings from becoming conscious, that they are actually defense mechanisms. But when one looks, or rather listens, more carefully one discovers a tragic feeling, a sense of being, without any sort of protection, at the mercy of a more or less natural and unyielding power, an instance of fate; this particular feeling, no matter how paradoxical this may seem, emerges from a position that lies outside of the realm of guilt or innocence. When one dissects the process of what happens to the pedophile into the individual steps that make it up, one encounters first admiration for the object: the beautiful bodies of children and youths, the innocent and pure expressions (Lacan says that perverts are "the victims of beauty always classed as incomparable [as well as unalterable]").[1] Descartes says admiration is the first passion and a precondition for all other forms of passion. This admiration leads to being seduced, which, in turn, provokes feelings of powerlessness, submissiveness, and dependency. The subject reacts against this passive position with action and now seduces the seducer. Accordingly, one pervert said to me, "When I am not provoked, I can easily keep myself under control. I never imagine anything, but when the provocation that I never imagined appears, I have to go for it."

Here, too, in a superficial analysis, one may think that we are dealing with the subject of lack: the object reminds the subject of its lack in the field of guilt, duty, and exchange (you have seduced me; in order to cover up the lack that you have thereby uncovered in me, I seduce you; through your culpability, I am confronted with my own lack, that is, my culpability; therefore I make you culpable in order to exculpate myself). But this is not really where we are. Even if the pervert is indeed confronted with his own lack, this lack has nothing to do with guilt or with being contaminated with culpability. One could almost say that it is pure. *Pure lack*. In order to categorize this lack, it might be helpful to consider the particularity of the pervert's use of metaphors. Noticeably often he chooses his similes from the realm of fauna, flora, and minerals. Think of the *uomo di sasso*, the stony guest in *Don Juan*. In his *Don Juan*, Molière writes, "He who has no law, lives like a wild animal." "He (Don Juan) would have married you, his dog, his cat," says Sganarelle Guzman. In his *El Burlador de Sevilla*, Tirso de Molina compares his protagonist with minerals or animals more than once. Doesn't one of the most frequent practices of sexual perversion in both men and women consist in sexual intercourse with animals, that is, with "sexual partners" who are situated outside of both culture and guilt? Can one deduce from this that the pervert lives in closer proximity to nature, so to speak, than does the neurotic for whom culture lays a grid over everything? I would like to define this realm of nature as dominated not by the Law but by the *laws (of nature)*, which cannot be transgressed without incurring a threat to life; they are unchangeable and absolute. They have nothing to do with those *laws* with which the obsessive neurotic struggles in order to circumvent *the* Law; they have existed and continue to exist before and after the establishment of the Law and have—this, by the way, is suggested by perverse urges—more to do with need *(besoin)* than with desire *(désir)*.

As paradoxical as this may seem, the realm of nature can be categorized as tragic. For the world of *tragedy* is not the world of the mistake, of sin, of hubris. Quite the contrary: tragedy is bound to misfortune, to an inexorable, unmitigable destiny, to Ate and Ananke: it is radically chained to the unrelated *[le sans-rapport]*, to the absence of relationship, to the lack of both mediation and mediator.

The world of culture (for the sake of clarity I am using the millennially old terms of culture and nature, of *noumos* and *physis*, knowing full well that it was precisely psychoanalysis that subverted the disjunctive use of these terms; the pervert, on the other hand, preserves the disjunction) is essentially the world of the mistake (*faute*) more than it is the world of lack [*défaut*], of guilt and culpability, of the relationship between mistake and punishment, between guilt and atonement, of the *do ut des*, of exchange. In short, it is the *world of law* [*Gesetz*], which, as soon as it establishes [*setzt*] itself, also establishes [*setzt*] the possibility of its own transgression. The realm of guilt is the realm of symbolic guilt, which, as we are used to saying, is structurally tied to lack and loss. But lack and loss are primarily marked by a tragic element of powerlessness, of being delivered up to arbitrariness. The Symbolic has two sides: on the one hand, the maternal Symbolic with its elements of presence/absence, death/life—the *tragic-Symbolic*; on the other, there is the paternal Symbolic that penetrates and traverses the former by belatedly [*nachträglich*] adding mistake and guilt to it. Only then do we have the *guilty-Symbolic*. Of course, we are not dealing here with a process of development but rather with structural processes.

In the psychotic patient this paternal Symbolic is missing (foreclosure); the neurotic inscribes himself within it and for him it takes precedence over the other. For the pervert this world of law is preserved as a world of whose existence he is aware but which he does not want to enter; it remains terra incognita, a blank spot, for him. He attempts to tear his object out of this world, out from the object's interrelatedness with the networks of duty and contract. The breakout is staged and has an apotropaic and derisive function. Don Juan seduces only women who, in Tirso, are tied to other men by the chains of marriage or engagement, and in Molière, who are bound to God by their religious vows. Don Juan has again and again been interpreted as the liberator of the women he seduced, but shouldn't one consider instead that he desired to abduct these women into his tragic world? In Don Juan's stagings one can see the stagings of the perverse subject who takes on the roles of both mother and father as they presented themselves to their child, the future pervert. The seductive mother who is now to be seduced herself appears in the *mille tre*, and with her, the *jouissance* of the maternal Other, which is no longer considered to be only conceivable; now it is also realizable. In the perverse staging the pervert plays the role of the seductive mother to whom he ascribes the *jouissance* of the Other, while the object takes on both the place of the mother as incestuous object and the place of the child as the object of maternal desire. But this staging, this transposition into action (*mise en acte*) invariably leads to a humiliating defeat, to a failure which takes on a comic—a comic/painful—coloring. Doesn't Mozart call his Don Giovanni a *dramma giocoso*? Doesn't this recall the way in which the Greek tragedies were performed, where three tragedies were followed by the representation of a satyr's play in which the preceding themes were treated in a comic fashion? Couldn't one also recognize in this comic element the laugh or laughter of the mother that the pervert knows so well? After all, he is the one who has experienced a mother who laughed at him after she snubbed him when he was drawn into her game of seduction. It is here, too, that one comes across the arbitrariness that I mentioned before, as well as the pervert's specific attempt to extricate his object (in this case, the mother) from its ties to the world of the Law (the father).

But this father, as I have shown elsewhere, is always culpable as he engages in compromises and compromises himself within the Law. In Tirso's Don Juan everyone is guilty—especially the father figures who want to circumvent the Law. In this connection it is fruitful to think of two exemplary passages: one from Plato's *Republic*, the other from Diderot, cited also by Freud. When Plato discusses wishes,[2] he says that the soul feels no inhibitions about joining with the mother or anyone else—human, god, or animal—in sexual union. In *Oedipus Rex* Sophocles writes, "How many men, in dreams, have lain with their mothers!"[3] Striking about both these quotes—the second one is spoken by Jocasta, by the way—is the absence of the father, who then appears, however, holding Diderot's opinion that, if the boy were strong enough, he would kill the father so as to be able to sleep with his mother.

Jocasta, on the other hand, could serve as prototype for those mothers who don't believe in the Law, but rather in the pseudonatural laws of fate. She attempts to calm Oedipus, who has been frightened by the Oracle and by Teiresias's prophecies, by telling him that "marauding strangers"[4] killed Laius. "Oedipus will use the term 'marauders' in order to engage with the future as an already known universe."[5] He feels involved, he is afraid of being implicated in the events both personally and causally. Jocasta, on the other hand, accepts the unrecognizability of the future as such; in this manner, she disengages herself from her guilt as an active subject. Oedipus's attitude turns him into a neurotic, despite Jocasta's attempts at persuading him, into someone who is established, by a discourse, as a responsible subject who is personally involved, someone who feels interpellated as an addressee by the Oracle, which reveals his culpability to him. It is thus that Oedipus steps from the tragic world into the culpable one. He inscribes himself into the Symbolic and takes both of its sides onto his shoulders. The *or* in the title of my paper is, for the pervert, a disjunctive *vel* (I am referring to Lacan's Seminar on *The Four Fundamental Concepts*[6]) and for the neurotic becomes an *and*, which, at least virtually, includes both sides of the Symbolic, even if the "tragic feeling" then decreases, and shrinks like a shagreen.

In Sophocles' text, Oedipus's "Ah! sadness"[7] resounds against Jocasta's "From now on never think of those things again."[8] Immediately following that, Oedipus speaks of his father's murder. Jocasta does not participate in this development, in this transition to the father.

> Oed.: Why should a man respect the Pythian hearth, or
>   Give heed to the birds that jangle over his head?
>   They prophesied that I should kill Polybos,
>   Kill my own father; but he is dead and buried,

And I am here—I never touched him, never,
Unless he died of grief for my departure,
And thus, in a sense, through me. No, Polybos
Has packed the oracles off with him underground.
They are empty words.

Jo.:   Had I not told you so?

Oed.: You had; it was my faint heart that betrayed me.

Jo.:   From now on never think of those things again.

Oed.: And yet—must I not fear my mother's bed?

Jo.:   Why should anyone in this world be afraid,
       Since Fate rules us and nothing can be foreseen?
       A man should live only for the present day.
       Have no more fear of sleeping with your mother:
       How many men, in dreams, have lain with their mothers!
       No reasonable man is troubled by such things.

In contrast to Oedipus, Don Giovanni remains untouched by recognition with his "No!" which he hurls out against the Commander's *"Pentiti!"* He knows no mediation, no recognition of the Symbolic father, while the real fathers in the Don Juan plays (as also in the story of Oedipus) make themselves culpable by not obeying the law. Laius also did not kill his son in spite of the Oracle's prophecy, but instead, as a kind of compromise, handed him over to the shepherd. In this sense Laius's action is radically opposed to that of Abraham who obeyed God's order and was prepared to kill his son. The knife that already touched Isaac's throat, in Oedipus's hands was directed against himself, even if—and this is hardly insignificant—it has taken on the shape of Jocasta's golden brooches.

Oedipus moves in the realm of neurosis in that he gives his drama a meaning, a meaning that always has to do with guilt, and which he opposes to the non-sense, the coincidence, of blind fate, which the pervert always resorts to for an explanation. The latter does not find expression in Freud's statement from *The Psychopathology of Everyday Life:* "I believe in real, external coincidence; I do not believe in psychic, internal coincidence."[9]

Yet, one should consider the pervert's attitude not only from the point of view of a deficit, a lack, a lack understood merely as a development that did not take place: he rescues a truth for us, and of this truth Montaigne says, "The opposite of truth has a hundred thousand faces and an infinite field." Against this multiplicity the pervert manages to preserve singularity—for instance, in his single and unchanging staging of his sexual activities, even if the objects in it are exchangeable, since he looks at them without seeing them and because to him they are merely witnesses or spectators in his theater. He doesn't see his object; he is incapable of seeing it; he is blinded, because he was too heavily seduced by the object—by his mother, that is.[10] The admiration of, the fascination with, the submission to this wonderful object, a submission that goes hand in hand with total dependency, total submissiveness and powerlessness, make it impossible for the pervert to break away in order to be penetrated by the phallus as the signifier of lack, or, to be more precise: he has access to the paternal Symbolic only at the price of the splitting that Freud discusses in "Fetishism." The function of his stagings is, in the last analysis, not to help him sew up a tear, but rather to bring to life again and again a derisive attitude toward a father who either was or was thought to be incapable of neutralizing the tragic world. The primary maternal object is recovered in the *mille tre* and thereby the world is made to see the father's incompetence. "The pervert belongs to nature, while all of his actions are aimed at breaking through its horrible practice" (Lacan). The pervert counters the tragic aspect of [the sentence], "There is no sexual relation" with a denial and thereby underlines its truthfulness; the neurotic, on the other hand, attempts to explain the sentence with guilt feelings ("There is no sexual relation because I am culpable"). Don Juan doesn't exert himself, doesn't toil—he exhausts himself, he dissolves (the *jouissance* of the Other—tragic *jouissance*).

It would be interesting to examine the development of the relationship between tragedy and guilt in the Greek world—where the latter concept was, at least in the beginning, meaningless—and in the Jewish world, where guilt was omnipresent. Perhaps it is because of this omnipresence of guilt that there are no tragedies in Judeo-Christian culture, with the exception of Racine's tragedy, which was, of course, rooted in Port Royal, and therefore in Jansenism, which knew a tragic God, not a God of guilt, but a God who either gives or does not, and never rewards or punishes anyone according to merit or guilt. But another question that emerges then is whether or not this world in which everything is permeated and marked by guilt is required in order to establish perversion as perversion. I refer to Greek homosexuality, especially in its pedophilic form.

In the pre-Socratics and in Homer it is destiny, fate, and later chance that fell human beings like trees (note once again the vegetable metaphor). Greek tragedy, in its development from Aeschylus to Euripides, marks the transition from tragic entanglement to entanglements of culpability, and therefore carries within itself the kernel for its own neutralization (dissolution). It neutralizes itself by introducing the dimension of sense, and thus of guilt, and by gradually replacing non-sense with sense. Antigone has no guilt and her sacrifice makes no sense, while Hyppolitus, according to the assertions of Aphrodite already in the first verses of the play, is culpable of having paid no attention to the goddess of love. Today there is much talk about the return of tragedy.[11] But aren't we actually faced with a monstrous inflation of sense, a gigantic vesicle of the Imaginary in which, not least within medical and psychosomatic discourse, what is being sought is guilt and the guilt ridden? (One dies and falls ill only because one has smoked, drunk and eaten; one becomes neurotic because mother or father have made themselves culpable). But perhaps it is precisely the non-sensical nature of this flood of sense and guilt that marks the return of the tragic which is once again claiming its rights in the realm of nonsense.

What conclusions can one draw from these thoughts on the position of the pervert vis-à-vis the Law and guilt? The psychoanalytic process implies and presupposes recognition of the Law. This recognition takes on shape in the fundamental rule, for example, which it is impossible not to transgress. Differently from the obsessive neurotic who knocks simultaneously at the door of the mistake and of guilt in order to encounter castration, while he also runs away from it, the pervert refuses to acknowledge guilt. He turns psychoanalytic treatment into a simulacrum, he mocks it the way Don Juan mocks the Commander when he invites him to dinner. By saying "No!" to the analyst, he rejects the paternal Symbolic, he remains faithful to the mother by identifying with her "no" and thus saves the world of tragedy, like a certain analysand who began his analysis three years ago because of an array of complaints and because of perverse forms of behavior. After two years he breaks off this analysis, which in retrospect has to be classified as a perverse staging. He ridicules it by claiming to have discovered the cause for all his complaints in the fillings in his teeth—this is his way of not relinquishing tragic *jouissance*.

Notes

This is a revision of a paper given at the second Kongress APERTURA, October 24–25, 1992, in Strasbourg.

1. Jacques Lacan, "Kant avec Sade," in *Écrits* (Paris: Éditions du Seuil, 1966), 775. Published in English as "Kant with Sade," in *October* 51 (winter 1989), 63.

2. Plato, *The Republic*, 571 c/d.

3. Sophocles, *Oedipus Rex*, trans. Dudley Fitts and Robert Fitzgerald, in *The Harcourt Brace Anthology of Drama*, ed. W. B. Worthen (New York: Harcourt Brace College Publishers, 1996), 2–72.

4. Ibid., 2.222.

5. J. Bollack, *L'Oedipe roi de Sophocle* (Lille: Presses Universitaires de Lille, 1990), 632.

6. Jacques Lacan, *The Seminar of Jacques Lacan: Book XI: The Four Fundamental Concepts of Psychoanalysis*, ed. Jacques-Alain Miller and trans. Alan Sheridan (New York: W. W. Norton, 1981), ch. 16.

7. Sophocles, 3.54.

8. Ibid., 3.64.

9. Sigmund Freud, *The Psychopathology of Everyday Life. The Standard Edition, Volume 6*, trans. James Strachey (London: The Hogarth Press, 1960).

10. The reference is to Sarah Kofman, *The Enigma of Woman: Woman in Freud's Writings*, trans. Catherine Porter (Ithaca: Cornell University Press, 1985), 79–80 passim.

11. See, for example, the work of Pierre Boutang.

4

Identification in the Name of Lolita

JOACHIM SAALFRANK

Current lexical or psychological definitions circumscribe identification as a person's emotional or other "equalization" with another person. In addition, the concept of identification can be applied to that of transference where what is at stake, according to current psychoanalysis or psychotherapy, is the equalization, at a given moment in the analysis, of the figure of the therapist or analyst with another figure of the analysand's past or present.

It is clear that even if this were the case, an identity—no matter of what sort, whether limited in terms of time or place or not—can paradoxically be attained only at the price of a split. Allowing an other to act in one's own place, or acting oneself, but with the motivations and emotions of an other, is logically possible only on the premise that a part of the self is split off; for example, one does so by leaving the action on the stage to the figure with whom one identifies, while one's own body, sitting more or less at ease in the spectators' area, remains removed from the action. At the moment of identification one is forced to remain on the outside at a crucial point, a point that is yet to be specified; as far as emotional equalization is concerned, one question that demands to be asked is, under what sorts of conditions can one actually ever have the feelings of an other? Can one really have the feelings of an other just by thinking about doing so? And at what point would one again be "oneself"? At what point would one be capable of jumping off the stage in order to reclaim one's own identity—that is, to stop dreaming in order to wake up in reality? Just as that point could not be the sound of an alarm clock for a dream when, say, the sound is transformed into dream images during sleep so as not to interrupt sleep, it could never be the end of the performance—that is, the identification—for the spectator in case any sort of identity had come into being between the signifier of the identification and the person who was identifying.

Just as the dream deals with the day's desire, and just as the desire enters sleep, so the object *[Figur]* of identification is someone who has to do with a desire and with the desire for identification. Thus the signifier of identification, like every signifier, is the signifier of a split, a cut: "*[L]a fonction de signi-fiance . . . nous pouvons la définir par la fonction de la coupure*" [The function of significance . . . we can define it by the function of the cut].[1]

Identification, then, is not a fusion, but, on the contrary, the realization of a split, a cut, which both the desire for identification and the desire of the figure who is being identified with enter into. Surely, the realization of one's own desire through an other would be of questionable worth for oneself if what is at stake were not a desire that is itself disunited. If another is desiring for me I could no more be identical with myself than an other could act identically with myself or with a role that has been imposed on him; something always remains split off into the unconscious.[2] I can be identical neither with myself nor with an other as long as there is desire, and desire (here) is the desire for identification. Beyond the boundary of the other begins the desire for identification which lies hidden within desire: "*[L]e désir s'institue en transgres-sion. . . .*" [Desire institutes itself in transgression].[3]

What kind of desire is this desire; what is it that forces one, like the sirens' song, always to return to the place of the event, of identification, while, on the other hand, neurotics and Odysseus, as Maurice Blanchot says,[4] refuse to tolerate these places? On the one hand, there is the attempt to evade the encounter, and, on the other, as in the case of Nabokov's main protagonist, the long-winded search for an encounter. Not the encounter with the respective subject or object of identification, because that could be realized only at the price of a split—or rather, precisely of the exclusion of a third (term) which *could* lead one to the object of desire. And finally, this intolerance manifests itself when in an intended encounter what is sought is this irrational fusion—no matter with which figure: say, for example, the embodiment of a figure from a person's early existence.[5]

Desire is as a matter of principle aimed at a lack, that is, at something one lacks; it props up its lack in order to continue to exist. Identificatory desire is aimed at handling or realizing, lack. The agent of identificatory desire would then be the song of lack, as Blanchot says, the voice of the abyss, and not the voice of he who articulates his desire. What is at stake is the place that is shunned but nevertheless fascinates—fascinates the neuroticized Odysseus to the extent that he allows himself to be bound in order to hear about or from the abyss, which the pervert regards as an object which is to be possessed from as many perspectives as possible. What is at stake is the place where speech and song cease to be alluring, as Blanchot says. Handling lack through the other gives rise to identification, which inscribes itself as a cut into the fantasm. In the transgression of its desire the signifier of identification uncovers the desire of he who identifies, without either of them knowing this. In Nabokov it is the silhouette of Lolita as the oedipal knot of the perverse hero transformed into a figure. The language of lack is here aimed at what one doesn't have and what Lolita herself is. It is the figure of Lolita as the object of desire per se and *per vers*, as the pervert's object of desire, that embodies his lack and that is he himself; it is the oedipally prohibited signifier which she is because she doesn't have it for someone else.

Can we say that it is the place of desire as the place that is bare of all song, of all speech, "as if the core land of music were a realm bare of all music,"[6] the realm where desire is no longer the desire for anything other? Just as the sirens' song increasingly recedes, so the signifier of identification disappears, and the object of desire cuts through the subject in the fantasm (the struck-out subject/object: $\$ \diamond a$). In this manner Lolita's silhouette, and in another place, Ophelia's name emerge as objects of desire, of anxiety, and of an always imaginary castration.

Just as the oedipal knots form an imaginary space, the object of desire, of anxiety, remains imaginary; the cut of the signifier is realized in the fantasm, and identification remains as fantasmatic as any other transference. In this manner identification can turn into the repetition of the oedipal knot, with the signifier unveiled as the figure of Lolita as the guarantor of desire, for example.

As far as the Imaginary is concerned, identification always also deals with a demand, with an ideal—whether aesthetic or otherwise. As long as the object of desire is not sought in an (inter-)subjective inside-outside, but rather in a steadily repeated demand of a transcendental ideal or object, the road is cleared also for so-called group identificatory processes: "[T]he class struggle is situated on the level of identification."[7]

Just as the repetition of a demand only refers to the desire lying behind it, the permanent repetition of mythical knots shows that there is another desire, which could be reached only with the destruction of the desire for repetition. The sado-masochistic or perverse short circuits exhibit this desire-become-figure openly; it is even more apparent in necrophilia where an object of desire is sought where it obviously can no longer be.

En-chor, /*encore*/ *en-corps*/ *en-coeur*/ *en-kore*,[8] still, desire seeks embodiment precisely where the latter fades. Identification with another desire imputes to a signifier knowledge concerning its desire; but this signifier just keeps on handing this question, the *"che vuoi,"* on; the symbolic knot of identification congeals into a demand for the embodiment of a desire in an object.

Notes

1. Jacques Lacan, "L'identification," (unpubl. Seminar of 5/9/1962): "The function of significance [meaning] . . . we can define it by the function of the cut." [trans. E. S.]

2. What a total identification with the ideals of a given figure or of a role, an identification, in other words, which represents no lack at all, leads to, or where it comes from, we know from history. One example is Ludwig II of Bavaria, who felt a little too much like a king: "que si un homme qui se croit un roi est fou, un roi qui se croit un roi ne l'est pas moins" ["that, when a person who believes himself to be a king is insane, a king who believes himself to be a king is no less so"]. Jacques Lacan, "Propos sur la causalité psychique," in *Écrits* (Paris: Éditions du Seuil, 1966), 170.

3. Lacan, "L'identification" (5/9/1962).

4. Maurice Blanchot, *The Sirens' Song: Selected Essays by Maurice Blanchot*, ed. and intro. by Gabriel Josipovici and trans. Sacha Rabinovitch (Sussex: Harvester Press, 1982).

5. To suppose that this desire is directed at the first person one relates to, for example, would, on the one hand, lead to the problem of how diverse identities could come into being at all; on the other, it would result in the misrecognition of tendencies or impulses in childhood or later. Such a misrecognition can occur during the course of any therapy when it is simply assumed that the concrete oedipal frame of reference is also valid for the sub-sequent life story, which results in the confusion of homo- and heterosexual tendencies, for instance. Another example is the psychotic or hysterical fit at certain points of the analysis that some analysts describe. The question that poses itself here is to what extent, on the one hand, the hypothesis that re-pressed homosexual tendencies are to be sought as causes in such events, and, on the other, an identification with another person, provoked by the analyst, play into these processes themselves.

6. Blanchot, 12.

7. Jacques Lacan, "La psychanalyse à l'envers" (unpubl. Seminar of 6/18/1970).

8. *Kore* is the old Greek name for Lolita/ young girl and, etymologically, the name Ophelia has the same meaning.

5

The Beauty behind the Window Shutters

AUGUST RUHS

In one of the sections of *Seminar XI*, entitled "Presence of the Analyst," Lacan once again criticizes the cemented conception of the analysis of the transference, according to which the transference is based on an alliance with the healthy part of the analysand's ego. Lacan has this to say about this "subject," this analysand:

> I am referring to the conception which would have the analysis of the transference proceed on the basis of an alliance with the healthy part of the subject's ego, and consists in appealing to his common sense, by way of pointing out to him the illusory character of certain of his actions in his relation with the analyst. This is a thesis that subverts what it is all about, namely the bringing to awareness of this split in the subject, realized here, in fact, in presence. To appeal to some healthy part of the subject thought to be there in the real, capable of judging with the analyst what is happening in the transference, is to misunderstand that it is precisely this part that is concerned in the transference, that it is this part that closes the door, or the window, or the shutters, or whatever—and that the beauty with whom one wishes to speak is there, behind, only too willing to open the shutters again. That is why it is at this moment that interpretation becomes decisive, for it is to the beauty that one must speak.[1]

Early on, Freud had had the presentiment that what is at stake in psychoanalysis has less to do with health and common sense than it does with passion and lovesickness. In his July 10, 1900, letter to Fliess he wrote, "The big problems are still wholly unresolved. Everything is in flux and dawning, an intellectual hell, with layer upon layer; in the darkest core, glimpses of the contours of Lucifer-Amor."[2]

41

We know this: in analysis the analyst functions as the object and cause of desire of an other, by way of which, once traversed, the production and the process of becoming conscious of a signifier, which essentially constitutes the subject, are enlisted, which, consequently, leads to the construction of a knowledge that demands for itself the status of truth and that represents the history of the conditions for love.

Freud's vision of Hell, Lacan's comments regarding the "beauty" to whom one must speak, but also metaphors like those circumscribing the inflammatory character and the inflammatory effect of interpretation in analytic practice— they all contribute to characterizing the enterprise begun by Freud as a sublime fire raising for the sake of setting in motion the love fire of the transference.

It seems that Lacan was inclined to misplace his matches or at least to have trouble finding them right away. For, precisely in the passage in the Seminar I mentioned, in which Lacan addresses the issue of the analyst's presence, and where he defines the unconscious as a beauty, something occurred which could function as a motto to what I am about to say. There is an anecdote that Lacan had been presented by one of the participants in his Seminar with a box of matches of an apparently impressive size. The event would probably not have merited mentioning had this object that changed hands not been the bearer of a text. Inscribed on it was the phrase, "The art of listening is almost as important as the art of speaking well."

Perhaps this inscription defined a relationship by way of the act of giving and taking; perhaps it did so in such a way that the giver, who worried about the acceptance of his gift, tried to maintain the gift receiver's good favor by adopting a phrase which, within that realm of praiseworthy faculties, places taking on the same level with giving.

But this is not the direction I want my presentation to take. For, on this side of all possible forays into the intersubjective realm, which would carry the presentation off in the direction of a wholly different meaning, this really quite banal sentence refers literally to a state of affairs that is capable of contributing something to a successful characterization of the psychoanalytic affair. The comment Lacan is reported to have made—"So our labors are hereby divided"— may also refer to the situation of the Seminar itself, where the distribution of speaking and listening doesn't seem to be particularly worthy of being problematized; however, as a broader gesture, it is aimed at the distribution of two disciplines within the arrangement which is that of psychoanalysis itself. At stake here are two arts—two techniques of speaking and listening—that are enriched by an ideal. In anticipation, let me say that I am referring, on the one hand, to the position of rhetoric and, on the other, to that of aesthetics within the framework of analytic treatment.

Let us begin with the first, since, probably, it seems more self-explanatory. Rhetoric in psychoanalysis includes the art of good speaking on both sides, even if, were one to consider a quantitative factor, its greater weight would have to be ascribed to the analysand. The technique of free association in which she or he is, according to the fundamental rule of analysis, to train him- or herself, intensifies to the point of rhetoric at the moment that, in the sense of Lacan, from the *parole vide* [empty speech] there emerges that full speech which carries the signifiers of the analysand's alienation from the moment of the birth of his or her subjectivity and which in turn is carried by those signifiers. Lying at a great distance from the surrealist aesthetic, which originated in a different automatism of speech, analytic speech is also capable of transmitting an educational impetus, which brings the analysand into proximity with the aesthete. It may be this that Lacan had in mind when he said somewhere that perhaps the only thing that psychoanalysis can teach is style.

On the side of the analyst, however, rhetoric is the art of good speaking, which is structured around the figure of interpretation; this, together with all of the work leading up to it—allusion, suggestion, confrontation, and so on—is the traditional understanding of good speaking. The rhetorical task of the analyst is an impossible one, because it cannot be transmitted by any sort of empirical knowledge or technical guidelines. The analyst's art of interpretation is to be distinguished from hermeneutics also by way of that artistic content which comes closest to being poetic art. Aside from its always individual development, one really cannot assume that the culture of the analytic art of interpretation is not also indirectly determined by the styles, trends, and aesthetics of literature ("literature" is here to be understood in its most general sense) dominant at any given time, which, together with a dependency on internal variations due to different theoretical positions as well as implicit and silent pedagogies and ideologies, determines its almost infinite multiplicity. When we think of Freud we are forced to note that he is not too favorably disposed to the concept of interpretation; rather, he wished to see it replaced by the concept of construction:

> If, in accounts of psychoanalytic technique, so little is said about "constructions," that is because "interpretations" and their effects are spoken of instead. But I think that "construction" is by far the more appropriate description. "Interpretation" applies to something that one does to some single element of the material, such as an association or a parapraxis. But it is a "construction" when one lays before the subject of the analysis a piece of his early history that he has forgotten, in some such way as this: "Up to your *nth* year you regarded yourself as the sole and unlimited possessor of your mother; then came another baby and brought you grave disillusionment. Your mother left you for some time, and even after her reappearance she was never again devoted exclusively to you. Your feelings towards your mother became ambivalent, your father gained a new importance for you," and so on.[3]

The discursiveness and closure of these interventions force one to remember that Freud's literary and aesthetic models were precisely those of his time, which were closely connected with the closed forms of the novel, the novella, the drama, and the representational poem. Just as, from the very start, Freud's case histories could be read as novellas, just as his texts were received by Krafft-Ebing as "scientific fairy tales," just as the neurotic destinies were placed by him within the framework of the great classical tragedies, his interpretations within the analytic treatment tended to take on, as constructions, the shape of stories, narratives, and epigrams. After all, one of the very few public acknowledgments he received during his lifetime lay in the bestowal of a great prize for literature, which was not by chance tied to the name of Goethe.

The rhetorical position of Lacan in analytic practice is—to my knowledge, which is derived from anecdotes and textual transmissions—from the very start a different one. One aesthetic principle which characterizes him particularly, as we will see, and which has to be understood from two distinct perspectives, has helped form his particular attitude behind the couch from the start. As a contribution to the art of good speaking, and this is its first characteristic which I will discuss here, its conception of the ideal is historically, culturally, and geographically distinct from Freud's position. To begin with, Lacan is a Frenchman. His interpretations, which, most of the time, probably consisted of a short illumination, his playful manipulations of signifiers, which testified to a faithfulness not only to the formal veil of the symptom but also to its object— the unconscious itself—, his devotion to and his permeability vis-à-vis the essence and immediacy of language can surely be understood fully only in connection with currents in Surrealism, Concrete Poetry, and other avant-garde movements in literature and the arts of his time. They must certainly have made their contribution to Lacan's character and to his appearance—the appearance of an aesthete.

Then, however, there is the second, and perhaps more essential, aesthetic, which plays a part in psychoanalysis as it is understood by Lacan. If one were to go back to examine the etymology of the range of meaning commanded by the word "aesthetic," one would come across the Greek word *aisthesis*, which means "perception." And, in fact, Lacan turns out to be an artist of perception who, with good reason, keeps the art of listening, which in its original sense is thus one aspect of aesthetics, within his own court according to his strict division of labor, in order to leave, to a large extent, the art of good speaking to the other, the analysand. One would, by all means, have to add to this the fact that he was not tied to suggestion, which lies at the origin of psychoanalysis in the form of hypnotic suggestion, as much as Freud was, and that he was perhaps also subjected to other ideologies.

From the start—and, again, this distinguishes him from Freud—Lacan's powers of perception included both of the most important sensory qualities: the visual and the auditory. Enough has been said about Freud's ambivalent attitude toward the Imaginary, to the image, and only late in the game, when Freud could neither keep the question of narcissism out of his field of vision any longer nor deny the existence of the visual media, which were demanding recognition, did the eye penetrate his theoretical structures in a way that he could find acceptable. It went differently with Lacan, who was in the picture from the start. He is a creature of the gaze, just like his only teacher in psychiatry, Clerambault, who was a creature of the gaze as well. Lacan's perceptions of what was coming from his patients' mouths was not just a matter of listening, but of reading as well. Learning from Lacan also means recognizing the close relation between image and tone, between language and writing, retaining one's awe of the letter and perhaps gaining recognition of the fact that an analyst is to be a blind seer and a deaf listener. Lacan's thought inhabits places in which, somewhere, there is always an eye present. This is the reason for the status of all of those objects categorized under the *petit a*, which makes them stand out— especially in the Seminar on the fundamentals of psychoanalysis, where a chapter, a whole discussion, is dedicated to the gaze—before the unconscious appears as the beauty behind the shutters.

In consideration of this in every respect close relation of Lacan to aesthetics we can now perhaps better understand why he uses this image of the beauty behind the shutters: in view of this context, it is more than just a pretty metaphor to characterize the unconscious, because it suggests that the unconscious shows itself only in oscillation, that it likes to close itself off, and that in its irrationality, it is opposed not really to logic but to common sense.

If it is the beauty who must be addressed in the act of producing meaning and who has no other wish but to show herself, then what is at stake in interpretation is the beckoning which assembles on the balcony the ideal, the gaze, femininity, and the transference.

This beauty is present not only in Lacan but perhaps also in Nietzsche. It has very little in common with Hegel's "beautiful soul"; indeed, if I may be allowed to make this conjecture as a nonphilosopher, the latter may actually be its very opposite.

In *The Gay Science* Nietzsche ponders: "Perhaps the truth is a woman who has reasons for not revealing her reasons? Perhaps her name is—to put it in Greek—Baubo?"[4]

There is no doubt that what is at stake in psychoanalysis is the truth, the truth which Lacan opposes to the *episteme* in the sciences—should we say the other sciences?—as *doxa*. Would it be going too far to speak in this respect, in regarding the unconscious in this way, of a final truth? The path leading there is, for psychoanalysis, at the very least, a claim, an ideal. In view of the experience which we have psychoanalysis to thank for, it has become a necessity to think of this truth in terms of the senses rather than in terms of common sense.

While German idealism attempted to reconcile aesthetic judgment (of taste) and universally valid and certifiable cognitive judgment, sensuousness and common sense (understanding), while Freud, on the other hand, aimed at (re-)dissolving them, Lacan positions them as opposites and as opposing forces, because for him it is common sense which continually closes the door, the window, the shutters, behind which the beauty, who is at stake in interpretation, in the transference and in the interpretation of the transference, conceals herself.

In relation to this pretty simile, Nietzsche's understanding of the relationship between aesthetics and truth converges with Lacan's answer to the question regarding the essence of the unconscious. In Nietzsche's attempt at completing the history of aesthetics, beauty is not the reconciliatory mode of appearance of truth as it is in Hegel, nor is appearance understood to be the self-manifestation of Being; rather, the opposite is the case: truth is understood to be the result of tragic beauty and Being as the defining interpretation of appearance—so that aesthetics becomes the self-perception of the world of contradictions.

The unconscious cause (*Ur-Sache*, "primal thing") in Lacan's definition is not something that is, nor is it something that is not, but rather it is this Greek *me on*, what should not be, what emerges from the prohibition, which brings something that is into being in spite of its nonarrival. For Nietzsche, the truth as woman has good reasons for not revealing her reasons; don't Baubo and the beauty represent the hole which is in the end unfathomable, unfillable, no matter what one tries to stuff into it, that wound around which everything turns to the point of vertigo and with which everything which is at stake in psychoanalysis either stands or falls? Castration?

Let us return to the point at which the secret of the dream was unveiled to Dr. Sigmund Freud, and let me quote a passage from the dream of Irma's injection. There we read the following:

> I took her to the window and looked down her throat, and she showed signs of recalcitrance, like women with artificial dentures. I thought to myself that there was really no need for her to do that.—She then opened her mouth properly and on the right I found a big white patch; at another place I saw extensive whitish grey scabs upon some remarkable curly structures which were evidently modeled on the turbinal bones of the nose.—I at once called in Dr. M., and he repeated the examination and confirmed it. . . .[5]

In Lacan's analysis of this dream, in the Seminar, *The Ego in Freud's Theory and in the Technique of Psychoanalysis*, this first part of the dream represents the moment "when the world of the dreamer is plunged into the greatest imaginary chaos."[6] And Lacan says, "There's a horrendous discovery here, that of the flesh one never sees, the foundation of things, the other side of the head, of the face, the secretory glands par excellence, the flesh from which everything exudes, at the very heart of the mystery, the flesh in as much as it is something which provokes anxiety."[7]

Whereas the goddess had simply laughed at the appearance of Baubo, Freud experiences sheer horror. This is why in the dream he appeals to his friends, and it is only with difficulty that the three of them—Lacan refers to them as a trio of clowns—are able to find a formula, a word to rescue them from what they have seen, a chemical formula. Is this the expression of the failure of his psychological abilities, of flight into the realm of biology?

In fact, the life of the conqueror who had begun to colonize an extensive country was too short for him to discover a continent which remained dark for him.

As a visual person, his descendant Lacan was able to bear better the sight of "the abyss of the feminine organ from which all life emerges, this gulf of the mouth, in which everything is swallowed up,"[8] and was, in fact, capable of lending it the appearance of beauty. Of course, he was successful in doing so only by allowing her to speak and not, as it happened with Freud and Dora, by interrupting her.

I wish now, in finishing, to make it possible for a beauty—in some sense, another Irma, who was willing to open up her mouth even more—to speak.

A beauty who, in her so-called more mature years, but nevertheless demonstrating that childlike temperament that characterizes hysterics, entered analysis with me a few years ago as Mrs. M. At the start of one session, before she had even relaxed, she said, in her distinct Berlin accent, that she'd "had once again one of those stupid dreams" of hers. She had dreamt that she had gone to a store to buy a box of laundry detergent, the brand OMO, to be precise. Attempting to get the jump on any kind of intervention on my part, she declared roundly that it was obvious what this meant. OMO meant: an M between two zeroes; M is she herself, and the two others, the zeroes, had to be her husband and her friend.

Here we had something like the image of the beauty between two window shutters, which, to her, always the commonsensical one, obviously meant nothing. M. and her clown duo, as Lacan would perhaps have said, unified in a formula. A formula that is not chemical, but that perhaps comes from the realm of advertising. Possibly it is Borromean.

Two zeroes hanging on to an M. On the one hand, this is perhaps an image of three discourses in which two of them, that of the Master and that of Knowledge, are concerned with the third, the Hysterical one, and its taming.

But, on the other hand, this is perhaps also an image of people, no matter whether they are male or female, as beings of lack, attached to that primal signifier, which carries them and which is capable of calming them and propping them up. M, as the anxiety-provoking head of the Medusa, but also M as *mors*, *maître absolu*, God. If we wish to follow Lacan, we know that this means language.

So that, in the end, language, too, is the beauty to which we must appeal in our interpretation.

From this perspective, then, language is also that *dieu-femme* who, in feminist circles, has lately been conjured up again and again.

Notes

1. Jacques Lacan, *The Four Fundamental Concepts of Psycho-Analysis*, ed. Jacques-Alain Miller, trans. Alan Sheridan (New York: W. W. Norton, 1981), 130–131.

2. Sigmund Freud, "Letter of July 10, 1900," in *Letters of Sigmund Freud to Wilhelm Fliess 1987–1904*, ed. and trans. Jeffrey Moussaieff Masson (Cambridge, Mass.: Harvard University Press, 1985), 421. German Letter #138; new version letter #251.

3. Sigmund Freud, "Constructions in Analysis," *The Standard Edition, Volume 23*, trans. James Strachey (London: The Hogarth Press, 1968), 261.

4. Baubo: A primitive and obscene female demon; according to the *Oxford Classical Dictionary*, originally a personification of the female genitals. Friedrich Nietzsche, *The Gay Science*, trans. Walter Kaufman (New York: Random House, 1974), 38.

5. Sigmund Freud, *SE* 4, 107.

6. Jacques Lacan, *The Seminar of Jacques Lacan: Book 2: The Ego in Freud's Theory and in the Technique of Psychoanalysis, 1954–1955*, ed. Jacques-Alain Miller and trans. Sylvana Tomaselli (New York: W. W. Norton, 1988), 170.

7. Ibid., 154.

8. Ibid., 164.

Part II
Sexual

Introduction

Maire Jaanus and Elizabeth Stewart

Bernet's essay, "Sexual Identification and Sexual Difference," in ways refers back to Widmer, Borens, and Saalfrank and their emphasis on pathological stasis and the disavowal of the gap, of substitution, and the mobile nature of desire. All four point to a static and fetishistic defense against traumatic perceptions of lack, loss, and castration. (The murderousness parents feel regarding their children as described by Widmer, their imaginary imprisonment and binding of them, should also be seen in this light.) Bernet, in his essay explaining why "there is no sexual relation," points to the desire- and reality-destroying properties of pornography. Since sexual identity is not naturally given but symbolically (and differentially) produced (the man asks the woman for what she does not have: the phallus), the pornographic representation of sexuality and sexual identity as biological and fully present to the senses, essentially and a priori, produces anxiety. Since desire is the effect of concealment of the fact of the symbolic nature of sexuality, confronting the supposed "reality" presented by pornography, without a symbolic/imaginary veil, results in reality loss and, thus, anxiety. Bernet suggests that this is an anxiety that is produced by a schizogenically automated and high tech society, characterized in this case by an excess of images of the total, and totally present, body. The subjects of pornography allow their sexuality to be determined by standardized, prefabricated fantasms, which further the repression of singular, unique sexualities and enable a flight from the anxiety of one's desires and drives. The pornographic body, then, is also an essentially static and pathologically full (or empty) body that signals a malfunctioning of the symbolic trauma-binding structure and that points to pornography's enmity towards personalized sexual desire.

Also dealing with the play that constitutes sexuality and the play of sexual difference in the symbolic order is Fehr and Sträuli's essay, "The Joys and

49

Suffering of So-Called Interpretation, or: The Soul of the Dress's Fold." Its main thrust is to undermine the idea of the possibility of gaining transparent knowledge (on the part of the analyst) by showing how the symbolic order is "disorderly" and trips up even those who are "supposed to know." The two authors tell the story of how symbolic disorder infiltrates imaginary meaning by way of a story Freud tells of his examination of a young woman appearing in consultation dressed in disorderly fashion. They treat the story as a sort of parable that in some ways is similar to Lacan's famous return to Freud's "Dream of Irma's Injection." While what had stared Freud in the face in the latter dream, according to Lacan, was the difference between imaginary knowledge and the symbolic murder of the Real by the "Word," that is, by the play of signifiers, in this story it is Freud's encounter with the Symbolic which infiltrates imaginary full knowledge, and which he perceives as disorderly—filled with desire—apparently too disorderly for his "obvious" interpretation of the consultation. In general this essay performs three deconstructive gestures and it yields one ethical imperative that are fundamental to the other essays in the collection: it points to 1) the illusory and compulsive nature of full knowledge and the impossibility of the truthfulness of signification; 2) the ethics of the recognition of misrecognition; and 3) the sacrifice of the "subject supposed to know" by way of psychoanalytic discourse itself, which sacrifices it to the Other. The "subject supposed to know" is the Other's pawn, and wears the symbolic on its skin; this sacrifice to the Other protects the subject against the Real.

Anne Juranville's essay, "Hysteria and Melancholia in Woman," is set up beautifully by Fehr and Sträuli. The inscribed—ornamented, painted, marked, lined, veiled—body of the woman takes center stage, just as Freud's young visitor had. And just as the visitor had pulled the rug of Freud's own making (his master's knowledge) out from under his feet, as Fehr and Sträuli so aptly demonstrate, the hysteric that Juranville paints for us is just as fascinating at identifying with the man by understanding and manipulating the symbolic order better than the men do, by making them forget its illusoriness for her own gain, and by doing it all *for another woman (the mother)*. And yet, she plays the woman to perfection. These two essays ought really to be read in conjunction. Juranville defines "Woman" by way of the operations of the "masquerade." A notion already widely disseminated in academic circles, specifically in feminist theory, Juranville brings it into relation with the melancholy and the hysteric woman respectively: the masquerade is the fiction whereby a woman "becomes a woman," marks her body as a "woman's body." The melancholy woman rejects fiction as such, and thus finds herself within the realm of the psychoses. She refuses the hysteric's theatricality, style, and aplomb, refuses the fiction in its entirety, and therefore finds herself off the stage (of the Symbolic). While the hysteric makes use of the theatricality of the masquerade, she continues to believe in the absolute femininity (embodied in the mother) beyond fiction for which she performs. The tension between fiction and nonfiction, the site where play breaks down in a demand for enjoyment and satisfaction, finds expression in her symptoms (while the masquerade already involves mourning for and a leave-taking of a nonexisting authenticity).

The difficulty posed by the mother, the question of "What does she want? What is she looking for?" on the part of the child, leads us into the next essay.

Regula Schindler's essay, "Symbolic Mother—Real Father," is exemplary of these essays' ability to move from the very clinical and theoretical, to the level of the individual subject's existence in the real world, to the collective, both historical and contemporary (here too a warning signal to a global culture too attuned to a heavy and absolute primal and maternal symbolic order characterized by the same binarism that characterizes digital culture). True to the slant of the rest of the essays, Schindler's centerpiece in this essay is the late Lacan—specifically the late, difficult, and almost unspeakable notion of the *sinthome*, a notion that is often presented by other authors in almost mystical terms, but which Schindler examines lucidly. Most of all, this essay is very successful at laying bare the truly *knotted-and-chained* mode of Lacan's thought. Through the notion of the *sinthome* Schindler makes clear how irretrievably interwoven the mother and father functions are, and, in both theoretical and concrete form, what the ramifications of the failure of these functions are not only for the subject, but for culture as such. She overturns the facile association of the father function with the Symbolic and the mother function with the Real and elaborates on the father's relation to the Real and to the symptom in contrast to the mother's introduction of the child to an elemental symbolic binarism of presence and absence. Certain aspects of her hypothesis are highly relevant to current theories regarding the psychology of totalitarianism in fin-de-siècle central Europe that turn on the notion of the decline of the father function, of the foreclosure of the Name-of-the-Father. The *sinthome* as an absolutely unanalyzable concept that "repairs" and "saves" is always a fascinating and immensely rich one, especially in the context of an individual or collective hyperrigidity and maddening of the law on the one hand, the image of the devouring mother on the other—*and* the fact that the two supposed extremes are always already also interchangeable, in the context of the history of modernity and its postmodern continuation. With its references to Western literature and to digitality, to sexual and parental functions, to clinical issues, as well as the profound treatment of Lacanian ethics, this essay hovers over all four of our categories. We place it here, and allow it to lead into an essay with equally many cultural echoes and which is also concerned with symbolization and heaviness in symbolization.

6

Sexual Identification and Sexual Difference

Rudolf Bernet

It seems appropriate to me to approach the question of the human subject's sexual identity in this paper first by way of the abstract problematic of sexual difference and only then to discuss the concrete forms of interaction between the sexual desires of different persons. My presentation concerning these two correlative questions emphasizes above all symbolic arbitrariness, that is, the conventional and nontransparent character of the symbolic legalities that coercively determine the subject's sexual identity and desire. Other aspects concerning the relationship between sexuality and subjectivity will be treated either more marginally or not at all. Thus I will not probe the way in which the symbolic structure of sexuality imprints itself onto the subject's physicality. The reason for that is of course not that I believe that sexual identity and sexual desire have nothing to do with a naturally determined physicality, but rather that, even more than is generally suspected, they have to do with an artificial symbolic system. One other consequence of this consciously one-sided treatment of sexuality is that preverbal forms of sexual experience and sexual communication will be left aside. The transcendence of sexuality—that is, the resonance that sexuality has with the subject's encounter with death and his religious and, above all, mystical experiences—will not be discussed either.

Sexual Difference

The structure of sexual experience threatens the traditional concept of the subject directly and from a variety of different angles. It is said that sexual desire is blinding and that sexual *jouissance* means self-loss, a *petite mort* that dissolves the boundaries between myself and the other. We will first concern ourselves with the structure of sexual difference, which implies a primary and surely also most fundamental problematization of the traditional concept of the subject.

53

We will also assume—which, by the way, is not as self-evident as it may seem at first glance—that sexual difference is a question of being either a man or a woman. What that implies, however, is that there is no communal *hypokeimenon*, no neutral human subject. Put more precisely: the concept of a neutral human subject implies a misrecognition, even a disavowal, of sexual difference. Usually this disavowal of sexual difference takes the shape of denying the singularity and difference of woman: man (*homme*) represents the human subject (*Homme*, one, *man*).

Traditional philosophical thought has always attempted to evade the alternative between a neutral human *hypokeimenon* on the one hand, and the compulsion to be either man or woman, on the other. Thus, sexual difference was regarded as the division of an original whole.[1] Man and woman are different but they belong together; they complement each other and together realize, in communion and union, the concrete essence of the human being. The sexual union of man and woman is a precondition as well as a metaphor for human fertility and creativity, for human institutions, and even for the relationship between human being and God. Some philosophers even go one step further and conceive of the unity of man and woman not only as the aim of human love and self-realization, but also as its origin. The best example for this is Plato's *Symposium*: in Aristophanes' speech the human being is represented as one half of an original whole, and love as a desire for the complementing, lost other half (*symbolon*).

It would appear that only the modern philosophies of human finitude brought about a true transformation of these "holistic" or "totalitarian" conceptions of sexual difference. In Feuerbach's anthropology, for example, the problematic of sexual difference is given a privileged position. Being either man or woman imposes considerable limitations on human knowledge and makes people dependent on one another. One desires an other whom one doesn't really know, and one knows oneself only as an other's love object. Feuerbach's analysis of sexual difference, however, remains in duty bound to Hegel's thought: the irresolvable difference between man and woman continues to be determined by opposition, by contraries. The same is true, by the way, for most of the modern apostles of philosophies of finitude, be they feminist in nature or not. It is true that there is less emphasis on the complementarity between man and woman, but that has merely reinforced the importance ascribed to their oppositionality. On the one hand, it is asserted that it is impossible for a man to understand a woman, and yet, on the other, woman is still understood as a not-man. It is said that, as a woman, one ought not be guided by male frameworks of expectations and at the same time the attempt is made to prove that a woman is capable of being as much a "man" as the next in any branch of work. With one breath one announces emancipation and liberation and with the next one locks oneself into a normative usage of antagonistic role patterns.

These contemporary modes of thought are not only marked by traditional and totalitarian thinking; they are also extremely inconsequential, not to mention dishonest. How can one, on the one hand, represent sexual difference as a fundamental form of the finiteness of human cognition, and, on the other, wish to determine it as being universally valid and preferably even as normative in content? Thinking in conceptual oppositions here too seems merely to point to difference in order to then deny it more thoroughly; it demands regard for what is foreign in order to be that much better equipped to appropriate this foreignness as one's other. It is not surprising that such a dialectical rape of sexual difference leads to few original insights: the difference between man and woman is viewed as being part of a row of very general oppositions, such as active/passive, aggressive/narcissistic, public/private, polygamous/monogamous. The psychoanalysis of Freud and Lacan, together with contemporary thought that bases itself on it, represent, in contrast, more promising approaches to the secret of sexual difference.

Even though Freud continues to use oppositional conceptual pairs like active versus passive, aggressive versus narcissistic, he surely does not do so, like the modern ideosexologues, in order to divide the human world into two equal halves. The opposition between being a man and being a woman for Freud is the result of a rationalization. Rationalization is what Heidegger and Derrida call metaphysical thinking, that is, making the incomprehensible comprehensible. Sexist rationalization exorcises the anxiety that emerges with the insight into one's own *bisexuality*, which is simultaneously a result of remembering the deep-seated conflicts (especially the so-called Oedipus conflict), out of which one's own sexual identity has emerged. Freud turns against the allegedly self-evident fact of sexual difference when he says, for example, that the unconscious does not yet know of this difference. In reality, this statement is based on the assertion that the drive is naturally masculine and that, therefore, there is no such thing as a purely natural or drive-determined femininity. Freud was not thanked for this assertion. Lacan is one of the few thinkers who took this hypothesis seriously and tried to explain it. Lacan, like Freud, does not regard an individual's sexual identity as a natural given, but rather as an effect of a symbolic articulation of desire and an imaginary clothing of the subject of this desire. In Lacan, the thesis that the signifier "phallus" takes on a privileged position in the symbolic articulation of desire and of *jouissance* corresponds to Freud's assertion concerning the originally masculine structure of the drive.

The assertion that the image or fantasm of the male sexual organ plays a central role in imaginary representations of *jouissance* and in the symbolic articulation of sexual difference is certainly not simply the verbalization of some visible biological fact. According to Lacan, the subject is originally nothing but its own desire; this desire is "lack" and the desiring subject is therefore "nothing," a gap, or "*béance.*" The original subject of desire is neither man nor woman, simply because it does not (yet) possess a content-specific identity. Desire has no original name any more than a subject has; rather, it is an anonymous process, a self-functioning machine, a self-regulating cybernetic system. The problematic aspect of this system consists in the fact that in reality it is a patchwork of different self-regulating systems, which Freud calls partial drives. Not only is the desiring subject driven by violent impulses then, but on top of that, these impulses often conflict with one another. In order to offer resistance to the violence of these antagonistic strivings, the desiring subject develops an instance of control that filters the impulses before they enter consciousness. This instance is the ego (*moi*). So the ego is not simply the subject, but rather a subject that is fleeing from the anxiety-provoking experience of its own splitting and nothingness by determining itself as something, by bestowing upon itself a determinate identity.[2]

The content-specific identity of the sexual subject is then something secondary: a form of self-protection against the overwhelming power of the sexual drive. But the ego has thereby not yet been set down as sexually either man or woman. That is not surprising when one considers that this ego is not in the first place a desiring ego, but, on the contrary, a construct of the subject which is defending itself against being annihilated by desire. It is therefore only logical that Freud should have conceived of this ego as the principle of an independent, nonsexual self-preservative drive. Even if with the introduction of narcissism the ego is included in the libido, this occurs with the intent that self-love will protect the subject from self-loss and self-destruction by the objects of the drive. Lacan has pointed out that identification with an image of the self plays a very significant role in the genesis of such an ego. But this *stade du miroir* [mirror stage] is merely a first form of the Imaginary, that is, the reassuring identification with an image or with a word, a story, and so forth. The Imaginary is the domain of content-specific identity, of knowledgeable consciousness and of assured self-recognition. In reality, however, imaginary rationality is rationalization, consciousness is repression of the unconscious, and subjective identity is a protection against one's own nothingness. And yet, the Imaginary does not necessarily cause problems; on the contrary, it furthers human happiness, at least as long as it doesn't become completely unmoored from the unconscious and fall victim to the delusion of its own autonomy.

In reference to the problem of the sexual identity of the human being as either man or woman, Lacan's analysis of the Imaginary has the following consequences: (1) the identity of the ego is originally—that is, during the mirror stage—not yet sexually differentiated; (2) when sexual difference becomes something self-evident, the legitimate suspicion arises that one has allowed oneself to be guided by a purely imaginary determination of difference. Traditional philosophical discourse that defines difference as opposition is a good example of this type of rationalization of the incomprehensible within sexual difference. For Lacan, on the other hand, sexual difference is symbolic in nature, since sexual desire is itself symbolically structured.

We will return to this symbolic structure of desire. For now we will limit ourselves to the reminder that both the subject and the object of desire owe their significance to a symbolic system. Lacan understands this symbolic system as a system of linguistic signifiers and explains its structure by referring to de Saussure's theory of signs and Jakobson's theory of the double axis of language. There are good reasons for identifying the symbolic system, which articulates desire, with language. Language not only determines what happens in psychoanalytic practice, but it also determines human existence as such in a wholly decisive manner. But it is still not clear why the symbolic structure of sexual desire should not be understood more inclusively by referring to culturally determined life forms and lifestyles, the way Foucault does, for example, in the last two parts of his *Histoire de la sexualité*. It is not the question whether sexual desire is determined by an infinite chain of signifiers, or by the rules of public life, or by a historically contingent power structure that is decisive. It is much more important to make it clear that the structure of sexual desire, of the desiring subject and the object of desire, cannot be adequately explained by biological factors alone.

Sexuality is then a cultural phenomenon. Lacan doesn't stop at this rather trivial assertion, however. It is clear, for instance, that he does not regard the symbolic structure of human sexuality as a sign of human superiority or freedom. On the contrary, human beings are symbolic beings by coercion, because otherwise they cannot survive. For, differently from animals, human beings cannot depend on their natural drives; their striving after *jouissance* is boundless; it becomes absolute and thus threatens natural survival instead of simply making it more enjoyable. The fact that the symbolic structure of human life is not proof of human superiority or spirituality is also made clear by the fact that the human individual experiences this symbolic structure as a determination that is to a certain extent external to the individual's own existence, which is what makes a continuous knowledge of one's own identity impossible. Lacan emphasizes again and again, and legitimately so, that the symbolic system is determined by laws and that these laws are in principle never completely discernible and can never be fully legitimated.[3] Laws, commands, and rituals function correctly only when they are also experienced as being more or less arbitrary, conventional, or even cruel. (Just think of the test case of the incest prohibition!) Only a self-fabricated law can be fully discernible. But a self-fabricated law always exists in the service of private interests and can therefore make no claim to general, and certainly not to absolute, validity. It is rather a pseudo-law, usually created for the sake of manipulation, meddling, and often even of sadistic usage. Perverse sexuality is the best example of how such pseudolaws function. The noticeably moralizing rhetoric of perverts always has to do with such pseudolaws whose function it is to both justify and conceal the refusal to recognize an arbitrary and absolute law (see also Sade).

What does all this mean, now, in terms of our question about the sexual identity of man and woman? First, that "masculine" and "feminine" are signifiers and as such are part of an infinite and unsurveyable chain of expressive signs. The meaning of sexual difference can therefore never be established and unequivocally determined. The meaning of sexual difference slips and slides and displaces itself into infinity. Secondly, as a symbolically determined difference, sexual difference also has a conventional, even arbitrary, character. It is not by chance that one speaks of a "small difference" (*petite différence*), and it is not immediately clear why so much significance is attributed to it. It is precisely because of the difficulty of recognizing the slippery meaning and the arbitrariness of sexual difference that one tries to find shelter in an imaginary determination of sexual difference and hence also of one's own sexual identity.

The illusion afforded by such a sexual identity may have a reassuring effect, but it in no way furthers sexual *jouissance*. On the contrary, most sexual frustrations and neurotic symptoms originate precisely in this imaginary disavowal of the symbolic character of one's own sexual identity. Disavowal of the slippery character of sexual difference often leads to a cramped identification with sexual role behavior and to a fantasmatic fixation on the ideal man or the ideal woman. Anything in the ego that does not correspond to this ideal is repressed or projected outward. Other people can then appear only as unconditional idolaters of our own ideal, or as persecutors who accuse us of not being the ideal man or woman. Hysterical frigidity and the foreclosure of latent homosexuality in paranoia are clinical examples of what I am describing.

The best example of an imaginary disavowal of the symbolic arbitrariness of sexual difference, however, is pornography. Acceptance of the arbitrariness of sexual difference leads to liberating laughter, to relaxation, or at least to compliance with its inscrutable character. Pornography, as is well known, allows for everything except laughter. It is also not a coincidence that pornography often hides behind the mask of "sexual enlightenment." Pornography depends on the expectation that the arbitrary nature of sexual difference can be made intelligible by showing everything that happens in the sexual act. It is therefore most likely not a mere coincidence that pornography often has much in common with a sort of detached introduction to a specialized realm of human anatomy. Even in the subtler forms of pornography a cool, dominated, and dominating gaze is turned on sexuality. But neither pornography nor the most highly specialized forms of medicine and sexology are capable of making the exact meaning of one's own and the other sex even vaguely clear. Fairy tales and Greek tragedies—the story of Oedipus, for instance—are much better at doing that.

Interaction between Different Desiring Subjects

Human sexuality is, then, in large measure imaginary, even deceptive, and always derivative, that is, derived from the symbolic structure of desire. Sexual identity emerges from the symbolic relationship, the dependency, and the playful struggle between desiring and being desired. Desiring and being desired are expressly brought into correlation with sexual difference through the Oedipal relation and the incest prohibition. Desiring and being desired necessarily means desiring and being desired as a male or a female subject. Sexual *jouisssance*, too, attains a new meaning when it is related to sexual difference, because the question that demands to be answered, then, is whether the sexual union between heterosexual partners is experienced as a dissolution of their sexual difference or rather as its confirmation. First, however, we must return to the problematic of the symbolic structure of desire.

The originally symbolic nature of the object of desire rests on the fact that it always refers to a lost object. Already in Freud the wish is the libidinal investment of an image or a sign that points to a past and more original experience of *jouissance*. The object of desire is, then, always the substitute, the representative, the sign for a lost object. This relationship between the sign and its object, however, is of the sort that the original and lost object owes its meaning as "thing in itself" of desire to its representation by the sign, and not vice versa. The object of desire, then, is either an original but lost and unreachable object or it is its representative. In principle, any object can function as such a substitute; the substitutive object, then, is an arbitrary and interchangeable representative of the original object (just like the sign). The original and lost object (*grosso modo:* the mother), on the other hand, is by no means arbitrary; it is not a sign and is, therefore, for the subject, moving on the symbolic level, an "impossible" object. This essentially interchangeable nature of the representative object of our most intimate and heated desire does not exclude the fact, however, that contentwise it is quite differentially determined. This specificity in terms of content is, however, dependent on this sign's reference to other signs. The representative object of desire owes its meaning to the place it has in the chain of signifiers. The arbitrary nature of the representative object must then be more precisely characterized as symbolic arbitrariness. The movement of desire, then, is guided by a symbolically regulated absence. Desire is a lack (*manque*, which, through the thicket of the phenomenal multiplicity of representative objects, points to an unreachable "thing in itself" [*"la Chose"*]).

The subject of desire has a symbolic structure as well. The subject, too, owes its meaning to the open-ended system of linguistic signifiers, that is, to its own representation at a specified point within the never entirely surveyable symbolic order. The subject, too, has always already lost itself, or more precisely: it is nothing but a having-lost-itself. Lacan clarifies this by making recourse to the linguistic distinction between the *sujet de l'énonciation* [the I of the enunciation] and the *sujet de l'énoncé* [the I of the statement]. The speaking subject can make itself evident only via a generally valid linguistic code—as a subject, that is, about whom others speak by means of general concepts. While on the one hand, the subject is the mere effect of language, or of the discourse of the

Other, on the other, it remains fascinated by the dream of a speech in which it is fully and transparently present, in which, in other words, the *sujet de l'énonciation* and the *sujet de l'énoncé* completely collapse into one another. Desire for an intellectual perception of oneself, then, corresponds to the "thing in itself" of desire. In a constitutional use of this regulative principle of subjective desire one not only gets wrapped up in paralogisms, but also ends up in psychosis.

Lacan examines the symbolic splitting of the desiring subject from another point of view as well. The subject is not just a chance product of a generally valid system of signifiers, it also constitutes itself in interpersonal relationships. In these relationships, dependency and striving for independence play an important role; independence, which yearns for recognition by the Other, leads to a new form of dependency. In this context Lacan often makes recourse to Hegel's master/slave dialectic. The splitting of the desiring subject also originates in the dissolution of the original union between mother and child. This separation is symbolic in nature because this splitting up of mother and child occurs in the name of a symbolic law—the incest prohibition. This separation, too, represents a loss, but not a loss of self, since the desiring subject always already exists as a split subject. Only where there is lack is there a desiring subject, and this lack has now taken on a double meaning: 1) to do without the mother as an essential "thing in itself" (*la Chose*), and 2) to experience the mother herself as a desiring subject whose lack one cannot cancel. All of this implies a symbolic or cultural revolution through which human sexuality attains a new meaning: the father has become the representative of the law instead of being a tiresome rival; perception of anatomical difference in regards to the presence or absence of the penis is translated into desire for the phallus; castration receives a symbolic meaning (it is impossible to be man and woman simultaneously). Without this symbolic revolution there can be no sexual identity and a fortiori no heterosexual relations either. While it is true that the social order limits the possibilities for sexual relations (Freud talks about "cultural denial"), it is no less true that without culture there would be no sexual relations at all.

The symbolic structure of the relationship to one's father and one's mother certainly does not neutralize the arbitrary character of sexual difference, but it does point one in the direction of a nonimaginary identification with one's own sex. One's own sexual identity is not derived from some sort of theory about anatomical difference (see Freud's theory regarding infantile sexual theories), or from an ideal male or female image. I am either a man or a woman, because the symbolic order does not allow me to be both, and I am made either a man or a woman through the desire of the Other. This Other is originally always the father and the mother. Disturbances in the child's sexual identification therefore always lead back to the influence of the unconscious desire of the father and the mother. As subjects of desire, by the way, mother and father are not merely

"Mom" and "Dad" but, like Greek tragic figures, representatives of different family histories and subcultures.

In spite of the symbolic-arbitrary character of sexual difference, the child encounters this difference first in the difference between mother and father. Both the boy and the girl discover the mother's castration and the significance of the phallus in the mother's desire for the father. This is where the roads of boy and girl part. The boy accepts the law that the father represents; he renounces his oedipal attraction to his mother, he identifies with the symbolic Name of the Father and goes off in search of sexual objects that confirm his new male identity. The decisive element here is that the father is no longer seen as a rival by the boy but rather as a symbolic initiator into the boy's own sexual life, which from now on takes place outside of the family. Many clinical symptoms, especially of obsessive neurosis, have their source in an imaginary misrecognition of the symbolic significance of the prohibition that is spoken by the father: symbolic castration, which by necessity is closely correlated with the absolutely valid (for the father, too) incest prohibition, then turns into the threat of punishment through which the father keeps his exorbitant privileges and tyrannical power intact and forbids his son all sexual *jouissance* whatsoever.

It is probably (even) more difficult for the girl to recognize the necessity for symbolic castration, because she often imagines that her body is sexually at a disadvantage. While for the boy the (imagined) threat of castration leads to a revolt against the father, the girl usually blames the mother for her own (imagined) castration. In this way the girl enters into an often ambivalent relationship with her mother as well as into serious conflict, because this same "bad" mother is also the original and total love object. In addition to that, this ambivalently determined, lost love object is not replaced by a female substitute the way she is for the boy. This is where the sometimes lifelong (but often overcompensated) hatred for the mother and simultaneously the search for the motherly element in men, which is most of the time frustrated, originate. The relationship with the father is also structured in a more complicated way than it is in the boy: the father is representative of both the law and the new, oedipal love object, who often appears in the guise of seducer. It is here that the assertion that women have a less developed or less cruel superego than men do originates. Quite often the contradictory wish that the father may undo her (imagined) castration (for example, in the form of being impregnated by him) comes into existence in the girl.

The heterosexual relationship between the adult man and the adult woman is also a complicated matter, and perhaps it is, as Lacan says, not a "relationship" (*rapport sexuel*) at all. Even though the woman, like Penia in Plato's *Symposium*, knows what she wants, she never really gets it. She wants to be desired, she wants a man, she wants a son, she wants to become rich like Poros. But when she is desired, she is desired as Penia, and for her lack and poverty.

Hence a woman's seductiveness often contains something mysterious for the woman herself and hence she easily falls victim to whoever is selling female seductive sorcery. Not infrequently one also finds in woman a (hysterical) inclination to use her own power of seduction phallically. The man, for his part, asks the woman to give him something that she herself does not possess and which he possesses only insofar as the woman demands it—the phallus, that is, the key to sexual *jouissance*. He yearns for recognition of his masculinity and is for this reason dependent on the woman's desire and *enjoyment*. As symbolic identity, then, his masculinity is not a substantial possession, but rather the effect of the woman's desire and pleasure. For this reason the man is very dependent and vulnerable in his masculinity. He believes that he knows the secret to his own seduction, but this lonely knowledge does not reassure him.

The idea of a sexual union or even fusion between man and woman is therefore hardly more than an imaginary and idealizing fantasy. As it often happens in the context of human sexuality, here too a biological model plays the role of a reassuring fiction. One does not always have to think of it and one is, after all, able to live with it, but, still, the result of the symbolic determination of male and female desire is that all sexual relations in principal carry within them the possibility of conflict. Man and woman never get what they demand and what is demanded of them contradicts what they themselves demand. Penia wants to become rich herself instead of submissively idolizing Poros's greatness. Poros, on the other hand, wishes to be drunk and yet still potent; he fears that the sobering experience of his own dependency on Penia will bring about his impotence as well. If even Poros and Penia don't understand each other too well, is it surprising that we don't understand their child Eros any better than we do?

Proof through the Example of Pornography

Only contemporary commercial pornography pretends to understand it all and creates a spectacle of its understanding of human sexuality. It is precisely not, as is often claimed, this as-if behavior that is most typical of pornography. Simulation is a specifically symbolic action and therefore also an essential element of the sexual game. It is impossible to conceive of sexual seduction without this as-if behavior; what is manifested in as-if behavior is both the symbolic character and the arbitrariness of sexual behavior. The attraction of pornography is limited also because the as-if behavior of the actors naturalizes it and thereby destroys the symbolic and arbitrary character of their actions. This antisymbolic mode of operating of pornography originates in the human wish to be free of the symbolic dependency of one's own sexual desire on the desire of the Other. This dependency is that much more difficult to bear as one has no influence over the desire of the Other and really will never understand it.

Pornography promises to heal this suffering; it pretends to be able to offer insight into the incomprehensible. To a great extent pornography owes its power of attraction to the illusion it promotes that it is possible to experience *jouissance* in the position of an absolute lord and master. It constitutes a defense against one's own sexual stimulation, against the vulnerability of one's own sexual identity, and against the dependency on the desire of an imaginary other. Pornography is the staging of the detached overpowering of woman, of the domination of one's own desire by the deferment of satisfaction, and of the overcoming of one's own sexual ignorance. Contemporary pornography is above all characterized by the fact that it operates primarily with images. The reason for this is not just that consumers are becoming increasingly more illiterate but also the specific effectiveness of the pornographic image, which differs in an essential way from the erotic or pornographic text. Words and texts have an essentially evocative effect; they suggest more than they really say; they place the reader into an atmosphere that varies from text to text. In a way that is similar to an actual seduction, readers often do not quite know what is happening to them; they are carried away by the narrative and surprised. The pornographic image, on the other hand, functions more like material evidence that confirms spectators in their expectations and therefore soon becomes tedious. This trivial factualness, this loss of all suggestive power, is also what distinguishes the pornographic image from the erotic one.[4] The pornographic image is characterized by its far-reaching or even absolute homogeneity, by its schematic treatment of the represented scene. There is neither imagination nor pleasure; it lacks mischievousness and levity. Instead of being the expression of increased *joie de vivre*, it petrifies the gaze through its deadly serious and almost ritualistic representation of a horrifying machinery of bodies that have lost all individual or human expressive power.

One should also note that in many representations of "dirty" fantasies the people in those pornographic images do not indulge in their own sensuality but strenuously attempt to represent a stereotypical image of "vice." They illustrate the schematic image that one has of human lasciviousness. They confront consumers with an unimaginative mirror image of their alleged sexual fantasms. Consumers, on the other hand, are stimulated by these images only if they pretend to believe in their veracity. The erotic effectiveness of pornographic images is based, then, on a double pretense: the actors pretend to be driven by true desire while they really illustrate mere schematic pictures of an alleged collective unconscious; the consumer pretends to believe in the veracity of the pornographic images, and then in his real sexual life allows himself to be directed by the pseudoreality of these images. This pornographic representation of human sexuality leads in the end to a total reality loss. Actors and consumers allow themselves in equal measure to be led by schematic images in their actual sexual behavior; the reality of their sexual experiences consists precisely in the simulation of these normative images.[5] Contemporary visual pornography is hence not only the result of the pathological sexual frustrations of a few odd people and their commercial exploitation. It is rather a faithful representation of a historical era in which the image has become the norm of reality.

In psychoanalytic terminology, pornography promises exquisite *jouissance:* the *jouissance* that results from the transgression of the law. From the point of view of its structure, pornography is always connected to perversion, even when one uses pornography in order to defend oneself neurotically against one's own perverse inclinations. The law that is transgressed in pornography relates both to the symbolic-arbitrary determination of sexual identity and to the heteronomy of sexual desire. The pornographic transgression of symbolic signification confronts one with the uncanny reality of a meaningless and stereotypical sexual behavior. The primary reaction to this violent destruction of the symbolic signification of human sexuality is anxiety. Bad conscience is a secondary reaction to pornographic transgression; it is, like fear in Heidegger, already flight from anxiety, that is, the trauma of the meaninglessness of reality. Pornographers know about this panicky anxiety and tend to reassure viewers' feelings by the inclusion of idyllic images of nature or of boring interviews.

What from the Lacanian perspective appears as a transgression of the law can also be understood philosophically as a flight into objectivism and empty formalism. Contemporary pornography, industrially produced and reproduced, is doubtless the brainchild of scientific objectivism and the technological civilization that has necessarily followed it. It is true that pornography implies a transgression or disavowal of the essential laws that constitute the finite subject of human sexuality. Yet, if pornography doesn't lead directly to the psychotic self-loss of the subject, that is due above all to the fact that it doesn't even allow this subject to gain consciousness regarding itself and its own potential downfall. As long as the deceptive illusion that pornography is the product of the dirty fantasy of the Other remains intact, consumers need not worry about their *jouissance* or about the possible loss of their symbolic humanity.

An especially clear and grave consequence of pornographic objectivism and its industrial use is that people of today increasingly allow themselves to be determined sexually by anonymous and prefabricated fantasms. It has frequently and correctly been noted that pornography furthers the repression of sexuality. It is now possible to say more precisely that pornography is a form of objectivism that disavows the individual subject of sexual desire and replaces it with automated programs for stimulation. The consumer of pornographic products is thereby not only in the position to be both man and woman, voyeur and exhibitionist, masochist and sadist, actor and director, but he also disappears more or less into events that arouse him but no longer concern him personally. To quote Heidegger, "The Who is not this one and not that one, not oneself and not some and not the sum of all. The "Who" is neuter—the "one." . . . We experience pleasure and joy the way one experiences pleasure. . . . It "was" always the "one," and yet one can say that "no one" was it."[6]

Of course, in every "normal" sexual desire there is also the wish for the dissolution of self-consciousness, for anonymous voluptuousness, which Schiller wanted to attribute only to the worm. But it is precisely this extreme experience and the self-loss that it implies that is evaded in pornographic pleasure by replacing one's own fantasms with generally effective, standardized, and usually also unimaginative fantasms. With the detached visualization of erotic events as well as the constant chatter about sexual techniques, the abstract generality of modern science now also invades the intimate sphere of the individual person. One has difficulty understanding this search for shelter in allegedly generally effective means of stimulation, which remain standardized even in their differences, as anything other than flight from the self, from one's own desire, from one's own impotence vis-à-vis the drive. One flees into spectacle in order to drown out the fluttering of one's own heart; one is satisfied with what everyone else is happy with, because one doesn't know what one wants oneself; one flees into a dream scene in order no longer to have to bear the tension between one's own fantasms and the symbolic reality of the Other.

Where the subject with its symbolically determined identity and its simultaneously individual and general desire goes up in smoke, precious little remains of the possibility for sexual *jouissance*. Pornography is in reality less a means of stimulation than it is protection against stimulation, or more precisely: a means of stimulation that serves the function of protecting against stimulation. Pornography resembles a self-service store in which one preventively loads up on *jouissance* in order not to be suddenly caught unawares and helpless by the power of desire. Pornography grows out of the wish to overpower the drive completely and for that reason it also necessarily leads to a kind of sexual immunization or frigidity. Pornographic disregard of the law of the dependency of one's own desire on the desire of the Other is therefore hardly as unproblematic and inconsequential as it may at first seem. The pornographic transgression, which had promised *jouissance* without repentance, in reality furthers the repression of symbolic human sexuality. Sexual *jouissance* is exiled into the dark room of the secretive and in many ways solitary enjoyment with the bitter aftertaste.

Pornography as a means of the repression of sexuality shows its true face above all when it promises quick *jouissance* and then in fact tortures its victim with endless frustration. Especially in contemporary visual pornography one soon begins to feel like a child in a toy store who is shown the most desired goods in beautiful wrapping but is simultaneously told not to touch anything. The victim of pornographic seduction is soon made to feel like the unsuspecting vacationer on the roller coaster: he has been promised that he'll be tickled by this form of enjoyment but can't get out when he begins to feel frightened and sick. If it is true that the consumer's *jouissance* is to some extent masochistic, then one must also assume that the production of pornographic products is spiced quite heavily with sadism.

An especially horrifying consequence of pornographic enmity toward sexuality is the naturalizing objectification of the sexually determined body's anonymity. One knows from one's own experience how the beloved one's body can suddenly turn into unconscious and impersonal flesh during sexual contact. This simultaneously frightening and sublime *jouissance* produces pleasure only when it lasts no more than a moment. Inversely, one dares to go to extremes within sexuality and to play dead only when one is sure that one is alive and that one will awaken from the intoxication. The dreamlike experience of total self-loss soon turns into a nightmare in pornography. This is because the experience of fleshly anonymity in pornography is visually objectified, is temporally terribly drawn out and reproduced at will in nonsensical repetition. To quote Sartre: the dialectic that animates the body between the *pour soi* and its *en soi* is raped in a sadistic manner so long until the only thing that remains is the dead *en soi* of just any impersonal material body. Pornographic images sometimes remind us of the terrible scenes that we know from concentration camp photographs in which people were methodically degraded to the level of anonymously vegetating and decomposing flesh. The seemingly innocent, because detached, objective gaze of the camera stages with clinical cleanliness the crimes whose narration renders every reader of the Marquis de Sade's novels speechless. In the constant change of perspective and focus of the camera, as well as in the disturbing magnifications of the sexual organs, the symbolic cohesion of body parts is torn asunder. When the sublime moment of the silent anonymity of the sexual body turns spectacle, one soon gets a feeling of uncanny dread.

My critique of pornography can easily be conceptualized within the terminology with which Husserl criticized scientific objectivism.[7] Like scientific discourse, pornography, too, abstracts from the subject, or rather, from the individual, historically contingent point of view from which the subject approaches reality. The subject is then no longer bound by the finiteness of his or her sexual identity and the resulting limitation in being able to comprehend the Other and itself. It has toned down its most secret yearnings and fantasms to general norms and a concept of normality that is correlated with it. Individual affects are sacrificed to general expectations and standardized role playing. Sexual relationships are channeled into an artificial univocity, which, in an emergency, will allow for the intervention of an external expert. Such an idealization of both sexual relationships and the appropriate attitude towards one's objects of desire also makes it possible to develop generally valid processes for bringing about effective stimulation and satisfaction. Once again, the pornographic industry is a good example of erotic "calculation" of this sort. Just as calculation frees one from having to think, individuals of today have, in case of need, prefabricated fantasms at their disposal all around the world, fantasms that enable them to reach the aim of drive satisfaction quickly and easily. But just like scientific technology, erotic technology too must struggle with the phenomenon of wear and tear. Like technology, pornography too gets enmeshed in the vicious circle of endlessly pushing back the boundaries of the possible and thus also of the constant escalation of the inhuman.

Husserl's remedy for the crisis of European humankind consisted, as is well known, in attempting to relate science and technology back to their original worldly contexts, as well as in a call to human responsibility, which is founded on the presence of individuals and their readiness to take a position. Here too there are once again obvious points of comparison with the contemporary crisis within human sexuality. It is true that as sexual subjects of desire, both man and woman are determined by generally valid and scientifically formulatable symbolic legalities. But the individuality of the subject cannot be derived from this generally valid formal legality. The individuality of the sexually desiring subject results instead from its own particular history, from its place in a contextually determined social community. The subject becomes an individual subject only when it becomes conscious of its own particular situation, when it relates in a personal manner to the general legality which determines its own being symbolically. This individualization of the subject results only when there are personal dealings with other human individuals within a common environment. The experience of one's own individuality and thus also of one's own sexual identity is a phenomenon that belongs primarily within the realm of affect. Even though each and every affective experience of self presupposes the meaningfulness of a symbolic framework, it can never be totally integrated within this general framework. Within the sphere of affect one is directly struck, touched, and seduced by the Other. There emerges a self-referentiality that exists on this side of all symbolic univocity, and there emerges an experience of self in which self-consciousness and self-loss are irretrievably wound up in each other. So, do sexual identity and sexual desire have something to do with feeling and with gentle touching after all? One can at least dream about countering our contemporary sexual misery with a query about the lost presence of affect.

Notes

1. See, for example, René Descartes, *Les passions de l'âme:* "En sorte qu'on imagine un tout duquel on pense être seulement une partie, et que la chose aimée en est une autre." [So that one imagines a whole of which one thinks oneself only a part and that the thing loved is the other part.] (Paris: Adam & Paul Tannery, II, 1996).

2. It is striking how strongly this psychoanalytic description of the genesis of a subjective identity resembles Heidegger's analysis of an essential relationship as opposed to an unessential relationship of the subject to itself.

3. Cf. Rudolf Bernet, "Gesetz und Natur. Der kategorische Imperativ bei Kant und Lacan," in *Schriftenreihe zur Psychoanalyse* 34 (Dec. 1990), 185–205.

4. Roland Barthes, *Camera Lucida: Reflections on Photography*, trans. Richard Howard (New York: Farrar, Straus and Giroux, 1981) 57–9 et passim.

5. Ibid., 118: "Pleasure passes through the image: here is the great mutation. Such a reversal necessarily raises the ethical question: not that the image is immoral, irreligious, or diabolical . . . , but because, when generalized, it completely derealizes the human world of conflicts and desires, under cover of illustrating it."

6. Martin Heidegger, *Being and Time*, § 27.

7. E. Husserl, *Die Krisis der europäischen Wissenschaften und die transzendentale Phänomenologie* (Hamburg: Meiner, 1977).

7

The Joys and Suffering of So-Called Interpretation or: The Soul of the Dress's Fold

Johannes Fehr and Dieter Sträuli

> da helpt keen tüten oder blasen
> [neither tooting nor blowing will do any good there]
>
> —Grimm, *Deutsches Wörterbuch*

It is almost the last of the stories in *The Interpretation of Dreams*. It appears in chapter 7 of the book, in "The Psychology of the Dream Processes," and has the status there of a sort of bonus.

At stake in these last pages of the *Interpretation of Dreams* are "the intimate and reciprocal relations between censorship and consciousness."[1] With the report of two examples which are supposed to illuminate these relations, Freud desires to "end" "these psychological reflections." We will deal here with the first of these examples:

I was called in to consultation last year to examine an intelligent and unembarrassed-looking girl. She was most surprisingly dressed. For though as a rule a woman's clothing is inspired down to the last fold (*bis in die letzte Falte beseelt* [modified from Strachey's "woman's clothes are carefully considered down to the last detail" to bring it closer to Freud's German text—E. S.]) she was wearing one of her stockings hanging down and two of the buttons on her blouse were undone. She complained of having pains in her leg and, without being asked, exposed her calf. But what she principally complained of was, to use her own words, that she had a feeling in her body as though there was something "stuck into it" which was "moving backwards and forwards" and was "shaking" her through and through: sometimes it made her whole body feel "stiff." My medical colleague, who was present at the examination, looked at me; he found no difficulty in understanding the meaning of her complaint. But what struck us both as extraordinary was the fact that it meant nothing to the patient's mother—though she must often have found herself in the situation which her child was describing. The girl herself had no notion of the bearing of her remarks; for if she had, she would never have given voice to them. In this case it had been possible to hoodwink the censorship into allowing a phantasy which would normally have been kept in the preconscious to emerge into consciousness under the innocent disguise of making a complaint.[2]

No further remarks follow this report in the text of the *Interpretation of Dreams*. Not only does everything there is to say seem to have been said, and the consultation thereby ended with the significant glance exchanged by the two doctors, but the "example" has also fulfilled its function within the *Interpretation*'s argumentative process, for Freud begins his next paragraph with the words, "Here is another example." Then, by narrating this other example as well, he quickly moves closer to the end of this book dated 1900; only three more printed pages remained to be written.

Perhaps it is precisely this urge to finish, aside from the conflicting impression this story leaves behind, that awakens in us the need to read it again.

Let us begin with the circumstances. Freud seems to have been called to a consultation by a medical colleague—nothing, by the way, points to the fact that this is really the doctor from Graz, the surgeon Dr. Friedrich Leid[3]—by a doctor unknown to us, then, and asked for a "second opinion."

Should there have been any doubts regarding the causes of the patient's sufferings before the consultation, it seems that they were completely removed afterwards. At least to the ears of the two male physicians, or the two males who happen to be physicians, the nature of the patient's complaints is unmistakable. Indeed, "she had a feeling in her body as though there was something 'stuck into it' which was 'moving backwards and forwards.'" From the patient's main complaint, quoted word for word, the text moves directly to the silently eloquent look that the two experts exchange. Nothing more is said; apparently, nothing more *needs* to be said: we can supply the rest ourselves. Whoever has been reading this big book up to this point needs no step-by-step explanation of what is going on here. As readers, we too, in the role of imaginary "present medical colleagues," are invited to make the classic psychoanalytic diagnosis, preferably even in the words of Master Charcot: "Mais dans des cas pareils c'est toujours le chose génitale, toujours . . . toujours . . . toujours" [But in such cases it is always the genital domaine, always . . . always . . . always].[4]

Let us also imagine that Freud pronounces what he reads in the girl's behavior. He says to her, "What you are feeling is nothing other than your desire." And let us further imagine the astonishment of the surgeon, his disbelief, when he has to witness how the symptoms in this case of his, about which he had up until a moment before been racking his brain, disappear without the least intervention, perhaps only by the repetition of a sentence, as if they'd been blown away. Had Freud articulated the fact that what was at stake here was sexuality, the girl's desire, the resistance to association controlled by the censorship would have crumbled, and the complaint would no longer have had to wear the disguise of symptoms; it would have been a true "dream" interpretation, a dream of an interpretation, playing itself out in our fantasy.

However, no part of this "doctor novella" or "analytic daydream" actually takes place in the "example." On the contrary: Freud seems to have proceeded carefully and discreetly in the presence of this "intelligent and unembarrassed-looking girl." For, in spite of the first impression, he leaves the diagnosing and interpreting to others: he emphasizes the fact that the complaint does not seem incomprehensible to his colleague, and it is up to us readers to guess what the colleague has wordlessly understood. Whatever Freud might be thinking, his interpretation is limited to reproducing the patient's words literally. But by placing them in quotation marks, he also characterizes this speech as writing, as a text to which one may return, which one can read repeatedly.

Because Freud on the one hand emphasizes and on the other is elliptic, the text—we now become aware of this—powerfully pressures us to fill in the blanks. This pressure can also be found in his sketch of a sort of topography of knowledge: on the one hand, there are those who know "it"; on the other, those who don't know "it." This becomes clear also in the following sentence in which Freud reinserts himself into the duet with his colleague: "But what struck both of us as extraordinary was that it meant nothing to the patient's mother. . . . " Wherever many people are in agreement, a person to whom "it means nothing" must be that much more conspicuous, especially when the following can be said of her: "She must often have found herself in the situation which her child was describing." A strange sentence, convoluted, somehow indecent, even rude. Freud continues to succeed in not verbalizing what kind of situation he means. Instead, he determines, almost in critical fashion, that there is a person who does not wish to confirm, even though one ought to have been able to expect that from her, what cannot be misunderstood.

But what makes our physician think he knows that "it meant nothing to the patient's mother"? He seems to reach this conclusion simply by way of the fact that it is not possible to exchange a knowing glance with her as he had done with his medical colleague.

Two people know "it," know something that we too are cordially invited to know. One person seems not to know it, even though she ought to, based on her own experience. But yet another one does not know "it," because if she did, she would not speak and behave the way she does. I quote Freud, not Lacan: "The girl herself had no notion of the bearing of her remarks; for if she had, she would never have given voice to them." Freud does not seem to consider even for a moment that the alleged not-knowing on the mother's part could be directly linked to the daughter's behavior, and vice versa: that the daughter's behavior is linked to the mother's not-knowing. Wouldn't it be possible to imagine that the object of the daughter's complaints is nothing other than this apparent not-knowing or not-wanting-to-know of the mother? The fact that the daughter suffers from, suffers under, her mother not responding to any of the questions that she stages for her?

How would Jeffrey Masson and Alice Miller read the mother's silence? One can also imagine totally different interpretations of this silence: perhaps the mother is simply rendered speechless by the fact that once again two young physicians have been taken in by the obvious if clumsy seduction attempts on the part of her daughter and feel so smugly smart because they have noticed that it is sex that is at issue.

Or finally: wouldn't it be possible also to think that here are a mother and her daughter who want to rib two physicians, one of whom is famous for his sexual theories—a little local ambush in the global war between the sexes?

At this point we are very sorry that Dr. Leid, if that is even who this medical colleague was, published nothing about this case.

We must make do, then, with the following statement: what was so dreamily pacifying about the first interpretation was that sexuality, desire, could be shown to inhabit the patient in such an unequivocal, such a clear, fashion. The physician who can locate the hysterical symptom in such a way is not affected by this desire. This is not the case with the interpretations we suggested afterwards: here all the people present, the mother, the physicians and we readers, are unmistakably involved in the desire.

In retrospect one can recognize the naïveté of the interpretation in the psychoanalytic daydream: it thinks of itself as the revelation of a concealed meaning—"Here it was revealed . . ." and so on—but discusses only what the patient had at the very first and in a completely explicit manner held up to medical attention. What the interpreter overlooks in this interpretation is that perhaps he isn't revealing anything in the other at all, but is instead being involved in something.

The extent to which *Freud* is involved in the story can be judged by the sentence with which he describes the patient's appearance: "She was most surprisingly dressed. For whereas a woman's clothing is inspired down to the last fold, she was wearing one of her stockings hanging down and two buttons on her blouse were undone."

"Whereas a woman's clothing is inspired down into the last fold": suddenly we get this generalization about "women's clothing" in this otherwise hurried narrative, a generalization which is, after all, superfluous in terms of argument. What "last fold" is Freud talking about here? What "inspiredness" of clothing?

Well, now we have gotten to a point that we interpret—or perhaps it would be more correct to say "suggest"—by simply reproducing Freud's speech word for word and setting it between quotation marks. In the meantime we have learned to see this procedure not as just wriggling about and as an avoidance technique, but rather as an appropriate procedure. If the text seems, as we showed above, to pressure us to say finally what is actually at stake here, it simultaneously warns us against doing so. It would be unsatisfactory to be content with the conclusion that here too it is sexuality that lies at the bottom of everything. By doing so we would lose out on the possibility of asking what is at stake when the issue is sexuality.

Perhaps a different section from the text of *The Interpretation of Dreams* can give us greater insight here. For the "example" has an astonishing counterpart in the dream of "Irma's Injection," the first story of the *Interpretation of Dreams*. Together they form a kind of concealed frame for the book. In the protodream of psychoanalysis, for the interpretation of which Freud believed he had reason to expect a memorial plaque, there is also a consultation that takes place between medical colleagues who are on friendly terms, and there too there is a female patient. But while the "example" appears to present itself as easily understandable and clear to an uncritical gaze, everything in "Irma" is from the start unsure, unclear, even uncanny. Whereas the unembarrassed-looking girl seems almost to extort an examination, Irma struggles against one. And most important for us: while in the "example" so much is unexpectedly revealed, here the examination of the female body occurs through the clothing: "My friend Otto was now standing beside her as well, and my friend Leopold was percussing her through her bodice and saying: "She has a dull area low down on her left." He also indicated that a portion on the skin of her left shoulder was infiltrated. (I noticed this, just as he did, in spite of her dress). . . ."[5]

Here are Freud's associations to this part: "*In spite of her dress.* This was in any case only an interpolation. We naturally used to examine the children in the hospital undressed: and this would be a contrast to the manner in which adult female patients have to be examined. I remembered that it was said of a celebrated clinician that he never made a physical examination of his patients except through their clothes. Further than this I could not see. Frankly, I had no desire to penetrate more deeply at this point."[6]

Does Freud, at the end of the dream's interpretation, again run into what he did not want to get more deeply involved in the Irma dream: the instance of the girl's offensive clothing?

In any case, the physicians' urge for discovery runs up against a serious obstacle in the woman's clothing. A disrobing would be theoretically and technically possible, and also desirable. It's just that it coincides in a fatal way with another wish fulfillment to which Freud too has to admit; he does so in a letter he wrote to Fliess: "I can only indicate . . . that later (between two and two and a half years) my libido toward *matrem* was awakened, namely, on the occasion of a journey with her from Leipzig to Vienna, during which we must have spent the night together and there must have been an opportunity of seeing her *nudam*. . . ."[7]

If at that time it was perhaps a matter of snatching a secret and guilty glimpse at what he presents to us as the trigger of his libido, it seems that something naked forces itself on his adult gaze from all nooks and crannies: here is one quotation from the *Interpretation of Dreams*: "One can scarcely pass through a country village in our part of the world without meeting some child or two or three who lifts up his little shirt in front of one—in one's honour, perhaps."[8]

One must admit, this sounds almost like, "A decent scientist can hardly go anywhere anymore under these circumstances" and it is echoed by, "She was most surprisingly dressed. For whereas as a rule a woman's clothes are inspired down to the last fold, she was wearing one of her stockings hanging down and two of the buttons on her blouse were undone."

The patient's clothing is disturbing not only because it stands in the way of an examination but also because it reveals too much of something that is not to be the object of the examination. The half-opened, disorderly dress reveals, in the *Interpretation of Dreams*, not the biological-physiological body, but the erotic body, a body within society. Irma's and the girl's complaints are directed at this body, and it is in face of it that medical knowledge fails as far as this knowledge is limited to what, in the credo of Freud's teachers, is referred to in the following way: "'Brücke and I,'" writes Du Bois-Reymond, "'have sworn to lay stress upon the truth that no other forces are at work in the organism aside from the common physical-chemical ones. . . .'"[9]

Freud seems still to be paying homage to this knowledge when he reacts to Irma's complaints—"If you only knew what pains I've got now in my throat and stomach and abdomen—it's choking me"—with, "I was alarmed and looked at her. She looked pale and puffy. I thought to myself that after all I must be missing some organic trouble."

What is not to be overlooked in the end—the end of this dream as well, we might add—is the formula from organic chemistry written in bold, the trimethylamine. Let us recall where Lacan placed the significance of the dream of Irma's injection: "What gives this dream its veritable unconscious value, whatever its primordial and infantile echoes, is the quest for the word, the direct confrontation with the secret reality of the dream, the quest for signification as such. In the midst of all his colleagues, of this consensus of the republic of those who know—for if no one is right, everyone is right, a law which is simultaneously paradoxical and reassuring—in the midst of this chaos, in this original moment when his doctrine is born into the world, the meaning of the dream is revealed to Freud—that there is no other word of the dream than the very nature of the symbolic."[10]

Perhaps the "example" at the end of the *Interpretation of Dreams* does not give rise to such pathos. It isn't a dream text like the one about Irma's injection, and it doesn't have its dark promising charm. Its effect is rather irritating, both for Freud and for the reader. Freud is unfavorably impressed by a girl's appearance. Even if in the eighties of the twentieth century most blouses have two buttons undone and an artfully hanging stocking is entirely plausible as an element in a punk outfit, there is something we must not forget: that with every piece of clothing we are literally wearing the Symbolic order on our skins.

Every child must learn to dress right. Which one of us has not ever had to hear the phrase, "You're not going to school looking like that!" But just how coercive this aspect of the Symbolic is brought before the eyes of us adults especially in those moments when we ourselves discover on our bodies a run in our stocking or a shirt button that has torn some of the surrounding material. Because it is then that we are looking directly at the texture, at the pattern consisting of loose threads, from which every piece of clothing is woven.

Freud's text allows us to see an order's complex system in his own language in which single buttons are obviously undone and single subordinated clauses hang down untidily like stockings.

Perhaps it is this truth which is staring Freud in the face out of the disorderly clothing and with unembarrassed-seeming and intelligent eyes: that in most cases the Symbolic order is encountered by the subject as disorder while it continues to remain largely invisible as an orderly order.

If at first it looked as if there are those who know and those who do not, that, on the one hand, there are specialists and, on the other, women living in ignorance, we are now looking at a completely altered topography. In a theory of knowledge that is not imaginary in this way it is the signifiers—words or clothes—which produce and carry knowledge through their play. But this knowledge is no longer—fault for this lies with the play—simply available for the subject; rather, the subject is offered up to it. (This is the meaning of Freud's concept of the "unconscious.")

In this scene the disorderly dress is the place where Freud is confronted with the unavailability of a knowledge, which at the same time forces itself on him: "[W]ithout being asked, [she] exposed her calf." For us readers, however, this place is located in Freud's speech—specifically where it is irritating in its obvious "disorderliness."

Should one wish to describe the complex relationship between signifier and subject by way of the elements of dress and body, that is best achieved with the image of the mythical Nessus shirt, that shirt which, once one has put it on, cannot be removed because in the meantime it has grown together with the skin and bones.

In the *Studies on Hysteria* Freud compares the pathogenic psychic material in the unconscious to a foreign body. Here, then, the foreign element has grown together with its environment in the interior of the body, or, as the case may be, in the psyche's center. But it is precisely here that the comparison with the histological foreign body fails, for "[a] foreign body does not enter into any relation with the layers of tissues that surround it, although it modifies them. . . . Our pathogenic psychical group, on the other hand, does not admit of being cleanly extirpated from the ego. . . . In analysis the boundary between the two is fixed purely conventionally, now at one point, now at another, and in some places cannot be laid down at all. . . . In fact, the pathogenic organization does not behave like a foreign body, but far more like an infiltrate."[11]

What Freud feels through Irma's little bodice is that her "skin" has been "infiltrated."

One last experiment, one last comparison: the "last fold," deep down into which, according to Freud, women's clothing has "inspiration": the fold creates interruptions in the otherwise undifferentiated continuum of a fabric. These result in places, in concealed and unconcealed spaces, in a signifying order. The fold in the fabric creates a backside without thereby making the seamy (reverse) side, the so-called "wrong side" of the fabric, truly accessible.

Instead of speculating now as to whether one can see in the "last fold" that signifier par excellence which, according to Lacan, represents the subject for another signifier, we would like to refer to Mallarmé's journal, *La dernière Mode*, that *Gazette du monde et de la famille* in which the poet, under the name of "Marguerite de Ponty" or "Miss Satin," chatted about the cunning details of women's clothing. He ends one of the leading articles, in which he speaks to fashion-conscious women as one of them, with the following words: "[P]armi cette enveloppe, somptueuse ou simple, plus qu'à aucune époque va transparaître la Femme, visible, dessinée, elle-même, avec la grâce entière de son contour ou les principales lignes de sa personne (alors que, par derrière, la magnificence vaste de la traîne attire tous les plis et l'ampleur del'etoffe." [Amidst this envelope, sumptuous or simple, more than at any other period, Woman is going to show through, visible, limned, herself—with the whole grace of her contour or the principal lines of her person (while, behind, the vast magnificence of the train draws all the folds and massive fullness of the material)].[12]

Notes

The German title of this article begins, *Freud und Leid*, an untranslatable pun. In addition to meaning "joy" and "sorrow" respectively, "Freud" and "Leid" are also the names of the two protagonists in the story told by Freud in his *Interpretation of Dreams* which is the focus of this essay.

1. Sigmund Freud, *The Interpretation of Dreams, Standard Edition, Volume 5* (London: The Hogarth Press), 618.

2. Ibid.

3. *Leid* = suffering. –translator

4. Sigmund Freud, "On the History of the Psycho-Analytic Movement," *Standard Edition, Volume 14* (London: The Hogarth Press), 14.

5. Sigmund Freud, *Interpretation*, 107.

6. Ibid., 113.

7. Sigmund Freud, *The Complete Letters of Sigmund Freud to Wilhelm Fliess, 1887–1904*, ed. and trans. Jeffrey Mousaieff Masson (Cambridge, Mass.: Harvard University Press, 1985), letter of October 3, 1897, 268.

8. Freud, *Interpretation*, 244.

9. Ernest Jones, *Sigmund Freud, Leben und Werk*, vol. 1 (Munich: dtv TB Nr. 4426, 1984), 61f. [trans. E. S.]

10. Jacques Lacan, *The Seminar of Jacques Lacan. Book II: The Ego in Freud's Theory and in the Technique of Psychoanalysis 1954–1955*, ed. Jacques-Alain Miller and trans. Sylvana Tomaselli, notes by John Forrester (New York: W. W. Norton, 1988), 159-160.

11. Sigmund Freud and Josef Breuer, *Studies on Hysteria*, trans. James Strachey (New York: Basic Books), 290.

12. Stephane Mallarmé, *Oeuvres complètes* (Paris: Bibliothèque de la Pleïade, nrf, Gallimard, 1945), 833. English translation by Cary Plotkin.

8

Hysteria and Melancholia in Woman

ANNE JURANVILLE

It is not a matter of course that one should speak of women. Lacan's well-known phrase, according to which "woman does not exist," seems to stand at the end of a whole cultural tradition for which woman is an illogical being, incapable of understanding, and lacking both identity and soul. Nietzsche says in this vein, "Woman is thought to be profound. Why? Because one can never plumb her depths"; Jacques Derrida, too, returns to this thesis: "There is no essence of woman."[1] According to Lacan, she does not exist because she is "not fully" addressed by symbolic castration, and this affords her a positive definition in the shape of a "supplementary" pleasure, or a pleasure of the Other. It is this that marks her contribution to the constitutional madness of *the Thing*, just as it also simply marks her madness.

That woman's relation to the Symbolic order is endangered and incomplete was already established by Freud in his own way. One logical consequence that apparently results from this is that nothing can be said about woman. Paradoxically, however, there has been a huge crop of texts about the feminine, a veritable wave of conceptual discussions of the topic. A phenomenon of this sort deserves to be examined and it also warns one to be cautious, since it is often women who have demanded the privilege of talking about themselves. In this vein, one female Lacanian analyst ends her article, entitled "On the Search for Woman" (*"Chercher la femme"*), with the question "whether contemporary hysteria might consist in contributing something to this gesture of awarding woman an existence, and this, in a sense, is really a new kind of masquerade."[2]

I wish to refer to this statement, but will do so by giving it another direction; because for woman the state of affairs of being "not fully" marked by the phallic function does not mean that she is not marked by it at all. In other words, I want to try to show to what extent woman exists. This means paying tribute to hysteria (*faire la part belle à l'hystérie*), as it is woman's constitutive neurosis, her normative neurosis. In contrast to this, melancholia, the psychotic structure itself, represents the failure of femininity, the missed entry into feminine identity, an identity that needs to be *produced*, developed. This is the hypothesis to be presented here. Hysteria and melancholia are considered to be opposite in nature, so that the melancholic position in woman finally proves to be incompatible with the femininity through which she "exists." Of course, this does not change the fact that the definition of woman, if such a thing is possible, is not identical with the definition of femininity, because, aside from the sexual identity that she achieves, she remains "the thing" as which she "does not exist."

But to return to where she does exist, namely in hysteria: here one can draw on a famous formulation, "One is not born a woman, one becomes one", and thereby inquire into her access "to artificiality as regards her gender" (Lacan). The term "artificiality" ought not to be understood in its negative sense: we find ourselves here neither in the ontological order of nonexistence, nor in the logical order of falseness, but rather in a special dimension of being which Lacan calls the "Imaginary" and which can be characterized as "illusion," as "fiction," but as a "real" or "objective" fiction. How this imaginary dimension functions was described by Lacan from the beginning of his teachings. To do so, he at first employed a model from the realm of optics, the "science that endeavors to produce images," then the model from topology, the "soft logic," the nonmetric geometry of surfaces and holes. At stake here, then, is the production of images; in other words, we will enter the realm of representation (mental, specular, theatrical); surfaces will be thematized as well.

For we must trace the Imaginary insofar as it refers to the category of appearance (the imaginary aspect of the signifier). This path moves briefly in the direction of phenomenology and anthropology: here it is possible to observe and describe the comedy of sexual relations as it is played out on the world's stage, a comedy in which one must nevertheless believe. It is here that one encounters the masquerade—a term that must not be understood in its derogatory sense, as it constitutes a central category of the feminine Imaginary—as well as the symptom. Both are subject to the gaze, that is the least one can say, since their register is constituted mostly by provocation and by showing.

Even if hysteria and melancholia should prove to stand in opposition to each other, their semiological descriptions bring topics to the fore that, at first glance, at least, clearly intersect. Let's look at three of those.

Depersonalization and the Question of the Body Image

In every psychosis, but in melancholia especially, one is confronted with the radical absence of the Imaginary, whose paradigm resides in the body image (the so-called kinesthetic disturbances, "negation deliria," long since described). The work of Gisela Pankow on the psychotherapy of psychosis develops along these lines. It is based on an attempted "dynamic structuration of the body image," beginning with the construction of a single "fantasm." Melancholia seems to be prototypical of this primary identification that is not possible, an identification with a specular image which can be terminologically defined as a "structured totality" (which Pankow contrasts with the part taken as the whole), as "boundary," "form," and finally as "surface." Archaic identification, termed "incorporation" by Freud and Abraham, emerges not from the Imaginary of the body but from its Real.[3] Pankow describes this confusion between "substance" and "image" by way of the riveting literary example of the "abysmal mirror," into which the patient wants to immerse himself and against which she rams her head.

On the other side, the hysteric is marked by a large number of different disturbances that concern the body's representation: aside from the rich supply of phenomena which, as different varieties of conversion, have been classified as somatic, authors have exhaustively described conditions of ego modifications which range from vertigo, deafness, insensitivity, paralyses, and pains, to feelings of strangeness, unreality, deformation of the body, even to a sense of body fragmentation. In the realm of identification Melman describes the hysteric as "imageless," and he refers to her failure in terms of identification.[4] But are all these conditions of depersonalization of the same type? If the "person" can etymologically be led back to the "persona," which originally denoted the actor's mask, then one may assume that identity is a mask (which is what Lacan says about the ego, which, paradoxically, brings him into proximity with social psychology); depersonalization would then signify the dropping of the mask. We need to clarify the nature and function of this mask. This will allow us to avoid improper adulterations in the realm of diagnostics.[5]

The phenomenology of melancholia and hysteria respectively could justify another approach, which is correlated with a second topic.

Integrity

Woman, it has been said, is "subjected to melancholia" because of the logic of a structure that is geared towards everything or nothing. The moment of the mirror reflection (*moment spéculaire*), which signifies the subject's entrance into the phallic function, marks an irreversible split between boys and girls, a split that will never achieve complementarity. The phallic function (termed Φ by Lacan), which affects both genders in the same manner through the mechanism of primal repression, introduces this fundamental body image that specifies both genders. These nonsymmetrical types of emerging desire are echoed by the difficulties which analysts encounter in patients and which were described by Freud: fear of castration for the boy, penis envy for the girl. In the register of the Imaginary, which is where we find ourselves right now, the male sexual organ embodies "something supplementary," which "allows the man to gamble with only a part of himself. The woman, on the other hand, looks for her balance entirely in between her own double and nothingness." This is Lemoine's thesis in *Partage des femmes*.[6] This "entirely" is a theme that has been conjugated in a variety of ways (for example, in the realm of *jouissance* that in woman is characterized by diffuseness and noncontinuity, because she, in contrast to the man's "instrumental" enjoyment, does not perceive it as concretely localizable). In a paper on hysteria Perrier turns this topic into one concerning the realm of the girl's "phallic narcissism": "To be whole, to be the 'Phallus-Girl' in its statuesqueness," he writes, "that is where she exhibits her highest point of development. This is the source of her predilection for the theater, for dance. When she speaks, she is whole."[7] What is at stake for her, then, is "to be whole and to remain so by any means deemed necessary," even if that means enduring depression and even melancholia.

Authenticity

The melancholic affect consists of a nostalgia which is fed by images of our culture—the Golden Age, Earthly Paradise, and Utopia, for instance—as well as by all those variations on the theme that are concerned with what lies concealed: purity, depth, the inside, the kernel, the origin, the untouchable. The statue of Glaucon, disfigured by smeary and corrosive algae, symbolizes a lost nature. In Rousseau the deceptive mask of appearance is termed imagination. It is well known that with this term Rousseau condemns to damnation anything that is associated with artifice: urban life, the mundane, the arts, the predilection for luxury and the unnecessary; they are all causes of our misfortune.

To the melancholic nostalgia for the absolute, mythical object (the Thing) there corresponds, in hysteria, the complaint that, measured against a "true" femininity that she does not possess and in the face of which she feels inadequate, she does not feel real. This lament goes hand in hand with a question which Lacan places at the center of the hysterical structure: What is that, a woman? An impossible question, it "does not prevent her from searching for the reflection of the mysterious object which keeps the desire in the gaze of him whom she loves upright, leading her to continue to imagine the representation of an ideal woman."[8]

The concept of authenticity, then, underlies two different psychic configurations: on the one hand, longing, or nostalgia, etymologically means "suffering from return," the missed mourning for the absolute which in melancholia is experienced as a sort of exile; on the other, the search that circles around a riddle, that suffering from appearances on the part of the hysteric who, as we shall see, again and again asks herself how she "becomes an object": "On that side on which femininity bases itself there is a demand for an authenticity the realization of which would reveal the fetish where one had expected the essence *(l'être),*" Melman continues in this context.[9]

The apparent connection between melancholic and hysterical suffering surrounding the topics of depersonalization, integrity, and authenticity might excuse diagnostic errors[10] and even legitimize attempts to use categories like "hysterical psychosis," "hysterical insanity," and other borderline conditions which often hide a hyperbolic eagerness to apply labels rather than to analyze. My thesis here is that there is in fact a radical break in continuity between melancholia and hysteria: they are two opposing structures that lie at the two ends of the spectrum, a spectrum which could symbolize the construction of an ontologically imaginary female identity, the focal point of this discussion. The melancholic woman does not achieve that female identification which would allow her to experience desire and to exist within society. The constitution of hysterical desire, on the other hand, is situated at the origin of that Imaginary which makes one think of the categories of play, illusion, and masquerades—in a word: the "artificial."

Let us record some of the central differences in a schematic, maybe even a somewhat cavalier, way. Like every psychosis, melancholia is determined by a fundamental failure of the inscription of the subject into the linguistic order (a failure which Lacan for a long time now has described as the mechanism of repudiating symbolic castration, that is, as the foreclosure of the Name-of-the-Father). What ensues is chaos within the signifying chain; this chaos is characterized by the lacking construction *(montage)* of the mirror image with regard to the body image. What this means is that it is the constitution of reality itself that is at stake. Lacan has shown in his teachings that the world is based on a fantasm (a screen, frame, or window) which is formed by withdrawing a piece of the Real, which he calls *objet a.* ("The field of reality . . . is sustained only by the extraction of the *objet a.*")[11] The formula for the fantasm $\$◊A$, which marks the gap between the diagonally barred subject of the Unconscious (the side of desire) and the object (the side of pleasure) in the form of the double logical operation of alienation and separation, symbolized by the punch $◊$—is especially enlightening in the case of melancholia. And it is true: melancholic incorporation points to the failure of the forming of the fantasm and its correlate, the *objet a,* which has not been extracted, does not exist outside of the body. The mad person, to whom one rightfully refers as *alienated,* is the other, but not in the sense of a specular, narcissistic relation to the "alter ego" which characterizes the Imaginary, but rather in the sense of a confusion with an undetached other and a lost/not-lost object. Melanie Klein calls that object the "inner object" which fantasmatically destroys the interior of the body, which in turn has not been able to empty itself out on the level of the Symbolic and become surface, and whose holes would then define the realm of the drives.[12] In this sense the melancholiac's body image disturbances, which emerge from this delirium, can be related to the category of *depth* (or the Real) of the body. This has nothing to do with the hysteric's disturbances in body image, which represent *symptoms*, effects that do not result from a foreclosure of castration but rather from its repression.[13] In order to simplify one could say that in hysteria the construction of the Imaginary is merely defective, because what happens at the same time is that the structure of hysteria (as opposed to the structure of melancholia) comes into being wholly within the realm of representation (theatrical representation, to be precise) where, in some sense, desire more or less realizes itself in an exemplary manner.

Let me proceed in my analysis by referring to two symmetrical quotations, which reiterate what I've said so far. One of them is by Racamier: "It is illusion that, more than anything else, the psychotic lacks."[14] The other is by Melman: "The (female) hysteric is allergic to appearance."[15] Illusion and appearance are two forms of the Imaginary. How are they to be understood? In reference to what has been said about the failure to form a body image (which I first defined as boundary and surface) in melancholia, it would seem that one is here confronted with the failure to form a female identification, a sexed, that is, desiring, but symbolically castrated image of the self. The existence of woman can be only at this price. Now reality, which rests on the fantasm, is a stage; the actors on it represent people in the sense of personalities; social existence is constituted by the play, and sexual relations are a comedy. The melancholic woman is incapable of playing this play; like all psychotics she is not part of the "game." There is no room for alterity for her. Lacan says that the psychotic believes in the Other and that, as far the psychotic is concerned, the Other is incapable of lying. It is in this sense that one can understand the expression, "There is no game." (Surely this is the level on which one must situate Winnicott's therapeutic attempts.)

The hysteric, on the other hand, knows what desire entails in terms of play and possible deception. Desire unfolds in the articulation of the signifying chain as a deeply rooted riddle (just think of the "questioning figure," the sphinx, which embodies it). Lacan, who in his Seminar on anxiety refers back to the marks of the signifier, defines the latter as an extinguished trace which he distinguishes from the traces of an animal, because "the animal does not leave seemingly false tracks. . . . When a trace has been left, if one is to consider it a false one, we know that it comes from a speaking subject."[16] The hysteric is a specialist in laying false tracks. It is precisely for this reason that she must never forget that she herself is implicated in the deceptions of the other, and, as she does not believe in the Other,[17] she "never believes in her symptom." The hysterical woman defines the rules of the game of desire; she is glamorous in this role in a staging that befits her. But she hides in this play and gives it away. Even after praising hysteria in this way one can still not evade having to speak of the troubles of hysteria for which femininity as appearance or artificiality has to pay.

Let us attempt to approach this femininity, which has been circumscribed with the already mentioned terms "artificiality," "illusion," "faith," "appearance," "falsity," and "deception," from the perspective of the masquerade. In order to do so, we must survey the problem from an anthropological point of view.

What is at stake here is to categorize the masquerade into the ranks of the symbolic inscriptions of the body within the social field. The human body represents itself to conventional perception as always already provided with a symbolic sign, with a trait, a cut, an incision *(trait, coupure, entaille)*. Lacan writes the following in reference to tattoos and ritual scars: "The tattoo cut *[l'entaille]* certainly has the function of being for the Other, of situating the subject in it, marking his place in the field of the group's relations, between each individual and all the others. And, at the same time, it obviously has an erotic function, which all those who have approached it in reality have perceived."[18]

All human cultures define themselves via special procedures of corporeal ritualization, which can be summarized with the word "decoration" *(décor)*. It is possible, by the way, to make a little word game with the word *décor:* every ritual is indeed ordered around some process of decorporation *(dé-corps)* through which human beings offer up their "pound of flesh" (a loss of *jouissance*) in order to enter both culture and sexual desire. The body is thereby sectioned *(sectionné)* and sexed *(sexionné)*, to use the expressions of an author who has researched the main types of body rituals throughout time and place.[19] This voluminous work, which Maertens presented in his *Ritologiques,* contains differential analyses ordered around the axes of binary oppositions, such as "historical society"/"traditional society" and "men"/"women." He alternates between a number of criteria, such as, on the one hand, "the most 'incorporated' *(incorporé)*" (sexual maimings, sacrifices, tattoos . . .), "the most abstract" (the most detached: masks, clothing . . .), "the established," the "forever more" (tattoos, bodily deformations . . .), and, on the other, the more fleeting criteria (bodily drawings, make-up, clothing . . .); he also uses differential criteria, such as the gesture and the trace (which applies, for example, to make-up).

In this way the manner in which the human body turns itself into an object and even into a fetish for the sake of the staging of desire are determined and ordered. These traits of identification, which are essentially symbolic (there is a *writing* of the body), at the same time belong to the imaginary order (the body is conceived of in its function as semblance, as a signifying wholeness, as image). They define every individual in a gender role, which is mixed in with one's social personality. All of this depends on the belief in the complementarity of the sexes, which Lacan has termed the illusion of the existence of sexual relations. This illusion, this deception, in turn also depends on a sort of faith, which is necessary for forging a social tie. This illusion is comparable to the play or fairy tales that children believe in without really believing them. It depends on the fact that there are two opposed positions present in the psyche at the same time: on the one hand, the demystification of an original belief; on the other, the persisting and (by the other half) disputed belief itself. This juxtaposition depends on a split in the ego and corresponds to a *denial* whose effects Freud analyzed in his work on fetishism. Mannoni has shown by way of his analyses of masks in socièties containing initiation rites that the formula for perverse desire—"I know that . . . but still"—is true of all collective beliefs that found a cultural identity.[20] Beyond their symbolic and imaginary dimensions the body offers itself up to these rituals in its real dimension as fetish. It is "offered up for use" as "the object side of the signifier of the law," as "the Name-of-the-Father turned object," to use the terminology of Alain Juranville.[21] The body also fetishizes itself insofar as it becomes the real surface for a signifying writing (in contrast to the art work).[22]

This representation of bodily rituals makes clear, then, in what sense the definition of the ego is indebted to the metaphor of the theater. One could turn Rousseau's theory on its head and claim that the subject, far from being disfigured by the imagination, is, on the contrary, indebted to the Imaginary for its representability [or figuration]. "Figure" (the word derives from *fingere*, which then leads to "fiction") must be understood here as a border, a boundary, which lends direction and sense, as "configuration" in the sense of being "etched in": as the incision of features or of letters on the surface of the body or the ground (littoral, "litturaterre," after the word created by Lacan)[23] which also paves the way toward geometry. Just think of the expression "to be disfigured," which means to have lost the visible signs of one's ability to be recognized by the other; or, think of the sense, derived from the latter and used in the theater, of "figuration" (representation) from which it is possible to derive evidence of the cohesiveness of this imaginary identification.

Let us determine what it is that the author calls *logique tégumentaire* ("enveloping logic") in these *ritologiques*: it is the logic of the skin as surface. This logic is really a contribution to Freud's theory of the ego as the "projection of the body surface," or to Lacan's theory of the ego as the "sum of the subject's identifications." Both Freud's and Lacan's embryologies are at times supported by visual props such as "the superimposition of coats" or "onion skin covers." In his book, *La pensée et le féminin* ("Thought and the Feminine"),[24] W. Granoff develops Freud's representation of the theme of the membrane as a long semantic row ("partition wall," plane, border community, interface, side, veil, cover, skin, skin cell . . .). Its source lies in what Granoff calls a "logic of the hymen." The book is of interest because it brings together the question of femininity and the topological treatment of the issue, a problem that Freud represented with concepts like "outside-inside," or with concepts having to do with the transition from inside to outside insofar as it determines the constitution of reality (this is what is at issue in his essay "Negation").

To summarize the topology in one word, let us say that Lacan defines it as an "elastic logic" because of its malleable surfaces; they are structured around holes and organize themselves around a gap. "A signifier's locus is always a surface," Lacan says in the seminar on "Identification"; a signifier is an incision into a surface: "Around the signifier of the incision that which we call a surface comes into being."

I see two very fruitful paths opening themselves up here:

First, as far as psychosis is concerned, psychotherapy, as it is practiced by R. and R. Lefort, for example,[25] attempts to reach a rimlike structure throughout all of the stages of the mirror phase (whereby the "significance of the image" is evoked). The rim or torus, a surface produced by a cut, which is characterized by its rotatability, its dissymmetry in the mirror, and its differentiation between inside and outside, contains all of the characterizing elements of a body image as a holey surface.

Generally speaking, the central emptiness that is constitutive of all topological figures (rim, cross-cap, Klein's bottle, and so forth) represents a point of transition between inside and outside, a place where the drive circles around its object (the so-called *objet a*) as Lacan describes it in his Seminar XI. This means that this hole of the drive in the body is not some sort of bloody gaping wound, which is how the psychotic sees it, but rather an erogenous zone marked as rim.[26]

Secondly, as far as woman is concerned, the "logic of the hymen," as it is represented by W. Granoff (who quotes Derrida plentifully), makes it possible to discuss woman's special relationship to castration. That woman has a "natural," "readily apparent," "immediate" relation to separation and to loss, as Lacan determines in his Seminar "Le désir et son interprétation," may correspond to some "original truth"; one must, however, say so in a "correct and clear manner"[27]: "For her," he writes, "the point of natural objects, insofar as they are objects from which one separates oneself, is to realize the function of being objects of desire in the most natural way possible," and, in the same breath, he says, "This phallus, which she doesn't have, is what she is in a symbolic way, as the object of the desire of the Other." (This Latin word *separare* Lacan years later significantly transformed into *se parare*—*se parer* [to decorate oneself]—which fits rather well into our context).[28] Other authors, like S. Leclaire, emphasize to what degree "the respective gender, corresponding to an apparently anatomic determination, is characterized by the manner in which it enters into the discourse, by how a fundamentally subjective position, whose source lies within the structural heterogeneity of the phallus, constructs itself."[29] Around the especially important term of *evidence* (with which one could associate the term *l'évidement* [the emptying out]) W. Granoff develops the thesis of a "relative dispensation" of woman as far as judging is concerned. The feminine is constructed from a foundation of certainty. "She is immediately done with her judgment and with her decision. She has seen it, knows she doesn't have it, and wishes to have it," says Freud. Without evasions or indecisiveness woman *knows*, and the result of that is a singular relation to knowing: "The corner stone of the theory does not lie within them. Instead they are the corner stone . . . of the entire movement of thinking and acting."[30] Man is given the detour toward judgment, the research, the difficult work of *theory*, in order to reach the judgment, should he attempt to comprehend "this apparentness which is not visible." It is the passion of seeing and knowing that is typical of him. S. Leclaire also writes that it is up to him to "articulate the proofs for the existence of the phallus through tiresome work." Forced to judge, he turns himself into the inquirer, the inventor, "into the constructor of families, of wealth, of streets, of dams, of cities, of realms. . . ."[31] All of this stands in a close relationship to the masculine structure of melancholia, which we will not develop here. Woman does not inquire. To parody Picasso: she doesn't search, because she has already found.

What about the melancholic woman? Melancholia, a disease of mourning, represents the impossible mourning for a lost object. In terms of the logic of the fantasm, we have already referred to the "missing separation from the *objet a*"; in topological terms we have referred to the "missing signifying incision which produces the body's surface." Insofar as the girl experiences symbolic castration, the vagina becomes in effect the significant place in the sense that one must represent for oneself emptiness there where one would expect completeness. It is beginning with this emptiness "that the Symbolic will find its place," says Lacan, "which is difficult." Quite so: while this symbolization of the body in an image is difficult for the hysteric, for the melancholiac it turns out to be impossible.

One could illustrate this point with the article that F. Perrier dedicates to the Amatrides,[32] those women who were exiled from the mythical earth, the mother as thing.[33] For desire implies perversion (also in the sense of *Père-version* = *Version du père*, Version of the father), which consists in the creation of an exile without return—the work of mourning. The separation which the subject in melancholia, by making itself into the object (compare, once again, the formula $\$ \lozenge A$), does not want to enact, this nonaccepted separation is directed at the original other, the "real other,"[34] incorporated by the intact, noncastrated, and absolute mother. What is at stake here is, to use an expression used often by Lacan, a disavowal of "the loss of the thing in the object." Perrier formulates this as the incapacity to "accept that one has come out of a hole that one has oneself."[35] This hole, which has not been symbolized as the point of transition for the sexual drive, turns into an abyss, into a broken eye, the evil eye, the Medusa, and into everything that inspires us with dread and horror in the face of the unrepresentable, the unnamable, this "archaic anxiety that belongs to the petrified silence of nature before the appearance of humankind, the anxiety that is evoked by the image of reptiles rigidified on a stony earth."[36]

What is missing is the imaginary dimension of the gaze as it is taken up into the Symbolic, the gaze that was described in the mirror stage ("of a point in time of spectacular importance in which a child, carried by its mother, whose gaze it looks at, turns around and finds this very gaze which establishes it"[37]), and, in addition to that, the gaze which "aestheticizes" and "idealizes" and which would make it possible to envision and conceptualize sublimation in the feminine sense of the word, a capacity in the relation to herself, to her mother, to her femininity, to the femininity of her being, to the Real of her body, to the desire of the man, and simultaneously to the love and pleasure a woman has. "But for this"—this is how Perrier ends—"traditions, dramas, wars and death" were necessary, and, above all, "necessary were three generations of women, three generations of gazes."[38]

In this way women don't hand down a name, but rather an imaginary identification, which Perrier thinks is symbolized by the beautiful gaze, which has a double function. The beautiful appears as a last fortress against death and as a "transfiguration which veils the nonrepresentable as the Lacanian *objet petit a.*" Insofar as she is its vehicle, woman has to accept being this *objet a.* In her identification with her castrated mother, woman makes herself beautiful as partial object; she thereby makes possible, in the words of Perrier, "an objectifying and reifying fetishization of herself." This is the definition of the masquerade.

We can speak of masquerade in terms of two of its aspects: 1) from the point of view of a *script,* insofar as this corresponds to a work of mourning, to a "playful work" (*travail de jeu*),[39] in which woman presents (creates) aesthetic forms and even, going out from nothing, *represents them for herself.* The action of the masquerade can, in this sense, be compared to the art of pottery, in which a surface is created around an emptiness that is both the pot's cause and its effect. It can also be compared to architecture, which constructs surfaces around a central emptiness. This is the minimal definition of sublimation[40] and, beyond that, an illustration of the logic of weaving, an image of which Freud was reminded in the context of woman's relationship to castration. It is there that woman finds the source of her capacity to create, to invent, even to fabulate and tell stories; all of these categories originate in the artificial. What is at stake here is not so much deception, but seduction: seduction has to do with "play" and not so much with disfiguring; the play of concealment/revelation which is practically identical with the art of enticement (think of garments and especially of the veil). The masquerade functions as a *trompe-l'oeil* for the sake of creating an illusion in which, of course, no one believes—all of which is not dissimilar from wearing a mask "in order to designate with it who one is so that no one be deceived."[41]

The body image created through the feminine masquerade may be understood as a described body image: what we're dealing with here is a play of differential signs which produces a meaning or which has an aesthetic effect (think, once again, of clothing and make-up which are exclusively reserved for women who are themselves excluded from the wearing of masks which belongs to the male domain); or, perhaps, we are dealing with the peculiar writing of gestures in the realm of coquetry (posture, gait) which is most purely embodied in dance. Here the writing is no longer inscribed on the body as surface, but rather it is the body itself which makes itself a letter, a letter, which displays itself like writing, on a page produced by the space of representation. In dance, however, woman's body does not remain merely at the level of object, but also moves into the sphere of artwork.

The masquerade is an act of representation, of the *figure*,[42] also in the sense of "rhetorical figures" as they were defined by the Ancients as the media of style, which supported a theory of *ornamentation*. From this perspective it would be possible to comprehend the female image as the effect of a *metaphor* (induced by the metaphorical function of the Name-of-the-Father, which is exactly what is missing in psychosis). Without spending too much time on this point and the following one, we could say that this allusion to rhetoric could serve as an argumentative basis for underpinning the thesis about the truth of appearance in the masquerade, the source of which lies in a critique of the theory of expression. Against this latter dualistic theory, which opposes form and content, whereby the former is reduced to being the cover (or garment) for the latter, one could construct a theory of truth according to which form is inseparably tied to content: a work's *style* is evidence that the essence consists of the form. Nietzsche says so in a most astonishing manner in relation to the Greeks: they are "superficial because of their depth."

These statements about surface are not meant to sing the praises of evanescence or of the surface: human language, which resorts to the expression "to reemerge" *(refaire surface)* when depression or even melancholia are about to be surmounted, is not deceived in this sense.

2) The other aspect of the masquerade manifests itself in relation to perversion. Phenomena like the striptease or the "star" speak for themselves. On the imaginary level, perversion would have to be examined from the perspective of *narcissism*, which, because of its irreducibility, really and specifically marks woman, as Freud saw clearly. Rilke can describe for us the "Woman in the Mirror":

> Reflections: O beautiful glow of the shy reflection!
> How it is allowed to shine, because it lasts nowhere . . .
> We [men] fall into the reflecting glow
> as into the secret draining of our being;
> they, however, find theirs there: they read it.
> They must be double; then are they whole.[43]

This is just another way of saying that in woman appearance comes out of being, or that, for structural reasons, it is predestined to dwell in the realm of an Imaginary which contradicts all melancholia. Therein lies its strength (Freud was not wrong about this), but also its limitation. "Nothing determines woman to reduce the phallus to a mere signifier";[44] the concept of the real surface of the body as the locus of symbolic inscription can throw light on this sentence by S. Leclaire. Even dance, the most developed and most highly sublimated instance of the masquerade, does not detach itself from the body on which it depends. It is here that problems concerning the transmission and conservation of dance originate; these problems are also its inherent limitations as art form.[45]

It is at this liminal point of what can be written that the continuity between woman and her mother as Thing manifests itself, where the Other loses its dimension of otherness, the condition for desire, in order to remain the *same*. Reduced to the condition of being a cover insofar as it is fetishized, the body, as the Real, is the limit of the representable, the symbolizable. It draws woman onto the side of the so-called supplementary *jouissance*, with its bent for madness, witchcraft and "idiocy" in Michel de Certeau's sense of the word, on the one hand, and, on the other, with its inclination for plenitude and for devotion it draws her in the direction of the saint (through child bearing, through her mystical relation, through the gift, through mercy, unselfishness— through everything that roots woman in the otherworldly).[46] It is here that we enter the territory where "woman does not exist." We will say nothing more about this, since our endeavor is, in contrast, to explore to what extent woman does exist. If the melancholic woman is excluded from this special way of existing, then the hysteric stages it with that much more noise and clamor.

The time has finally come to sing the praises of hysteria.

If, as far as *jouissance* is concerned, the girl at first and fundamentally stands in a relation of continuity to the real Other, the mother, she has to undertake to do something in order to free desire, which lies on the side of the Other of the signifier, and in order for her to become "this Other for herself as she is this Other for him." Lacan makes this point more precisely: "We wish to say that the defense becomes tangible at first here in the realm of the masquerade which is emancipated into the sexual role by the presence of the Other."[47] What is it, in other words, among the various types of neurotic desire, that marks hysterical desire which, through Freud, opened up the space of psychoanalysis and which stands on the threshold of the true entrance to analytic work? (One often hears talk about "hystericization.")

It is possible to extricate from hysterical desire a first period, which one could call "the appeal of the Other to desire."

Desire, defined by the signifying cut (the cut between two signifiers), marks the subject of the unconscious as a *split* subject. This splitting of the subject is fully accepted by the hysteric; she shouts it out and makes a show of it by representing herself as incomplete, as suffering from the lack of an object which cannot be (ful)filled by any ordinary object. She thereby demonstrates a difference between demand and desire which Lacan established a long time ago: desire cannot be reduced to demand; in other words: desire strives to be the desire not for an object but for a desire (the other is desirable as object because he himself desires). The dream of the beautiful butcher's wife analyzed by Freud and picked up again by Lacan demonstrates this: she desires something without wanting it. In her dream she desires smoked salmon or caviar while unconsciously desiring that there will be a lack of smoked salmon and caviar. Demand is directed at the object (which can be the analyst), while desire is directed at a lack. The hysteric knows, then, that desire is based on a structural and essential insurmountable split. This is what constitutes Dora's power vis-à-vis Freud, her advantage: no matter what Freud suggests to her— the ideal of marriage (the boy instead of the girl) or knowledge concerning her unconscious—her response is always the same: "That's not it." She reminds Freud of the nullity of the sort of knowledge that belongs to a discourse that pretends to master the truth of *jouissance:* "So what really has been established?" is her response to Freud, who, in exchange for her associations, offers her knowledge of the unconscious as if it were a secret brought out into the light of day. But the hidden truth consists of nothing other than the emergence of desire as a tear; that is the real meaning of the interpretation. And yet Dora, who like all hysterics assiduously obeys the ground rules, knows how to seduce the other into desiring; one could even go so far as to say that she masterfully knows how to manipulate Freud by kindling his desire for knowledge, a knowledge that is also the locus of his enjoyment. (Let us remember that it was a hysteric who suggested to Freud the rules for what we call free association). Like Freud's homosexual girl, Dora plays the card of provocation: a challenge in the form of mockery, which is the same thing as a caricature of *irony,* that Socratic irony which belongs to the definition of desire as a search.

According to the logic of the structure of the fantasm, the relation of the hysteric to desire necessitates her identification with the object: partial object, lost object, the object as the cause for the desire of the other, the Lacanian *objet a.* She offers herself as object to the Other by identifying with lack, that is, by offering her castration in a seductive, lamenting, and submissive manner. This is the "I don't know, I don't have, I am not" of the hysteric, the making a show of her lack, her incompleteness—in short, her phallic privation to which she is indebted for her prestige as imaginary object. For we are here in the imaginary dimension of the fantasm, which regulates desire by reacting to it through the medium of appearance. Making oneself the *objet a* implies the double edge of seductive attraction and rejection (turning oneself into waste material, into something insignificant *[petit rien]*, which, if it cannot be the absolute object of desire, stands in as object *for* desire).

Such seductive play, which sets in motion all sorts of combinations and maneuvers (one presents oneself as at times amenable, at other times stubborn), begins to resemble something of the order of stage directions. The point is to plot, to simulate, to come up with strategies, to be in control of the ropes, even while pretending to have fully surrendered to the game; in short, it seems that we find ourselves fully in the realm of the feminine masquerade. And the appeal to desire, the call to arms is, we recall, the aim of the masquerade as I described it above.

By bringing the other to desire in this way, the hysteric desires herself. But we have still not come full circle, because the analysis of the hysteric implies a second phase as well: the phase of *evasion*.

If it is possible to speak of the masquerade in hysteria in a deprecating manner, that is because in reality the hysteric's offer of desire is deceptive. Like all neurotics, the hysteric wants to "flee from aphanisis, the implicit fading of desire. . . . The neurotic accepts an absence which nothing can fill, but not that he himself could be absent," says Alain Juranville.[48] In order not to disappear oneself as absence (which is what the effect of symbolic castration consists of), the hysteric constitutes her desire as a *dissatisfied* desire, just as the obsessive compulsive fabricates an *impossible*, and the phobic a *prohibited*, desire. "Desire is maintained only through the lack of satisfaction that is introduced into it when he eludes himself as object," Lacan writes, and he continues, "She, the hysteric, attempts to block desire with situations which she herself concocts. She prevents desire from arriving in order to be at stake herself in this game."[49] Desire eternalizes itself instead of erasing itself in the sexual act (in connection with Dora, Freud mentions "her inability to be commensurate with the real demands of love"). In this way the hysteric makes herself into the ruler of the desire of the Other: by attacking desire with desire, she supports the man's desire, through which she then supports herself. It is here, in this dissatisfaction of desire, that she finds her enjoyment, not as object that causes desire, but rather as the subject in her symptoms. In reality, the hysteric removes herself as object by making herself into a subject through a male identification with the father's trait: this is what her "masculinity complex," which Freud relates to the unsurmounted penis envy, consists of—a masculine function, which, in contrast with the homosexual woman, she fills only "ad interim," to use Melman's expression. Making oneself into a subject, by the way, is a characteristic of all neurotics, while the pervert presents himself above all as object. By identifying with the father she enters into a relationship of rivalry with him and challenges him to show his stuff. Opposed to the idealization of the father in a seductive play of machinations there is, in relation to the gaze of the mother for whom this play is put on, a mocking of the father, as it has been represented by Alain Juranville in his schema:[50] in an imaginary fashion the hysteric is, as subject, identified with the symbolic father; the real father is in the position of an object, while the mother takes up the position of the Other. To sum up, one could say that the hysteric represents herself as "deceptive object," "marionette," "mannequin," in a position of seduction towards the father, a position which she deceptively veils with the mantle of femininity in order to deceive the man who himself is in the position of a ridiculous, foolish, and myopic master, like the king in "The Purloined Letter," who understands nothing and who, as Lacan says, is "a simplistic and castrated partner." The masquerade is a swindle, it is a *parade* (Lacan reserves this term "parade" for the man) offered to the mother: vis-à-vis the man, she plays the woman; vis-à-vis the mother, she "provides the man." In this game she remains within the realm of falseness (this is what represents her "faithless side") wherein she paradoxically rebuffs the "apparent" in order to find out about "true" femininity, precisely that femininity, in other words, through which woman does not exist and in relation to which she feels inadequate.

Her special status among the other neuroses is the result of her occupying two fields, and this bisexuality manifests itself in her symptom: while in its essence it is masculine, it nevertheless betrays its own femininity, because the so-called conversion symptom is a signifier become body, a language inscribed in the Real of the body. Earlier we saw that the transformation of the bodily Real into a signifier is the result of a symbolic identification present in corporeal rites of which, in my estimation, the masquerade is one. And yet these two types of inscription, both of which are the result of a metaphorization and develop within the realm of representation, are not of the same kind; nor do they have the same function. Let me attempt to show how, by ending my presentation with a comparison of the masquerade and the symptom, the hysteric turns the masquerade into a symptom.

The masquerade may be conceived of as a sort of norm, while the symptom is a defense, a compromise formation. In the masquerade the subject represents itself as an aestheticized object in a play of presence and absence, of concealment and revelation, comparable to the structure of the opening and closing of the wings of a butterfly, whereby the flight of the *objet a*, its pulsating and vanishing, is evoked, that phenomenon which, as gaze (the object of sight), "as play of light and opacity . . . always takes on something of the ambiguity of a jewel."[51] The hysterical subject has been called a "phallus girl," since she offers to the gaze the phallic splendor of her body and because her bodily symptoms have not become phallic signs of this body. These are all dissimulations that attempt to hide the fact that it is she who determines the law.

Where in the masquerade a minimal amount of *sublimation* manifests itself (on the basis of perversion), which is characterized by a *writing* of the body which has resulted from an emptiness, we come face to face with the *symptom*, with the repression of symbolic castration.[52] The symptoms inscribe themselves on the surface which the body represents in a way that corresponds to a fantasmatic geography; they obey the laws of symbolic exchangeability in the representation, displacement, and condensation that are typical of the language of the unconscious. One can also speak of a fantasmatic geography when one thinks of the drawings that Hans Bellmer made, basing himself on Lombroso's descriptions of young hysterics. These drawings, which attempt to represent the superimpositions of organs, their substitutions, and so forth, make possible a nonlinguistic understanding of what could be the disturbances of depersonalization in relation to body image, of which we have already spoken.[53]

Within the medium of the masquerade woman finds a point of reference for her game in phallic enjoyment. In the symptom there is confusion between phallic *jouissance* and that other *jouissance*; phallic *jouissance*, which she there encounters against a traumatic backdrop, is experienced as unpleasure. In the pantomimic spectacle of the body (just think of the great hysterics who had their so-called crises *à la Charcot*), the symptom brings the fantasm onto the stage as the fantasm of seduction or as the fantasm of the primal scene. In any case, "the bisexual meaning of hysterical symptoms" and the "contradictory simultaneity" of their corporeal representation of which Freud speaks in the case of one particular patient, who "pressed her dress up against her body with one hand (as the woman), while she tried to tear it off with the other (as the man),"[54] are astonishing.

In the masquerade the woman addresses a worldly, social Other; her theater is the world's stage. But even if the hysteric turns her body into a stage, this theater remains private. The spectacle addresses—we said this already—the Other who, for the subject, is almighty and divine: the mother, a personality whose rule, however, hardly extends beyond the borders of the inner fantasmatic world of the subject. It is this that drives Lacan to say, "The hysteric gives herself over to a theater which apparently can be no more than a charity performance."[55]

Finally, the masquerade is the creator of a feminine identification which results from an "artificiality of gender," in which woman *believes*, but does so in the form of a "Yes, I know . . . but still." This belief makes possible the partial sublimation that marks social affiliation, even if it seems to result from the "discourse of the master." The hysteric does not believe in her femininity and turns her masquerade into a disguise in which she feels she is comically made up. Wearing herself out by playing the man, she nevertheless holds on to (the idea of) a horizon of absolute femininity beyond the phallus. It is here that we see, among the various types of *belief*, as Lacan has defined them, her particular manner of "believing in the Other."

And thus we see that the masquerade is situated, as a fiction, in between the missing illusion in melancholia and the missing belief in hysteria. Finding its source in the Imaginary, in the instance of the ideal, it becomes increasingly more fragile when it moves toward either one of the two poles of the spectrum: psychosis and neurosis. There is the danger of the deadly idealization of the Other in *passion* or in erotomania, into which melancholia can lead; there is also the danger of idealizing femininity as something divine. Dora finds this perfection embodied in the "enchanting white" of Madame K., whom she worships, unless what is at stake here is not really a threat that she may be narcissistically fetishizing herself, a sterile primness (affectation), which is always possible in a perverse use of the masquerade.

But these illnesses of idealization should not conceal the other aspect of the Imaginary which involves positive and necessary illusion, and which became the driving force behind Winnicott's psychotherapy of the psychoses. This illusion exists in art as well; it also provides a space for death and allows it thereby to become *possible*. In psychosis, in other words, the Imaginary tends to have itself introduced via the dimension of the transition, the in-between, play. This occurs in neurosis as well. When Lacan says that at the end of one's therapy one "knows how to handle one's symptoms" (*savoir y faire*), one may take this to mean that what is at stake is being capable of "handling them playfully" (*savoir en jouer*).

Notes

1. Jacques Derrida, *Epérons* (Paris: Champs Flammarion, 1978), 38: "Il n'y a pas d'essence de la femme parce que la femme écarte et s'écarte d'elle-même."

2. D. Silvestre, "Chercher la femme," *Ornicar?* 25 (1982), 62.

3. If the three dimensions (the Real, the Imaginary, the Symbolic) are constitutive for all structures, it would be appropriate to suggest, as Alain Juranville does, to distinguish three types of the Imaginary: if in psychosis the Imaginary of the body is the Real of the body perceived as totality and completeness, then in perversion the issue is the "Imaginary of the image," which is the subject of the following examination (Juranville, *Lacan et la philosophie* [Paris: Presses Universitaires de France, 1984], 421: "The psychotic immerses this absolute *jouissance* of the body in the Imaginary. . . . He himself wishes to form a whole," while in the perverse structure "the Symbolic separates itself off from the Real. . . . The body empties itself out. But the Real is imagined. Hence the importance of the fantasm of the wholeness of the castrated body, of beauty in perversion" (423) [trans. E. S.]; cf. also 418. It is this opposition on which we draw in order to talk about *depth* and *surface*. D. Vasse (*L'ombilic et la voix* [Paris: Seuil, 1974]) in this connection speaks of this depth in reference to childhood psychosis when he uses terms like "substantial image"

(85), "imaginary identification with the body-thing" (119), or "imaginary identification with the Real" (128).

4. C. Melman, *Nouvelles études sur l'hystérie* (Paris: Clim/Denoël, 1984).

5. Mixing up disturbance of the body image in psychosis with those in neurosis always poses a threat. When one reads through the impressive list of Anna O.'s hysterical disturbances as they were described by Freud, one could almost be tempted to see in them disturbances of the psychotic type. Several papers along the lines of this problematic which question any given diagnosis of psychosis in order to replace it by one of neurosis have been published in the last few years. See, for instance, the case of Susan by Marion Milner, which C. Soler reconsidered ("Une passion de transfert," in *Ornicar?* 29 [Paris, 1984]: 31–57).

6. E. Lemoine-Luccioni, *Partage des femmes* (Paris: Seuil 1976).

7. F. Perrier, "Structure hystérique et dialogue analytique," in *La Chaussée d'Antin 2*, no. 10/18 (Paris 1978): 65.

8. C. Melman, 129.

9. Ibid.

10. See note 4 regarding the differential diagnosis of psychosis and neurosis. Cf. J. C. Maleval, "La destructuration de l'image du corps dans les névroses et les psychoses," in *Folies hystériques et psychoses dissociatives* (Paris: Payot, 1981). This author contests a number of diagnoses of psychosis.

11. Jacques Lacan, "D'une question préliminaire à tout traitement possible de la psychose," in *Écrits* (Paris, 1966), 554. English: "On a question preliminary to any possible treatment of psychosis" in *Écrits: A Selection*, trans. Alan Sheridan (New York: W. W. Norton, 1977), 223, note 18.

12. Alain Juranville, *Lacan et la philosophie.* (Paris: Presses Universitaires de France, 1984), 405.

13. Ibid. Cf. also the chapter on "Les structures existentiales," insofar as all four of them are marked by a process and a phenomenon (237ff.).

14. R.C. Racamier, *Les schizophrènes* (Paris: Petite Bibliotheque Payot, 1983), 113.

15. Melman, 223.

16. Jacques Lacan, *Le Séminaire X (L'angoisse)*, (unpubl., June 12, 1962).

17. Juranville, 422.

18. Jacques Lacan, *Le Séminaire XI: Les quatre concepts fondamentaux de la psychanalyse* (Paris: Seuil, 1973), 187. English: Jacques Lacan, *The Four Fundamental*

Concepts of Psychoanalysis. The Seminar of Jacques Lacan, Book XI, trans. Alan Sheridan (New York: W. W. Norton, 1998), 206.

19. J. T. Maertens, *Ritologiques* (Paris: Aubier, 1978).

20. O. Mannoni, "Je sais bien, mais quand-même . . . ," in *Clefs pour l'imaginaire ou l'Autre Scène* (Paris: Seuil, 1969), 9–33.

21. Juranville, 262.

22. Ibid., 291 f.

23. Jacques Lacan, "Lituraterre," in *Revue Littérature* 3 (Oct., 1971).

24. W. Granoff, *La pensée et le féminin* (Paris: Minuit, 1976).

25. R. and R. Lefort, *Naissance de l'Autre* (Paris: Seuil, 1980).

26. Juranville, 175 and 405.

27. Jacques Lacan, *Le Séminaire VI: Le désir et l'interprétation* (unpubl., 6/17/1959).

28. Ibid.: "For her the point of natural objects, insofar as they are objects with which one decorates oneself, is to realize the function of desire in the most natural manner possible." Cf. also Lacan, *Les quatre concepts fondamentaux*, 194; English: Lacan, *The Four Fundamental Concepts of Psycho-Analysis*, trans. Alan Sheridan and ed. Jacques-Alain Miller (New York: W. W. Norton, 1978), 213–4.

29. Serge Leclaire, *On tue un enfant* (Paris: Seuil, 1975), 39. "One comprehends that the 'Phallic' phase of the girl inscribes itself in a row of similar experiences of loss, of separations or of lacks, which *in a wholly natural manner*, to put it his way, is situated in the structure of the Unconscious determined by castration. . . . It is for this reason that she is situated on the same plane as primal repression" (37); "[I]n this immediate relationship to castration she finds a support for a process of identification *of a sexual nature, which, to begin with, unconsciously characterizes her as woman. . . .*" (38 f.) [trans. E. S.]

30. Granoff, 289.

31. Leclaire, 42–43.

32. F. Perrier, "L'amatride," in *La Chaussée d'Antin 2*, no. 10/18 (1978): 195–209.

33. The significance that the earth has in melancholia is well known (in the theory of the elements, in the tie to Saturn . . .).

34. Jacques Lacan, *Le Séminaire IX: L'identification, 1961–62* (unpubl., 6/20/1962): "The psychotic's desire has to do with the body." ("Le psychotique dans le désir a affaire au corps.")

35. Perrier, "L'amatride," 205.

36. Ibid., 206.

37. Ibid., 204.

38. Ibid., 208.

39. Following an expression which P. Felida uses and has developed (*"L' objeu' Objet, jeu et enfance, l'espace psychothérapeutique,"* in *L'Absence* [Paris: Gallimard, 1978], 98).

40. Cf. also the theory of sublimation as it has also been developed by Alain Juranville, 276ff. (and elsewhere). See also C. Millot, "La sublimation, création ou réparation?" in *Ornicar?* 25 (1982). See also the topic of sublimation as it has been developed by Laplanche, which takes a completely different direction: as "the continual restarting of an excitation and not the channeling of an already existing energy" ("Faire dériver la sublimation," in *Psychanalyse à l'Université* 2, no. 8 [Sept., 1977]: 609).

41. Expression of J. Clavreul who discusses the topic of the masquerade in reference to the article, "La féminité," in *Le désir et la perversion* (Paris: Seuil, 1987), 83.

42. We are here not concerned with the term "figure" in the sense in which it would have to be defined from the point of view of a reflection on art, namely in the sense of "figural" as J.-F. Lyotard does, for instance, in *Discours figure* (Paris: Klincksieck, 1978).

43. Rainer Maria Rilke, *Werke in drei Bänden, Band 2: Gedichte und Übertragungen* (Insel Verlag, 1966), 181. (The excerpt here comes from *"Drei Gedichte aus dem Umkreis: Spiegelungen."*). [English translation E. S.].

44. Leclaire, 50.

45. M. F. Christout, "L'écriture de la danse," in *Corps écrit* 1 (Paris: Presses Universitaires de France).

46. Cf., for example, F. J. J. Buytendijk, *La femme, ses modes d'être, de paraître, d'exister* (Paris: Desciée de Brouwer, 1954).

47. Jacques Lacan, "Pour un congrés sur la sexualité féminine," in *Écrits*, 732. English: Lacan, "Guiding Remarks for a Congress on Feminine Sexuality," in *Feminine Sexuality: Jacques Lacan and the école freudienne*, ed. Juliet Mitchell and Jacqueline Rose, trans. Jacqueline Rose (New York: W.W. Norton, 1982), 93–4.

48. Juranville, 241.

49. Jacques Lacan, "Subversion du sujet et dialectique du désir," in *Écrits*, 824. English: Lacan, "The Subversion of the Subject and the Dialectic of Desire in the Freudian Unconscious," in *Écrits: A Selection*, trans. Alan Sheridan (New York: W. W. Norton, 1977), 321; and: "Le désir et son interprétation," (unpubl., 6/10/1959).

50. Juranville, 247, which is then explained on pages 248–249.

51. Jacques Lacan, *Le Séminaire XI*, 90. English: Lacan, *The Four Fundamental Concepts of Psychoanalysis*, p. 96.

52. See note 14.

53. Hans Bellmer, "L'anatomie de l'image," in *Le terrain vague* (Paris, 1957).

54. Sigmund Freud, in "Hysterical Phantasies and Their Relation to Bisexuality," *Standard Edition, Volume 9* (London: The Hogarth Press), 166.

55. Jacques Lacan, "D'un discours qui ne serait pas du semblant" (unpubl., 6/7/1971), where Lacan also comes to speak of the "usual clinic with which the hysteric fills out the yawning absence of the sexual relation." [English trans. E. S.]

9

Symbolic Mother—Real Father

REGULA SCHINDLER

translation for a German-speaking public, of a paper given at the Franco-Belgian conference, "Le pére—un symptôme?" of the Association freudienne, September, 1990, in Brussels. Consequently, it moves with some difficulty: polemical allusions to the current jargon had, it seemed to me, to yield to bumpy attempts at explanation. Even worse: the Lacanian "topology" without its connecting links does have a rather abstruse effect here; and yet, it by no means consists simply of learned accessories: it is the consequence of that lack or loss which, by talking about it, one goes on to drown in meaning.

How is it possible to transmit "Lacan"? Hardly this way. But if someone or other has the urge to chew through all of this and in the process perhaps encounter an illumination or two, I'll be satisfied.

Introduction: Two Functions One Doesn't Want to Know About

The search for contributions to this number of *RISS* enabled us to establish that one topic that is missing in the conferences, books, and journals of the *École Freudienne de Paris* and its followers is that of the mother, and this very much in contrast to the ubiquitous father. When the mother does appear, she does so as a figure subjected to questions concerning the feminine, or rather, the *Other Sex*. Within this framework something can often be found on the mother-daughter relationship, usually from a female point of view; and it seems that there is a general tendency to banish the mother-son relationship to the ghetto of perversion.

Does this mean that normality—*norme mâle*, the male norm—depends on the mother's disappearance? We know that she is prohibited by the father, and, because the father corresponds to a highly complex nodal point of functions, no one can get enough of making him the focus of examination, untroubled by this mother who is to remain where the paternal metaphor has banished her: below the bar.

101

That she reappears at the most central point where "the woman" is viewed "only *quod matrem*," that she "functions in the sexual relation only as mother," these are "massive truths," which "analytic discourse brings into play"[1]—in other words, for which we have Freud to thank. Strange that this analytic discourse should shroud these massive truths in silence.

The announcement of my title already provoked a degree of discomfort and some doubts in the audience in view of my title's two protagonists' right to exist. But no one can deny that the *symbolic mother* and the *real father* appear in the seminars and texts of Lacan in the later 1950s. Is this a concession of Lacan's to his listeners of that time? An aberration? Is that Lacan to be ranked retrospectively as a matrophilic heretic in his own School?

It is true that these two figures lie diagonally opposed to the current connections father = Symbolic, mother = Imaginary/Real. When one furnishes this bipolar breakdown with bivalent signs one gets: father = Symbolic = good; mother = Imaginary = dubious/dangerous. Then and only then can the idea establish itself that *symbolic mother* and *real father* tend toward mother cult and devaluation of the father. Nothing of this sort is to be found in Lacan.

The interest in this figure—or better, this function—*symbolic mother* lies in the fact that it is located on this side of any sort of valuation. Strictly speaking, it mediates nothing but the auto-difference of the signifier: +/-, o/ a, (*fort/da* is already an interpretation). This is the "first symbolic order," introduced by the mother:[2] a Symbolic Order which generates the object as a lost—or better, frustrated*—object. This frustration leaves a question mark behind which the child then tries to decipher: the riddle of the mother's desire. In this way this *first symbolic order*, in which the symbolic mother-child relation is situated, already brings the ubiquitous and nonexistent maternal phallus into play.

In order to turn this first order into an inhabitable world it is necessary that there be the *real element*, which is introduced by the father:[3] a real answer to the question of the mother's desire that makes it impossible for the child to think that it itself is the answer. The aim is to open up the wonderful prison of the mother's desire, to make that impossible phallus handy, manipulatable, and negotiable.

Symbolic mother and *real father* are not persons; no Mommy *is* a symbolic mother, no Daddy *is* a real father. Lacan dissects and transforms the fetishized parental figures, which outline psychoanalytic knowledge and which are guarded by that knowledge, into *significant functions*. By doing so he subverts any sort of person or essentializing cult as well as its moralizing offshoots. It would be

---

**Versagung* = frustration, failure; *versagtes Objekt* = object that the subject is frustrated of through speech.—E.S.

equally wrong to understand these functions in the sense of (psychosocial) roles which a subject can assume or cast off: those who find themselves in the position of mother or father will have to act out that function for better or for worse, even when they attempt to withdraw from them. Mothers and fathers, whether they want to or not, function as agents of the order of signifiers.[4]

Far from disappearing, these two functions reemerge in the nodal Seminars of the 1970s; as the symbolic *and* real cords of that Other, which now has the consistency of the "knot," they form the foundation, the base matter, of the subject's identifications.[5] In parallel fashion the *father function* displaces itself: it becomes a symptom. But note: the symptomatic nature of the father function is absolutely not incidental; it is necessary: the symptom (or more precisely, its "half-*saying*"—I will return to this) is now the *"only guarantee of the father function."*[6] From this one can measure the extent to which Lacan has distanced himself from an allegedly purely symbolic father function. That things have always been more complex than that dogma would have liked will become apparent: especially that the famous Name-of-the-Father has always already had one foot in the Real. The necessity of developing the father function into a symptom saw its beginnings in the Real of the father of the 1950s, in a Real about which people seem to want to know as little as they want to know about the maternal Symbolic. Why is that?

The "Symbolic Mother," Signifier of the Paternal Metaphor

Statements of the sort that the father "introduces the symbolic," and thereby "symbolizes" a mother who up to that point had been imaginary, obscure Lacan's differentiations relating thereto and mislead one into simplifying the understanding of the paternal metaphor.[7] And who doesn't know, leaving the formulae aside, that the maternal signifier, the desire of the mother, which refers to her castration, in no way disappears but rather returns as a more or less repressed signifier in the symptom?

In "The Signification of the Phallus" (1958) this signifier regulates not just symptoms, but structure as such: "Clinical experience has shown us that this test of the desire of the Other is decisive not in the sense that the subject learns by it whether or not he has a real phallus, but in the sense that he learns that the mother does not have it. This is the moment of the experience without which no symptomatic consequence (phobia) or structural consequence (*Penisneid*) relating to the castration complex can take effect."[8]

The most incisive of the experiences of childhood, that of the mother's castration, can be understood neither in a naturalistic nor in a cultural manner. These explanatory modalities are not just wrong; they are analytically insufficient. The nature/culture distinction can be found only in a discourse in which the paternal metaphor has been at work for a long time. Even the most "natural" child-mother relationship is inscribed in the paternal metaphor before and outside of the intervention of a real father.

Frustration [*Versagung*] and Phallus

The mother—any mother—has always already been backed by that *symbolic father* who is nothing but the "always necessary condition of speech":[9] in short, she speaks and is spoken—that is, she desires. Is everyone silent about her in order to get her to be silent?

But in spite of all of these exertions she does not stop speaking: she speaks and speaks, be it at home, be it in analysis: her theoretical nonexistence does not prevent her from expanding through speech. Perhaps this is why analyses are so difficult to terminate. From the very beginning she should have designated the father as the custodian of the phallus and thereupon she should have shut up. Instead she continued chatting—about everything, nothing, anything. Does this inexhaustible desire to speak stand in any sort of relationship to that knowledge that Lacan, at least, ascribes to her as woman: the knowledge, that is, that the phallus stands *beyond* the sexual relation? In any case she constantly addresses, via others and especially via her child, this phallus. And when husband and children withdraw she continues talking; any prey that crosses her path turns into a pretext for her address.

Let us admit, at any rate, that insofar as she speaks, she does not intend to reincorporate her product. On the contrary, it is in her interest to preserve her product as her phallic relay for as long as possible. We reproach her with succeeding in this only too well.

Let us admit that any given mother is propped up by that language which has always already cut mother and child off from the Real of the object and which has made the object into the plaything of the treacherous dialectic of the demand for love and the proof of love. "The satisfaction which is at issue in frustration appears against the fundamentally disappointing background of the symbolic order and is here simply substitute, compensation . . . ," "the alibi of the frustration of love."[10]

The knot[11] of frustration (S-I-R) has always been connected with the knot of privation (I-R-S) and the knot of castration (R-S-I). It is the frustration of the presence of the object that evokes absence.

The beginnings of such a connection can already be found in Freud. Freud tells us that the child "never gets over the loss of the mother's breast," that "the child's yearning for its first nourishment is altogether unappeasable."[12] And later: "I have the breast, that means I'm not it."[13] How can I get over something, which, strictly speaking, I have never "had" (because when I "had" it, "I" did not yet exist)? How can I get over something, which I "was" in the *deferred nature (Nachträglichkeit)* of speech, thanks to a "being" which is the name of that empty place on which my existence is founded? Let's remember that Freud refers to this impossible grief as the cause of the later "reproaches and complaints against the mother."[14] "The child's demands for love are excessive, they demand exclusivity and allow for no sharing." We cannot forgive her, this mother, and the fact that she denied us that mythical "first nourishment." In a certain way the daring metaphor of desire for incest shrouds this gap in early childhood which could perhaps be articulated in the following way: what is she, this mother, looking for when *I* am here? Why can't she be satisfied with the miracle of being, mine and hers?

And if the mother is so successful at preserving her product as a phallic relay then that is also because this product has some difficulty with the renunciation of representing that constantly threatened phallus for the mother.

One can make a simple deduction from what has been said so far: this mother whom one generally prefers to not speak about is the *symbolic mother*, that is, the mother insofar as she exercises the symbolic function: the function of saying what is always already an unsaying. Neither the prohibiting nor the silent father is capable of restraining her; even worse, the less people want to know about her, the more she reappears in the well-known forms of the omnipotent phallus. The evil devouring mother *[Krokodilmutter]* who lurks, waiting for the right moment to devour children and father, is one of these imaginary shapes her reappearance takes, and its modern metonymy is the women's libber with her burning desire to squash the Name-of-the-Father in order to present her children with a meal that is dedicated to *her* totem. Since there is no cause for the gap in the subject, the mother is always welcome to step in. Was it not she who seduced the father and offered him, "cut off in the blossom of his sin" (*Hamlet*), up to eternal damnation?

How is one to encounter her, how to manage living with her? Let us present the one whom alone we can expect to have some sort of effect on her: the *real father*. And as we will see, the result is a perhaps infernal, in any case symptomatic, couple.

The "Real Father"

"In contrast to a normative and typical function which one would like to give him (the father) . . . the salient point of what takes place around the castration complex is to be ascribed to the real father."[15] In the Seminar *La Relation d'Objet*, especially in the sessions of March 6, 13, and 20, 1957, Lacan repeatedly gets back to this: in contrast to the mother, who has introduced a first symbolic order, a first symbolic dialectic, which brings the phallus as a symbol of desire into play, the father intervenes as he who introduces the real element.[16] The maternal phallus is everywhere and nowhere and therefore the plaything of a placeless and timeless pleasure between mother and child. Only a father can "put it to the test of the

Real" (*mettre à l'épreuve du réel*). "He (the father) is the one who has it, this master-of-all, and who *knows* that he has it." Between the symbolic mother and the real father there is sometimes, in this Seminar, an almost sexual relation.

But the attribute *real* already announces the fact that this issue of castration approaches the impossible. It has neither cause nor object: "The phallus functions everywhere except where one would expect it: on the level of genital mediation. For this reason anxiety is the reality of sexuality."[17]

It is the task of the real father, or rather, because such a father does not exist, of the *Real of the father*, to rupture the seduction by the maternal symbol—the symbol of privation, which is everything and nothing, everywhere and nowhere—and to substitute it with the imaginary phallus which guarantees the circulation of the objects in the world of discourse. This is no easy task—hence the eternal alibi of a symbolic father whom one addresses but who, unfortunately, neither responds nor intervenes.

The task of the real father is almost impossible. To the degree to which he believes he must separate his descendants from the maternal phallus the whole thing has already been missed.

The Failure [*Versagen*] of the "Real Father"

This is the case with the father of *Little Hans* who cares lovingly for his son, who attempts to explain to him what can and cannot be, who, in pedagogical fashion, forbids him to enter the mother's bed, and who even tries to achieve a pedagogical rage: as Lacan puts it succinctly, Hans "has no real father." "This rage is not a real rage, and little Hans hits the nail on the head: you should be really enraged, really jealous."[18]

This may have horrified quite a few people at the time and it still has the capacity of shaking the security of those who want to conceive of the paternal castrative intervention as a symbolic *enunciated* (*énoncé*). Hans is the classic example of the fact that the success and the failure of this intervention are independent of the enunciated and that it depends on the *Real of the enunciation* (*énonciation*): on the How and Whence. This *Real of the father* is not unconnected to the *Imaginary* and the *Symbolic*; what is crucial is the position, the place, from whence it speaks—in other words, its style, its tone. It is well known that children have an excellent ear for what sounds fake.

Lacan has pursued this issue by way of the voice. In the Seminar *Angoisse* (1962/63) the voice is "the Other (*l'alterité*) of what speaks itself," and "that which does not assimilate, but rather incorporates." There would be far too much to say about the *objet a* "voice" as the cause of the Freudian "longing for the father": the famous phrase "God is unconscious" belongs to his context.[19]

Little Hans's father failed in his attempt to play the "god of thunder" (*faire le dieu tonnère*). But how can one play the god of thunder when it is precisely the voice that cannot deceive? "Playing the god of thunder" is not an act of will; it is an *act* and as such is subject to those aporias which Lacan developed by way of the *Acte psychanalytique*.[20] In distinction to just any kind of action, any given deed, *l'acte* is a significant event, a cut, which makes possible a new beginning, and which opens up a whole new field: but such an action is still not a conscious act of will, as it is carried by the *objet a*, by that paradoxical "object one does not have." (The insufficiency of the alternative spontaneous versus planned acting, which is at stake here, is eminently related to practice; what analyst doesn't know that?) A father exercises his real function when he is in a certain way (and this is where the difficulty lies) capable of surrendering himself up to the unconscious; when he doesn't at all believe himself to be in possession of the factotum, he misses his father function, but when he is totally convinced that he has it he runs the risk of installing himself as a perverse master. We know that perversion exists not only in those circles said to be "perverse" but also, and especially, in normality, in the normal family, and it is here that its effects are that much more devastating, because here the factotum conceals itself behind paternal ideals, be they professional, national or religious. Throughout his life Lacan had very sharp words regarding this issue: in "acts of faith such as the professional ideal the instrument of *jouissance* is confused with the instrument of power."[21]

The sharpest and most brilliant tirade regarding the father as the carrier of ideals occurs in "On a Question Preliminary to Any Possible Treatment of Psychosis,"[22] which one should, however, read in the original: at issue here are "the ravaging effects of the paternal figure," "whether in fact he is one of those fathers who make the laws or whether he poses as the pillar of the faith, as a paragon of integrity and devotion, as virtuous or as a virtuoso, by serving a work of salvation, or whatever object or lack of object, of nation or of birth, of safeguard or salubrity, of legacy or legality, of the pure, the impure, or of empire, all ideals that provide him with all too many opportunities of being in a posture of undeserving, inadequacy, even of fraud, and, in short, of excluding the Name-of-the-Father from its position in the signifier."[23]

What doesn't come through too well in the translation is the inclusion of "negative" contents of faith: what is at stake is not only *du pure* (purity) but also *du pire* (the worst), not just some sort of object (*objet*) but also a lack (*manque d'objet*, which seems to have been coined precisely for those analysts who make "lack" their credo . . .).

The older Lacan returns to this tirade in the Seminar "R.S.I." (1/21/75): "Anyone can appropriate the father's function of exception. We know the result: his foreclosure or rejection in the majority of the cases . . . , which the father brings about, with the psychotic effects to which I have referred." How can one then expect his wife, the mother to support his position if not from that position which defends the paternal ideal a priori? One can only welcome the fact that mothers à la Mother Schreber have become scarce.

The "Half-Saying" of the Symptom as the Only Guarantee for the Father's Function

How is the father supposed to fix this? What kind of father would be a "good enough" father? Only a Solomonic logic is capable of fulfilling the impossible task of mediating castration—it's impossible to say it, impossible to avoid it. "The guarantee for the father's function," Lacan says in "R.S.I." (1/21/75), "is the version of the père-version belonging to him . . . , which leaves what is at issue in castration at a proper "half-saying" (*mi-dire*), or, if I may put it this way, at a 'demigod-saying' [half-god-saying] (*mi-dieu*). . . ." The dictum that the truth can be said only halfway is one of Lacan's household words. But what of this *mi-dieu?* The more than accidental metonymy *dire-dieu* leaves us in a lurch in German [and English]. The context: at issue is a father's version (*père-version*) who "alone has a right to our respect, if not even to our love." This version is determined by the particular manner "of making a woman into a symptom." At best, "the woman he has procured to bear his children is his *objet a*," the cause of his desire. But she does not allow herself to be reduced thus. "Unfortunately, confusingly, a woman is—just like a man—not an *objet a*. She has people who belong to her, whom she cares about. . . . [M]aking her a symptom means placing her there where phallic *jouissance* concerns her as well. A woman is subjected to castration no more and no less than a man is."

That a woman is man's symptom "is a result of the structure," the structure of the big Ø as "matrix with a double entrance": one entrance "emits small a"; the other "the One," that One, "which inscribes itself in the unconscious as letter, and to this degree it is his symptom." "There is no conjunction, no copulation, between One and *a*": no sexual relation.[24]

One should recall here, as far as the logic of numbers and letters is concerned, which we cannot go into here, the detailed example in *Encore* where Achilles stands for the One and the tortoise for "a": that tortoise which Achilles can never catch up with. The impossible relationship between *1: a* is valid for the man-woman relationship and also, in this context, for the female subject-object, the division of which does not make a whole, neither for herself, nor for the man.

At issue always is the nonrelationship between signifier (1) and object (a). The subject, subject of the signifier, is denied the object: what appears as "sexual nonrelationship" has the structure of that frustration whose agent is the "symbolic mother."

And it is here that the *mi-dieu* can be clarified: "demigod" is the status of that woman "who has a function in the sexual relation only as mother"; she is a symptom insofar as she refers to the maternal "One," or more correctly, to the status, split between "1" and "*a*," of the mother-wife of the father and wife of the father's father. Somewhat crudely one could say: *because* the maternal signifier has an eminent symbolic position, that of the One that molds every symbolic relationship, there is no sexual relation, and *because* at the same stroke the mother has always already represented every prohibited love object, the sexual relation is always incestuous.

Back to that "father, who deserves our respect, if not even our love": this would be a father who, "in the favorable case," "intervenes with the children only exceptionally in order to keep what is at issue in castration in repression, in a half-saying, demigod-saying, proper not-saying."[25] In this context it becomes clear that *mi-dieu, demigod,* is due to that woman who is a symptom to the extent that she refers to the maternal *One*, or, more correctly, to the status of the mother, split between "1" and "*a*."

The Incestuous Sexual Relation

That the sexual relation is incestuous, "that the woman is always only taken as *quod matrem,*" is an old Freudian truth. The Lacan of the 1970s makes his last turn here in his return to Freud; at this central point this truth undermines his dictum of the nonrelation between the sexes. What at best keeps the symptom at a "half-saying, demigod-saying, proper not-saying" are the "points of suspension of the symptom, which query the nonrelation." In "Moment de conclure" (4/11/78) the statement is even made that the sexual relation *does* exist, between parents and children; this is *parried* by the incest prohibition (aside from "to protect" and "to bend forward," *parer* also has the meanings "to adorn," "to prepare").

The effect of this protective as well as adorning and structuring prohibition: incest is normally fantasmatic. "Only" fantasmatic, but necessarily so. Compare this to Freud: "It sounds not only disagreeable but also paradoxical, yet it must nevertheless be said that anyone who is to be really free and happy in love must have surmounted his respect for women and have come to terms with the idea of incest with mother or sister."[26]

The salient point of this half-saying and demigod story seems to me to be this: the necessarily incestuous symptom of the father should not speak too explicitly, but neither should it deny itself. The father, who deserves our respect, perhaps even our love, is a man who desires his woman, who covers the nakedness (of the *objet a*) of himself and her with *Noah's cloak*, with the veil of love, without deifying her completely and without making her into the impossible incarnation of the One-Signifier; rather, her status is that of the *symptomatic One*. When the *père-version* of the father allows for the maintainance of things in a *mi-dire, mi-dieu,* and otherwise "intervenes with the children only exceptionally" (this in noteworthy contrast to current pedagogical ideologies), then, Lacan says, he can afford to have other perversions as well. But success in the "*juste mi-dieu*" is unfortunately "rare": and there is nothing less than failure of the paternal function as such. "There is nothing worse than a father who proclaims the law; it would be better if he withdrew from all master positions." The father, too, is subjected to the law, the law of the incest prohibition and incest desire. *Juste mi-dieu* would mean hiding neither one of the sides of the coin completely nor pluming oneself with one of the sides—the law or its transgression (in our jargon one would say, "to act it out").

The Sinthome: Saving the Father

What these two signifiers, the symbolic mother and the real father, rig up together is neither happiness nor the sexual relation. The effect of the seldomly half-said, often said too loud or unsaid symptom of the father is the *sinthome* of the son or the daughter. Sinthome: the sin (the fall), the mistake, the stain, the irreducible guilt, which connects the subject to the stain, the guilt of the father—with a guilt in which the father's mother carries much weight. The *sinthome* is the very special sexual turn of the subject that connects it with the father's turn, with the father's *jouissance*, which has necessarily surpassed the matrimonial bed. Lacan continues: from the *symptom*[27] of the father from the perspective of his nuclear family to the *sinthome*[28] which is transmitted in the succession of the generations. This *sinthome* forms the "necessary fourth term or circle (*rond*) of the knot."[29]

The sinthomatic turn to the father is based on the "mad idea of salvation" (*à propos de James Joyce*). "The conception of the savior is the prototype of what I write as *père-version*. To the extent to which there is a son-father relation, and that has been the case for a long time, the mad idea of salvation has emerged."[30] To save the father . . . from what? Perhaps the different answers converge in the following: at the stigma of the maternal birth—"*être né de ce ventre-là*"[31]—which inescapably leads him, the father, to being swept away in the blossom of his sins.

Saving the father—that could only fail. *Saving the Name-of-the-Father*, however, is *the* topos of Western dramatic literature. When one pursues this topos it seems that *saving the Name-of-the-Father* necessarily entails the destruction of a Name-of-the-Father that has stiffened into an ideal and its reconstruction with the help of a female knowledge which is tied to the Real of the father: recall Antigone, King Lear, Michael Kohlhaas. I cannot pursue this thread, but I will use two of the most famous psychoanalytic cases to illustrate this thesis a little and to test their clinical usefulness.

The Sinthome of Little Hans

The case of *Little Hans* demonstrates the connection between the symptom of the father, which notoriously revolves around the father's mother, and the *fatherwards (père-vers)-sinthome* of the son. After the removal of his phobic symptoms Hans retains a *sinthome*, which one could call the "knight *(chevalier)* of phallic women"; he emerges as a chevalier for the type of woman to whom his father was subjugated. This *sinthome* is his irreducible symptom, his very special sexual turn, which connects him to his father, and does so precisely where the father has failed: the Real of this father had been crushed, so to speak, by the symbolic weight of his mother-symptom. Hans resumes this connection the other way around; he really dominates those women who incarnate the maternal phallus in order to take the weight of his father's guilt upon his own shoulders, in order to reestablish this father who has been subjected to the symbolic domination of his mother. Hans's *sinthome*—"domination of phallic women"—is his dominant Name-of-the-Father; a trait that marks the failure of paternal castration and which, at the precise point of this failure, repairs, connects, and solders it.

Finally, in the end Hans *did* have a sufficiently *real father* for him to have gotten away with merely a rather banal neurotic symptom. Since we know very little about Hans's subsequent life, what I am saying is speculative. But what one can maintain with a degree of certainty is that here the father's *proper half(god)-saying* was not successful: there was a *saying-too-much (trop-dire)* and an excessive deification *(trop-dieu)* of the mother, of Hans, of Freud.

The Father-Symptom as Necessary Fourth Term in the Borromean Chain

With the engagement with the work of James Joyce[32] Lacan's topological work takes an incisive turn at and with the *Borromean knot*: the fourth circle *(rond)* of the symptom is necessary in order to hold the Borromean chain (which is no longer a knot) together. "The triple knot is a knot no more, it is held only by the symptom," by the father-symptom which, in its utmost reduction to the *sinthome*, "cannot be analyzed." "There is no radical reduction of the fourth term (of the *sinthome*). Freud—we know over what path—was able to pronounce it: there is a primary repression, a repression that is irremovable. It is in the nature of the Symbolic to bring this hole with it—this hole, which I see, I recognize, (as lying) in primary repression."[33] This hole in the Symbolic corresponds to the irreducible *Real of the father*, the stigma of his birth. The speaking being, "born from this belly—is cut off from his origin."[34]

And yet, there are subjects who foreclose this concealment of the hole, the father symptom: paranoiacs. "Without that fourth term," without the father-symptom, "this chain constitutes a paranoia." "When the subject connects the Imaginary, the Symbolic, and the Real as a threesome, it is carried only by their continuity. The Imaginary, the Symbolic, and the Real are of the same consistency, and this is what paranoid psychosis consists of." Even worse: "Paranoid psychosis and personality[35] have no relationship with each other: they are one and the same thing." The range of these sentences, which are absolutely not aphoristic tidbits, but are strenuously constructed, is enormous.[36]

Without a father-symptom, a *sinthome*, a subject is *paranoid*. In the triple knot the Real, the Imaginary, and the Symbolic are indistinguishable (it is helpful to think of surrealist art here): paranoia and personality are one and the same thing. The father-symptom is, so to speak, the only possible salvation: the "fourth circle, differently from the three others, specifies itself as a neurotic symptom: with it, this chain no longer constitutes a paranoia, except a communal one."[37] A subject without a father-symptom is a paranoid personality, a subject with a father-symptom is neurotic and not paranoid, unless (by having the father-symptom) it participates in the communal, general paranoia.

Effect of the Father Function: the Eroticization of the Ego Ideal

A reader not very familiar with Lacan may think, what is all of this supposed to mean? I will try to say something about the clinical pertinence of these theses. Clinical pertinence is social pertinence: what other analyst aside from Lacan has come to terms with the simultaneous untrustworthiness and indestructibility of the oedipal structures of the twentieth century now reaching its end? Some believe they have come to terms with the father, while others talk nonsense about the stabilizing father imago.

How, then, is one to specify this *father-symptom*, which saves the subject from paranoia and allows it to join the pleasures of a *communal paranoia*, clinically? One clinically isolatable trait of the connection of the subject with the *Real of the father* is—this is my hypothesis—the *eroticization of the ego ideal*. "The ego ideal does not correspond, as is commonly thought, to a progressive neutralization of the functions—but is rather always accompanied by an eroticization of the symbolic relation."[38] The symbolic child-mother relation (I-M in Schema R),[39] matrix of the ego ideal, does not suffice to stabilize the subject's world. Lacan shows by way of Jean Genet (*Le Balcon*), that lack of the eroticization of the symbolic relation between the ego ideal and the world of discourse relation makes it impossible to enjoy any kind of worldly position, whether it be a professional position (it is its grotesque eroticization that is at issue in the *Balcon*), the position of a marriage partner, the maternal or paternal position. Even when a subject formally accedes to such a position, it is not permitted (*père-mis*) to enjoy it. The position is abandoned, picked up again, or another one is picked up and again abandoned: the specific abnormality of such a fragile personality, which, in a different terminology, are referred to as "borderline," seems to me to be the lack of that *eroticization of the symbolic relation*, which makes the ego ideal a sufficiently flexible foundation for a more or less stable ideal ego. As we know, the number of subjects who withdraw from the *communal paranoia* of the oedipal—or better, as Lacan says, the *fatherwards*-neuroses—in favor of a "personal" paranoia is increasing.

The paternal function consists, then, in making sure that the eroticization of the ego ideal and the symbolic relation connected to the ego ideal (the relation to a world which is simultaneously internal and external) takes place. Once more: if the only guarantee for the paternal function is the *proper half-saying* of the father version (*père-version*), which belongs to the father, this has very little to do with the father's good intentions. What it really presupposes is that the father desire or deify his children—in a prolongation of the status he had recognized in regard to their mother, so to speak—neither too much nor too little.

What one encounters in women who have experienced paternal incest seems to me to correspond very precisely to the destruction of that eroticization of the ego ideal, an eroticization which props itself up on the *fantasmatic* incest. The narcissistic ego ideal does not lack a symbolic anchoring but a symbolic erotic cathexis: it has turned into pure pretense, artificial jewelry which can be attached and then stuffed back into the closet; often the attaching and stuffing process fails, and it attaches and removes on its own. The opposite of incest, the lack of a real, that is, an eroticizing, paternal cathexis, seems, by the way, to have very similar, even if less pervasive, effects.

The common denominator of all *fatherward*-neuroses, which all fall under the category of *communal paranoia*—everything from the real father trauma (as far as it can still be neurotically processed), and phobia, to hysteria—seems to be a faulty soldering, especially when it comes to soldering the Real with the Symbolic. The tear between gender and subjectivity is a structural one; hence the ubiquity of a symptom that repairs it. The "paranoid personality" should be distinguished from these *fatherward*-neuroses, where the *proper half-saying* has more or less failed but has succeeded at least to the extent to have had an effect in the sense of neurotic symptom formation; the "paranoid personality" is an extreme case of the failure of a proper half-saying and has the effect of foreclosing the paternal symptom.

From the start Lacan related the failure of the paternal metaphor not to a missing father in the familial reality, but, almost the opposite, to his crushing presence: to an all too masterlike father proclaiming the law and salvation, to a father in a deceitful position who thus gave "occasion to shutting out the Name-of-the-Father from its position in the signifier."[40] Here already it is clear that what is at stake is *the position of the Name-of-the-Father in the Symbolic* and not, as is constantly being hawked, *the Symbolic* (in the unspeakably reductive version the phrase that "the psychotic forecloses the Symbolic"). The older Lacan said very clearly that the identification with the Name-of-the-Father moves through the Real of the father.[41] Accordingly, a father who denies the

Real is psychoticizing: a usurper of the Symbolic, one who maintains that everything is sayable, doable, "symbolizable." Unfortunately, certain versions of psychoanalysis are moving in this ideological direction.

"Wholly in the Signifier"

This emphasis on the Real in the Name-of-the-Father throws a new light on that earlier statement, that "the presence of the (father)-signifier is more than compatible with the absence of the real father."[42] More precisely, it sharpens this last statement: the signifier is in such cases in a state of purity, which makes the eroticization of the symbolic relation more difficult and which leads into other than normal paths.

The fact that the biographies of writers are so extraordinarily often marked by a missing real father, be it that he was really absent or that he was incapable of taking up a real paternal position, is of course no coincidence and in fact well known. It seems that practically all of German literature of the nineteenth and twentieth centuries is the work of fatherless sons: Kleist, Hölderlin, Büchner, Keller, Bernhard, and so on. The daughters are missing; here there is a different effect of this lack.

It seems to me that Lacan contributes quite a bit to explaining the logic of this phenomenon. These men, "wholly in the signifier" (as Lacan says about André Gide), who were incapable of occupying mundane positions, or who found such positions insufficient, nevertheless occupied that purest and simultaneously most real effect of the signifier—writing. We must study this material waste of a *fatherwards* society in order to lay bare its workings. Even the laying bare of the *communal paranoia* of the oedipal symptom addresses a real father who can be trusted: sound, rhythm, voice.

Sexualization emphatically belongs to the mundane positions: a subject declares itself "man" or "woman,"[43] and in the same breath renounces full *jouissance*. The half-saying of the real father can also be understood this way: as a dividing up, a cutting in two of *jouissance*, as the mediation of the imperative that says, "Enjoy like a man like me, or enjoy like a woman, like the not-me, cause of my desire!" To subject oneself to this imperative means to subject oneself to the semblance of the signifiers "man" or "woman"; one does this, I believe Lacan suggests, only because of the promise of a pleasure prize, that of being connected with the *jouissance* of the father.

Whoever extricates himself from this imperative hardly fares any better, as he falls under the crueler imperative of that superego which harks back to the first agent of the signifier, to the symbolic mother: "*jouis*," enjoy boundlessly, enjoy everything and nothing, everywhere and nowhere. What is called creativity in this view consists in the necessary invention of barriers, be it those of the perverse pact or those of the arts.

The Daughters: Dora

But what is valid for the sons, as far as it *is* valid for them, is valid for the daughters only in a very qualified way. The failure of the *half-saying* of the father seems here to be neither paranoia-inducing nor perverting nor something that promotes creativity; it is, rather, inhibiting. Those women who distinguish themselves, who make a name for themselves in the public sphere, including that of the arts, are often the daughters of strong, that is, *symptomatic*, fathers. This is also valid for so-called perverse women, Freud's "young homosexual," for example.[44] It would be necessary to examine the reasons for this asymmetry in more detail.

I will close with the typical female case of a little father-misery, the case of "Dora." This "little hysteria," as is well known, made it possible for Freud to broaden and deepen psychoanalytic knowledge and psychoanalytic technique. As a classic female *fatherwards*-neurosis, it is still and always again relevant.

The unifying symptom of the father is missing at first; its place is taken by those diverse somatic symptoms with which the daughter, *faute de mieux*, identifies. But finally a unifying substitute symptom is found for father and daughter in Frau K.

In this way the father, ill and impotent with his wife, Dora's mother, becomes a possibly potent lover in the daughter's eyes. Poor Dora: she can find no support in her mother in the way in which the latter is mediated by this father. From the perspective of the father's desire, the only genuine thing about this mother is her jewelry. No wonder that Dora attempts to eroticize this dead material with all her might. Frau K., of whom she suspects that she knows how to animate her father, serves as the support she needs in order to ask her question: What is a woman? What do people want from her, this unhappy little girl, and what good could it do? To consider her to be homosexual because of her fancy for Frau K. would be a mistake. She loves the Other via her identification with the desire of her father. She makes of Frau K. the subject supposed to know, "she who would know what is necessary for the man's enjoyment."[45] That the father's mistress "has" that hidden object of the father's desire is of little use to her; she believes that Frau K. possesses *the knowledge about it*, and in this supposed knowledge she seeks that material support, that maternal signifier that is missing in her own existence. When Frau K. withdraws the promise of this knowledge from Dora for diplomatic reasons and rejects her, Dora's hope naturally transforms into pure hatred.

And this occurs after Herr K., the fourth term in this quartet, fails on his part: with the unforgivable remark, "I get nothing from my wife," he repeats word for word the father's remark in reference to his wife, Dora's mother. The quartet Dora/Frau K./Herr K./Father, propped up by Dora's hysterical identification with the supposed object of the men's desire, violently collapses. What is left is the pain of a girl who has had the foundation of a fragile desire pulled out from under her feet. Together with the ego ideal, which had propped itself up on the erotic knowledge that was imputed to a maternal Other, her virile ideal ego shatters: "For if he is taken away, man can no longer even sustain himself in the position of Narcissus. As if by elastic, the anima springs back on to the animus and the animus on to the animal."[46]

This is the meaning of the famous slap Dora regales Herr K. with: *Animal*. Since this Herr K. represents her ego, this occurs with a boomerang effect: according to the testimonials of Felix Deutsch, whom Dora turned to later in life, she complained of a chronic neuralgia around her right ear as well as of all men except for her brother. She was to have been the most repulsive hysteric this gentle man and analyst had ever encountered.

"The hysteric plays the man who would suppose, expect, the woman to have knowledge. That is why she emerges on the scene through an entrance which brings the man's death into play."[47] The conditional form is important here: "would suppose" (*supposerait*): what is specifically hysterical here is that she or he plays the man who does not, but should, exist: the one who believes in the woman. The existing man, the one who doesn't believe in *the woman*, or doesn't believe in her enough, sooner or later gets in the way of the hysterical project: this is how the man's death comes into play. Compare Dora's second dream which she told to Freud: the death of the father in order for her to do a better job, in order, without being hindered by paternal indolence and paternal not-wanting-to-know, to approach that omniscience which the ideal symbolic mother, the madonna, is supposed to have; to approach it without a male companion, but with the intention of teaching him, the man, the knowledge that he lacks to make his *jouissance* possible. Dora pursues her investigations with the encyclopedia: even when she leaves Freud, she still has the hope that she might be able to save the father.

Had there been more *half-saying, true not-saying*, on Freud's part—who knows, perhaps it could have protected Dora from having to represent in her own flesh and blood the truth that "M," the symbolic mother, knows nothing; that without the father, who designates her as the symptomatic One, she cannot exist.

The symptomatic half(god)-saying on the father's part corresponds to his statement about femininity: the father's failure relating to femininity seems to concern a daughter in a perhaps less dramatic, but all the more inclusive, way. Is "femininity" the prototype of what Lacan calls real metaphor[48] in his commentary on the "*Meninas*" of Velasquez?[49]

Final Remarks

The functions of the *symbolic mother* and the *real father* are far reaching: they go all the way back to the abyss of the primal scene and endanger its manifold veilings. The primarily *symbolic* function of frustration is more easily projected onto the father to the extent that we are attached to the representation of a mother who has always been there for us, who has always loved us unconditionally. And how could one ever rely on the *Real* of the father? Who, if not the father, guarantees us an order, a meaning?

"The oedipus complex is a symptom":[50] a necessary invention of the speaking being. That "god" is a symptom we think to have known for a long time. Lacan radicalized Freud: *the* symptom, even Freud's, the symptom which holds the world together, is the erotic turn to the father. Aren't there a number of signs that the much discussed "decline of the (Name-of-) the Father" in no way excuses us from the symbolic but rather propels us into the arms of that "mother" who represents the binary principle of the symbolic in its purest form? What does she want, this electronic *mother*? As the tightest accomplice of the *symbolic* father she wants what he does: nothing.

Topology of the Schema
Castration/Frustration/Privation, and Connection

In the Seminar "Relation d'objet," there are two versions of the schema castration/frustration/privation, an earlier and a later one. The change, as is always the case with Lacan, is not an arbitrary one; I will discuss this in the second section.

Here is the first version:

(1) Schema castration-frustration-privation, 12/12/56

Agent	Lack	Object
Real Father	Castration symbolic guilt	imaginary = phallus
Symbolic mother Symbolic father	Frustration imaginary lack	real = breast
Imaginary father	Privation real gap	symbolic = child

Figure 1: Schema 1

The schema consists of a symbolic, an imaginary, and a real operation: symbolic castration, imaginary frustration, real privation. Every operation consists of three elements R, S, I: agent, lack, object.

In castration the agent is real, lack is symbolic, and the object is imaginary. In frustration the agent is symbolic, lack is imaginary, and the object real.

In privation the agent is imaginary, lack is real, and the object is symbolic. This results in the following distribution of R, S, and I:

	Agent	Lack	Object
Castration	R	S	I
Frustration	S	I	R
Privation	I	R	S

In retrospect, from the viewpoint of the nodal Seminars, the Schema can be read as a Borromean chain of three triple knots; as a chain that consists of the knot RSI (castration), SIR (frustration), and IRS (privation). This is my assertion; what authorizes me to make it?

A long time before the Borromean phase Lacan had talked about *knots* and *nodes (noeud, nouage)*; thus, already in "The Signification of the Phallus," castration is conceived of as a knot. Should this, in contrast to the later topological investigations, be designated as "only metaphorical" language? The topological access investigates metaphoricity: how does it come into being? To what extent does the knot hold, consist, and ex-sist? I cannot go into the connection between knot and metaphor any more deeply here. It seems to me that the attempt at a clean separation misrecognizes the real elements of metaphor (sound, letter) as much as it does what the topological manipulation owes to linguistic metaphor.

The discursive elaboration of the schema frustration/castration/privation allows for no doubt around the fact that none of the real, imaginary, and symbolic elements can be deleted without the ensemble unraveling; this is the definition of a Borromean knotting. It concerns different levels:

- On the horizontal level, each one of the three operations: no castration without the triple knot *real father, symbolic guilt, imaginary object*, no frustration or privation without the corresponding knots.

- Less obviously and more importantly: if one gets rid of a single element, the ensemble of the operations unravels. Castration, frustration, privation—formally a triple knot S-I-R—are developed as a strictly interdependent operation in the text of the Seminar. This is the salient point of Lacan's reading of Freud in this Seminar: the conception of genetic phases which lead into a mature sexuality is opposed by a logic of the signifier. Castration, frustration, and privation are three logical phases, three stages that bring forth the subject. The subject, caught in the logic of interdependence/knotting of signifying elements, does not step up from "preoedipal" lowlands to "oedipal" heights. Even the sequence castration-frustration contradicts such a conception: from the very beginning the subject finds itself in a castration that has effects on the level (often designated as "central") of frustration and of privation. Castration in its narrower sense is not a dissolution of frustration and privation but rather their transformation: to frustration it lends "a law," "a different value," and it "legalizes the level of privation."[51] No "overcoming" of these levels takes place; what determines differences in single clinical cases could at most be conceptualized with the Heideggerian term *Verwinden* ["recovering from"].

I have attempted to examine this non-Euclidean topology of castration/frustration/privation in more detailed fashion in another place,[52] and did so in response to Freud's insurmountable difficulties with the *inside/outside* opposition. Lacan cuts through the bipolar thought schemas inside/outside, before/after, frustration/castration. Each one of the three levels in some way precedes the other two. For example, the *real gap* of privation always already presupposes a symbolic order (female castration is real in relation to the Symbolic): on the other hand, the *symbolic guilt* of castration and its object, the *imaginary phallus*, are unthinkable without the real gap of privation. And both castration and privation presuppose the lost, or better, the prohibited, real object of frustration. Frustration, conceived of as a signifying prohibition, and posited as central, precedes the two other levels in the sense of primary repression, though a primary repression which always remains effective: if one wishes to avoid falling back into a temporally linear schema, one would have to speak here of the *most inclusive* of the three levels.

At least for the sake of a thinking aid one can distinguish between two levels of castration: that of frustration/prohibition, whose agent is the *symbolic father*, that is, the signifier as such, represented by the *symbolic mother*, and that of castration in the narrower sense, whose agent is the *real father*, he too an agent of the signifier. The second version represents these nuances much more clearly, and it makes a connection with the *sinthome* possible:

(2) Version of 3/6/57: the symbolic father as fourth term

In the first version, from a topological point of view, the triple connection R,S,I held together on its own. In this second version, one term, that of the *symbolic father*, has been removed from the "Agents of frustration" column and moved to the left. From here it presides over all triple knots: as *fourth term*.

By doing so Lacan formalizes what he develops in his text: the *symbolic father* does not function on the same level as the other agents; he stands

Symbolic father	Real father	Castration Symbolic guilt	Imaginary Phallus
	Symbolic mother	Frustration Imaginary lack	Real object breast, penis
	Imaginary father	Privation Real gap	Symbolic object child, phallus

Figure 2: Schema 2

"behind" them, especially "behind" the *symbolic mother* (in the first version he was a coagent). This symbolic father "is unthinkable, he is nowhere, he intervenes nowhere," he is "a necessity of symbolic construction . . . almost in a transcendence which can be conceived of only in a mythical construction."[53] This has paved the way for the discursively logical conception of the *symbolic father* as "logical complement of the discursive world".[54]

In the 1970s this logical term is incarnated in the father-*sinthome*. The positional value as the fourth term, which makes possible and holds together the triple knots, remains the same:

(3) Symbol—Sinthome

The abstraction of the Schema castration/frustration/privation, second version, 1957—

$$S \quad \left|\begin{array}{ccc} R & S & I \\ S & I & R \\ I & R & S \end{array}\right.$$

—is taken up again in the Seminar *Sinthome*, 12/16/75, in the following way:

$$\begin{array}{ccc} R & S & I \\ S & I & R \\ I & R & S \end{array}$$

SINTHOME

One difference: *the sinthome (1975) replaces the symbolic father (1957)*. This is something quite a few followers of Lacan do not like to acknowledge:

"the Symbolic" guarantees nothing. "The only thing in the symbolic that does not become imaginary is the gap"[55]. Did the *symbolic father* of the 1950s and 1960s have an existence different from that of the signifying empty place from where a voice comes? The connection is established in the *sinthome*.

I have explained in the text that the father-*sinthome* of the late Lacan carries enormous weight: it is only this *fourth term* that rescues the subject from paranoia or from the paranoid personality, and it is only this *fourth term* that makes it possible to distinguish between R, S, and I. Effective fathers and mothers have to carry this weight on their shoulders.

In retrospect, perhaps the following question must be asked: does the schema castration/frustration/privation constitute a paranoia? Indeed, the differentiation R,S,I in "Relation d'objet" is anything but unproblematic, especially in regard to the phallic object. Is this slipping the exclusive problem of a Little Hans? Isn't it rather this that the art of this century confronts us with, especially surrealism and its descendants?

Opposing the slipping of the dimensions R,S,I, their indistinguishability, increasingly thematized in the nodal Seminars, is the symptom as that which guarantees a "psychic reality," found again *beyond* the signifying fragmentation: the reality of "the Freudian subversion, which we are encouraged to carry out, that of the *être-pour-le-sexe*."[56] *Être-pour-le-sexe*, Sexual being, Being-to-the-sex, in contrast to that *être-pour-la-mort*, the Being-to-death of Heideggerian coinage, which veils castration philosophically. "When there are two of you, being-to-death (*être-pour-la-mort*; also: death-being), in spite of what those who cultivate it want to believe, allows one to hear in even the smallest of slips, that it is the other's death that is at stake. In contrast, analytic experience proves that when one is paired, the castration which the subject discovers can only be one's own."[57]

The analytic differentiation from a *symbolic castration* conceived in a Heideggerian fashion could not be clearer. The movement corresponds to the movement from the symbolic father or symbolic mother to the symptom/*sinthome*. Still, the psychic reality of the Lacanian *être-pour-le-sexe* is a post-Freudian one—the passage of the *être-pour-le-sexe* through the signifying fragmentation of the *être-pour-la-mort* is obligatory: no one evades the *symbolic mother*.

The Lacanian movement, *être-pour-la-mort—-être-pour-le-sexe*, signifier—symptom, is not a linear movement, nor is it a sublating movement [*noch die einer Aufhebung*]. Even Heidegger "cannot be superseded."[58] But it is, it seems to me, closer to the movements of contemporary artistic production than it is to the philosophical and scientific discourses of which it makes use. An eminent example for a late work that is "symptomatic" in the Lacanian sense and which presupposes a passage through the signifying fragmentation is the work of Alberto Giacometti; here one speaks of a "surrealist" and "postsurrealist" phase. These are parallels that should be studied; I mention them here in order to contradict the conception that Lacanian psychoanalysis is placeless and timeless. It seems to me that what it owes to the most intensive and specific transference—not only onto Freud, Heidegger, Marx, Kant, and so forth, and not only onto Saussure, Peirce, Frege, and so on, but also onto contemporaries such as Giacometti—has hardly been acknowledged.

"Le désir s'inscrit d'une contingence corporelle." [Analysis presumes that desire is inscribed on the basis of corporeal contingency.][59] Loosely translated this means that desire, including and especially analytic desire, is time-, place-, and body-bound; it is necessarily symptomatic.

Notes

All of the translations into English of the author's German translations of Lacan's unpublished materials are my own.

1. Jacques Lacan, "The Function of the Written," in *On Feminine Sexuality, The Limits of Love and Knowledge, 1972–1973. Encore: The Seminar of Jacques Lacan, Book XX*, 1/16/73, ed. Jacques-Alain Miller, trans. Bruce Fink (New York: W. W. Norton, 1998), 35.

2. Jacques Lacan, "La Relation d'objet" (unpubl. Seminar, 1956–57, 3/6/57) (see quotation in note 3).

3. Jacques Lacan, "La Relation d'objet" à propos the paternal intervention: "It is the introduction of this real element into the symbolic order, in opposition to the mother's first position, which is symbolized via her presence and absence in the real" (3/6/57).

4. Cf. Appendix, 59ff., the schema frustration/castration/privation.

5. Jacques Lacan. "R.S.I.," (unpublished Seminar, 1974–75, 3/18/75): "One identifies with the Symbolic of the real Other: this produces the identification that I have designated "single trait" [or "single stroke"]. One identifies with the Real of the real Other: this results in what I have indicated as the Name-of-the-Father, and here Freud shows what identification has to do with love." This was to be completed with the third type of identification: "One identifies with the Imaginary of the real Other: this is how one gets the identification of the hysteric with the desire of the Other." The real Other is at this point in time "nowhere outside of the knot and to that extent there is no Other of the Other."

6. Jacques Lacan, "R.S.I." (unpubl., 1/21/75).

7. Jacques Lacan. Schema R in "On a Question Preliminary to Any Possible Treatment of Psychosis," in *Écrits: A Selection* (New York: W. W. Norton,

1977), 197. The symbolic mother-child relationship (M-I) forms the basic axis of two triangle relationships: the imaginary triangle mother-child-phallus (M-I-I) and the symbolic triangle mother-child-father. This fundamental *symbolic* axis is currently being suppressed and subsumed by the axis of the *imaginary mirror relation* (m-i). M is the "signifier of the primordial object," *I* the matrix of the ego ideal, the first symbolic marking which connects the child desired as such or as different with the world of discourse. *I* founds the "innermost" part of the subject as something "external" (of the signifier). *m* and *i* represent "the two imaginary terms of the narcissistic relation . . . , the ego and its mirror reflection."

8. Jacques Lacan, *Écrits*, 289.

9. See more about this in the Appendix.

10. Jacques Lacan, "La Relation d'objet" (unpubl., 2/6/57).

11. Knot: see Appendix, 59.

12. Sigmund Freud, "New Introductory Lectures on Psycho-Analysis," *Standard Edition, Volume 22*, trans. James Strachey (London: The Hogarth Press), 123.

13. Sigmund Freud, "Findings, Ideas, Problems," *Standard Edition, Volume 23*, trans. James Strachey (London: The Hogarth Press), 299.

14. Freud, *Standard Edition, Volume 22*, 123.

15. Jacques Lacan, "La Relation d'objet."

16. Ibid. Cf. the quotation in note 3.

17. Jacques Lacan, "L'angoisse" (unpubl. Seminar, 5/29 and 6/5/63).

18. Jacques Lacan, "La Relation d'objet," 3/6/57 and 3/27/57.

19. On the voice and belief in the father see also in particular *Les Noms-du-Père*, the only lecture given in the Seminar of 1963 which was cut short (unpublished in German). [English: "Introduction to the Names-of-the-Father Seminar," in *Television: A Challenge to the Psychoanalytic Establishment* (New York: W. W. Norton, 1990), 81–95.

20. Jacques Lacan, "*L'acte psychanalytique*" (unpubl. Seminar, 1967/68).

21. Jacques Lacan, "L'angoisse" (6/5/63).

22. Jacques Lacan, "On a Question Preliminary to Any Possible Treatment of Psychosis," in *Écrits: A Selection* (New York: W. W. Norton, 1977), 179–224.

23. Ibid., 218–19.

24. Jacques Lacan, "R.S.I." (1/21/75).

25. Ibid.

26. Sigmund Freud, "On the Universal Tendency to Debasement in the Sphere of Love" (1912), *Standard Edition, Volume* 11, 186.

27. Jacques Lacan, "R.S.I."

28. Jacques Lacan, "Le Sinthome" (unpubl. Seminar, 1975–76).

29. Ibid., (1/9/75).

30. Ibid., (2/10/76).

31. Jacques Lacan, "Réponse à M. Ritter" (unpubl., 1/26/75).

32. Jacques Lacan, "Le Sinthome" (12/9/75): "In his art Joyce, in a privileged manner, takes a bearing with that fourth term which is essential to the knot; he got as close as possible to it," and "by proceeding in a very special artistic manner he refers to the *sinthome* as something that cannot be analyzed."

33. Ibid. (12/9/75).

34. Jacques Lacan, "Rèponse à M. Ritter" (1/26/75). This improvised speech on primary repression, perhaps the densest of all Lacanian texts, ought to be translated and commented on on its own.

35. This is an allusion to Lacan's *"thèse"* of the title, *"De la psychose paranoïaque dans ses rapports avec la personnalité,"* in *Le champ freudien* (Paris: Seuil, 1973).

36. I refer readers interested in more precise details to the Appendix, 59 ff.

37. Jacques Lacan, "Le Sinthome" (12/6/75).

38. Jacques Lacan, "Formations de l'inconscient" (unpubl. Seminar, 3/5/58).

39. Cf. note 6.

40. Cf. Jacques Lacan, "On a Question Preliminary to Any Possible Treatment of Psychosis."

41. Cf. the quotation from "R.S.I." in note 5.

42. Jacques Lacan, "On a Question Preliminary to Any Possible Treatment of Psychosis."

43. Jacques Lacan, "Petit discours aux psychiatres" (unpubl., 1967).

44. Sigmund Freud, "The Psychogenesis of a Case of Female Homosexuality" in *Standard Edition, Volume 18,* 147–172.

45. Jacques Lacan, "D'un Autre à l'autre" (unpubl. Seminar, 6/25/69).

46. Jacques Lacan, "On a Question Preliminary to Any Possible Treatment of Psychosis," 195.

47. Jacques Lacan, "D'un Autre à l'autre" (6/25/69).

48. The "real metaphor" is a "metaphor whose element is a real one." The thesis of the paternal metaphor being a "real metaphor," which during the course of my work has become increasingly more apparent, is something I would like to pursue; I would like to know whether anyone has worked on this or on the question of metaphor in Lacan in general.

49. Jacques Lacan, Seminar "L'objet de la psychanalyse" (1965).

50. Jacques Lacan, "Le Sinthome" (11/18/75).

51. Jacques Lacan, Seminar "La Relation d'objet" (1/9/57).

52. Regula Schindler, "Topologie der Versagung" in *RISS* 13/14 (spring 1990).

53. Jacques Lacan, "Relation d'objet" (3/6/57).

54. Jacques Lacan, "L'Étourdit," in *Scilicet* 4 (1973).

55. Jacques Lacan, "R.S.I."

56. Jacques Lacan, "Discours de clôture des journées sur les psychoses chez l'enfant" (1967) in *L'Enfance aliénée*, ed. Maud Mannoni (Paris: Denod, 1987).

57. Jacques Lacan.

58. Jacques Lacan, *The Seminar of Jacques Lacan, Book VII: The Ethics of Psychoanalysis, 1959–60,* ed. Jacques-Alain Miller (New York: W. W. Norton, 1992), 206: "One never goes beyond Descartes, Kant, Marx, Hegel and a few others because they mark a line of inquiry, a true orientation. One never goes beyond Freud either. Nor does one attempt to measure his contribution quantitatively, draw up a balance sheet—what's the point of that? One uses him. One moves around him. One takes one's bearings from the direction he points in."

59. Jacques Lacan, *On Feminine Sexuality, The Limits of Love and Knowledge, 1972-1973. Encore: The Seminar of Jacques Lacan, Book XX,* ed. Jacques-Alain Miller, trans. Bruce Fink (New York: W. W. Norton, 1998), 93.

Part III
Clinical

Introduction

Maire Jaanus and Elizabeth Stewart

The image of a silent, captated, and perhaps deadened figure that was suggested by Widmer to be present in the fantasy of the parent, and that structured the essays of Borens and Bernet returns in a different guise in Christian Kläui's essay, "'But It, the World . . . It Shames My Mute Pain': Some Thoughts on Melancholia and Depression," as the relatively unsymbolized, isolated, and insulated body of the melancholiac. Its lack of symbolization has already been introduced by Anne Juranville. Melancholy proper, as distinguished from other depressive disorders, Kläui argues, is a narcissistic disorder within the field of the psychoses. At its root lies that form of identification that takes the shape of a destructive search for origins, quietude, and rest—the death drive. The melancholiac knows—and is, perhaps, fuelled by the enjoyment this knowledge provides—that at the root of desire lies death: the ultimate restoration of identity, the undoing of loss, and thus the (illusory) site of "full knowledge," and the end of the signifying chain, producing a "mute thing." Melancholia exerts a fascination, however, as it is profoundly connected to a supposed knowledge of origins and produces a heightened sensuous experience that is not structured into language. While one result of melancholia is that corporeal sensations are heightened, it also covers up the erogenous zones, limiting the symbolic organization of the drives, locking up an internal emptiness, and foreclosing meaning. While both psychotic melancholia and nonpsychotic depression are marked by a narcissistic illusion of completeness, the depressive does not deny desire, but notes, simply (and lucidly and truthfully), that all objects are equivalent; thus he relinquishes desire. He sees desire as worthless and "desires to evade desire." Kläui takes pleasure in referring to the significance and prevalence of melancholia in artistic representation (the "horrible pleasure" produced by the poetry of home- and origin sickness, for ex-

127

ample). It would be fruitful to read his essay with the relationship between melancholia and allegory, as it is presented by the modernist Walter Benjamin, in mind: for example, in the latter's theory of allegory in the German Baroque. Kläui is interested in the elements of brokenness, muteness, petrification, fragmentation, melancholic collection—all as indicators of the silent drive toward the end of language and blissful suicide. Kläui poses the question as to the therapeutics of melancholia and depression: Is it possible to bind the melancholic wound to meaning within the symbolic register? He also addresses the relationship between the depressive mode and women: as woman, not only within Lacanian discourse but also in Western literature, is imaged as the hole, as emptiness, she stands in closer relation to melancholia and depression, which are both constituted by a hole in the signifying chain. That hole and the feminine/maternal hole form the matrix of trauma in the "nostalgia" that stamps the depressive and melancholic dispositions, and are always irretrievably linked to suicide, regressiveness, and conservatism (in the sense of the radically conservative nature of the death drive).

More purely clinical is Monique David-Ménard's essay, "The Act of the Interpretation: Its Conditions and Its Consequences," which bears on the differences between interpretation and construction and on how each relates to the transference as well as on the relationship between signification (imaginary, and constituted by empty speech) and meaning (symbolic, full speech), and further on how, from this constellation, arise effects which are beyond the analyst's control. She concludes that the intervention becomes an *act* only when the patient recognizes the repeatable element within his childhood history in the transference, but also that the moment of coalescence of signifier and signified can only occur in silence, paradoxically with a loss of knowledge. This blanking out of intention, certainty, and representation in general as marking, as it were, the moment of illumination characterizes the focal point of many of the essays in this collection. In the silent act itself, knowledge seems to be achieved precisely by relinquishing the pretenses to knowledge, a moment that is similar to the end of analysis and therefore closely associated with Lacanian ethics.

Elisabeth Widmer's essay, "Castration and Incest Prohibition in Françoise Dolto," on the one hand, provides us with an example of the effectiveness of nonverbalization in the clinic, of nonarticulation (of the actual incest prohibition), and relying on the emergence of an interpretation in the context of the transference (cf. David-Ménard); on the other hand, the clinical example could be used by the active reader as a concrete situation to which to apply Regula Schindler's theory regarding the functions of and the dangers posed by the symbolic mother and the real father, in that we get a concrete idea as to how the symbolic and real aspects of the mother- and father-functions are irretrievably mixed. Widmer's initial question, whether spoken incest prohibitions are seductions, is answered by her case study, which gives us a concrete example of what it means to be capable—or incapable—of acceding to "worldly positions," as opposed to remaining stuck within the presence/absence binary opposition of the primary maternal symbolic function. It is advisable to read these three essays together. In itself, with its transferential detail and the sense it provides of the sequence and the actual events of "signification" and "meaning" (cf. David-Ménard), Widmer's essay offers a fascinating look into the practice of child analysis.

Lucien Israel's essay, "Demand and Wish," is concerned with clinical matters as well, though this time with the clinic of the teaching analysis. The teaching analysis is, perhaps more so than the regular analysis, marked by a paradox: "professional analysis" does "not exist." As soon as a teaching analyst sets himself up as teacher, he confuses himself with the embodiment of an aim, with the real object, and the learning analyst sees him as such as well. The quandary produced by the impossibility of the teaching analysis—which, when it goes wrong, and the transference is not dissolved, undermines the very idea of psychoanalysis—points to the fundamental subversive structure of psychoanalysis: it can neither turn into a profession nor institutionalize itself; it is marked instead by constant self-dissolution. Therefore, finding itself located in impossibility characterizes it. The clinical example that Israel presents—not from a teaching analysis, but from his own practice—provides a powerful cautionary tale for psychoanalysis (which is, ideally, marked by its own impossibility of existing): the mother who forestalls all of her son's demands, who therefore can never have a forbidden object, makes it impossible for the son to develop his desire or the symptom that would form in the gap between demand and desire. The result is foreclosure of the Name-of-the-Father and, with that, of the imagination. Israel seems to be saying that psychoanalysis dies in such conditions, as it is the imagination—the production of the gap and of the symptom, in which the wish lives—that keeps its utopian potential (that is, that which does not exist) alive.

With Michels's essay we move into the realm of the clinic of the psychoses, and his essay prepares us for the collective and social perverse and psychotic variants of the pathological relationship between the body and the letter of the signifier, the theories concerning which go into full bloom in the last "Philosophical" section.

Michels's essay, "Psychosis and Names," probes the area of the embodied letter and the literalization of castration on the body from the clinical perspective. He emphasizes the analyst's need to have a poetically trained ear, to be attuned to the sheer sound of letters in the psychotic patient's speech, which enacts for the analyst first, the psychotic's distrust of symbolic speech (which murders the Real), second, the way in which that patient experiences language as an actual attack on his body—a constantly threatened and often imaginarily realized bodily disintegration—and, third, the way in which he inscribes psychically the letter of the signifier not in symbolic, but in concrete form, on his own body in the form of concrete rims, cuts, and edges. These letters are the "bones" of the paternal metaphor that house the potential for linguistic metaphoricity. Michels shows this mostly by way of the world's most famous psychotic: Judge Daniel Paul Schreber. The essay is itself an almost surreal piece whose rhetoric attempts to approximate the density and torturedness of the psychotic relation to language. Fascinating in this essay is the relation Michels draws between this psychotic interrelation of language, writing, and the body and modernist "traumatic" art forms such as Cubism (the emergence of letters on the bodies of Picasso's and Braque's human figures) and Symbolist poetry. The persecutory nature of the letters that appear on the fault lines of the psychotic's body may in fact be deeply related to the "persecutory" nature of such art. From the clinical point of view, Michels's insights are integral for an understanding of hypochondria when he explains that the hypochondriac forces the inscription the psychotic has foreclosed (that is, symbolic castration) onto his body, thereby handing the body over (sacrificing it) to the letter's cruelty. The cruelty of the signifier and the tyranny of the Symbolic are experienced by the hypochondriac on his as it were literal body in the form of actual pain.

And here we have touched, as already a number of times before in the preceding essays, on the pervasive and fascinating topic of sacrifice.

10

"But It, the World . . . It Shames My Mute Pain"

Some Thoughts on Melancholia and Depression

Christian Kläui

Were I to deliver to you a melancholy paper, I would have to remain silent. I would say nothing to you; or, maybe I would say to you, "Everything is nothing." In order to talk about melancholia, one must protect oneself against it, said Robert Burton, author of the splendid *Anatomy of Melancholia*, at the beginning of the seventeenth century. And he emphasized that he wrote about melancholia precisely in order to ward it off, as self-therapy.

Having safeguarded my soul I can only hope that my paper will not deliver you up to melancholy despair.

I will first talk about *melancholia*, not *depression*, in order to evade being hampered by the precipitous limitations that current psychiatric terminology may impose upon us. The concept of melancholia establishes a relation to Freud's work, "Mourning and Melancholia," and to his categorization of melancholia as a narcissistic neurosis within the field of the psychoses. The term "melancholia" has also had a cultural and historical background ever since antiquity, a background from which no psychoanalytic consideration of melancholia ought entirely to extricate itself.

In the second part of my paper I will distinguish between melancholia and the "depressive ill humors" that belong to the field of neurosis in its most general sense. This classification follows psychodynamic criteria instead of phenographic ones. For this reason it does not necessarily conform to American psychiatry and its *DSM* phenography.

The work on melancholia is located at a key juncture in Freud's work: it lies in between the work on narcissism of 1914 and the great works of the

1920s, especially *Beyond the Pleasure Principle*, *Group Psychology and the Analysis of the Ego*, and *The Ego and the Id*, in which Freud reorders the structure of his theory in his so-called second topology. The twofold revision of his concept of the drive—first in the work on narcissism and then in the groundbreaking introduction of the death drive—had been a prerequisite for that reordering.

One theoretical question intersects all of these works: the question of identification. In Freud's theory the "normal" and the "pathological" are always thought simultaneously and are distinguishable only within this (fundamental) unity. It is in this sense that the process of identification with the ambivalently cathected object, which Freud originally described in the context of melancholia, later (namely in *The Ego and the Id*) becomes the precondition for the development of the instances of the id, ego and superego.[1] Freud, who in this instance bases himself on the work of Abraham, determines this mode of identification to be "oral":[2] at the origin of melancholia Freud places the unconscious loss of the object through a "real sleight or disappointment."[3] But now, in *The Ego and the Id*, loss has become the precondition for development. The origin of the psychic subject requires this loss. In 1925, in his short and momentous text "Negation," Freud says that the purpose of reality testing actually is the recovery of the lost object, the determination of whether or not reality permits the recovery of the always already lost object in the shape of actual object cathexes.[4]

Freud structures the theme of the impossible "lost" object into his appropriation of two myths that take up crucial positions in his thinking: the myth of Oedipus and the myth of the slaying of the original father and the totem meal. The Oedipus myth organizes the renunciation of the first object cathexis and the establishment of sexual fantasies via the intervention of a law, of a prohibition—the incest prohibition. The Oedipus complex represents a grid, a matrix, without which melancholic identification and the processes of the constitution of the subject as Freud describes them cannot be understood. (It is impossible to reduce such processes simply to a psychology of the different phases of development.)

The other myth, which Freud develops in *Totem and Taboo*, concerns the instance of the law which regulates the loss inherent in the Oedipus complex: it is a fantasy about the original conditions of a human society that is ruled by a violent and jealous father, who, in a state of boundless *jouissance*, keeps all the females for himself and drives away his sons as they grow up. Until "one day" the brothers get together, kill, and then devour their father. "[I]n the act of devouring him they accomplished their identification with him, and each one of them acquired a portion of his strength."

"They hated their father, . . . but they loved and admired him too. . . . After they had got rid of him, . . . the affection which had all this time been pushed under was bound to make itself felt. . . . A sense of guilt made its appearance, which in this instance coincided with the remorse. . . . The dead father became stronger than the living one had been. . . . "

In "deferred obedience" they now prohibit themselves what he had previously prevented through his mere existence.[5] Access to *jouissance* inaugurates its simultaneous restriction. In this way the law originates in the identification with the dead father and is handed down from generation to generation.

By the way, Freud later drew a parallel between this story and melancholia and mania. Mania, in this conception, would correspond to the jubilation over the elimination of the powerful original father (*Ur*-father), and melancholia would correspond to identification with him, the result of having previously mourned him.

The close relationship between this myth and the Greek Kronos myth is obvious—Kronos, who in obedience to his mother Gaia's command has castrated and overthrown his father Uranus and who then devours his own children because it has been prophesied that he himself would be overthrown by them, until his wife Rhea protects the youngest son Zeus by hiding him with shepherds and feeds Kronos rocks clothed in diapers instead. It will then turn out to be Zeus who will overthrow Kronos and establish the reign of the Olympian gods. In Western culture this legend has been intimately related to melancholia, which in medieval astrology is associated with Saturn-Kronos.

Now, of course you may ask yourself what is going on when Freud introduces mythical narratives at critical points in his theory. Should you grant yourself the pleasure of reading Freud, you will discover many junctures of this sort, points where Freud breaks off a thought process, a scientific explanation, moves onto another plane, and resumes his discourse with a discussion of myths or with literary allusions. In contrast to scientific discourse, myths are ambiguous, less geared toward closure. In his earliest psychoanalytic researches, his *Studies on Hysteria*, Freud looked for the "kernel" of things, the kernel of pathology. Again and again he searched for the "primary," for "beginnings," for the "origin," while at the same time writing texts that never led him to the kernel, or whose kernel was irremediably constituted by the ceaseless search itself, a search for what can reveal itself only in disguise—the disguise of the mythical narrative, for instance. Hölderlin says, "We are nothing, what we look for is everything." As the Freudian text weaves a texture around a gap, which he calls "loss," he encircles it in a constant searching motion and still necessarily always misses it. Because he was unable to find the "kernel" anywhere, Freud stepped in his work onto the path of desire, which then led him to all of his most important insights.

Allow me now to tell you a story: in his *Cratylus* Plato addresses the question of whether the names of words issue from the nature of what is being designated or whether the signifier and the signified exist independently of each other and are brought into relation with each another only by convention.

Plato has Socrates represent the onomatopoeic thesis, namely that the names of people, heroes, and gods derive from their meaning, as is the case for the name of the ruler of the underworld, Hades: Ἀιδησ—παντα τα καλα αει ειδεναι. [panta tà kalà aei eidénai. "And so the name Hades is far from originating in the invisible; rather it comes from the fact that he knows everything that is good." —E. S.] This then is the connection: Hades is he who for all eternity knows everything that is beautiful and rational. By way of this knowledge he is able to bind souls for all eternity, because he takes possession of them by appealing to their desire to know. The strongest desire of all is the one that binds humans to death, that place where everything is known.

Freud's story of the lost object is the story of the move away from "total truth"; it is the story of displacement and substitution, which is the story of Eros. It is in this way that the death drive is forced into the *détours* of life by its tendency to restore identity.[6] In our culture the Oedipus complex is the omnipresent fantasmatic structuration of this story: the original object is prohibited; the search for its recovery turns into a failure that consists of substituting the forbidden object with all other allowed objects through the process of displacement.

One could say that the Freudian Oedipus complex theorem serves as a protective screen over the abyss of the unnamable, the unimaginable—the Real, as Lacan calls it. The mother who takes the place of the "lost (object)" has already been pushed into that space, is already a "substitution by displacement."

An intimate connection obtains here between an epistemology that is active in the categories of origins, of beginnings, and the topic of melancholia. One could ask to what extent this connection is obligatory in our culture. For Hildegard von Bingen humanity is weighted down with melancholia because it lost paradise: "When Adam sinned gall was turned into bitterness, and melancholia was transformed into godlessness."

The melancholy fluid in Adam's body originates *de flatu serpentis* [in the serpent's breath]. It is a fluid, "qui tenax est et qui se ut gummi in longum protrahit" ["that is sticky and stretches out far, like gum"], as Hildegard, having fully taken on the voice of the physician here, suggests.[7]

If Freud derives the concept of melancholia from the identification with the (ambivalently cathected) "lost object," one sees now, however, that it is not all that easy to determine the nature of this object. We experience what frightened children experience at night when they clearly recognize the strange intruder standing in the shadows of the curtain who dissolves into thin air as soon as the light goes on. Lacan confirms, "The essence of the object is failure."[8]

Melanie Klein has illustrated this status of the object in relation to the death drive quite nicely. According to her, psychic development is always the result of the processes having to do with the "bad part object" whose paradigm is the absent mother's breast. The "good object," the breast that provides satisfaction, for example, can only have a modulating function without determining the dynamic. In her child analyses Klein uncovers a number of fantasies that are concerned with the absent, withdrawn object, from which the child has experienced a separation. A search is now set in motion which, in a truly destructive manner, is aimed at destroying and thereby appropriating what withdraws, in turn putting itself in danger of being destroyed. The child then requires the regulating instance of the Oedipus complex as a shield against this destructive dynamic; the Oedipus complex is capable of channeling it.

While Melanie Klein concretizes the "lost object" in the mother's body, Lacan emphasizes its impossibility, its status as the absolute Other of the subject, as the Other that has detached itself from the subject,[9] and by way of which the subject can orient its desire along the lines of an impossible recovery. It is here that ambivalence—which, for Freud, is a precondition for melancholic identification—is at its most incisive. Beyond love and hate, it is structured into the destructive potentiality of the unsatisfiable desire that evades all libidinal homeostasis.

It is the order of language itself, in which the subject must constitute itself, that creates the problem of the "lost object"—this absolutely Other that lies outside of symbolic meaning, this mute thing. Language is inhabited by mourning,[10] mourning for the nameless thing, of which, at the very beginning, the Logos says that it is absent. Where language creates itself, it does so around a gap. There is a relationship of identity between the shaping of the signifier and the introduction of a gap in the Real, says Lacan,[11] who refers to Heidegger's jug, whose very emptiness is the actual object of the potter's creation.[12]

Sublimation is then enabled to emerge from this instance of mourning. By never ceasing in its search for the "lost object"—in itself already a metaphor— language finds the radiance, the "dignity" of the "Thing" in its own poetry, its musicality, its rhythm.[13]

I don't know how this inextinguishable nostalgia could be expressed more beautifully than Hölderlin does in his "Hyperion," when he finds in the "chameleon colors of men," in deceitful and befooling language, the poetic phrases to express the poetry he looks for in the infant, the speechless child, even as he acknowledges that this poetry has been lost:

> Yes, divine is the being of the child, so long as it has
> not been dipped in the chameleon colors of men.
> The child is wholly what it is, and this is why it is
> so beautiful.
> The pressure of Law and Fate touches it not; only in the child is freedom.
> In the child is peace; it has not yet come to be at odds
> with itself.
> Wealth is in the child; it knows not its heart nor the
> inadequacy of life.
> It is immortal, for it has not yet heard of death.[14]

The relationship between melancholia and artistic and intellectual creativity has been a topos of Western thought since the *Peripatos*. While in the case of the poet it is his play with melancholic nostalgia that enables him to mold that divine being, the lost Thing, into the figure of the child, for instance, the melancholiac doesn't take part in this game at all: the melancholiac is incapable of paying out the *obolus* to the linguistic order; he is incapable of renouncing the Thing. In melancholia a failure of the process of mourning for the "lost object" has occurred, a failure of the instance of separation sealed by the intervention of the dead father's law, a failure of the instance of mourning that inheres in language.

Taking this instance of mourning upon oneself means entering into discord with oneself and into the insufficiency—and paltriness—of life. The coercion of the law and of destiny befalls the subject who is forced to submit to a linguistic-symbolic order to avoid becoming psychotic. In the sense that the subject is identified by the signifier, which can represent it only for another signifier—as Lacan tirelessly emphasized[15]—it is dependent upon the differential referentiality that characterizes the relationships between signifiers.

The subject is always incapable of finding its way to itself; all it can do is invent the fantasmatic representation of the "nevermore," the fantasy of paradise lost. As such its constellation is that of desire; it is marked by lack, which simultaneously forces and enables it to form its fantasms within the realm of substitution, around an emptiness, and in the modalities of displacement and metaphorization which characterize both language and the unconscious.

It is within that space of identification under the dominion of the signifier—where the subject finds its ego ideal[16]—and by being forced to substitute the forbidden Thing with objects of desire, that the subject is constituted in its own desire. In contrast, in melancholia the failure of the separation away from the Thing makes it impossible for the space in which the subject could constitute itself to open up.

The notions of "heavy spirit" (*Schwermut*), "despondency" (*Bedrücktheit*), and "dejection" (*Niedergeschlagenheit*) all allude to something in melancholia that weighs down. The melancholiac is incapable of developing weightlessly within the referential function of language. Connected to this failure is what Freud described as "the self-tormenting in melancholia, which is without doubt enjoyable."[17] There is the presence here of an extra-symbolic, a horrible rather than enjoyable "pleasure," which in melancholia grows rankly. The patterning of the immediate corporeality of the processes of excitation and release into the network of language miscarries. The at first unnameable and purely corporeal sensations fail to be structured by the paths of desire within the framework of the Symbolic order. The "melancholic complex," says Freud, conducts itself in the manner of an "open wound."[18] The gaping wound, however, is not the same as the gap within the subject that constitutes itself in the linguistic-symbolic order. The gaping typical of melancholia is immediate corporeality; it is experienced as real. What fails in the symbolic process returns as rank pain. The "wound" as real, unmediated corporeality persists where, through the function of the Symbolic, an emptiness should have come into being as the "zero point of the Imaginary."[19] The formation of the fantasm miscarries because the body image is incapable of organizing itself as an imaginary surface whose openings in the erogenous zones make it possible for the drive's activities to orient themselves. Just think of the various disturbances in body image that one encounters in melancholiacs. The spectrum reaches from delusions of nonexistence to delusions of temporal and spatial limitlessness,[20] and all of these phenomena are marked by the failure of symbolic patterning into the categories of "limit," "form," and "surface."[21] Emptiness for the melancholiac is not the emptiness of a surface on which the imaginary body projections can establish their outlines like a mirror reflection; rather, the emptiness lies inside the melancholiac himself.

The emptiness of the melancholiac—who accuses himself of being nothing, of inhabiting the lowest rung, and of being a burden to his entire environment—this emptiness is a plenitude of emptiness. The melancholiac is filled to the hilt with emptiness. He is the thriving wound, pain in its pure state.[22] This is most obvious in the case of profoundly apathetic melancholiacs who, veiled in stench and excrement and in a sort of state of autoerotic megalomania, refuse to put to waste their waste products and thus do not suffer a loss. In the erogenous zones, where, orchestrated by desire, a pulsating opening-up of the drive's movements ought to occur, a kind of autoerotic mud bath is engaged in covering them up.

This can become unbearable for the (melancholiac's) environment, be it the home or the clinic that tends to him. All of you know what sorts of aggression the melancholiac patient is capable of provoking. But be careful here: the aggression that a melancholiac provokes when he is in the condition I have described is not the same as that set in motion by the "depressive" who takes sadistic delight in doing so. The type of aggression at stake here is conditioned by the fact that you cannot reach these melancholiacs. This is no "sadistic-masochistic game" as is true in the other case. Rather, it consists in the lack of both appeal and response to you. It does not depend on a mutistic collapse of language but, on the contrary, becomes the most unbearable with patients who seem constantly to want something from you, who bombard you with questions, but then are not even capable of listening to what you say because language has lost its signifying function and has atrophied, like a broken record, into a stereotyped repetition of the same.

The melancholiac is incapable of accepting the gap that opens up within the psyche between the elements of meaning, the statement, and the phonetic elements of the statement which, in themselves, are meaningless. And it is precisely in this gap, in the interstices of meaning, that, from the very beginning, Freud situated the unconscious: in parapraxes, in dreams, in the double entendre of a joke that suddenly breaks into consciousness, in the repulsive senselessness of the symptom. The immanent uncertainty that obtains on the terrain of meaning drives the melancholiac to foreclose meaning as such as he reduces everything to one single meaning: everything is senseless, empty, and null. Lacan once briefly spoke of a "reject of the unconscious."[23] This refers to speech that takes place within a condition of meaninglessness, speech that lies on the melancholic wound like an affective Band-Aid. The road to sublimation has been barred.

Within the "nothing" of meaninglessness there is also nothingness—death. Suicide, then, comes to mean actual success in terms of finding completion in unnameability, of completely stepping out of the order of the lacking, the missed, the postponed, the gap in language. Suicide addresses no one and is not appellative in nature. It is an imaginary fulfillment that is really transposed into the fulfillment (*Voll-Endung*) of life in death.

Melancholic failure affects the ego ideal and the superego as well. If we recall once more Freud's story of the cannibalistic identification with the primal father, we see that he found a basis for these identificatory processes in the Symbolic, in the linguistic-symbolic order. He effected the shift from "oral" ingestion to "oral" linguistic process in this mythical story about the origin of the law of the dead father in whom the flesh became word—the word of the law. This identification that takes place in the Symbolic underlies the ego ideal, which Lacan has set off against the identification (that takes place within the superego) with the imaginary father of the oedipal constellation, who is ambivalently cathected in the subject's imagination. Even though the law of the dead father is not arbitrary, it can still take on tyrannical features. And Freud has taught us that the more we give in to the superego, the more it demands of us.

In melancholia the symbolic basis of identification in the ego ideal—within which the superego could lodge itself and by which it could be softened—is disturbed. It is here that that peculiarly rigid strictness that characterizes the purely imaginarily anchored "superego" typical of melancholia originates. "What is now holding sway in the super-ego is, as it were, a pure culture of the death instinct," says Freud,[24] who sees in the superego a reaction formation against the strivings of the id, which is strengthened by the energy of the drives at which the counter-cathexis is aimed. As an identificatory instance in the realm of narcissism it has become the representative of the death drive. It is here that those cruel, torturous acknowledgements of guilt, the self-humiliations, the delusional self-incriminations, and indeed omnipotent confessions of guilt on the part of melancholiacs find their sustenance. This unstoppable and unchannelable thriving of the superego is what lends the nonsymbolic, unspeakable, but nevertheless unquestionable *jouissance* of melancholia its imaginary content.

Allow me now to refer quickly to the fearful and agitated form of melancholia. Here fear constitutes for the subject one last line, so to speak, to hang on to—a kind of screen whose function it is to protect it from total fusion with the unspeakable Thing. This screen is not the kind of fantasm we know from the neurotic, that is, the fantasm that forms around the emptiness where, on the level of the signifier, the subject experiences its identification as the cut which means separation, a separation to which the Thing is sacrificed; the separation from the mythical maternal body, the separation that confronts the subject— where it attempts to grasp its own meaning—with a fading. Instead of submitting to lack and constructing an ideational world of representation by the signifier and within the logic of substitution and displacement, the melancholiac is left standing without any orientation before the nothingness that opens up before him. It leaves him, so to speak, speechless.

Perhaps this could be compared to something we all know: to that moment, that is, right before we are inspired with an idea—be it a witticism, be it the sudden brainstorm (the analysand's or the analyst's) in an analytic session which paves the way for interpretation. What takes place in moments of this sort is a semiunconscious emptiness lasting a fraction of a second, a lightninglike, purely physical change of condition. Perhaps by imagining this almost inconceivable, always already past moment as drawn out, as stretched out to the point of losing all perspective, it is possible to suggest something of the agitated torture typical of the fearful melancholiac.

In one particular melancholic phase a young woman is filled with a "No, No, No, No," which "screams itself inside her," absorbs her thinking and makes her incapable of acting or making a decision. She is the single mother of an approximately two-year-old son who is stubborn and from whom she is "simply incapable of distancing" herself. She is no longer capable of loving the child and is compelled to think of collective suicide. She observes that her son is being taught to speak by other people and not by her. The "No" that is called upon here because of the necessity of breaking up the deadly "enmeshedness" of mother and child and enforcing recognition of symbolic castration, this "No" is incapable of finding its place. The "symbolic working out of loss"[25] does not take place. Instead the "No" thrives in this woman in such a way that she is forced to ask herself whether perhaps she "actually feels pleasure" in it and whether she should allow herself to be "directed inside the boundaries of health" or linger in this "pleasure."

Here we must also ask the therapeutic question of whether or not this symbolic working out of loss can succeed. Is it possible to extricate the "pleasure" of the "No, No . . . " from its immediacy and work through the process of mourning which introduces the mediating distance of the linguistic exchange into the relation to the child? Is it possible to bind the melancholic wound, the "cry," to meaning—and thereby to objects of desire—within the symbolic register? Liberating oneself from bondage to the archaic Thing is possible only by being able to signify desire.[26]

Finally we want to turn to the nonpsychotic field, where "depression" is the diagnosis that is most frequently made: neurotic depression, reactive depression, exhaustion depression . . . The term "depression" is often used in a wholly uncritical manner, and the diagnosis is often made precipitously by following purely phenographic criteria. Despondency, aversion to work or sex, generalized dissatisfaction with life all become "depressions."

It is perfectly possible to distinguish between and determine these "depressions" in terms of their symptomatic appearances and how they are subjectively experienced. In my opinion, however, they are not based on a specific depressive or depressive-narcissistic neurotic structure; rather, these are phenomena that can occur in all of the neuroses. They are especially close to hysteria, this most misrecognized of the neuroses. But they also appear in obsessional neurosis as well as within the spectrum of so-called normality. Depressive ill humors occur here at certain moments and are to be evaluated within the context of such moments.

Such moments occur mostly when a highly cathected fantasm can for one reason or another not be kept standing and the subject is overcome by emptiness, by a "fading," in that place where it has constituted itself within this fantasm. This effect can also occur in an analysis at those moments when a transferential constellation dissolves.[27] In these moments of depressive ill humor something happens that is different from the neurotic symptom as compromise formation caused by repression, and which I would like to describe as instances of a "shift" in thinking.

By this I mean a shift in one's orientation around unconscious desire. Desire orients itself around a "lost object," the unreachable—we've discussed that. There, the subject always exists in a torn condition. Narcissistic images of integrity, the narcissistic ideal of wholeness and completeness, and the narcissistic illusion of knowing who one is and what one wants, are in a position of discrepancy with the effects of the unconscious that come from another, noninfluenceable, never completely appropriatable, place. This inability to constitute an identity with oneself, this being intersected by a desire that affects one from a "different scene," is irretrievably connected to this concept of identity.

And it is this identity that is at stake in depressive ill humor. This ill humor could be understood as an attempt to constitute and fasten identity. This, however, binds it unyieldingly to the loss of the search for wholeness and identity. It is for this reason that the depressive is trapped and hopelessly smothered by his incapacity to develop nostalgia. "I don't suffer at all—that's the worst of it," says one patient; "Were I suffering, I would renounce my depression—but maybe it is really the reverse that is the case: maybe I would suffer were I to give up the depression."

Where the path of desire confronts us with the sad truth that no object is any more valuable than any other[28]—Freud says that the object is the most variable aspect of the drive[29]—depressive ill humor shows us the other side of the coin: desire itself is worthless, because it does not take us to the place where the desired object *is*. In other words, the depressive process is an attempt to take up a position that has nothing to do with contradictions, irresolvables and incompletenesses, but rather one that looks for freedom from contradiction by avoiding the search and by avoiding a confrontation with the search's own desire. It wishes to know nothing of the unconscious, which confronts the subject with lack and scarcity.

The depressive process belongs to the order of illusory misrecognition. The individual who has no interests, to whom everything appears worthless and empty, does not feel the pinch of scarcity, desires nothing, is lacking in nothing. *That* is the narcissistic illusion of completeness. But, in contrast to melancholia, the register of desire has not been left behind here. The depressive desires to evade desire. I have described this process as a shift in thinking in order to point out that the one position of the switch, if you will, is possible only in relation to the other position. Only through it does it take on its determination and its meaning (hence, also, the almost ubiquitous appearance of depressive symptoms).

It is time, now, to catch up on making an observation I promised to make a long while ago, a reference to the differences between the sexes: how can one explain the fact that women are more prone to switch into the depressive mode than men are? Freud made a differential determination for the two genders concerning the limits of analyzability, the "grown rock" that no cure is capable of removing. While in the man it is his resistance to the passive, feminine attitude toward the other man, rejected because of its significance in terms of castration, in the case of women it is the wish for the penis that cannot be renounced; this can lead to "outbreaks of heavy depression."[30]

The Symbolic order, in the face of which the sexes are equal in terms of lack, can never extricate itself from its enmeshment with the narcissistic register, in which the wish for wholeness is tied in with the attempt to find what is lacking in the love partner and where images of one's own completeness and incompleteness take root. For this reason the feminine, insofar as it images itself as hole, as emptiness, stands in a closer relation to the emptiness of the depressive mode. The different position of the genders vis-à-vis the chain of displacements of phallic objects and, therefore, vis-à-vis *jouissance* on the level of desire is what led Lacan to the assumption that women, in contrast to men, are "not entirely" situated within this register of phallic desire and still experience another, unnameable *jouissance*. He compares this other *jouissance* to mystical experiencing. From here the road to the unspeakable affect (typical) of depressive ill humor and melancholia is not very far.

What I have represented as a "shift" in the depressive process applies to widely different types of this condition. Depressive ill humors can be momentary (often, for example, in therapy, they act as a sort of entrance ticket into the session), they can persist over days, weeks, and months, or they can turn into a character trait in their own right. They can exhibit extraordinary sluggishness since the depressive condition pretends to be a solution to lack. A considerable secondary gain may lie in this characteristic.

Among those patients who have a tendency to develop depressive ill humors it is to be expected that one particular difficulty in terms of their therapy emerges frequently: I mean the difficulty that these patients, who have little access to the unconscious, have when one calls their attention to slips of the tongue, for example, or to an ambiguity in their statements; they refuse to accept that and just say, "Oh, that doesn't mean anything; I wanted to say only this." These are patients who stick particularly stubbornly to the narcissistic integrity and closure of their statements. One finds this inertia vis-à-vis the unconscious especially frequently in depressive individuals.

There is a correlation here with the process of denial characteristic of perversion, especially when one thinks of the dull persistence of some depressives.

The depressive turn away from the "phallic" organization of pleasure that characterizes desire can lead to a difficult struggle on the level of demand, that is, where one is entitled to something: love, recognition, help. The statement "I have a depression" represents both an invitation and a demand for help, which unfortunately is accepted all too often and all too quickly by medical polypragmatism (*Polypragmasie*). No matter with how much help, love, and attention you respond to the typically depressive demands—"No one likes me," "Everyone always abandons me"—it will get you nowhere. At best—and most often—it will land you in some sort of malicious and tough clinch. In such cases the therapist who can no longer bear the situation is in danger of making recourse to all sorts of pills in order to calm himself. The aggression in what is generally and somewhat thoughtlessly referred to as "countertransference" has a different cause here than it does in melancholia: it is the aggression typical of the love relation, where it constitutes itself as sadomasochism. Only when it is possible to evade such a perversion within the therapeutic situation does the path for performing analytic work on the fantasms on the level of desire open up.

It is also the case that these patients' suicide attempts are directed at the Other and that their function is, perhaps, to keep desire going precisely where it can't seem to find any more space[31]—strangled, perhaps, precisely by help, love, and "understanding," by an understanding that is a misunderstanding of the unconscious desire, dictated by the patient's own narcissism and, perhaps, also by that of the environment or that of the therapist, both attempting to calm themselves in their understanding instead of listening to the disturbance, that otherness that doesn't fit the picture. "It is only through suicide that I can take the floor," was the paradoxical formulation of one hysterical patient.

The only thing left is to repeat that depressive ill humors are to be placed within the sphere of narcissistic misrecognition, the sphere of the illusion of wholeness and the illusion that always characterizes our conscious ego when we believe that we know ourselves and intend actually to direct our own behavior.[32]

The illusion that there is a lack that is missing also correlates depression with love where the love partners are wrapped up in the delusion that they complete each other, often resulting in the most horrifying misunderstandings and aggressions. Narcissistic illusion, the illusion of love, depressive illusion— all these illusionary conditions make a good companion piece to any neurosis, and every one of us, cross my heart, has experienced them sometime, somehow. We are found out in our illusionary misrecognitions and wishes just like the hypochondriacal depressive patient of the famous joke, who goes to see his doctor to complain to him, "Doctor, I am so despondent, I have terrible ill humors, I have stomach aches and headaches. And, you know, all of my joints hurt—I have pains here, pains there. Doctor, please tell me, *"Was fehlt mir?,"* which in German means at once "What's wrong with me?," "What ails me?," or "What am I lacking?," And the doctor says, "My dear friend, you're not lacking anything, you've got it all already!"

Notes

This is a revised version of a paper given at the Kantonale Psychiatrische Klinik Liestal on September 12, 1991.

1. Sigmund Freud, *The Ego and the Id, Standard Edition, Volume 19,* trans. James Strachey (London: The Hogarth Press), 28.

2. Sigmund Freud, *Group Psychology and Analysis of the Ego, Standard Edition, Volume 18,* 105.

3. Sigmund Freud, "Mourning and Melancholia," *Standard Edition, Volume 14,* 249.

4. Sigmund Freud, "Negation," *Standard Edition, Volume 19,* 237–8.

5. Sigmund Freud, *Totem and Taboo, Standard Edition, Volume 13,* 141–6.

6. Sigmund Freud, *Beyond the Pleasure Principle, Standard Edition, Volume 18,* 38–9.

7. Cf. R. Klibansky, E. Panofsky, and F. Saxl, *Saturn und Melancholie* (Frankfurt: Suhrkamp, 1990), 141 (translated by Cary Plotkin).

8. Jacques Lacan, *On Feminine Sexuality, The Limits of Sexuality and Knowledge, Book XX Encore 1972–73*, ed. Jacques-Alain Miller, trans. Bruce Fink (New York: W. W. Norton, 1998), 58.

9. Jacques Lacan, *Séminaire VII, L'éthique* (Paris: Seuil, 1986), 65. English: Lacan, *The Seminar of Jacques Lacan, Book VII. The Ethics of Psychoanalysis*, ed. Jacques-Alain Miller and trans. Dennis Porter (New York: W. W. Norton, 1992), 52.

10. J.-B. Pontalis, *Aus dem Blick verlieren* (München: P. Kirchheim, 1991), 203ff.

11. Jacques Lacan, *Séminaire VII*, 146. English: 121.

12. Martin Heidegger, *Das Ding*, in *Vorträge und Aufsätze* (Pfullingen: Neske, 1990), 161.

13. Jacques Lacan, *Seminaire VII*, 133. English: Lacan, *Seminar VII*, 111–2.

14. Friedrich Hölderlin, *Hyperion, or the Hermit in Greece*, trans. Willard R. Trask (New York: Frederich Ungar, 1965), 24.

15. Jacques Lacan, *The Four Fundamental Concepts of Psycho-Analysis*, ed. Jacques-Alain Miller, trans. Alan Sheridan (New York: W. W. Norton, 1978), 198 and passim.

16. Ibid., 256-7.

17. Sigmund Freud, "Mourning and Melancholia," 251.

18. Ibid., 253.

19. Julia Kristeva, *Geschichten von der Liebe* (Frankfurt: Suhrkamp, 1989), 29.

20. Jean Starobinski, *Kleine Geschichte des Körpergefühls* (Frankfurt: Fischer, 1991), 73ff.

21. Anne Juranville, "Hysterie und Melancholie bei der Frau," *Riss* 11, no. 55. [See p. 000 in this volume.]

22. Jacques Lacan, "Kant with Sade," *October* 51 (winter 1989).

23. Jacques Lacan, *Television: A Challenge to the Psychoanalytic Establishment*, ed. Joan Copjec, trans. Denis Hollier, Rosalind Krauss, Annette Michelson, and Jeffrey Mehlman (New York: W. W. Norton, 1990). [In the German edition of *Television* (Weinheim: Quadriga, 1988) the translation given, *Verwerfung* (77) (foreclosure of the unconscious), is a slip in light of the fact that the original French is "*rejet.*"—E. S.]

24. Sigmund Freud, *The Ego and the Id*, 53. Cf. also S. Cottet, "La 'belle inertie,'" *Ornicar* 32 (1985): 84, and E. Laurent, "Mélancolie, douleur d'exister, lâcheté morale," *Ornicar* 47 (1988): 5–17.

25. Julia Kristeva, *Soleil noir* (Paris: Gallimard, 1987), 58.

26. Ibid., 69.

27. S. Cottet, 84.

28. Jacques Lacan, *Séminaire VIII, Le transfert* (Paris: Seuil, 1991), 460.

29. Sigmund Freud, *Instincts and Their Vicissitudes, Standard Edition, Volume 14*, 122.

30. Sigmund Freud. *Analysis Terminable and Interminable, Standard Edition, Volume 23*, 252.

31. Lucien Israel, *Die unerhörte Botschaft der Hysterie* (München, 1983), 186.

32. One advertisment for NLP training reads, "Sit down in the driver's seat of your brain."

11

The Act of Interpretation:

Its Conditions and its Consequences

MONIQUE DAVID-MÉNARD

To interpret could mean that one listens to the play of meaning and of the signifier in the patient's discourse with passive sensitivity. But in analytic treatment listening is never passive. The specificity of analytic listening consists in the fact that it submits the patient's discourse to a hypothetical reading which, in turn, always lends this listening the quality of an act: from the clinical point of view, the hypothesis of the unconscious means that a discourse consists of the variable relation between what a subject can hear within its own assertions and what it cannot hear. The analyst's listening always refers to this relation, and this is precisely why it is never passive. But within this listening to a subject's discourse there are gradations in the degree to which one can intervene in the relationship between the conscious and the unconscious.

The first point that I would like to shed some light on are the varying degrees of activity involved in the process of intervening or interpreting. In other words, interpretation is an act because it is never merely a matter of listening to the signifiers of desire or to the meaning of the discourse, but rather a more or less profound transformation of the relationship between the conscious and the unconscious.

My second point will be a clarification of what the analyst does and does not have control over. How are we to understand this? Is it enough simply to oppose the "logic of treatment" to what is coincidental in interpretative intervention—and to any kind of discursive intervention, for that matter—or could it be that it is necessary that the analyst master the range of his act only partially, even when he has thoroughly thought through all of its principles?

I. The Zero Point of Intervention

I will be concerned here with a patient who is a psychiatrist and who went into analysis because he had become seriously worried about and bewildered by his relations with women: he had fallen platonically, yet also very powerfully, in love with a number of women without having been capable of ever approaching them in a sexual manner. It is "like a current of air" which "whirls around" the papers over which he is leaning. When the draft dies down he is "exhausted, everything is messed up, in vain."

At the beginning of the treatment he had the following dream. The administrator of an island had received a delegation of visitors of which he was one and was showing them a sailing boat which was lodged in the building; it was a prototype that had never been completed and had never left the island. The patient was observing this scene—that is, he was simultaneously a visitor and the gaze that was observing this meeting from the outside. In fact, in one other dream image he hid so as to avoid having to join a team of people going off on a journey.

His associations led to people in the military who fascinated him and who had recently been in the newspapers, people who, in contrast to him, went on trips.

Some time ago the patient told me hastily about his evenings and conversations with a female colleague. It seemed like he had arranged them in such a way that I would share them with him and become curious to see whether this time something would happen. Since he had also told a friend of his about these encounters with great relish and continued to feed this friendship with descriptions of intimate situations, I asked myself how the obsessive and perverse elements were being articulated in this patient.

I associated for myself: *à voile et à vapeur* (literally this means "with sail and with steam," that is, with the sailboat and the steamboat; in French this is a very common expression for "bisexual"). However, this association seemed somewhat massive to me, and, by thinking of that gaze from the outside which did not get involved in the scene represented in the dream, and which, in the construction of the two dreams, produced the connection to the not-traveling, I said: "Ce bateau n'avait jamais pris la mer" [This boat never went out to sea/ This boat never took to the mother (mère), without really thinking of the incestuous content of such a sentence.

Strangely enough, my patient had no particular reaction to it. His associations went from how he constantly hesitates in his work and with women, to how he really does always "drift" in muddy waters, never daring to go out to the open ocean, and to the time when he had learned to ride a bike in spite of his mother's fears. Then he returned to the ship and to his predilection for constructions. I now risked asking, "Was it a sailboat?" (while thinking "à voile ou à vapeur").

"Yes," he said, " I don't belong to the era of steamboats. And my movements are driven and determined by an external element, just as the sailboat is by the wind. Motor boats are like cars, after all; I'm incapable of such independence."

The patient's groping is not very conclusive in terms of my interpretation's hypotheses. Of course, he himself could have come out with the expression *à voile et à vapeur*; in any case, it is by no means certain that its latent presence was a determining factor in the dream's development.

My interpretation took the form of a discrete probing, and the purpose of my play with the signifiers was to avoid leading the patient in his associations. In addition, this slight intervention was of no particular significance in terms of the transference. That is, nothing of these signifiers was actualized in the elements that the patient could have gathered from the frame or the space of the analysis. For this reason the intervention retained a "theoretical" quality. I would say that this was a kind of discrete plumbing of my patient's psychical processes or the signifiers of his desire. It did not involve a significant modification of that part of his desire that the patient was able to accept.

II. The Transferential Moment of the Interpretation

Interpretation carries a completely different significance in the following sequence, where, within the subject's discourse, the analyst interpreted by referring to the transferential element as it related to the subject's mythical story; she did so at the moment that the subject himself became capable of hearing the transferential element in his discourse.

Olivier Olms has been a filmmaker for twenty-five years. A first segment of analysis had occurred under the following circumstances. He had left his parents at the age of fourteen, because he had found unbearable a situation his father had accepted without any opposition: after the end of World War II his mother had taken a woman into their home with whom she lived and still lives today. My patient's father had accepted this exclusion of himself, and the children had always blamed him for doing so. My patient, on the other hand, had left at age fourteen and, in a sense, had never recovered from that: after a suicidal phase which, thanks to a first phase of analysis, he was able to overcome, he became a filmmaker, even though he doesn't really see what the purpose of his work is; he would like to soar higher, but has so far been prohibited from doing so. In his relationships with women he always places himself into extreme and unbearable situations; for example, he fell in love with a disabled woman and developed a paranoid jealousy, which, his friends say, made him unbearable. The first analysis ended, as far as he was concerned, with an absurd comment on the part of the analyst, who had asked him, "Why do you want to sleep with my wife?" He had been deeply insulted, had married three months after the analysis was broken off, and gotten divorced just a short while later.

The problem that this treatment posed for me was that for a long time I was asking myself what it was the patient wanted: for months he told me about his upcoming scripts, about the present condition of the film industry and the world of publishing. He programmed his life: "I'm sick and tired of this unstable life; I want to meet a woman with whom I can have a child"—this was part of a long discourse of the ego, and he was once again trying to prop up its foundations. When he dreamed, the dreams were always anxiety dreams bordering on nightmares and often consisted of scenes of jealousy that made him worry that he might be homosexual. But he was unable to say anything about his dreams except that he didn't want to dream them and that perhaps he would lose his ability to make movies were he to analyze them. I often said to myself that this patient should really be thrown out and this pseudoanalysis—often he used pop psychoanalytical terminology—ended. But two things stopped me from doing so.

Sometimes the patient fell asleep during the sessions in a very specific way. He allowed himself to fall asleep. When he woke up he would be completely calm without saying much about his having fallen asleep, and was then immediately capable of continuing with and concluding his organized discourse, his agenda for his life.

The other element, the significance of which I was able to grasp and accept only after some time, consisted in his saying that he felt better now, that he could have his own apartment and return there without fear.

After four years I said to myself that, in spite of everything, the significance of this rejuvenating sleep would now have to become apparent. One day he fell asleep again. I said to him, "You always tell me the same things, but I do not doubt that you gain something important from this." There was neither a reaction nor an association to my interpretive remark. In reality I had a much more precise conception of this sleep of his: I thought that he unburdened himself with me, of a burden that consisted of programs, of organizational measures and mental projects, all of which he could then leave behind. And that he could do so without this [act of falling asleep] having the catastrophic consequences it had had with his mother: he had been a child during the war and she had been a heroic resistance fighter in a responsible position. When his father was imprisoned he had slept in the same bed with his mother. He was doubly chased out of this bed: first, when his father returned, and then again when shortly thereafter his father was himself chased out of his wife's bed by another woman. My patient had learned to speak about the time in between his father's return and his supplanting by this woman, whose name, by the way, was similar to mine. All of the unspeakable and unformulatable elements surrounding the mother's sexual position found their equivalent, on the one hand, in the way in which the mother's activities had been kept a secret during his childhood, and, on the other, in the unspeakable nature of the war on the whole for this child, for this was also the time in which the father's entire family, which was Jewish, was deported to different concentration camps. His first work before becoming a filmmaker had been a *silent* play about the war in Algiers and had been acted out by children.

I thought of this while the patient fell asleep on the couch. There was also a clearly seductive element in his attitude. One day he said, "When I came to you I came to an analyst who was in the process of becoming a mother. Now I have a pin-up girl facing me and I am the one who has gained ten pounds." This happened during the period when he was drinking too much. He came to me, marked by a provocative seduction, in order to get a rest from his organized roles. These roles became more organized the more he feared risking having to repeat, in the transference, his prehistoric dependency on his mother, who, through a double breach, had pushed him to the edge of catastrophe.

None of this has anything to do yet with interpretation. These are constructions. The fact that this construction had occurred to me during the course of the sessions is of course not a matter of indifference, but it was not interpretation. The construction, however, had for some time now been taking on shape, because something was changing; not so much in the patient's discourse but in his relation to the frame of the analysis. Olivier Olms strongly emphasized how important the analysis was to him: not just in terms of his ego, but in a manner that made it clear that he was accepting a continuous process which he could not name. With this the moment for an interpretation had arrived.

One day the analysand said to me, "You are my Wailing Wall. I have never been to Jerusalem but sometimes I dream of bringing my complaints to this wall like the old pious Jews did." At that time he was suffering from sciatica and back pains which, according to him, had begun twenty-five years earlier when, after having left home without any means of subsistence, he had been forced to do work that had been too strenuous for him.

"You are my Wailing Wall. The only difference is that I don't bring you prayers but money. Of course, you haven't stolen it. When I am here, you are at work."[1] Then he changed the topic.

This "being at work *[in labor]*" immediately made me think of a telephone call I had received recently during a session. When the phone rings I say either, "I'm working" or "I'm in a session." This analysand condensed the two phrases and thereby expressed what was happening in the analysis and what was ripening in my constructions.

I merely repeated, "At work *[in labor]*?" And with some trepidation, he returned to the life feeling of that earlier period in time—to the impression, that is, of having been born.

This seems to me to throw light on what makes an interpretation possible in all of its effectiveness. In an article translated by *RISS*, Roland Chemama posed the question of whether the act of interpretation consists merely in actualizing signifiers that are already (virtually) present in the treatment.[2] He concluded that that is not the case, that these original signifiers are produced as original signifiers in the course of treatment for the first time, that the original is that which is connected to an unformulatable primal wish that has to be relinquished.

I would agree with this formulation were it not for one thing: Chemama does not make it clear that it is possible to focus in on the articulation of a primal wish only at one specific moment in the transferential process. The interpretation remains abstract, ineffective, as long as what the analyst says or emphasizes in the analysand's assertions, that is, something insisting on expression, is not immediately linked to the relation between the signifier of desire and precise transferential elements. In the example that Roland Chemama gives, the analyst says in the context of a dream image, *"Vous êtes mordu"* [You are bitten]; in this statement the analysand can perceive how important what is at stake in his relationship to the man who bites him in the dream actually is. One of the signs of the accuracy and effectiveness of an interpretation, says Chemama—and this is a classical position—is that the play of the signifiers forms a knot of associations which is first planted by the analyst. Fine, but are there not, among the associations that have been freed in this manner, some which are inscribed primarily in the transference? Chemama, for example, quickly ignores the fact that this "You are bitten" points to the patient's orality. What does that mean? How is orality here brought into relation with the analytic space?

What is at stake here is not the very general statement that "no one can be killed in absentia," nor that, as Lacan and Freud remind us, the analyst "waits for the transference in order to interpret." What is at stake is whether or not interpretation can become an act without becoming indentured to the absoluteness of the patient's demand when the patient risks bringing this absoluteness of his demand into the treatment.

Allowing the absoluteness of the demand to flow out into the treatment has no interpretive function in itself. Nor do listening and allowing the signifiers of desire to express themselves. To interpret means using that or those moments in which a precise relation between the construction of the childhood myth, which is in the process of unfolding itself, and the details of the analytic frame, which have been cathected by transferential passion, is being formed. In view of this prerequisite for interpretation its modalities are, even if not unimportant, of secondary importance: do the analyst's words refer to an assertion made by the patient or do they refer to the frame of the treatment? Do they relate to purely signifying elements or do they also plant the element of meaning? Do they inevitably occur in the mode of surprise? In any case, the interpretation refers to the relation that obtains between the working out of the history, in which it is the constitution of a signifying structure of desire that is at stake, and that which, within it, is repeatable. The interpretation allows for this process to emerge at that particular moment when it becomes possible for the patient to hear it. Only when these prerequisites are fulfilled does it become an act.

III. The Interpretation that Goes Beyond the Analyst's Conscious Knowledge

I now get to my second point: when an interpretation becomes an act in a given treatment, that is, when it transforms the relation between the conscious and the unconscious for a given subject, this always occurs in situations in which the analyst loses some of his or her control. First of all, this is a distinguishing feature of interpretation, one that I have repeatedly noted in my work. I am trying to understand why this is the case. One wouldn't think that this loss of control is necessary if one contrasts the element of chance in the analyst's interventions with the "calculatedness of interpretations," as Marc Strauss recently did in his article, which appeared in *Ornicar?* In his Seminar on the "Analytic Act" ["L'acte psychanalytique"] Lacan wrote that the act consists of constructing the frame and making it possible to walk. Marc Strauss draws the following conclusion from this statement: "Let us suggest that interpretation is the verification of the execution of this act, the "I can make it" of the operation with its actual and diachronic value, constituted by its frame. The result is a definition that is more logical than phenomenological, a definition which corresponds to our formulation of the calculatedness of interpretation. It is, of course, not the effect of the interpretation that is calculated—it is rather difficult to calculate a wave—but the subject's position vis-à-vis his fantasm."[3]

This definition seems to me to be nominal rather than actual; that is, it categorizes interpretation among other psychoanalytic concepts, but makes it impossible to gain any ground in understanding the treatment. Contrasting structural necessity and the coincidental nature of what in the treatment would be its mere application does not lead to a better understanding of the fact that an interpretation which takes effect as act always means for the analyst a relative loss of control over the transferential effect of his or her words.

I will try to clarify this point by returning to two clinical sequences, the first one involving the patient I have already mentioned. My interpretation concerning his silence hit the mark and, as far as the moment of intervention is concerned, was at the same time clumsy insofar as it consisted too much of the application of a construction. On the other hand, the simple fact that I had repeated this "being at work *[in labor]*" and had thereby made it apparent that I had heard the analysand's lapse and had emphasized its significance put this new opening into the unconscious—which, as is usual, was transient and for that reason in need of being grasped quickly—to better use.

But there is something else as well. These two interpretations had a decisive effect also because they coincided with an event, an event that became analyzable in terms of its importance to the analysand; this increased the interpretation's effectiveness dramatically. A female friend, who was much older than he was and with whom he had once had a love relationship, died. They had been working together on a project and she belonged to that series of women who in his dreams represented what he was repeating in his analysis, a relation about which he was incapable of saying anything. These dreams were about an intimacy that was trust inspiring and untouched by absence, as is so often the case in phobia.

The death of this friend led him to dream about his relations with other men and to then talk about them. At his friend's funeral, her husband had said to him, "I hardly know you, but I do know who you are." Thereupon my patient dreamed that he was doing a shoot on a ship and that he was preparing this shoot for a friend. But when it was all ready, this friend said to him, "No, this belongs to me; this is my film." He was not very happy, thought that his friend was behaving very badly, and left the location. I said, "So, you're leaving?" This led him then to talk about film contests at which he had had to compete against this woman's husband, and this at a time when he had been in love with her. Above all, he remembered that during his first analysis he had not discussed this woman and her husband and that his alleged reason for this had been that he had not wanted to name anyone famous. He also remembered now that his analyst's heated question, "Why do you want to sleep with my wife?", had referred to this—for him impossible—rivalry with a man over a woman.

His mother's homosexual position had robbed him, so to speak, of the possibility of engaging in a rivalrous competition with his father. He was suddenly able to hear all of this, and—in connection with what I had said, which he was able to connect with the impossibility of being his father's rival—it had the character of a revelation.

The example of this death, the cause of which was unrelated to the analysis and which, unpredictably, brought into plastic relief what was beginning to be articulated in the analysis, shows that the analyst is unable to control the range of the effects of the analyst's statements even when the interpretations are correct.

Another example may illuminate, even if in a slightly different way, what it is that evades the analyst's grasp during the course of an interpretation-become-act.

After years of total anxiety caused by an incestuous relation with one of her brothers, Elise Maillot had embarked on an analytic treatment. In our preparatory conversations I was impressed by her love of words. She spoke softly and used subtle, complex, and literary language. She had inherited this love of language from her mother who was a professor of literature in a town in southern France. Elise was a translator of Slavic languages in the same area. This love of words was the result of a close and long intimacy between mother and daughter and was directed against the father of this family rich in children. The father was an engineer and he introduced the children to the physical and mathematical disciplines. At a specific point in her treatment Elise said that she hated her father and refused to enter into his world. Her mother had always confided in Elise and told her about her unrealized dreams. At this particular point in her treatment Elise said that her attitude toward her mother's initiative, which was both her support and her prison, was one of mistrust. The position of the outsider, of a third person who had to be present, was the constant element in her love life. Elise was able to maintain a lasting relationship with a man only if she was taking this man away from another woman and could keep her life together with him a secret. This was the case even when she lived under the same roof with the designated man and the woman who was to be displaced. In this manner she led a secret existence together with Antoine, who translated and published American poetry—in other words, who was also in the literary profession.

After several years of analysis Elise had broached all the questions that were important to her, but nothing in either her discourse or her life had really changed.

After a vacation she told me about a conversation she had had with her sister Louise. (Louise, Elise, and Marc, the brother with whom she had had an incestuous relationship, were the only ones of her many siblings who were doing relatively well. The others had difficult lives.)

During her vacation with her family, the mother had said to Louise, "I advise you not to leave your daughter (Armelle, two years of age) in the care of Agnes" (the oldest of the siblings, who was very depressed). At the same time her mother had given her the following "information": shortly before the suicide of her brother Paul, whom she had loved deeply, a female friend of his had been found dead. Investigations concerning this woman's death had been initiated, but they ceased after Paul's suicide.

Louise had been frightened by these disclosures and had discussed them with Elise. What had alarmed both of them was not only the thought of a possible crime which could be repeated over the course of the generations, but also the discovery that their uncle Paul, whom they had thought to be homosexual, had had serious relationships with women.

Elise often spoke of Paul, her mother's darling, as the "antithesis" of the mother's husband. Following this report of hers Elise had two dreams. In the first one she arrived at a family dinner, where Paul too was present, and said to her mother in a provocative manner, "I no longer believe in God." In the second dream her father and her brother Marc were playing volleyball and encouraged her to join them; she declined, however, saying that she didn't know the rules.

Elise's only comment about these dreams was that they reminded her of a remark her father once made. After Paul's death her mother had spoken of him with much emotion, and her father had said to her in front of the children, "I don't want you to place him before them as some kind of god."

After having said this, Elise was silent for a long time, which was very unusual for her.

I thought to myself that Elise was incapable of accepting that it had been precisely this father with his "imperialistic rationality," the father she had described as being uncouth, clumsy, and ordinary, who had nevertheless separated her a little from her mother's realm. It was, after all, him she had to thank for not having been completely suffocated by her mother's "gods." But I did not want to share my thoughts with her because it was precisely this sudden and massive falling silent of her discourse and her silent occupation of my workspace that was decisive in this treatment.

One day I said, "Talk about anything at all—the weather, for instance." Her response was passionate: "It is out of the question that I talk about harmless things here; it would make me feel like I'm profaning this analytic space which is significant to me—thanks to the lights of Paris, the colors of your clothes, and the flowers you have chosen for when I am here."

I thought of the intimacy which she had created by the magic of her discourse just at the moment that her dreams were beginning to say that she was capable of breaking away from this very pleasurable intimacy, and suddenly it seemed to me necessary to have her come more frequently. At the time she was having only two sessions a week. Occasionally it had seemed to me that the sessions were not sufficient because, without my really knowing why, all of my thoughts regarding this treatment disappeared from one week to the next. But up until that point this massive forgetting had been my own business: it had had something to do with my rhythm of association in this treatment, and my patient simply pursued her path from one week to the next without being affected by a similar phenomenon of effacement. Suddenly I had the impression that for Elise the analysis became increasingly more a space of enjoyment the more it maintained itself from one week to the next as this small island of sessions which had no connection whatsoever with the rest of her life.

I told her that she should think about having an additional session per week. The next day she said to me very quickly and clearly upset, "How did you guess? When I talked about your flowers and your clothes, I didn't tell you— that would have been too much—about another thing I had dreamed about: I had asked you to allow me to come three times because I had stopped going to see another woman in Fleurville [the city where her mother taught]." Elise then talked about how affected she was by my having seen right through her, just like her mother, who intruded into her thoughts. She had just received a letter in which her mother told her about her dreams, as if she had been told that Elise was in analysis. The letter contained the following sentence: "I am writing you only because I have a desire for your style (in case you will answer me)."

Surprised that my words had hit their mark so exactly without my knowledge, I thought to myself that it would be appropriate not to close up so quickly what had been opened up regarding a third session. For the first time Elise was speaking of her mother as if she were describing a threat and not just a source of bliss. Thus I left the question regarding a third session open and made no determinations regarding it.

In the following week Elise seemed very angry. Her tone of voice, her relationship to the discourse, had changed. This was the end of words that strove for intimacy with the other; in a coarse manner she reproached me for not having scheduled the third session. This was an almost delusional moment for Elise. I had become a being in whose power she stood: I guessed her secret thoughts, released a torrent in the realm of pleasure, which had striven to remain protected and hidden, and at the same time left her hanging and exploited her pleasure. One part of her self was incapable of distinguishing between what, according to her, I was capable of effecting within her and what she found to be imaginable in terms of my being: she said she didn't much care for these too sudden encounters, and that I am like her mother in the letter, that I had changed the ritual: at the end of the last session I had said good-bye to her next to the couch and not, as was usual, at the door. She said this was just like her mother who had suddenly changed her handwriting and had put down a "good bye" in beautiful calligraphy.

I remembered that in my surprise at having hit the mark so fully with my offer of a third session I had held out my hand *in front of* the door.

The same moment in which Elise had fallen prey to my words and the power to dominate her pleasure, which she suspected to be hiding behind my words, and in which what was at stake for her was in fact her renunciation of being included in her mother's desire, turned out for me, the analyst, to have been the moment of a kind of confusion: the correctness of my intervention regarding the necessity of a third session went hand in hand for me with a loss of knowing, with a loss of control. Even if in my construction regarding the patient's silence I had been in control of the knowledge concerning what this silence revealed, what had had the value of an interpretation went beyond this knowledge.

So the question I ask myself—and you—is this: is the loss of knowledge on the part of the analyst who deals in interpretations, which "act within the treatment," merely one chance appearance of speech among others?

I believe rather that one should attempt to think of this loss of knowledge or power as being similar to the loss that occurs at the end of an analysis.

Notes

This is a revised version of the paper "Modalitäten der Deutung," given September 27, 1988.

1. "Être en travail" means "to be in labor."

2. Roland Chemama, "Über die Deutung oder die Prüfung durch den Signifikanten," in *RISS* 3 (October, 1986): 24–37.

3. *Ornicar?* 40, no. 9.

12

Castration and Incest Prohibition
in Françoise Dolto

ELISABETH WIDMER

Justification for the incest prohibition, a central law in our culture, is something that is hardly ever questioned in the public arena. It remains unchallenged in Freudian psychoanalysis, and Françoise Dolto,[*] whose theory serves as a basis for me in my work with children, expresses, as far as I know, not a single word of doubt regarding this issue. She bases everything she has to say on the subject on Freud's theories.

The point that really engages me is the question of whether a spoken incest prohibition could turn out to be the same thing as a seduction. If the prohibition were to supply desire with an object and, on the other hand, transgression of the prohibition were to produce *jouissance*, then it would be difficult to understand why a child would renounce the object of its desire—the mother as representative of the Thing. As far as I can see, such a thesis would run counter to Françoise Dolto's conception and would be relevant to an essential element in my child therapies. Again and again Françoise Dolto emphasized in her theoretical expositions and in her case histories that an unspoken incest prohibition could cause disturbances to emerge and, conversely, that a verbalized prohibition, even if it finds expression only later, could repair such damage.

Would an incest prohibition spoken in therapy then be counterproductive? How important should we consider this question to be? Is the problem of verbalization or nonverbalization of the prohibition that central, or do other factors play a more decisive role?

---

[*] [Françoise Dolto (1908–1988) was a student of Lacan and a child analyst. Her work helped to change the perception and status of children in society. She produced numerous texts for the psychoanalytic community, for educators, and for the general public regarding mainly childhood issues. —Ed.]

159

I posed myself such and similar questions at a point in time when I began a therapy with a thirteen-year-old boy who, verbally, and in the drawings he did and the models he built, seemed to be communicating precisely this problematic to me. These questions pushed me to sift through the work of Françoise Dolto from this vantage point and to examine her understanding of symbolic castration and the incest prohibition. I asked myself: is it possible to find confirmation of a seduction theory among her many case histories, or do other factors perhaps prevent such a seduction?

The incest prohibition plays an important role in Dolto's work. Of all the symbolic castrations—she refers to a number of castrations in the child's development—it is the most decisive one in view of the subject's later genital sexual life. It is the last castration in the entire castration complex a child experiences in its first years of life, and, depending on the manner in which it "suffers" it, it leads either to so-called normal or to pathological psychic conduct.

In *L'image inconsciente du corps*,[1] in a chapter entitled "La notion de castration symboligène,"[2] Dolto examines the notion of the castration complex. She intends to determine Lacan's concept of symbolic castration more precisely with this adjective *symboligène*; that is, she tries to clarify the difference between a maiming and a humanizing castration. It is precisely the nuances that lie in between these two extremes, where a maiming castration is to be understood on the symbolic plane as well, that are decisive in the child's development. First off, castration presents the subject with a shock: the fulfillment of its desire for a forbidden object is prohibited. The subject comes face to face with the impossibility of continuing to desire the forbidden object.

It is possible that this work of repression may have a depressive effect. Since the subject must renounce the object of its desire as well as the satisfaction of that desire, a repressive condition of tension may involve even the very legitimacy of that desire and could have a definitively maiming effect on the psychic level. In this case one must speak of a traumatic injury, of a maiming that gives rise to hysteria.

The repressed drives, whose first aim has been prohibited, strive for satisfaction through new means. They can either find this in suffering—"une castration qui induit le désir de se satisfaire dans la souffrance, au lieu de se satisfaire dans le plaisir, est une perversion";[3] they can affect the body and lead to an inhibition of further development; or the castrated drives can be sublimated, that is, no longer strive for a fulfillment by way of the primary object, but rather seek satisfaction, after a process of transformation, in new objects that are not affected by the prohibition.

Sublimation, and therefore also the castration which introduces the process, is inevitable if development is to occur. For Dolto it is always language, speaking, and communication that make sublimation of the drives possible. During the weaning process this occurs through the playful communication that takes place between mother and child and through a gradual increase of distance made bearable by language. In anal castration, what is at stake, aside from hygienic education, is the child's autonomy and its placing of itself within a community, as well as respect for property relations and the property of others. Giving and taking are symbolized. The child is enabled to identify with an adult who is subjected to the same laws, who obeys them, and who explains their necessity.

Symbolization of castration in relation to the law orients the child toward the future, promises it a more encompassing satisfaction of its desire in the future, and awakens its creativity, which it develops in order to achieve this aim. Opposed to that there is the so-called short circuit, which is how Dolto refers to situations in which the child is allowed immediate gratification of its needs, which makes it impossible for a desire that is geared toward the future to manifest itself. In *L'image inconsciente du corps*[4] these two modalities of dealing with the problem are illustrated by the following metaphor. A first blossom blooms on a young plant and the plant believes it is the only one it will ever have. The gardener cuts it off. Were the plant able to think, it would believe that its reproductive organ, which the blossom represents, its whole reproductive system is being maimed. The gardener, however, who knows more about the life of a plant, bestows on the plant the possibility to develop its full vitality so that it will be able to create new blossoms.

Trust, faith in the castrating person, that is, in that person's experience and truthfulness, are decisive elements in every symbolic castration. Only when this occurs, when the child is aware of the well-wishing intentions of the adult, when it is consoled with words for the loss it has suffered, when the words and the actions of this adult agree with each other and when the childhood drives first "have found their rightful satisfaction in the child's body," that is, "when this pleasure, which is necessary for primary narcissism, has taken place at an earlier moment in time"[5]—only then will the child use its powers to become like that adult in the future. This precondition is more likely to be fulfilled the more the adult demonstrates that adults too are lacking and does not attempt to hide their own state of subjugation.

Now, what else must we add to these general statements about castration when we are talking about the incest prohibition?

Here—as opposed to when we were discussing these umbilical, anal and oral, castrations, where primary needs are at issue—the question is whether incest becomes a problem for the child or whether it only plays a problematic role for adults. Dolto is of the opinion that in a family in which the parents still have a relationship and respect each other the child will necessarily develop incest fantasies. In the case of boys, she explains this by pointing to the boy's identification with the powerful father and the child's pretensions to wanting to have everything that he possesses and to imitate everything the father does.

Things are a little more complicated with girls. After primary castration (the perception of sexual difference) the girl finds compensation for her bodily lack in the fact that she will be able to bear children. She, too, at first wants to marry the mother because she believes that the mother will give her children just as she had done for her husband. Her aim is to seduce someone who will turn her into a mother like her own mother. The incest prohibition that denies the child all satisfaction from a family member presents the girl with the impossibility of realizing her desired satisfaction from her mother. She can then only enter the oedipal situation by attempting to transgress the incest prohibition.

While the incest prohibition leads the boy out of the oedipal situation, it actually effects the girl's entrance into it—that is, it effects her desire to seduce the father, to make herself beautiful for him, to become her mother's rival. While in the girl the incest prohibition effects the sublimation of pregenital drives, in the boy it awakens his repressed drive for knowledge.

In this representation of the girl's Oedipus it is not entirely clear how it later resolves itself. Dolto writes that this occurs when the girl understands and accepts the impossibility of her desire for her father and when she widens the scope of her art of seduction to include other males of her own age. In the girl, therefore, the incest prohibition develops her femininity, a, as she puts it, as a *ça-être (paraître)*, while in the boy it develops his masculinity as a *ça-voir (savoir)*.

I will only very briefly go into the question of whether or not this conception of sex-specific attitude is justified, whether it is possible to speak of *a* femininity and *a* masculinity. In *L'image inconsciente du corps* Dolto maintains that "the dynamic genital body image"[6] in the woman is centripetal in relation to the penis as partial object, while in the man it is dynamically centrifugal.[7] The life drives and the desire which is tied up with them as well as with the subject, who is determined by this desire, would therefore necessarily have to manifest sexual differences.

Let us return to the incest prohibition, the most significant form of castration.

Even though the function of the father or his representative plays a role from the beginning of the child's existence as an instance of separation, this function must nevertheless be especially emphasized in the context of the incest prohibition. The child sees its sense of omnipotence threatened only by the father. It is he above all who represents an obstacle to being with the mother constantly. But it is also he who, because he too submits to the law, guarantees that the child will be oriented around deferment and towards the future. It is at this point that the child experiences the beneficial aspect of the incest prohibition. The latter is supported by a strong and consequential father in the process of learning, in engaging in physical exercise, in becoming an adult, in finding a significant other outside of the family. This second part of the incest prohibition, one could say, is just as important for Dolto as the prohibition itself. Again and again she insists that the two aspects should be connected and presented to the child simultaneously: "You are prohibited from satisfying your sexual wishes with father, mother, or your siblings, just as my parents and siblings are forbidden to me; but you will, as my son or my daughter, experience a much greater satisfaction with a woman or a man of your own age."

Such a statement contains at the same time the fact of subjugation to a law that applies to all members of society, recognition of the child as its own person, trust in it, and a promise for its future.

Dolto underlines here how important it is that the father take up this position as the agent of the Other so that there will be no doubt in the son's mind about whether it wouldn't be possible after all to demand and take up that position himself. Often pathological cases come into being as a result of such doubts and hopes that are closely connected with feelings of guilt and self-punishing anxieties, about which Dolto has a lot to tell us.

Another element, one which plays a role in the early castrations as well but which can turn into a big problem in the oedipal phase, is the mother's desire. Should this desire be directed solely at the child, should the mother have neither a partner nor a significant other whom she trusts and with whom she can deal on an adult level, there will be catastrophic effects. In such a case the child becomes her object, her phallus. It is then not in her interest to let it try out independence, to support it in its endeavour to find other significant others. Too many demands are placed on the child—on the one hand, because it must constantly face the impossibility of satisfying the mother's desire, and on the other, because it becomes the victim of this woman's seductions. It will give up all endeavors to ever leave this place where fantasm and reality merge. A situation in which the child becomes the aim of the mother's desire can even come into being when there *is* a man present in the family but this man no longer takes up his position as the mother's sexual partner. That is perhaps the situation Dolto describes in the story of Léon,[8] where the mother is frigid, takes the children to bed with her, and ties her son, who is a toddler, into his high chair for half of the day. The father may be present, but he is forced to be constantly hiding as he is a Polish Jewish immigrant in France (the story takes place during the period of the German occupation of Paris). He leaves important decisions, like the Catholic baptism of the children, entirely up to his wife, has even given up his mother tongue and Polish surname in favor of his wife's language. His wife does say that she loves him. This love, however, is childish and has nothing to do with sexual desire.

This case history refers to the knot of the two elements "the place of the father" and "the mother's desire." In this case the father, as a broken-French-speaking Jew, does not represent the Other. Nor can he be the representative of the law of a society that persecutes him.

In the case study of Léon there were additional confusing elements that had an effect on the element of sexual difference as well as the child's relation to the mother. Every Sunday morning the mother played "the game of the mama dog with her little puppies" in bed, while the father, who tolerated this game, made breakfast. The mother would pull her two children under the blankets with her and place herself over them on all fours like dogs do when they feed their young. This game had come into being when the father had been away at war and the mother had stayed with *her* mother with her two children. In this house there had been a female dog that had just had a litter of puppies produced with one of her sons from a previous litter.

The fact that the impossible relation between mother and son had not only never been spoken about in the context of this family situation, but had even been imitated in the game, is, in my opinion, directly related to the "place of the father" and "the desire of the mother." Dolto believes that this game, which always took place in the absence of a man, turned out to be indistinguishable from an imaginary permission of incest. In consequence of the fantasms that were brought to light via the figurines that Leon made in the analysis, she spoke with him about primary castration and the incest prohibition.

I am still, actually now more than ever, driven to ask myself whether or not the incest prohibition has to be verbalized. One could, especially in connection with this case, draw the conclusion that the presence of a genital male who takes up his position in the family as the woman's sexual partner and who is also the recipient of her desire would be enough to guarantee the children's development. Is it not true that uncovering the fantasms and talking about sexual difference also result in insight concerning the impossibility of incest?

Françoise Dolto insists that the incest prohibition must be verbalized. She maintains that, as in the earlier castrations, here too verbalization on the one hand either makes impossible immediate gratification of a desire or intercedes for an absent object; on the other hand, the child is recognized as a subject by way of this gesture of speaking with it; in this way, its desire is not denied by satisfying it.[9] Through the incest prohibition secondary narcissism comes into being, and, in general, that prevents sexual drives from remaining in society without having been subjected to a law that humanizes them. Through the incest prohibition the child finds out that it was wrong up until now to have believed that it could some day take over the place of the same-sexed parent, including all of the privileges associated with it, through total identification with that parent; for now it is forced to identify with the subjugation of one of its parents to the law and not with the image of the parent, or with the parent's affective mode with which he or she appears to others.[10] From now on the child must master its desire and differentiate between acting and thinking. It learns to act in its own name, which is what constitutes its identity as a subject within the group.[11]

According to Dolto, the points we have discussed—the place of the father, the desire of the mother, mutual respect—represent, so to speak, the ideal ground and preparation for a healthy resolution of the Oedipus complex. Within this configuration there are more or less appropriate times at which to verbalize the incest prohibition. The child has to learn about sexual difference. Dolto says, for example, that a girl who says, "That pee-pee-maker boys have is icky," is not ready for the incest prohibition.[12] It is during the phase of primary castration or maybe even sooner that the child becomes aware of family and kinship relations; it becomes capable of placing itself within the sequence of its fathers and mothers. The incest prohibition is then the next logical step in order for it to understand these correlations even better.

Dolto emphasizes again and again that an attitude of this sort on the part of the parents without a clear verbalization of the incest prohibition is not enough. She would be happiest if schools, too, addressed these issues with children, since they are, after all, social issues. In most schools, she claims, sexuality is addressed only with pubertal children while smaller children are left to their own devices with their sexual problems. This then leads to the creation of fantasms. The child, she suggests, can order all of the experiences it has had, can separate the Imaginary from the reality authorized by the Law, only with the verbalization of the incest prohibition. She claims that the anxieties emerging from all such confusions could then be resolved. For, " [Q]uand les enfants ne reçoivent aucune réponse au problème oedipien et aux questions sexuelles, [ils] débouchent toujours sur les fantasmes se rapportant aux pulsions génitales, mais issus des fantasmes archaiques oraux, passifs ou actifs."[13] When children are incapable of resolving their oedipus, this is, according to Dolto, often due to the absence of timely information, an absence, which, in the unconscious, represents a danger for desire and for genital pleasure. Falling in love with an extrafamilial object could then be experienced as something laden with guilt, which, in turn, leads to the subject's failure and unleashes psychic disturbances within him.

In order to discuss this problematic in terms of a concrete example—the already mentioned thirteen-year-old boy—I will now report on the material of the first session in abridged form:

Matthias was brought into psychotherapy with me because he suffered from a great deal of anxiety whenever he had to spend the night away from home. Since the birth of his brother, five years younger than he—he had been taken to the neighboring house of an aunt at the time of the brother's birth— he had never again slept away from home. The problem became virulent when one night his teacher invited her pupils to camp out in her yard. From that day on the boy was incapable of thinking about anything else. His schoolwork deteriorated; he sat in the corner and cried. On the appointed evening his mother picked the boy up before everyone went to sleep in the teacher's yard and took him back there the next morning so that he could spend the rest of the time with his classmates.

Matthias himself was not entirely sure whether or not he would have wanted to try to get through the night. His problem had not been solved by his mother's actions, especially because he knew that in secondary school, into which he was about to graduate, two-day school outings and class camping trips were part of the curriculum. Should he work towards attaining this higher level of schooling, which was a prerequisite for the occupation of his dreams (becoming an auto mechanic), and therefore repeatedly make himself vulnerable to these torturous anxieties? He had already tried several times to spend the night with his aunt, to whom he felt very close, but each time he had been forced to let go of this resolution when dusk fell because he was tortured by the question and the fantasy of what the rest of his family might be doing at home.

During the first therapy session, while producing a colorful drawing with great facility, he talks, on the one hand, about his fears of spiders and reptiles, of being alone in the dark, of the problem already mentioned, and, on the other hand, about the brother he takes care of when his parents are absent, and whom he had diapered and fed in the past; he also says that he loves his brother, that he hardly ever quarrels with him and that he is not at all jealous of him. He says that he never gets into fights with his classmates and that, in any case, he is the strongest and biggest among them. He says that when they laugh at him because of his advanced development and his beard—he looks like a fifteen-year-old—he just walks away and tries not to listen to them.

His family's house as drawn during this first session, has no windows, only a closed garage door. Leading up to it is a pathway covered with gravel and sided by flower beds and bushes. Smack in the middle of this path there is the red car of one of the neighbors.

I learned the following additional facts from his mother to whom I spoke alone, since the father was away in the military. At the age of three months Matthias had had warts on his tongue which over the course of his first two years of life had repeatedly had to be removed under anaesthesia. Because these irritating infirmities had often woken him up during the night, his mother had taken him into her bed; he had slept there all the way up until her second pregnancy.

Now, as her husband was finishing his refresher course in the military, she said both boys were back in the parental bedroom with her so that no one had to feel lonely.

The boy's father, she said, had had the same problems as his son: except for recruit school, he had never been away from home, not even for a vacation. During a later session Matthias tells me that his father always has tears in his eyes when he's off to rejoin the ranks in the military and that he himself then always cries for a very long time.

In my second therapy session with Matthias he produces a drawing of a big sailboat, which he draws in a longitudinal section so that all of the spaces in the hull are visible. On deck he draws the captain and a sailor, and inside the ship there is a sleeping cabin for everyone. In the kitchen a woman is cooking. He notes that he has no bed available for this woman. So he draws a structure on deck, which contains three more beds, and says about it that now, aside from the bed that belongs to the man in the lifeboat, there's one more bed available for a guest. Suddenly he sees that the lifeboat is attached to the wrong side of the ship—its bow. This makes him apprehensive, but he says that it's too late to change that now. At the same time he talks about another failed attempt at spending the night at his aunt's.

Right at the beginning of the third session he reports that he has been successful: he slept at his aunt's, in the room of the three-year-old cousin he often takes care of. He did, he admits, experience terrible pain at ten o'clock but overcame it. He was also forced to think again about his home and of what the others might be doing. I mention to him that during his father's absence he had slept in his bed. Yes, he says, he sleeps very well there. I remark that, surely, this is really the father's place, and he responds, his father had not protested; still, it is true, he goes on, after the father's return, he'd been glad to sleep in his own bed again.

While he says this, he begins to shape two balls and attempts to connect them with a rod. He says it's supposed to be a weightlifter's weight. He is dissatisfied with it and forms, from three differently sized balls, an initially conventional looking snowman with a big top hat, a large carrot nose, a stick, and a large bag. Then he adds two enormous finlike feet onto it (see figure 1). He says they are penguin feet. The snowman, he says, no longer knows what he is—snowman or penguin. He sometimes doesn't know that about himself either, he says. Often he thinks about the fact that even though he is so big he's incapable of sleeping away from home. True, he has recently heard about a sixteen- and an eighteen-year-old girl who also still have the same problem. That had comforted him somewhat.

In the next session Matthias molds an elephant—at first he forgets the trunk—with a long tail and huge ears. This seated and anthropomorphized elephant is eating a banana and holding a thick rope that is strapped around a baby elephant with a bottle in its mouth (see figure 2). The big elephant, he says, is the father who watches over the child with his big ears. The mother, who just now is cooking, will surely chide the father for having tied the child to this thick rope. Many fathers, after all, don't know how to take care of their children. He himself will know how to do so when he becomes a father—he had, after all, taken care of his brother and now often takes care of his three-year-old girl cousin.

Figure 1   The Snowman

In the following session he draws a bouquet of flowers and tells me that he has gotten new shoes and that he was laughed at in school because his feet are so big. His mother had gotten angry and said that one day she would tell his classmates just what she thinks of them. He says, though, that he would not want that, that his mother shouldn't get involved. Then he talks about his father, who has bought a new house (Matthias had been allowed to take part in the discussions surrounding this event and express his opinions) and who is going to give him a stereo system for his confirmation—a church ceremony that signals the church's acceptance of him as an adult member—which is to take place in ten days.

The sixth therapy session does not take place. Matthias's mother calls up shortly before the session to say that he is ill. She says he has a high fever and the shivers, and is vomiting.

Discussion

During his father's absence Matthias not only slept in his bed; he also took his place at the table. His mother saw nothing unnatural in this and the father handed his place over to him without a word. (Both father and mother had lost their respective fathers at the ages of thirteen and fourteen and left their mothers' houses only when they got married.) Matthias idealized his father; even though while modeling his elephant he had said that fathers often don't know how to take care of their children, his assertion had been formulated in an entirely general way. I had found out from his mother that his father really hardly ever spent much time with his children—at best off and on he took them to the bar when he went drinking. Whenever his father was actually the subject of conversation, Matthias never dared utter the slightest bit of criticism. In a later session he spoke admiringly about the father of a classmate of his who had earlier in life been a glider pilot and now operates a hot-air balloon; he immediately added that he did not admire the man for that, but instead admires his father who gets old cars to drive again and who earlier on had been a butcher.

While drawing the bouquet of flowers he first said that his mother should not intrude into his affairs; then he began talking about his father's financial possibilities and to rave about the gift—the stereo system—he was to receive soon. It seemed to me that he was trying to express with these examples that he actually wishes he had a different father, a father who perhaps cared a little more about his children, who had some daring, like his classmate's father, and who would provide him with a role model in terms of his difficulties in leaving the home. But he was able to admit all of this only in a disguised way.

I also believe that these doubts were relatively new and presented him with a conflict regarding his identification with his father (he did not want to continue talking and became ill). This identification had up until now been total; in his father's absence he took his place and he wanted to learn to have the same occupation as his father. And wasn't having to cry when leaving home also a form of identification?

But this seems to me to be only one side of the problem. The mother's desire is part of this problematic as well. She, who lived only for her two sons, who thought it was her duty [*Aufgabe*]—I mean that in the double sense of the word [*Aufgabe* translates both as "duty," "giving up," and "surrender."]. [Another meaning of the word is "homework"—E. S.]. When she told me about that she said that Matthias demands that of her; that he comes home and says, for example, "We (by which he means himself and his mother) still have to solve these arithmetic problems!" When he was asked about this, Matthias voiced the opinion that his mother wants to sit next to him; he said he, too, sort of enjoys that, and that that is the way it has always been. It was impossible to distinguish clearly here what was whose desire. Still, Matthias seemed to be perplexed by the question. Immediately afterwards he drew huge burning (rocketlike) engines

Figure 2   The Elephant

on an airplane which scorched the other flying machines in his drawing, a helicopter and a glider (figure 3). Did this signify, perhaps, that wanting to be independent, flying away, would endanger the others?

Matthias had often already indicated, even if in a disguised fashion, that becoming an adult would bring him into conflict with his mother's desire. She said proudly about him that he is always a sweet boy, that he helps her with the housework, that he looks after his little brother like a mother and never quarrels with other boys; also, that he wants her to come along when the father takes the children to the bar. Like his mother, Matthias suffers from migraines.

His questions concerning his own identity, which he expressed in his representations of fantasy figures, surely fitted into this context too. Was the elephant he formed, the one who tied the child to the thick rope, perhaps the mother and not the father? The elephant, whose phallic symbol, the trunk, he had almost forgotten to draw—or did he not know who it was who was holding on to him? Was it for this reason that he preferred to take the pain upon himself? (He had spoken of a terrible pain in connection with spending the night away from home.) Was it the mother, above all, who felt lonely when her husband was in the military? Matthias said that he was quite happy to return to sleep in his own bed after his father's return.

Matthias's drawings and models illustrated for me how his fantasy world was structured. By talking in therapy, through the recognition he was receiving as a person as he approached adulthood, and through the verbalization of his

Figure 3   Airplanes with other flying machines

fantasms, it became possible to unravel his anxieties, and the structure necessary for separating from one's parents began to take on shape.

In this phase of the therapy I was still not clear on how I should deal with the question of the incest prohibition. I invited his parents to meet with me and advised the father to speak with his son about sexuality, about his place in the family in connection with the incest prohibition, and about the experiences he himself had had at Matthias's age.

During the course of the therapy it became apparent how Matthias's initial total identification with his father increasingly changed. Pretty soon he was doing his homework on his own and in his own room. On one Sunday he went skiing together with two classmates for the second time; during his first attempt to go away without his parents a year earlier he had injured his forehead. Neither his father nor his mother knew how to ski; he assumed that I did. Another attempt to spend the night away from home was successful.

My interpretation that he had already realized many things that his father was not able to do emboldened him to do even more. First he went on vacation for a week with an uncle and then he added onto that another week with an aunt. The transition into secondary school no longer seemed to represent a problem (his father had attended the school at a lower level.)

How do we deal, then, within this concrete case, with the question of seduction?

That something changed within the entire family constellation is beyond doubt. By calling into question the legitimacy of his sleeping in the parents' bedroom, not only did Matthias begin to behave more independently and to extricate himself from the tight bond that had chained him to his mother, but the parents too seemed to breathe a sigh of relief. Matthias noticed that his mother was happy when he was able to spend the night away from home, and that his father was proud of him for being able to ski and for getting along better at school.

But was all of this the result of the incest prohibition having been verbalized? Had the father in the meantime spoken about it with his son? If he had, then there had in any case been no repeated rapprochement with his mother. On the contrary, he seemed relaxed and relieved. The massive anxieties and guilt feelings he had experienced at the slightest separation from his mother, turned out, for Matthias himself, to be groundless and allowed him to focus on other things, things more important in terms of his age.

Because I assume that in his therapy Matthias would have spoken about a father-to-son conversation having taken place—he always reported even the smallest incidents taking place within his family—I believe that the changes in his attitude must be ascribed to something else. In this case—as, to a large extent, in the case of Léon (which was characterized by much more massive disturbances)—what was much more important was sorting out the ambiguous relationships within the family: the "place of the father" and "the desire of the mother." The effect of clearing up these ambiguities was that the boy gained insight into the impossibility of an incestuous relation with the mother, without it having to be said explicitly, "You, like all people are forbidden to have sexual relations with your mother."

Half a year has gone by since the beginning of Matthias's therapy. My queries concerning the incest prohibition and its correlative seduction have taken on another coloring. Within the course of time—surely also thanks to my therapy with Matthias—I have reached the conviction that it is not the verbal-ization of the incest prohibition as such that is most important, but rather that the child find its place within the family, that it be recognized as a subject, and that, as far as the satisfaction of its sexual wishes are concerned, it be referred to the future. What is at stake in socialization is, on the one hand, the erection of structures, and, on the other, castrations, which are crucial for the child's development, which promote its desire for independence, lend it support, and confront it with laws that are binding for all humans. The incest prohibition is one of the laws that are in operation in our particular cultural field. I do believe, however, that one misses the crucial point when one makes its verbalization responsible for an either favorable or unfavorable socialization. Similarly, the question of whether the incest prohibition could represent a sort of seduction when it is verbalized within the therapeutic setting, for example, no longer seems all that important to me.

Notes

1. Françoise Dolto, *L'image inconsciente du corps* (Paris, 1984), 78.

2. There is no corresponding word in German; it can best be translated as "deriving from the Symbolic."

3. Françoise Dolto, 81: "A castration that induces the desire of satisfying itself in suffering instead of in pleasure, is a perversion."

4. Ibid., 79.

5. Françoise Dolto, *Praxis der Kinderanalyse: Ein Seminar* (Stuttgart: Klett-Cotta, 1985), 49.

6. The dynamic image, according to Dolto, corresponds to the life drives which hold together the three aspects of the body image—the funda-mental image, the functional image, and the erogenous image—and is con-nected to desire.

7. Françoise Dolto, *L'image inconsciente du corps*, 59.

8. Ibid., "Le cas de Léon," 288.

9. Ibid., 64.

10. Ibid., 203.

11. Ibid., 200.

12. Françoise Dolto, *Praxis der Kinderanalyse*, 49.

13. Françoise Dolto, *La difficulté de vivre* (Paris: Inter-Editions, 1981), 29: "When children receive answers neither regarding the oedipal problem nor to sexual questions, fantasms emerge which refer to genital drives but whose sources lie in archaic oral fantasms of either the passive or the active type." [translated from the author's German translation by E. S.]

13

Demand and Wish

LUCIEN ISRAËL

All Strasbourgers will tell you or must have at some point told you about the millet gruel. Once, in 1576, Strasbourg and Zurich were allied, and when Strasbourg was once being besieged by someone, I don't remember now by whom, the inhabitants of Zurich transported some millet gruel, still warm, to Strasbourg and broke through the siege.

Well, I'm not here to smear gruel around your mouths,[1] even if it *is* millet gruel. That is, I wasn't invited to spin folkloristic tales, but rather to talk about serious things; so many of these serious things have been bestowed on us provincials by Paris.

This too has occurred once before—this reciprocally fruitful collaboration between Zurich and Paris.

May I read a few verses to you?

> *Wir wachten auf ein letztes Abenteuer*
> *Was kümmert uns der Sonnenschein?*
> *Hoch aufgetürmte Tage stürzen ein*
> *Unruhige Nächte—Gebet im Fegefeuer.*
> [We're holding out for a last adventure.
> What do we care about the sunshine?
> Days stacked up high collapse
> Uneasy nights—prayers in purgatory.[2]]

This is the first stanza of a poem called "Morphine" by Emmy Hennings, and it appeared in 1916 in the first issue of the *Café Voltaire* in Zurich, at number 1 Spiegelgasse. But the true name of the periodical was *Dada*. Cabaret Voltaire was the inn where, thanks to Hugo Ball, Arp and Tzara, and Yanko and

Oppenheimer met. At the first French soirée poems by Apollinaire, Max Jacob, André Salomon, Jarry, Lafforgue, and Rimbaud were read.

So what does that have to do with our meeting today? Isn't it presumptuous to begin a serious evening of work by invoking ridiculous poets? But Lacan counted himself among the surrealists. This is a fact known probably only to his oldest—should I say "students"? Is the word "friends" blasphemous? More than twenty-five years ago, when I first met him, that was still allowed.

Ever since he has been deified, the oldest ones—I, at least—have distanced themselves. I am no "צבך סוככ'מ," no "slave of the stars," as they are called in the Bible, no slave to idols.

So what I have managed to take with me, and what I may even be able to share with you, belongs to the earlier Lacan, not the late one.

The founding of Dada in 1916 gives us one additional hint. Just as Zurich brought hope and support to the people of Strasbourg during the Thirty Year War, Dada brought a little light to the French in the middle of World War I as well as the promise that one day it would be possible to smile again; but a new kind of smile, a different smile, one which already takes account of what is unconscious in human beings.

Periodically analysts forget that it is this unconscious that is at stake in analysis; periodically ruptures, splits, crusades, and religious wars must flare up in order to remind them of the fact that analysis is and must be a struggle.

I am currently in just such a phase. You probably know that on January 5, 1980, Lacan dissolved the EFP (École freudienne de Paris).

A few years prior I had written that every few years—say, every fifteen—analysts should quit all analytic groups and movements. Was it my own fatigue that was speaking? Not only. The dissolution of the EFP had become a necessity, but it is not at all certain that Lacan himself hadn't become the reason for this necessity. Perhaps we can get a better look at this hypothesis if I talk about the issue of the teaching analyses.

I

Our friend Widmer gave me this task. Or perhaps he just gave me the impetus.

I should have apologized sooner for my bad German, but then the analyst really doesn't need to speak much. Just listen.

Listen. To listen [zuhören], to lend an ear [anhören], to prick up one's ears [horchen], to eavesdrop [lauschen]: how many words there are in German as opposed to the single French word, écouter. Does that mean that the French language isn't well suited for psychoanalysis? Freud said something along those lines. And it is true that psychoanalysis was introduced to France rather late. The first French psychoanalysts were amateurs rather than professionals. But, then, there is the question of whether or not there is such a thing as professional psychoanalysis.

Let us return to our French words. *Écouter, entendre.* That sounds very Cartesian. But is the unconscious Cartesian? I certainly hope not. Otherwise, after a few generations of analysts, we humans will all have been made as equal as ants. Efficient. Adapted to reality. But is it the aim of analysis to replace the pleasure principle with the reality principle?

Among the ants—and probably among all less evolved animals, and, for example, among the inhabitants of totalitarian or authoritarian countries—there is no difference between demand and wish. It is precisely the fact that in such societies language undergoes certain transformations that we pick up in analysis: no matter how much the powers that be, wherever they might be, wish it to be so: there is no perfect and precise fit between language and its objects. Between the expression and the thing to be expressed there is room for play; there the wish plays hide and seek. Prosopopoeically, the wish might say, *"Larvatus prodeo"* ["I move forward, masked"].

Take the child, for example. Anyone who has been blessed with children (in my case it would be grandchildren) has experienced this a number of times. The child goes to bed. After a while the child calls out, "Mommy, I'm thirsty." You get a glass of water. It is not necessary to be provocative and to offer juice, for example; because the child will, in any case, call out again a little later, "Mommy, I'm cold (or hot)." And then, "Mommy, I want a piece of chocolate." "Mommy, I forgot to brush my teeth," and so on. And if the parents still don't understand, or if they have a lot of stored up patience (it's said that "modern" parents are much more tolerant than we ever were) the children advance by a degree and switch to the phobic register before which every mother—or mother-father—capitulates: "Mommy, there's a noise; Mommy, I'm scared; Mommy, I had a bad dream." The fact that many parents are made uneasy by such appeals probably also has something to do with wish; but that is a different story, which I neither wish nor am able to tell you, as I have never worked with children. (Ha! What significant repression is silently at work here! Here one can see to what sorts of aberrations the Lacan cult has led! How is it possible for anyone to claim to be doing analysis without ever having worked with children? As if it were not indispensable, and not just recommended, in any sort of decent training to have worked with children! . . . But who demands this, who requests it?)

Let's get back to our child, then. What is it asking for with its incessant demands? With its requests? Because it is a request that is at stake. Every parent eventually learns that it is not the object that's being asked for that is at stake. And also that the symptom formation becomes clearer the closer one gets to the truth, even if we still find ourselves entirely within the range of normality. The shout, "Mommy, I'm scared!" or "Daddy, I'm scared!"—after all, psychologists have to make a living too (there is a saying in French: "Il faut de tout pour faire un monde" [It takes all kinds to make a world], which allows for everything— murderers, fascists, ayatollahs, Jews, even psychologists)—"Mommy, I'm scared" usually frightens the mother enough for her to seek out all sorts of explanations in order to pacify herself; and then she is no longer capable of understanding the request.

For what is at stake here? It's all about calling out for the mother's presence, to see her once more, to hear, feel, and have her. Which is the case with anyone who is in love. Here we see the wish, perhaps in its most original form. What does the child want? To have the mother there . . . for itself? It is a myth that one was happy with the mother, that one had no wishes then. The child is no happier than any lover. "That I should have to hear that!" said the mother of a schizophrenic to me once when I dared suggest that her son was probably not the model of normalcy. I was still very young then. Well, this mother may have been happy. But the son? Even today I find it impossible to determine that. But I don't want love to be limited to a schizophrenic mother-child relationship.

Demand and love probably belong to a single category. Both want to bring about a certain object. The child's request does not know this clearly and lovers think they know it. But they will all experience in a painful way that the potential object will not really suffice to free them completely of a given ten- sion. This tension, which is embedded in the request, which perhaps is the basis of the request, is precisely the wish. Don't think that I am denying love any possibility of satisfaction or enjoyment. But the French song, which claims that "Plaisir d'amour ne dure qu'un instant, chagrin d'amour dure toute la vie" ["Love's pleasure lasts but a moment, love's sorrow a whole life long"], is one of my lullabies. But this does not prevent me from preferring the principle expressed in a different song, in "Temps des cerises" [Cherry Season]. This song gives the following advice: "Si vous avez peur de chagrins d'amour évitez les belles" [If you are afraid of sorrow, steer clear of the girls]. As if that were enough to evade the torments of love. The end of the stanza goes, "Moi qui ne crains pas les peines cruelles, je ne vivrai pas sans souffrir un jour" [I, unafraid of cruel tor- ments, won't live without suffering one day].

What are we to pick up from this little song? That love—and I am talking about reciprocal, recognized love here, even, or especially, the most violent passion—love has nothing to do with happiness. Whoever surrenders to wish must renounce happiness. This seems rather immoral. "Are you suggesting there is no happiness in marriage?" you could ask me. No, there certainly is happiness in marriage. Love too. But since both concepts are somewhat imprecise there are enough cracks in which the wish can hide. And who can claim, what wife, what husband, even the most honest, the most reasonable, the most faithful, that he or she has never been surprised by the wish? What is done with this wish belongs to the realm of one's own personal morality. But this does nothing for happiness.

And please don't think that this has anything to do with any kind of malice on the object's part. All passions bring the same kind of torments with them. In his poem, "Il n'y a pas d'amour heureux" [There is no happy love], Aragon says it explicitly: "Et pas plus que de toi l'amour de la patrie" [And of you no more than love of a country].[3] Love for one's fatherland is no more comfortable than love for a woman or a man. Perhaps the love of God is somewhat more relaxed, but what we know about the mystics does not make this very likely.

Happiness must be conquered; that's why the damsels sent their knights out on the most difficult feats.

Happiness, love, morality—what does all of this have to do with psychoanalysis? I don't want to answer this question. I don't have the answer. I have been working long enough to get to the point where I can ask a few questions. Maybe it is more important to be able or to be allowed to ask questions rather than answer them. It is said of a certain Talmudic scholar that he always said to his students, "I have the answer. Who has the question?"

This question, impossible to pose, is probably the question of the wish. And the answer moves through castration. Perhaps we will get to talk about that. But first, a clinical example.

A thirty-year-old man, an engineer, a flight commander during his military service, a sports pilot in his civilian life, good looking and wealthy. In short, he lacked nothing, as they say, to make him happy. But he suffered from a stubborn phobia, which appeared as an isolated symptom: he was incapable of sitting in a restaurant or tavern. I will tell you right away that this was a case I took on twenty years ago and that after a three-year-long analysis nothing whatsoever had changed. I do not think I would be any more successful today. At most I might have become a little more experienced with the perversions now and would not have undertaken an analysis in this case. Or perhaps I *would* have, out of interest. Because you will have noticed that this patient was a pervert. But this diagnosis does not interest us today. The topic I have chosen to engage is a miniscule circumstance that the patient told me about several times in a stereotyped narrative, which was the way all of his sessions went. He had participated in a strenuous flight competition, and after his landing his mother was waiting for him; she had brought him his favorite cake. This is where in his narrative he got into the crudest, most violent rage. He who always spoke in a very educated, sensitive, even elevated, manner couldn't find words vulgar and hate-filled enough to scold and curse this mother who brought him his most beloved cake. He said to me, "And do you know what this pig, this bitch, this whore did?" At this point we could play out a little radio quiz or TV game show: "What could this horrible mother have done?" At that time I would never have guessed it. I wouldn't get it today either, probably, but it would not surprise me so much now and I would not remember it so clearly. What had the mother done? Let's let the patient himself speak. "Do you know what she had done? No, you could never imagine such a rotten thing. She had bought the cake in a different bakery, not the one I preferred."

Let us look a little more closely at the crime this mother had committed. We could, of course, think that a thirty-year-old sportsman would expect such an act of love from a woman or—let us not be misogynist—from a friend rather than from a mother. And there was no lack of women in his life.

Let us look at the scene carefully. The mother comes to meet this man, just as she might have come to meet her husband who was returning home from work, in order to bring him his slippers.

To come to meet. Is this the most fitting word to describe this maternal behavior? Actually, she doesn't only come to meet him. She brings him something. Something that we could label an oral object. As if she had known in advance what her son, climbing out of the airplane, would want. She does not give him the chance to express a wish. She has gotten the jump on [zuvorkommen, or *zuvor kommen*, to come before —E. S.] this wish. In French one would say "Elle a prévenu sa demande." *Prévenu*. Past participle of the verb *prévenir*. *Prévenir* is exactly the same word as *zuvorkommen*. But in French two nouns are derived from this verb. The first is *prévenance*. *Prévenance* is an act of cordiality, of amiability. No one would be offended by someone acting out *prévenance* in their regard. But there is a second noun that is derived from the verb *prévenir*, whose meaning is therefore contained in the original verb; this is the word *prévention*. *Prévenir* in the sense of *prévention* is to avoid something. There is something prophylactic about it. *Prévention du cancer* by stopping smoking, *prévention des maladies vénériennes* by no longer having sexual relations with just any partner, *prévention des accidents de la circulation* by renouncing the pleasures of fast driving. *Prévention*: it means to prevent, preclude [the German word *vorbeugen* also means to bend forward—E. S.]. I know that the German *Prävention*, in French *prévention*, can also refer to the act of being "prejudiced or biased." But let us leave it at that—we have our hands full with our two meanings.

I said that *prévention* means to "prevent" [*vorbeugen* = bend forward].

By satisfying the wish of her son before he could express this wish, this mother prevented what lay within the wish, that is, the actual spring of life, the wish, the unconscious wish, which expresses the essence of the subject. What happens to this prevented wish, to this not just inhibited but even avoided wish? It is not repressed; instead, it is ejected, repudiated, to use one of Freud's terms. Following the tracks of this repudiation, Lacan came upon the foreclosure of the Name-of-the-Father, which is where he thought to have found the cornerstone of psychosis. Foreclosure of the wish and foreclosure of the Name-of-the-Father—what is introduced into the private language between mother and child by the mother's wish—are closely related.

Does this mean that my pilot was psychotic? Certainly not. His scolding of his mother expresses the felt need for an intensification in order to salvage some of the wish after all, possibly through such violence in his expression that even the deafest father would have to hear it.

It is probably thanks to this mechanism, which did manage to open up a tiny possibility for the wish to find expression, that the patient did not become psychotic—just perverse.

And how could one describe the mother's behavior? We are probably dealing with a true castrating mother here. But the word "castration" has been misused to such an extent that perhaps it would be productive to query it and examine its relation to the wish.

Freud talked about fear of castration, the castration complex and, eventually, the threat of castration. And who, in this fantasy, was the agent of castration? The father. The way is long from this castrating father to the by now customary castrating mother.

Let us look a little at this castrating mother, for this final product is much simpler—one might even say, much more simplistic—than the originating concept. In the various transformations of castration, brought about by different psychological reflections, we have moved from the signifier "castration" to castration as a reality. This happens when one confuses word and thing, when one forgets that our words are signifiers, which have some room for play. De Saussure has already demonstrated this, and speaking of de Saussure in Switzerland is probably comparable to carrying coals to Newcastle.

In all sorts of discussions of castrating mothers the claim is made that her children, the children of such a mother, are really castrated, in other words that they behave . . . in what manner? Right at the start we encounter an ambiguity which may lead to all sorts of confusions. For how do these "castrated" children, products of a castrating mother, behave? It is—or at least, it was for a while—quite customary to hear expressions like, "He is thoroughly castrated; his mother didn't leave that much to him." One could deduce from this, if these expressions had any foundation, that castrating and phallic mothers are one and the same thing. But let us get back to the ambiguity I mentioned. Is castration the inability to follow the drive because the tool is missing or because the wish is missing?

The castration indicated by Freud is never carried out; that is, there is no such thing as a real castration, at least not in psychoanalysis. The father does not carry out the castration. But what does he achieve through his threat? That sons turn away from their mothers; in other words, through the prohibition of one woman all other women become fair game.

And the castrating mother? She does not carry out any real castration either. Yet she succeeds—and she has all sorts of means at her disposal to do this—she succeeds in making sure that her sons have no desire, no wish for other women; that is, that her sons remain with her, at least in their wishes. It is understood, of course, that this is an unconscious wish. This castration, then, which I have attributed to the mother only as an example, has an effect opposite to the first one I mentioned: in the first one, one forbidden woman and all others allowed. Now, no women outside of the mother are desired. As if all women were forbidden except for one. For sure, there is at the very least a neurotic structure at work here, but I am not concerned with psychopathology right now, and would like rather to introduce a few concepts which have stood the test of time, at least as far as I am concerned. How can we characterize this castration by the mother? When women are no longer desirable we do not have to look for a biological explanation—an endocrinological one, for example. Nor does it have anything to do with the physiology of the genital apparatus. This is not the place for sexology or sex therapy. Somewhere these men lack the impulse to imagine themselves in a sexual situation with women. It's as if the prohibition, the castration, had affected their imaginative capacity.

What I have in mind here is to introduce the various Lacanian concepts of castration. What I have just described is one way of imagining, of presenting, imaginary castration. This imaginary castration probably coincides with what one regularly designates as castration.

We have also seen that there can be an actual castration, but that this is not what is at stake in psychoanalysis.

How shall we now refer to this paternal threat of castration, whose normative function we have seen to be to create the conditions for a free choice of partners for the price of having renounced the mother? That is, its function is to provide the possibility of creating relations through this castration. The ancient Greeks testified to the relations between two families, two tribes, with potshards that fit together and whereby one could recognize one's relatives. These shards were called *symbolon*. Symbol: that which binds together. It is for this reason that Lacan suggested calling this castration symbolic castration: that castration which makes the tie possible after the lethal, incestuous, tie has been obviated by the father. How this symbolic castration comes into being is another story. It is understandable that the mother's wish should be directed at the father, that is, at her husband. But the important thing to introduce here is the manner of rehabilitation of castration. Castration is not what is to be avoided. On the contrary: symbolic castration is the condition which allows for the wish; it is what makes it possible.

If we return to our earlier example, we will be able to arrive at a few more conclusions.

Our young man insulted the mother who anticipated [*zuvorkommen*] his wish before he did, who, in other words, attempted to paralyze these wishes in order to keep her son to herself. And the shout, the insults the son used, were appeals to a father or father substitute. They were to be heard as "This woman wants to nail me down to a place where I don't belong. It is your place, father. Come and forbid her to me; come, speak, and prohibit this woman from laying claim to me."

Certainly we are dealing with an ambivalence here, because the symptom—the tavern and restaurant phobia—forced the patient to stay with his parents! The same ambivalence is at work vis-à-vis symbolic castration: the latter is inevitable if we are to have access to the wish; however, it does also separate us from the first love object. Is this maternal love object also the object of the wish? At this point we could attempt to go a step further.

What is this object's position vis-à-vis the wish? This model of all lost objects—whether they be partial or total objects is not that important for our metapsychological reflections—this model, then, has a completely privileged position, a unique role, vis-à-vis the wish. The lost object is not an object but the *cause* of the wish. Through loss, through symbolic castration, the child is introduced to the world of the wish.

For this reason all wish objects will be nothing but attempts to find substitutes for the first, lost objects. And for this reason they will never be fully satisfying. The need to seek satisfaction can be assuaged by no specific object. The object is always only a substitute object, which, through the illusion of passion, is recognized as being the only one, the only one that had been missing.

Thus we get back to passion, something about which every one of us, I hope, has much to say so that I need not stick to this topic any longer. Access to the wish through symbolic castration—perhaps this is the way to formulate the aim of analysis as well as the criterion of a successful analysis.

II

I now suggest that we apply our metapsychological reflections to the teaching analysis. For I am in possession of excellent material that would enable us to do so: the dissolution of the EFP and the circumstances that unfolded as a result.

What is at stake when someone comes to us to demand a teaching analysis? When I began my own analysis we were still living under the committee system. There was a Commission de l'Enseignement [Teaching Commission] on whose agreement it depended whether or not a given teaching analysis could be undertaken.

Of course, I didn't accept such a procedure and came to a direct understanding with an analyst, because at the time I neither had the slightest idea about what analysis was nor did I have definite plans as far as my future practice was concerned. But I certainly had sufficient personal reasons for undergoing analysis and my first analyst probably understood that. What happens when such a committee accepts a candidate and allows him to undergo a teaching analysis? The same thing that occurs at the French secondary engineering schools. If one is able to get in by way of a competition one has ensured one's graduation and secure employment in the industry, whether one has learned anything or not.

It is probably somewhat subtler in analysis. Nevertheless, something has been introduced which is related to the customary instructional process. And the teaching analyst becomes a teacher. And the candidate is frozen into the position of student. It is no longer a matter of loosening the reins on the unconscious—and we should all know that this is in any case not an easy thing to do—but it is rather a matter of pleasing the master. We could ask in this case what happens to the transference. Either the analyst is simply to be viewed as a teacher—and we know that in most cases teachers are not valued very highly, are actually looked down upon—or they are so worshipped, so deified, that a dissolution ("analysis" means "dissolution") becomes impossible because it is not desired. Most analyses oscillate between these two extremes, a situation that is sometimes made even worse by the fact that one's future career really, at least in part, depends on the teaching analyst. I have been led to believe that there are analytic societies which demand of the psychoanalysand that he not only work through his four weekly hours with his teaching analyst but also that he participate with this analyst, with a colleague, in different groups or study groups. And that the teaching analyst can then testify to the above mentioned teaching committee, whether the candidate had done so, and so on.

I know that this deplorable state of affairs has frequently been criticized without anyone having come up with a better plan. This is the extent to which people generally believe in the possibilities of a certain kind of training on the one hand, and, on the other, in social welfare, in the social protection of future patients. The point is to offer a guarantee for the practitioner and to base it on the Society's respectability, as is the case in every commercial enterprise.

There is no guarantee for analysis. At most there is, as Lacan said, an insurance against psychoanalytic speech. There are relationships that are incapable of guarantees, relationships that actually even lose their essence in guarantees. Try introducing the Oedipus into marriage. The renunciation of one woman, we said, makes all other women available. Is marriage, then, a kind of psychotic regression in which one single woman is available and is then guaranteed by the law, by morality, by religion—in short, by society?

But let's not get too far off track. There is no guarantee for either a good analysand or a good analyst; even less is there one for a good psychoanalysis.

And all of this happens not only in the conception, the imagination, of analysands. Analysts are complicitous. They share the same fantasies.

The French experience—and not only that of the EFP—shows that analyses have become longer and longer and this is in general the case, not just in those analyses that practice the short sessions "à la Lacan." Interminable analyses, one is tempted to say. I prefer to speak of an interminable transference.

Transference does not come to rest only upon the analyst who, as an illusory object, takes up the exact position of the wish object. The transference dissolves when the subject becomes capable of accepting the fact that the wished for object is never found and that he must be content with substitute objects, which sounds somewhat bitter but which in reality does not involve eternal suffering. One can mourn for the half empty glass or rejoice over the half full one. Castration brings emancipation from phallic compulsion. It has nothing to do with resignation. But when the analyst is confused with a real object, when he thinks he is really the teacher, how can a transference of that sort be dissolved? Either he (the analysand) joins the master, becomes his herald; he copies his style, his way of speaking, his style of dress. He imitates him; this is how aware he is of not having become a psychoanalyst—that he hopes to be recognized only by these deceitful means. For the unsuccessful dissolution of the transference results in the superego not having been touched and in the continued support of his belief in a loving/hating instance which can and will recognize him. Or he will have a tremendous falling out with the analyst, be the spokesman for opposite theories, and believe himself to be radically different in his practice. But in both cases the analyst as referent remains unassailable, and the transference is neither dissolved nor analyzed. Also, both cases can be found in the history of psychoanalysis, for instance, in the formation of sects where each party accuses the other of heresy. Anyone who is even a tiny bit acquainted with French psychoanalysis will recognize this phenomenon.

The question is whether such fixations can be avoided. Because, let's assume that we reject the committee on instruction and that the analysand comes to a direct agreement with an analyst and that the analyst says to him, "We will do an analysis, but we will be able to determine only after its termination whether or not it was a teaching analysis." In this case the analysand is once again in a position of being tested, and the situation is one in which the analyst once again takes up a real position—that is, a situation in which a dissolution of the transference is weighed down by the same sort of difficulties we examined earlier. Let's now attempt to formulate this situation theoretically with the help of all of the above.

The analysand arrives with a demand: "I want to become a psychoanalyst." Once, several years ago, Lacan put a sentence on the blackboard: "Je te demande de me refuser ce que je t'offre, parce que ça n'est pas ça." "I demand that you refuse me what I give to you, because it isn't that." This is a sentence that could be used by many lovers. Everyone here is requested to apply his or her own experience. Whether or not it is necessary in love to demand the truth is not immediately at issue. But the demand is indispensable in psychoanalysis, at least in so far as the truth can be grasped. "La vérité est toujours un mi-dire." "Truth is always a half-said truth," Lacan also said.

If the analysand's request, then, is accepted, he is led in a circle, into the unending cycle of escalation: of demanding more and more in order, in the best cases, to find out that that is not what is at stake; that there is no object which stills that request and with which one can be content.

Surely we all know that the request to become a psychoanalyst is to be viewed as a symptom, and like all neurotic symptoms it both conceals and, as it were, represents a repressed wish. Psychoanalysis has given this wish the possibility to be expressed. It is for this reason that the request must not be nailed down by taking it simply as an understandable request. "It is natural that one would want to become a psychoanalyst. Psychoanalysis is an interesting, even an exciting, profession. Also, it allows one to be so effective, to help people so much to feel better inside their own skins, to alleviate so many conflicts and fears . . . " Perhaps . . .

But I'm not sure that this psychoanalysis can be a profession. When it becomes exclusively a profession, a sort of Supreme Psychotherapy, one can say in advance that in less than one generation there will be no more psychoanalysis. It's true—Freud did employ analysis as a therapeutic means, but the resistance to analysis cannot be explained by the invention of a new psychotherapy, no matter how much more effective it may be.

Freud discovered immediately, simultaneously with the discovery of the unconscious, that the causes for his patients' sufferings were to be found in their environments. Thus, psychoanalysis became a sort of accusation of society, a condemnation of culture. Psychoanalysis, in other words, cannot become a form of social welfare, cannot strive to choose as its aim to adapt people to a criminal world. The traditional values of the culture have been in part shattered by psychoanalysis. In this way, psychoanalysis cannot be viewed simply as part and parcel of this civilization without losing its identity. Psychoanalysis is not an item of consumption and the psychoanalyst is neither an industrialist nor a businessman. Psychoanalysis was, is, and, as long as it wishes to continue to be psychoanalysis, must be revolutionary. Perhaps we are breaching an area here which scientists shy away from and reject—the boundary of the political.

As long as we remain fully conscious of this, we can be sure that our reception of a patient will not end up in an acceptance of him or her. And this is where we get to the most doubtful element in our educational systems: even when the analyst is successful in remaining an analyst for the analysand and nothing but, this analysand will still find sufficient means and ways to participate in so-called psychoanalytic instruction. In this way, even if his request is not satisfied by the analyst himself, it will be satisfied by byways, by secondary transferences.

And the wish that he had been attempting to register via the demand is strangled. This analysand who will perhaps become an analyst has never encountered symbolic castration; at most he is imaginarily castrated, something he will attempt carefully to conceal, because, as far as he is concerned, this is a blemish, if not a disgrace. You can imagine what sorts of things these future analysts will hear from their patients and will have to defend against. I know that this is all schematic, practically a caricature. But is it completely inaccurate?

Do I know of a certain means of avoiding and preventing such a sorry state of affairs and aberrations? Probably not.

But if we wish to keep psychoanalysis alive we must protect its adventurous dimension. We have to know that it is often precisely our knowledge that is nothing but resistance against the surprises of the unconscious, that our training is a directed one which pushes aside undesired, because unexpected, side branches, and that our institutions are in danger of being concerned *only* with their own survival.

The aim of psychoanalysis is not to equalize and adapt analysands, but, on the contrary, to make it possible for them to achieve their own maximum differentiation. This means leading them to their own wish and allowing them to follow it to the extent to which they desire, even if in most cases they leave us in the lurch. Just as I am about to leave you in the lurch.

Notes

This is a paper given at the Psychoanalytic Seminar in Zurich on December 3, 1981.

1. Idiomatic expression signifying "to spin stories."—E. S.

2. Translated by E. S.

3. All translation from the French by Cary Plotkin.

14

Psychosis and Names

ANDRÉ MICHELS

The following pages could serve as an introduction to a reading of Schreber, to Freud's text on Schreber and to Lacan's commentary on these.[1]

Above all I have concentrated on the ways in which the edge *[le bord]* and the letter *[la lettre]* can be located in the psychotic. There will also be a few preliminary remarks on the question of the transference in the psychotic. There is a transference, but it is of a very particular kind.

We need, at the present time, an innovative clinical method—not in order to exclude theory, but rather to open it up. To listen means to take into account the radically Other. This is a challenge that we encounter not only in the psychotic. Locating that radical Other also makes possible an opening on a textual level.

But one could also go further and say that the psychoanalytic clinic must be an original clinic as it is a singular clinic: it is impossible to generalize the symptom. In order to find access to that form of listening that could found a new clinic, one must be able to expect from an analyst that he have at least traversed another discourse. It is only in that way that he can find access to the originality of the Other's speech and to record what is radically Other within it.

Voice and Psychosis

I will begin with a reflection on psychosis and the voice—not on a theoretical level, but rather as it was evoked in me by the difficulties in speaking experienced by a psychotic woman. For many years this patient had been in a phase of almost total mutism. The diagnosis of psychosis cannot be doubted: the patient had been hospitalized for a long period of time because of her delirious and hallucinatory activities. When she came to see me after leaving the hospital, she struggled with the almost total impossibility of saying anything at all. One could also say that she delivered a text without voice.

In order get closer to understanding what is at stake here one could attempt to examine what poetry tells us about the text and about writing. Isn't it true that what in the best cases constitutes poetry is its reduction to traits which only the voice—its modulations and intonations—can then supply with meaning? In poetry the voice can be found in between the letters, sometimes in between the words. The voice is the condition for reading. Most likely there exists a creative tension *between the voice and the letter* that is present from the very beginning. The "creation" itself is already an interpretation of the letter. In fact, before it became alphabetical, before it could be written, this letter had already undergone a long development: at first by marking an edge, which is not unrelated to the castration by the Other; and then by a "translation" of this edge without which we would have no means of finding access to it.

Our psychotic patient had been driven up to an absolutely impassable edge, an edge that allowed me to understand the *articulation between voice and writing* a little bit better.

Isn't the voice to be found in the first place and above all on the level *of silence, of being quiet?* The voice is not necessarily what is audible, but its falling away *[chute]* is what makes possible the articulation of speech. The function of silence is above all to interrupt the flow of speech. I am not advancing anything very original when I say that an uninterrupted flow of speech doesn't necessarily have much to say.

We must distinguish this *mutism* first of all from the *aphonia* of the hysteric in order to grasp its significance. One could compare the latter to a silent cry, to a withholding of the voice, which nevertheless addresses the one who does not wish to hear—the demand for love, for example. But there is always still the hope of making oneself heard. When the one willing to hear arrives, this voice may fall away *[chuter]* in order to become audible.

The falling away of the voice produces blanks, perforations. It produces a speech that is full of gaps. And these gaps turn up where no guarantee can be given, where all certitude is lacking. They provide a space for what is truly Other. Perhaps this allows us to understand better what it is that disturbs us about the pervert: it is the *affectedness of the voice.* It is incapable of falling out (of dropping) *[chuter],* it is like an erect phallus without which the pervert would fear that he is no more. He is incapable of renouncing it out of fear of losing himself. Sometimes the gaps appear to be filled in a superegoesque way; in those cases the voice can become authoritarian.

This authoritarian character is not necessarily communicated via the words' contents but rather by their tone. Children aren't fooled: the same words that can make them laugh can make them cry when they are spoken in a different tone.

Speech inadequately veils—or rather, is a slow unveiling of—this object of anxiety that is the voice. In addition, the way in which a person handles his or her voice tells us much about his or her relationship to anxiety.

Resistance and Reticence

This function of the voice allows us to distinguish the *resistance* that is manifest in the neurotic from the *reticence* that one observes in the psychotic. The voice betrays *what the neurotic does not want to say*. When it begins to tremble and become emotional, for example, it reveals his *resistance*.

For the psychotic the question is posed differently. He is aware of the fact that, necessarily, as soon as he begins to speak, *he gives up what he wishes to say*. This is something entirely different. His *mutism* is the expression of this *reticence*, which is the only position that remains open for him. He has no other recourse the moment he realizes that opening his mouth means losing something. He finds himself driven to that limit which he is incapable of overcoming, the limit on the other side of which all speech is mendacious. It is precisely this that the patient I am discussing wrote down, being unable to say it: "I cannot say what I think because it is not the full truth, it is not everything that I think, and it betrays [is not faithful to] that which I wish to say." Mutism is the attempt to curb a voice that cannot help but be deceitful.

And Schreber . . .

Other clinical examples teach us the importance of the *edge* [*bord*] in the psychotic and the difficulty in stepping over it. For some it is definitively impassable. In order to advance a little farther into this topic, I propose to revert to Schreber's delirium. I will start with the beginning of Freud's text, which I will precede with a sort of introduction. One can distinguish three phases in Schreber's delirium.

In the first phase the body's wholeness is being threatened. The body is fragmented and the different organs are involved in the delirium. Schreber is aware that he survives despite these bodily injuries, which would have killed anyone else. And so he is, as he says, the most extraordinary human being who has ever existed on earth.

In the second phase he reacts against this fragmentation of the body, as he does, for example, in the following sentence: "As long as I am a man, I am immortal." This is the reaction of a man who feels that his virility is being menaced, and this brings the most vulnerable point into focus. This megalomaniacal response—that is, the "I am immortal"—always emerges at the point of the most extreme fragility. Everything that is said about the body and its different parts is a translation of the threat that is directed, above all, at the male organ. These are all displacements onto other body parts, or onto the body as a whole. The aim is to turn attention away from the organ that is really being menaced. The latter is safeguarded by this costly—because delirious—operation. We should establish here that what is called *fragmentation of the body image* is not a primitive psychotic phenomenon; instead, it already constitutes a reaction to another threat aimed at one very precise body part.

This part refuses to be made negative and therefore remains specular. The stroke of the cut *[trait de coupure]* is displaced onto other organs. When the psychotic speaks of the end of the world, he is simply translating this threat, because when the body is threatened in its integrity, everything dissolves. Schreber has saved his virility, but has done so at the price of the integrity of his body image.

The psychotic, then, is lacking an imaginary or narcissistic prop, which can function only when one part of the body is not represented. Or, to paraphrase Lacan: the body image constitutes itself around a central part which remains aspecular. One could say the same thing in yet another way: the unity of the body image is founded on the negatability of one of its parts. Only when this is the case can a totalizing image come into being.

The Birth of Art

In this connection one could formulate some reflections on the *birth of art*. Art comes into being the moment representation not only makes room for a gap, a blank, but also when it is determined by the unrepresentable, by that which can be neither represented nor recuperated in any shape or form. It would not be exaggerated to speak of an "umbilicizing" *[ombilication]* of the image.

What in the body image radically evades representation? It is the letters that are inscribed onto the body. One could go even further: it is *the letters of the name*. To go back to our discussion of art, one can see this in the exhibit, *The Birth of Cubism*, which is presently taking place in Basel.[2] At stake in this exhibit is, first, the dialogue between two painters, Picasso and Braque, who were later joined by a third painter, Juan Gris, who is the great absentee in this exhibit. The body does not necessarily become proportionately more stylized or abstracted as the work of these two painters progresses, but rather, it fragments into such a plurality of planes that it becomes impossible to reconstitute its unity. It is lost. In addition, the body now appears increasingly more complex. This complexity increases to the point that not only is the body split into different parts, but, in addition, these parts themselves are fragmented almost into infinity. The result is that the more one attempts to represent the different body parts, the more unavoidably one bumps up against the unrepresentable and the more numerous do the body parts evading all representability become.

On the one hand, then, loss of unity in the body image, on the other, loss of a perhaps infinite number of body parts. But things don't stop there. At a certain moment—I no longer remember which painting marks the beginning—letters appear on the canvas, and they appear at the edges of all those cut up planes of the body. They form neither a body nor unity or meaning, but they are open to interpretation.

What is a Letter?

If we now return to the more clinical realm, we can say that this letter is not necessarily an alphabetical one. It corresponds to an *edge (rim)*—Lacan says, a *littoral*,[3] a written *trace [trace écrite]*, whose function changes according to its structure.

I will review these different structures as rapidly as possible.

In *hysterics*, the traces of the cuts *[découpage]* in the body determine the lines of both their suffering and their *jouissance*. One can speak here of a *"lettre en souffrance."*[4]

In the *pervert*, one encounters the fetishized letter, the often *very important production of letters/texts* the aim of which is to withdraw them from translation. They correspond to a *trace* which must by no means be erased; translation would constitute the greatest danger for the pervert. But a trace that must not or cannot be erased is not a trace.

In the *psychotic* the letter appears on the level of the breaking points of the body image and menaces its unity. Here the letter has a *persecutory function*.

This is what the third phase of Schreber's delirium teaches us. It marks an important stage which Schreber himself introduces with the following words: "The month of November, 1895, meant a turning point in my life history, and ever since then I have been unable to accord my circumstances, my prospects for the future, and so on, the same meaning."

Schreber now accepts the idea of his unmanning, which is tied in with his becoming a woman. This third phase appears with extreme punctuality: in November of 1895 Schreber is exactly as old as his father was at the time of his death. Feminization is a sort of compromise, which he is now ready to make. At the moment that he accepts this cut, a cut that, he says, is terrible and unspeakable (these are Schreber's own words), the threats that had been aimed at his entire body cease. One can hypothesize that his hypochondria—the diagnosis that had been made during his first hospitalization—resulted from the displacement of the threat of castration onto other body parts.

Hypochondria

One can observe that in the speech of some men hypochondriacal worries appear at very precise historical moments. I am thinking in particular of a patient who consulted me for severe prostate pain. He had previously seen a number of urologists who had all submitted him to the same exam—a rectal examination, which embarrassed him.

He had experienced these exams both as attempts at seduction, and thus as connected with a degree of *jouissance*, and as aggression, against which he defended himself rigorously.

His first prostate pains had appeared towards the end of his adolescence, when he had begun going out with a young woman his age. He had invented all sorts of stratagems to avoid having to have sex with her. It is not difficult to see on what level he had felt threatened. The threat of castration had been displaced onto the most proximate organ—the prostate, in this case.

Of course, hypochondria can appear in other guises and can involve other organs. It can at times provide protection against delirium, as a sort of last rampart, and at other times be a first indication of delirium. In Schreber one can see that it can develop into an unequivocally hypochondriacal delirium.

One must distinguish three things concerning these somatic manifestations. The *hysterical symptom* is characterized by a certain *jouissance* of the trace, the markings on the body, which, however, in most cases, remains easily translatable as it is not fixed.

This is the opposite of what occurs in the *pervert*, who solders *jouissance* to the trace. For example, he leaves inextinguishable traces on the body of the Other in his vain attempt at "making an inscription."

In *psychosomatic phenomena* the somatic illness attempts to inscribe a real trace that up until then had not found the slightest foothold.

On the level of *hypochondria*, which we wish to study here, the inscription of the trace is experienced as aggression, in other words, in a persecutory mode. It is absolutely necessary to take account of the context, which alone allows us to recognize the true meaning of the somatic manifestation. There is a search for a compromise between a number of different demands. Hypochondria is the negative recognition of castration through displacement onto other organs. But the effort to find a somatic support for the cut, the trace, the letter, whose inscription is nowhere secure, is gigantic, sometimes even desperate.

This may allow us to say a word or two about the foreclosure of castration or the Name-of-the-Father. The psychotic suffers from the crucial absence of an inscription of the letter on the level of the body of the Other. It is as if he had to force this inscription onto his own body.

In order to correctly situate the originality of the psychotic's response, one must return to the manner in which the neurotic reacts to the question of castration. He encounters it on the level of the body of the Other; hence the crucial importance the encounter with the other sex has for him. For the rest, the manner in which the preceding generations have handed down castration is determining. If he is capable of taking his reading there, he will be able to transcend his own individual history.

The psychotic, we said, encounters the absence of an inscription, of the trace, in the realm of the Other. This is what one may call a *foreclosure of the letter*. He finds himself in the absolutely impossible situation of attempting to inscribe a letter that has never been there. It is as if he himself had to become the Other in order to make it exist, as if he had to wear the mark of the letter on his own body. The body becoming the material support of the letter also means handing it over to the letter's cruelty. It happens that the psychotic may actively mark his body through maiming or castration. One can encounter this in the melancholiac, who sometimes appears on the depressive side of paranoia.

Hypochondria is a phase that precedes this delirious behavior. It can last a long time, sometimes a life long. I now return to my clinical example and to the context of the appearance of its symptoms. It appears at a very precise point in the subject's history. A masturbation gone out of control during adolescence is accompanied by great feelings of guilt, coupled with the conviction that it will have deferred effects, that it will leave him with unerasable signs. On top of that there is an absolute refusal to have sexual relations with a woman. This is the cause of the rupture with his first fiancée. With the second woman, his future wife, he succeeds in postponing his first sexual relations with her until after marriage. A third factor that lends the situation its characteristic tone is the fear of being a homosexual. For a long time this fear lies at the center of his preoccupations. It emerges again and again during the course of his sessions. When this factor appears in a dream, he finally allows it to be transformed.

I here end my exposé of this clinical situation, which I have related in order to demonstrate and illustrate the meaning of hypochondria. It is a sign that announces paranoia and defends against it at the same time. Homosexuality plays an ambiguous role in this context. It is experienced with great feelings of guilt but is simultaneously meant to serve as protection against castration. It is not impossible that fear of homosexuality corresponds to an inverse form of the fear of castration.

The Delirious Metaphor

In closing, I wish to return briefly to the third phase of Schreber's delirium. His becoming a woman represents an attempt to either step over an edge or to translate a trace. This allows Schreber to take a decisive step but one that remains on the level of delirium. It is legitimate, therefore, to speak of a *delirious metaphor*. It allows Schreber to accede virtually to a castration that, in a distant future, will make him a woman. The point of this entire operation is to find access to a lineage . . . in a delirious manner. It is beginning with this primary demand for lineage—Schreber speaks of "the absolute imperative of a world order" that a reading of his delirium may be attempted.

Notes

1. Prefatory remarks by André Michels on his translation from French into German:

"The author works with a number of terms that are not in current use in German psychoanalysis. Beginning with the term letter/*la lettre*, they constitute a metonymic net: *bord*/rim, edge, seam *[Rand, Kante, Saum]*—*trait*/trait, stroke, line *[Zug, Strich, Linie]*—*trace*/trace, track, trail, remainder *[Spur, Fährte, Überbleibsel]*—*découpe*/cut-out *[Ausschnitt, Tranche]*—*découper*/to cut out, to punch out, to carve out *[ausschneiden, ausstanzen, tranchieren]*—*chute*/fall, dissolution, decline *[Fall, Auflösung, Untergang]*—*chuter*/to fall, to dissolve, to decline, and to go under, to disappear *[fallen, sich auflösen, untergehen, verschwinden]*.

"The step Lacan takes from the letter as the "material prop" for the signifier to the letter as the latter's "inner exteriority" shifts into focus the concreteness *[ein Diesseits]* of linguistic metaphoricity; what is at stake here is the concrete interwovenness [entanglement] of language, writing, and the body. What appears from the point of view of meaningful speech—from the perspective of "intellect" or "psyche"—to be external, incidental, or arbitrary—trait, trace, the rim of writing—turns out to be the kernel or bone of that paternal metaphor in which the meaning effects of linguistic metaphoricity are anchored. This step, so decisive for clinical "psychosomatics" in its widest sense, needs to be effected through a reading of the Seminars that are still largely unknown in this country: "L'identification," "L'angoisse," "D'un discours qui ne serait pas du semblant," "Encore," "RSI," and "Le Sinthome."

"A warning seems relevant here: an isolated translation of a clinical text runs the risk of being read in a remetaphorized register of the "like," "as if," "in the sense of." But what is at issue here, before these traces, rims, levels, and so on are translated into a "psychic" register, are in fact nothing but traces, rims and levels—the topology of the body, in other words. In order to urge for a reading that is as literal, bland *[geistkarg]*, and unspirited *[seelenlos]* as possible, I have often added the original key words in brackets."

2. 1991.

3. [Original translator's note]: littoral = coast, coastal strip; alliteration with *lettre* = letter (in both senses).

4. [Original translator's note]: a letter that has not reached its destination; *souffrance* in its usual sense, i.e., suffering; allusion to Lacan's famous text, "La lettre volée."

Part IV

Philosophical

Introduction

Maire Jaanus and Elizabeth Stewart

To Samuel Weber, in his essay, "Vertigo: the Question of Anxiety in Freud," "sacrifice" means primarily sacrifice of the metaphysical and essentializing notions of meaning, sense, time—even anxiety itself. He establishes anxiety and the legitimacy of anxiety relating to the persistence of meaning throughout time as the center of Freudian theory. This is in part an essay that is critical of Lacan, whom Weber accuses of imposing closure on Freud's rigorously deconstructive work on anxiety. Weber also advocates, somewhat polemically, perhaps, the return to Freud's German text in reaction to the closure that most of his translators have sought to impose on it. While Weber's essay seems in part to act as a foil to most of the other essays in this volume, as it moves somewhat away from the others' emphasis on the body and the Real, its focus is nevertheless trauma and the ethics that are founded on it. Weber's emphasis on the constant redissolving of meaning by the interplay of signifier and signified links this essay to that of Sebastian Leikert, but he goes on to link this to the death drive, the fundamental rhythm of the drives, and, most importantly, to anxiety. Anxiety in Weber's—and he claims, Freud's—theory is both the creator and destroyer of meaning and signification. Freud began and ended his discourse with anxiety: first in order to unseat the reigning authorities in the field of neuropsychiatry, and then in order to dissolve the growing deification and ossification of his discourse on the part of his disciples. What Weber decries—and this is one reason why he celebrates, in this early essay (1982), the dawning influence of Lacan on literary academics in the United States—is the forgetting of the fundamental "impossibility" of psychoanalysis: the anxiety-producing inevitable slippage of the signified under the "impossible" reign of the signifier is related to the impossible relation of the empirical ego to the pure law, as it is discussed by Bernard Baas in this volume,

197

as well as to the impossibility of the Thing which is the topic of Alain Juranville's essay. The core of Weber's essay is his ingenious understanding of anxiety: while anxiety refers to a traumatic hole in signification, a hole in the signifying chain, it also creates meaning when, belatedly *(nachträglich)*, anxiety attempts to bind excitation into meaning whenever traumatic dissolution threatens to return. Weber shows us that the structure of meaning mimics (rather than being identical with—an impossibility in itself) the structure of trauma and anxiety. This literally maddening structure is the seat of ethics: while misrecognition is necessary in order to create meaning, the ethical act is finally to recognize that binding, that creation of meaning, as misrecognition. Hence Weber's German title: in "Der Schwindel: zur Frage der Angst bei Freud," *Schwindel* means both "vertigo" and "swindle." The suggestion is, then, that the ethical act consists of the always repeated recognition of vertigo: feeling that one is falling into the abyss without actually doing so. The "danger" of vertigo is at least double as well: almost falling is "dangerous," but not doing so is even more so. This danger will be seen to be central to the final four essays in this volume.

Michael Jackson's cuts and scars (Leikert), the hypochondriac's bodily pain as sacrifice to the Other (Michels), and acts of self-mutilation in an attempt to "pacify," to hold things together (notably, a precarious body image), while they are the signs of a psychotic relation to the letter of the law, are also the signs of the subject's self-sacrifice to the Other. The central image of Hans-Dieter Gondek's essay, "From the Protective Shield against Stimuli to the Fantasm: A Reading of Chapter 4 of *Beyond the Pleasure Principle*," is the image of the scar: previously living tissue is deadened, turned into scar tissue, as a defense against (re-)traumatization. It is also Gondek's image for the act of sacrifice. He traces this notion of sacrifice, a sacrifice that is performed for the survival of the subject and the establishment of the subject's sense of time, back to chapter 4 of Freud's *Beyond the Pleasure Principle*. After following Freud's turn to Kant and his categories of time and space, Gondek goes on to show how these same categories are created by the subject by way of the fantasm, and are often embodied: Gondek reads Freud's "protective shield" the barrier against a traumatic onslaught of stimuli, as the "sacrificial lamb" of the "living vesicle," the *Bläschen*: it is a piece of "the inside" turned inside out and deadened, turned into a scar, and used to ward off death (trauma), so that the scar of death protects against death. This scar, which protects against the full encounter with the Real, and which becomes the prototype for the fantasm as barrier, even as it itself consists of what it wards off, establishes the subject's sense of time—a peculiar sense of time, discovered by Freud already in his work on dreams. This unconscious time is shaped by deferment *(Nachträglichkeit)* and repetition, that is, by primal trauma, experienced belatedly and defended against by repetition. In this sense time has been established on the basis of trauma and of a more or less literal scar. (Compare Weber's definition of the structure and function of anxiety.) Gondek does not go into this, but much could be made of the significance of this understanding of the constellation of trauma/anxiety/scar/ time given the present pervasiveness of "cutting" among young people, especially as the scar as fantasm is simultaneously imaginary, symbolic, and real, as Gondek proposes quite convincingly. We might ask why it is that our present culture seems to provoke the production and sacrifice of fantasms that are so directly related to a scene of trauma and so closely in contact with the Real. Whatever the case may be, the sacrifice Gondek describes is ultimately that of the subject making itself the object of the Other.

Bernard Baas's essay, "Sacrifice and Law," one of the most demanding essays in this collection and one of the essays directly relating to the Holocaust and the psychoanalysis of genocide, attempts to explain the fascination that the idea of sacrifice exerts. Sacrifice, for all of the theorists (Hegel, Kant, Sade, Bataille, Mauss, Hubert, Girard, Vernant, Détienne, Durand, and so on), including Lacan, that Baas examines, involves the "pathological object" and its sacrifice in an illusory attempt to reach the Sovereign, the Sublime, and this process of sacrifice is linked to the process of identification (the sacrificer's identification with the sacrifice itself, the drive to become one with the One, the Sublime, the Thing). When the goal is identification with the Thing itself rather than with the *objet a* or with its "scar" (to relate this argument to Gondek's), we might say, all hell breaks loose. Sacrifice is therefore closely associated with what Jacques Derrida in a similar context[1] has called "the worst"— a spellbinding fascination with reaching the Thing and with sacrifice as the extermination of difference and distance for the Other. It has also to do with attempting (illusorily) to obtain what is impossible: the purity of the law. Attempting to reach the latter always involves exceeding the limit of what is allowed to subjects; it means penetrating into, pushing through to, *extimacy*, which is what Lacan calls the process of choosing a sacrificial object that is both an object that is articulated within the chain of signifiers, the empirical order, but that as *object a* of the sacred, is also that which is "intimately excluded" from that order and which, by way of its sacrifice, pretends to promise access to "sacredness" *(Heiligkeit)*. This process is, of course, more commonly known as "scapegoating," or as the construction of the Jew, or any other, as "pathological object." Sacrifice, then, Baas suggests, would disavow the subject's split existence by way of the sacrifice of the idea of difference and distance and thus represent the worst temptation—what Lacan has called the "dark god." Baas writes, "This impossible Thing, which, in human experience, orders the sacrifice, is, in human experience, simultaneously its *source*, its limit, and its threat." Attempting to enter sacredness by way of sacrifice necessarily means the former's disappearance. This brings us back to Peter Widmer's reference to the *akeda* in his essay on Tell and to Yahweh's lesson for Abraham: the law demands sacrifice, but it does not mean real sacrifice. The extimate object belongs to the play of signifiers in both the empirical and symbolic orders so as to make symbolic play possible and guarantee it. As soon as the *object a,* which points both to the Thing and to the order of empirical objects, is made concrete and literally sacrificed, the sacred order loses its symbolic nature. It is now illusorily ruled by the Thing and becomes sheerly murderous.

Peter Widmer's second essay in this collection, "Freud and Democracy," takes the more explicitly political route in the context of the law and violence. He also sticks closely to the late pessimistic Freud in whom he finds the essential seeds for Lacan's late ethics of psychoanalysis. Widmer's reading of Freud's *Civilization and Its Discontents* represents the latter as a modernist text: civilization is a human impossibility, as the death drive silently organizes (and threatens) all human structures. The origin of democracy itself is found again and again in the act of killing the one who wants to be the exception and impose his authority, the primal father. Freud by way of Widmer thereby reveals an intractable Manichean structure within the human psyche, split into victim and victimizer, which translates into social structures in which the majority of humans love to cower before the cruel superego, the violent law, the despotic, murderous master. While obsessives struggle against authorities or become passively submissive, hysterics remain fixated on authorities and seek their protection. But, as Widmer says, neurotics have fundamentally a disturbed and distorting relation to democratic life. Thus, there can be no democracy. However, true psychoanalysis must take on a political role: it is to struggle to allow sublimation to confront symptoms and fantasms. This is something the psychoanalyst must learn himself (in his own analysis), and it is theoretically the aim of all analysis: to overcome the transference, to recognize the analyst as a fellow subject, a brother/sister with whom the analysand learns to interact democratically, instead of wanting to offer himself up, sacrifice himself, to the master. The truest democracy, then, is what emerges, theoretically, in psychoanalysis.

This last act—the analytical recognition of the commonality of symptoms—comes to define the act of sublimation: the ethics of psychoanalysis.

Alain Juranville, in his essay "The Lacanian Thing," sees that psychoanalysis, by its questioning of traditional sublimation and the sacrificial violence that characterizes it, opens history and inaugurates new possibilities for sublimation. Traditional sublimation hid the truth of the lack of truth for us in the world. Because psychoanalytic discourse, by contrast, exposes this and fundamentally grasps, and uncovers as well, the various ways in which the Thing, which cannot be encountered, haunts us and makes itself present in desire, discourse, and sexual relations as an impossible demand for infinite sublimation, it introduces the possibility of a break with the traditional world. Analytic discourse is in essence political, though this politics of psychoanalysis is a slow affair without campaigns and platforms. It lays bare the operations of the fantasm and its structure of the one who desires and the one who becomes the object of desire and describes analytic sublimation as that which effaces the Thing as the "Highest Good" (but also the worst) and forestalls the danger of literal sacrifice. This sublimation takes the shape of the subject's sacrifice to his neurosis that takes place at the end of a successful analysis. Surrender to neurosis, Juranville suggests, means deflection: being caught up in hatred for and rivalry with the prohibitor, thereby covering up the real desire for the Thing, which unleashes the death drive. Another mode of finite sublimation, writing (for there is passion at the heart of every signifier), refers us back to André Michels's essay. In comparing the two essays, we can see the difference between neurotic and psychotic writing. The psychotic relationship to the letter involves actual inscription of bodies: various individual and historical instances come to mind, from self-mutilation (cf. Hans-Dieter Gondek, Sebastian Leikert, and Christian Kläui), to branding, to the inscribed bodies in concentration camps, so uncannily previewed by Kafka, for example, in his story, "In the Penal Colony." Neurotic and sublimatory writing, by contrast, steps away from the body and to the piece of paper. Juranville is also implicitly referring to Lacan's fascination with Joyce and the function of non-sense in his texts to provide enjoyment beyond meaning, but an enjoyment that does not become real for that reason. The nonsymbolic makes its way into writing instead of writing making its way into the realm of bodies. Yet another sublimator, according to Juranville, is woman; whatever one may think of this definition of "woman" as somehow more mystical than "man," or the masculine insistence on sense, the analyst, in Juranville's scheme, takes the position of woman, though finally, the analyst is the Thing that must be sublimated. Analytic discourse is a third mode of necessary historical sublimation in that it undoes sacrifice to absolute sense and absolute truth, and demands instead sacrifice of absolute sense, a surrender to the irreducibility of non-sense, and the questioning of the "illusory character of this whole world where everything has been given meaning."

Notes

1. Jacques Derrida, "The Force of Law: The Mystical Foundation of Authority," *Cardozo Law Review*, 11 (1990).

15

Vertigo: The Question of Anxiety in Freud

Samuel Weber

I

In stark contrast to some other Parisian trends in the realm of the intellect, the name "Lacan" does not cease to fascinate. But it seems—at least, this has been the case in the last few years—that the nature of this fascination seems to be changing. In the United States, where Lacan became famous rather early on—around 1966, the year in which the Structuralism Conference at Johns Hopkins took place—this reception was largely due to the literary establishment, which in its reception of him branded him correspondingly. The first English translations of Lacan were encouraged by Romance scholars such as Eugenio Donato, whose doctoral student Anthony Wilden edited Lacan's *Discours de Rome* and published it in conjunction with an elaborate commentary which is still considered exemplary. The reasons for this reception of Lacan by the literary establishment, which was repeated somewhat later within the German-speaking academy, had, above all, to do with language: Romance literature scholars, and then, among them, only those who had studied Mallarmé, were the only ones who escaped becoming lost in Lacan's stylistic peculiarities because they were able to find in it the play-on-words tradition so deeply rooted in Romance literature. This was the case even when most of the same literary scholars had very little background in those other sources where Lacanian thought and writing find their inspiration—on the one hand, in Western philosophy, from Plato through Descartes to Hegel, Husserl, and Heidegger, and, on the other hand, of course, in Freud.

What does it mean, then, when a thinker such as Lacan is received positively by people who are largely lacking not only in the conceptual "background" but also in the theoretical and practical "foreground"—that is, in knowledge of the works of Freud and the psychoanalytic practice in which those works originated?

Once it has been verbalized, this question needs to be complemented by a second one, which ties in again with my initial observation. If it seems that the reception of Lacan's work has undergone a change in recent years then that is because the first reception, which had been shaped by literary scholars, is being not replaced but complemented by the interest of certain practicing analysts themselves (analysts who are only partially trained in literature, such as Stuart Schneiderman in New York, Norbert Haas in Berlin, or Peter Widmer here in Zurich). So my second question goes as follows: what does it mean when, as seems to be the case so far, a literarily shaped reception of Lacan is not exactly being "relieved of its duty" but complemented by a directly psychoanalytic—in the practical/professional meaning of the word—reception? And my answer is: it means nothing but a confrontation with the question of meaning itself—the meaning of psychoanalysis, meaning *in* psychoanalysis, the meaning of Freud, and meaning in Freud, as well as the meaning of the Lacanian "return" to him.

In short, by way of this shift in the reception of Lacan, one encounters again a question which is no longer new, especially not in the English-speaking world: the question regarding the "meaning of meaning," which had been investigated by the semanticists Ogden and Richards already in 1923 in their book of the same title.[1] But it is precisely this reference to what has long been known that can enable us to recognize what is special and new about this question to which Lacan has led us. The authors of the book, *The Meaning of Meaning*, dedicated a few of its pages to Saussure in which they suggested that the Genevan linguist was quite useless to the semanticists from Oxford because he was completely unscientific. They found this lack of scientificity to be apparent already in Saussure's conception of the sign, which they criticized, and they did so in a way that, in my opinion, is far more discerning than some of Saussure's disciples have been and which in some ways anticipated Lacan's reading of Saussure, even if theirs did so negatively. For what Ogden and Richards found fault with, and yet verified, in Saussure is the fact that his conception of the sign as the connection between signifier and signified was precisely not just *descriptive* but *interpretive*: "Without the concept [Saussure] says, the acoustic image (*signifiant*) would not be a sign. The disadvantage of this account is, as we shall see, that the process of interpretation is included by definition in the sign!"[2]

You will surely already have figured out in what way this determination of the hermeneutic moment in the Saussurian conception of the sign anticipates Lacan, but since this point is important for my further argument, I will permit myself to elaborate on it briefly. The conceptually meaningful dimension of the sign, Saussure maintained, becomes what it is only through a process of articulation that includes both the reference to and the movement of signifiers. There can be no signifier without signified, but neither can there be a signified without a signifier. But above all, it is impossible to conceive of either signified or signifier without the play of differences by which linguistic—semiotic—value is determined. On the other hand, if, as Saussure insists, "arbitrary" and "differential" indeed imply each other and are inseparable, the consequence is that state of affairs which was destroyed in the most astonishing manner by that grapheme of Lacan's which literally stands Saussure's formula for the sign on its head—on its head and not, as one might think, on its feet. For the gesture with which Lacan literally reverses the hierarchy of signified and signifier in which it is no longer the meaning—the signified—that sits on top, placed over the signifier, but the latter that sits on top of the signified—this reversal marks nothing less than a revolution in the history of thought which by itself lends Lacan's return, though not only his, its specific sense ("sense" is here to be understood in the "sense" of the French *sens*, "direction," or, following German etymology, in the "sense" in which *Sinn* once meant "journey," "way"—sint—and thus: desire).

In any case, one can understand the turning around (*Umkehrung*) of this return (*Umkehr*) fully only when one notes that it also and above all brings with it a turning upside down (*Verkehrung*): that is, it means reading Saussure's discussion of the differential nature of the processes of the sign in the way it was first read by Lacan and then by Derrida, with the understanding, that is, that, as Derrida already said in his *Of Grammatology*, the signified (as the product of the play of differential relations) must "always already have been a signifier" in order to have become a signified; this means taking up a position that can't really be taken, that can only be more or less occupied, and I mean that in Freud's sense of "cathected." A position of this sort is in itself fundamentally turned upside down, because the signified does not represent just any given concept but rather the linguistic possibility of conceptuality itself insofar as the latter is grounded in some kind of principle of identity. But once the signified, as the linguistic manifestation *and* the possibility of identity in general, becomes itself an effect of the signifier, the ground of all meaning is turned upside down, since it can no longer ground (or find the grounds for); it is no longer a First Cause, but may itself, from now on, be understood merely as something derivative without even allowing one to hope to ever get to the bottom [*Grund*] of this derivation, unless it be the bottomless abyss [this is an untranslatable pun; the German word for "abyss" here is *Abgrund*—E. S.]. But terms such as "abyss" or, in French, *béance*, still seem to me terms that are too determined and too static to articulate that motion of turning upside down that is being turned out (*hervorgekehrt*) here. Within this turning upside down one finds oneself in a sort of antinomy, since it is impossible to conceive of the signifier without it being grounded in the signified and vice versa. But when the signified depends in a radical manner on the movement of the signifier, it hangs suspended in the air, since in order to be or become movement, it must be oriented, it must measure itself against something other, something firm. Without such measurement all movement becomes not only immeasurable but also constant: in other words, it insists on its own way to such an extent that one can no longer determine whether or not it has become a dead end. So if there is no firm point that acts as a measure, all movement stalls and becomes what one usually refers to as "bare" (*bloße*) repetition—as if that explained matters. But within such "bare" repetition something does indeed get bared, something that has to do with rhythm and with death; in other words, with what Freud described both as the death drive and the pleasure principle, and about which he finally maintained that it ought to be understood as a *rhythmic distribution* of tension and release rather than as their quantitative increase or decrease.[3]

Formally turning the relation between signifier and signified upside down means that the latter can be determined only by not recognizing the fact that it belongs to the chain of signifiers. Where It (*Er*)—the signifier—was, there shall It (*Es*)—the signified—be [*er*, masculine pronoun, referring to der Signifikant (the signifier), and *es*, neuter pronoun, referring to das Signifikat (the signified). —E. S.]. Or more precisely, since this process does not develop according to conscious time but occurs unconsciously, one would have to say: "Where It (*Er*) was, It (*Es*) shall have become." But now we can see why we are not talking about a meaningful reversal but rather a turning upside down of meaning itself. For It (*Es*)—the signified—must simultaneously always already have been "there" so that there can be any signifiers at all, even though it must always already have been a signifier itself in order to have been capable of becoming a signified.

The ambivalence of Lacan's turning-upside-down is, in other words, the result of the fact that it poses the question not only of the signifier but of the signified as well. The significant question that poses itself from within Lacan's writings for us then goes: *How does a signifier become a signified? Or: How do signifieds come into being?*

My answer to this will be just as simple: through *anxiety*. Even more: the turning upside down that transforms the signifier into the signified occurs not only *via* anxiety, but simultaneously *as* anxiety. Theoretically it takes place—for us, at least, and here and now—in the writings of Freud. Practically, on the other hand, it actually takes place in the texts of Lacan. Allow me now to explain these astonishing statements a little. Only that way will I be able to return back to my initial observations concerning the present-day reception of Lacan in a way that may be helpful for future research.

II

But before we get to the topic of anxiety, let's for a moment think about how the emergence of a signified has to be conceptualized from a Saussurean point of view. The signified constitutes itself as the product of the play of differential relations to other signifiers: the meaning of *mouton* compared with the English "mutton," for example, is determined by the fact that French contains no words that mark the difference between "edible—inedible," while the English words "mutton" and "sheep" designate these different aspects of the same animal. This example, used by Saussure, shows, at least on the verbal level, how the process of differentiation which creates the meaning of a word (that is, the signified) also contains a play of the signifier. Or, more precisely: it is possible to maintain that the term "signified" designates only one or several signifiers which have been extricated from the differential relations to enable other signifiers to be determinable. By "determinable" I understand not only "meaningful," but rather generally articulable, that is, something that belongs to articulated language. Because if there were not at least the overall possibility of referring such constructions to a signified, one could hardly consider them signifiers; they would really be something more akin to arabesques, senseless figures. What results, however, is not only paradoxical but, even more importantly, ambivalent: namely, that in order to recognize signifiers their relation to signifieds has to be simultaneously recognized and misrecognized. For the condition for the possibility of being able to talk about definite signifiers and signifieds is that other definite signifiers and signifieds must *not* be talked about. Inclusion is possible only through exclusion; Lacan's Other—capital O—whose discourse, as we know, Lacan determined to be the unconscious, says nothing else. It is for this reason that the Other is described spatially, as the locked off area of the chain of signifiers, for instance, because this barrier and this someplace-else point to the delimitation whereby the subject constitutes itself linguistically; it does so always in reference to that place that can never quite be reached, a place [*Ort*] I have once described as an "outhouse" [*Abort* = privy].[4]

(Put differently: in order to determine signifiers, one has to relate them to a signified. But this signified consists of words. When one defines a word through the use of predicates, one determines it via other words. For these other words to have a defining, determining effect, their meaning has somehow to be viewed as rooted. The signified, in other words, has to be disentangled from the movement of signifiers even as it still remains related to it, because otherwise it would have no meaning. The result is something that I wish to call ambivalence: that one must remain in a state of reference to an other which one must simultaneously deny and misrecognize in order not to lose oneself in a sort of infinite regress. This process, by the way, seems to have much in common with what Freud called "isolation" in *Inhibitions, Symptoms and Anxiety*.)[5]

The fact that the signified must always be ambivalent in the Freudian sense of the word and the way in which it is so can be clarified by recalling two paradigms used by Saussure. Saussure, if you recall, compares *la langue*, the linguistic system, to both a dictionary and a game of chess; he does so in both cases in order to illustrate the synchronic boundedness of *la langue* in contrast to the diachronic effect of the *parole* [an utterance within that system of language—E. S.] as well as of writing. Saussure's determination of difference as the linguistic principle of articulation, that is, that which gives signs their specific linguistic value, on the other hand, turns these examples around into their opposites. Instead of demonstrating the synchronic nature of *la langue*, the examples really demonstrate their diachronic susceptibility—not just superficially by chance, but rather out of an internal necessity. So if *la langue* is comparable to a dictionary, immediately the question is raised whether one should imagine this dictionary independently of how the dictionary is used. By "use" I mean not some sort of special application but rather the general way and means that precede such a special use; the way in which every conceivable dictionary must be used when one searches through it for the meaning of a word, which occurs along the lines of Saussure's theory of signs. When one is looking for the meaning of a word one looks at the different definitions of that word in those places in the dictionary where they are given. But where are those "places"? For the definitions consist of other words or sentences or phrases. These, in turn, are made meaningful only by combining them with other words used predicatively, and so on. In the final analysis, in order to understand a word correctly, one is referred to (and dependent upon) all other words in a given language, to an inherently unlimited and unlimitable number of word combinations from which one must make a selection, but this means also *excluding* elements in order to be able to include anything to begin with. If this sounds abstract, all you need to do is think of what occurs when one learns a foreign language, where it is precisely the unfamiliarity of the language that makes the problem of correct selection when using the dictionary such a frequent experience (compare, for example, the use of a dictionary that translates a foreign language into one's own with the use of one that defines only within the foreign language). If one is not always conscious of this moment of selection, or exclusion, when using language, that is because one allows oneself to be led by certain conventions whose raison d'être is to limit the play of signifiers from the start. Such conventions concern not only the meanings of individual words, but also—and this is far more important—the expectation that language consist essentially of words, that is, of signs that are both homogeneous and meaningful. For if one identifies articulated language a priori with a language of words and sentences. (as one must and by and large does in everyday functional situations), one is obeying a powerful social convention, but one is also misrecognizing the process by which such words and sentences come into being: this does not occur by an isolated consciousness sighting an equally isolated object in order to then express it in language; rather, it occurs by way of a number of signifiers being brought together and included into a signified through the exclusion of others. It is only this inclusion that enables one to even conceive of what we call an object.[6]

So if *la langue* is a dictionary, then this book, like every other book, is inconceivable apart from its use, just as the value of a sign is constituted by its relation to other signs. But these relations, even if they are not created by single subjects as individuals, do not exist separately from the process of inclusion and exclusion which determines them. And each one of these inclusions and exclusions contains within itself a given relation to the Other, both to the other subject and to the other place, the "outhouse," a relation that can be nothing but ambivalent—ambivalent in the sense of an agonistic game. Because Otherness must always be excluded for inclusion to take place, it is always misrecognized in order to be recognized. But this can succeed only insofar as one misrecognizes not only what one does, but also *that* one does so. This model can be understood in terms of Freud's dream analysis, especially in relation to the function of "secondary revision"—I only have time to point to it here.

And now I come to Saussure's second example, the chess game, which also allows for a reading that is totally different from the one that was apparently intended by him. Within Saussure's argument, you may recall, the chess game is supposed to illustrate the synchronic condition of language. The value or meaning of the constellation of the chess pieces on the chessboard, Saussure maintains, can be understood without paying heed to the diachronic dimension of time. In this contention, however, Saussure excludes exactly what is essential to chess in this example of his: the fact, that is, that what is inalienably proper to the game of chess is that it is played by *two* players, and that they play against each other, and therefore that every "constellation" is inherently *split by the move*; in this way the chess game is agonistically split and simultaneously opened up from within to that diachronous heterogeneity which Saussure otherwise links only with the *parole* or with writing. This way, however, Saussure's *jeu d'échecs* turns into a true *jeu d'échec*, that is, a game of failure, but to a game which can really only succeed as failure. For it is because of it that Saussure's attempt to banish the signifier into the solid frame of a synchronous structure, and thereby to determine it as the object of a bounded science, fails. Simultaneously, however, it demonstrates that the power of the signifier cannot even be thought without such a failure, for the signifier can determine itself only by excluding others to which it then remains implicitly related.

All of this perhaps explains why the most radical insights like those at which Saussure labored, but also those of Freud and Lacan, necessarily allow themselves to be recognized as misrecognition, and that for this reason recognition and misrecognition are by no means simple opposites. For when the signified is determined only by that Other which it excludes, then every meaning would have to constitutively misrecognize that through which it is made possible to begin with and which is ultimately its aim. In other words, one can recognize something only by wanting to know nothing of the Other and by not knowing about this not-wanting-to-know.

III

We now turn once again to the question of anxiety, which engaged Freud from the beginning to the end of his work. Halfway through this work, in his synoptic *Introductory Lectures on Psychoanalysis*, Freud presented the problem of anxiety to his audience as follows: "[T]here is no question that the problem of anxiety is a nodal point at which the most various and important questions converge, a riddle whose solution would be bound to throw a flood of light on our whole mental existence."[7]

No one knew better that the problem of anxiety is a "riddle" and simultaneously a "nodal point" than Freud, who had been working on this riddle ever since the 1890s. In spite of this continuous preoccupation with the problem of anxiety it is impossible to maintain that either Freud or psychoanalysis after him solved the problem. What seems to weigh even more heavily is the fact that psychoanalysis has also not reached a consensus concerning the place that is attributed to anxiety. Is it something epiphenomenal, the causes of which lie deeper and in a different location? Or is anxiety itself to be considered an irreducible force with its own effects? Freud's description of anxiety as a "nodal point" leaves the question totally unanswered. As you well know, Freud himself exchanged one interpretation of anxiety for one totally opposed to it: first he thought that it was the result of repression; later that it was itself the cause of repression. I find the respective contents of these two theories less significant than the form they share, which is one of attempting to explain anxiety *causally*. In his late work Freud himself seems to have doubted the appropriateness of these causal explanations (without, however, ever having renounced them). At the start of chapter 8 of *Inhibitions, Symptoms and Anxiety* he offers us the following to consider as he engages in some self-criticism:

> The time has come to pause and consider. What we clearly want is to find something that will tell us what anxiety really is, some criterion that will enable us to distinguish true statements about it from false ones. But this is not easy to get. Anxiety is not so simple a matter. Up till now we have arrived at nothing but contradictory views about it, none of which can, to the unprejudiced eye, be given preference over the others. I therefore propose to adopt a different procedure. I propose to assemble, quite impartially, all the facts that we know about anxiety without expecting to arrive at a fresh synthesis.[8]

That it is possible to be totally impartial and completely renounce "expecting to arrive at a fresh synthesis" not even Freud believed, which is what he then wrote at the end of *Beyond the Pleasure Principle*. Any undertaking that aims at recognition must believe in the essence of what is to be recognized as the condition of its own possibility and be "partial" in that sense. To "assemble . . . all the facts that we know about anxiety" is strictly speaking already an inherently impossible demand. For how does one decide finally what it is we can say about anxiety without simultaneously saying what it is about it that *we must not say*? And this knowing again presupposes precisely what it itself is supposed to uncover: the difference between error and truth, that either/or about which Freud, precisely in terms of anxiety, is forced to admit that it is "not easy to get." But if "anxiety is not a simple matter," that may be because it is what brings the possibility of grasping into the picture and it does so by dramatizing the play of signified and signifier. Let me try now to explain this supposition at least by way of suggestion, by going back to those two texts on anxiety that stand at the beginning and at the end of Freud's preoccupation with the riddle of anxiety. The first text is entitled "Über die Berechtigung, von der Neurasthenie einen bestimmten Symptomenkomplex als 'Angstneurose' abzutrennen"[9] ["On the Grounds For Detaching a Particular Syndrome From Neurasthenia Under the Description 'Anxiety Neurosis'"] and was published in 1895 in the *Neurologisches Zentralblatt*. The second one is *Inhibitions, Symptoms and Anxiety*, which appeared in book form in 1926, published by the Internationaler Psychoanalytischer Verlag. The difference that characterizes these two organs of publication points to the history of the psychoanalytic movement which, in the thirty-year span that separates these two publications, succeeded in institutional-izing itself and creating its own network of communications. While in 1926 Freud was already writing for "his own [followers]," he had to establish his audience in his first publication concerning anxiety. In this light it is also possible to contrast the two texts' respective strategies and rhetoric. In his later texts—such as *Inhi-bitions, Symptoms and Anxiety*—Freud was forced to struggle against an increas-ingly stiffening acquiescence, against the sytematization, in other words, of his insights which, after all, were all concerned with problems that would precisely question all systematization; in his earlier writing, on the other hand, he was much more concerned with establishing approval. The text on anxiety neurosis was conceptualized in just this way. At issue here is the right to introduce new terms into scientific discourse. Freud desires partially to complement that old traditional term "neurasthenia" with a new one. But this also means removing some of the old term's power and to appropriate it. The following introductory observation shows very clearly what Freud was after in this endeavor:

> I call this syndrome "anxiety neurosis," because all its components can be grouped round the chief symptom of anxiety, because each one of them has a definitive relationship to anxiety. I thought that this view of the symptoms of anxiety neurosis had originated with me, until an interesting paper by E. Hecker (1893) came into my hands, in which I found the same interpretation expounded with all the clarity and completeness that could be desired. Nevertheless, although Hecker recognizes certain symp-toms as equivalents or rudiments of an anxiety attack, he does not separate

them from the domain of neurasthenia, as I propose to do. But this is evidently due to his not having taken into account the difference between the aetiological determinants in the two cases. When this latter difference is recognized there is no longer any necessity for designating anxiety symptoms by the same name as genuine neurasthenic ones; for the principle purpose of giving what is otherwise an arbitrary name is to make it easier to lay down general statements.[10]

The "originality" claimed by Freud is here—and we know, of course, that this is not the first time—disturbed by the presence of another, that of E. Hecker, in whose "interesting presentation" he finds "the same interpretation expounded with all the clarity and completeness that could be desired." But missing in this *"same interpretation"* (that is, of the symptoms of anxiety in neurasthenia) is something essential (one can almost hear Freud's sigh of relief!): the term itself, which designates the new element, thereby stamping it as the valuable possession of the designator. Hecker's "same interpretation" remains unsaid because it does not transcend the level of the symptomatic: it remains stuck in the signifier and does not reach the position of the signified. This signified, at this starting point of psychoanalysis, Freud still conceived of as the *cause*, in the sense of etiology. But then, Freud will never quite be capable of completely renouncing causal explanations.

As it does in Saussure, this early attempt of Freud's to grasp the problem of anxiety etiologically interests us particularly for how it fails. For, as is well known, Freud represents anxiety neurosis as "a deflection of somatic sexual excitation from the psychical sphere, and in a consequent abnormal employment of that excitation";[11] he thereby attempts to solve the problem of anxiety by understanding it from the point of view of his conception of hysteria, as its "somatic counterpart." But while he understands hysteria too as the result of an "accumulation of excitation" which places too many demands on the psyche and therefore experiences a "deflection of it into the somatic field,"[12] Freud distinguishes the two phenomena in terms of their respective *causes:* "[T]he difference is merely that in anxiety neurosis the excitation, in whose displacements the neurosis expresses itself, is purely somatic (somatic sexual excitation), whereas in hysteria it is psychical (provoked by conflict)."[13]

Freud's claim to have identified a new syndrome and thereby to have the right to separate it off from neurasthenia and to claim it for himself scientifically depends on an etiological explanation which, in turn, presupposes a completely different kind of separation, a separation that seems odd in light of the later development of psychoanalysis. For this separation severs the psyche as the medium of conflict (as in hysteria) off from—of all things—sexuality, which is here represented as a purely somatic process. Consequently, a sexual conflict would have to be thought of as separable from the psyche.

The theoretical inadequacy of this attempt at an explanation is evident throughout, because it does not explain; it simply "displaces" the problem onto the "somatic," which is represented as a simple exterior opposing an equally closed off interior space. How the sexual conflict, here presented as purely somatic, is to become effective psychically at all cannot even be thought within such a conceptual dichotomy, and that is why Freud was to drop it very soon.

But before we greet and accept this dropping as a simple and evident instance of theoretical progress which, after all, is an essential condition for psychoanalysis itself (which, as we know, was precisely not to allow this traditional opposition of body and spirit to continue without challenge), let us stick for a while with this first step, written before this "happy" turn of events. Let us linger for a while on this threshold into psychoanalysis proper and see how the text that has not yet become "happy" is nevertheless characterized by a peculiar *reeling*—a reeling, which, even though it is still "preanalytic," perhaps shows us something notable concerning psychoanalytic thought itself. I am referring here specifically to that passage at the beginning of the text where Freud enumerates in sequence and describes the different symptomatic expressions of anxiety. Two things continue to make themselves ever more noticeable in this enumeration. On the one hand, it seems that what Freud is so preoccupied with in the separate symptoms of anxiety is generally the case with all manifestations of anxiety; the fact, for instance,

> that the proportion in which these elements are mixed in an anxiety attack varies to a remarkable degree, and that almost every accompanying symptom alone can constitute the attack just as well as can the anxiety itself. There are consequently rudimentary anxiety attacks and equivalents of anxiety attacks, all probably having the same significance. . . . A closer study of these larval anxiety-states (as Hecker [1893] calls them) and their diagnostic differentiation from other attacks should soon become a necessary task for neuropathologists.[14]

Freud's attempt to separate off some symptoms from general neurasthenia as "anxiety neurosis" seems to fail precisely because of the variability of anxiety and its tendency to be mixed; when this anxiety is itself represented as "surrogates of the omitted specific actions following upon sexual excitation,"[15] the description of the symptoms of anxiety nevertheless demonstrates that they in turn "replace" anxiety itself *and* that they can represent one another; rudimentary anxiety attacks, in other words, can be replaced by their "equivalents," but equivalents in which anxiety as such—that is, as conscious affect—no longer even appears, but which, nevertheless, "probably all carry the same meaning." This strange phenomenon is most clearly demonstrated via "one of the most consequential symptoms of anxiety-neurosis", an equally strange type of vertigo:

"Vertigo" occupies a prominent place in the group of symptoms of anxiety neurosis. In its mildest form it is best described as "giddiness"; in its severer manifestations, as "attacks of vertigo" (with or without anxiety), it must be classed among the gravest symptoms of the neurosis. The vertigo of anxiety neurosis is not rotatory nor does it especially affect certain planes or directions, like Ménière's vertigo. It belongs to the class of locomotor or co-ordinatory vertigo, as does the vertigo in oculomotor paralysis. It consists in a specific state of discomfort, accompanied by sensations of the ground rocking, of the legs giving way and of its being impossible to stand up anymore; while the legs feel as heavy as lead and tremble and the knees bend. This vertigo never leads to a fall. On the other hand, I should like to state that an attack of vertigo of this kind may have its place taken by a profound fainting fit.[16]

Even though this type of vertigo attack is "not seldom accompanied by the worst sort of anxiety,"[17] it is not necessary that it be accompanied by it in order for it to be counted among the "most consequential symptoms of anxiety-neurosis" "with or without anxiety." What seems peculiar, however, about this most consequential symptom is precisely the absence of that consequence which retrospectively determines vertigo as itself: falling. Because in spite of the sense of "the ground rocking, of the legs giving way and of its being impossible to stand up anymore," and in spite of the fact that "the legs feel heavy as lead," that they "tremble and the knees bend," the expected result does *not* set in: "This vertigo never leads to a fall." Instead it leads to something else: it leads, for example, directly to its representation [with the added suggestion of "replacement"—E. S.] by a "profound fainting fit," a sort of unconsciousness, that is, in which one no longer knows whether one is walking, standing or falling . . .

But it is precisely this "condition" of flotation—and now I come to the second aspect of Freud's symptomological description—that also reflects Freud's way of proceeding in this early essay. His attempt to separate some symptoms from neurasthenia and to name them "anxiety neurosis" fails because those symptoms, like vertigo in this context, appear not only "with or without anxiety" but can also be represented by other symptoms. But the result of that is that the "grounds" by way of which Freud wishes to legitimate this separation become just as unstable as the ground under the feet of the vertigo-afflicted subject, who, nevertheless, is incapable of dropping, even though he is also not in the condition to remain upright. The result is movement which really doesn't go anywhere but which also does not simply tread in place, and which, just like Freud's description of vertigo, is really more comparable to a sort of *paralysis* than to any kind of progression; in other words, it is not unrelated to that "limping" that Freud cites at the conclusion of *Beyond the Pleasure Principle* (and also in an earlier letter to Fliess) in order to characterize the movement in [or progress of—E.S.] psychoanalysis. But that vertigo, which neither stands nor drops, should be compared to a "paralysis of the eye muscle" must point to the peculiar nature of those symptoms with which psychoanalysis concerns itself and the meaning of which remains completely concealed from the eye of the traditional clinician. The anxiety symptoms that Freud describes here also show us why that might be: like anxiety itself, which they replace, anxiety symptoms are "in a *freely-floating state . . .* and always ready . . . to link [themselves] with any suitable ideational content."[18] But what is "suitable" and what is not the observer on the outside is incapable of deciding; only the subject attacked by anxiety can do that.

But with all of this, anxiety becomes equally "difficult to grasp." For even though one can describe it, one can't discuss it, that is, one can't place it. This is demonstrated in Freud's vain attempts to situate the cause of anxiety outside of the psyche, that is, to separate anxiety off from the psyche in a causal way. But it is precisely because of its protean representability that anxiety seems to mock that very separation. Rather, it appears to be precisely what both creates and does away with the possibility of any type of separation. It may be "free-floating," but it is also connective, even if the connections it enters into are especially loose, often fleeting, representable ones. It is precisely this replacement and representation, which simultaneously includes both the inhibition of replacement and representation, that makes anxiety "so difficult to grasp." But still, one never ceases to attempt to take possession of it, even if only theoretically, as Freud does in this text and later as well. When one does this, however, it seems that one is forced to participate in it in a way that makes any sort of objectification questionable. Whatever one does in order to grasp anxiety, it always seems that it has already done so itself. The following passage, where Freud attempts to summarize the results of his exploration, is an example of what I mean: "The psyche finds itself in the affect of anxiety if it feels unable to deal by appropriate reaction with a task (a danger) *approaching from outside*; it finds itself in the neurosis of anxiety if it notices that it is unable to even out the (sexual) excitation originating from within—*that is to say, it behaves as though it were projecting that excitation outwards.*"[19]

The differentiation between inside and outside, between endogenous and exogenous, that is typical of Freud's later attempts to separate real anxiety from neurotic anxiety, is enacted here in this description of anxiety by anxiety itself—anxiety neurosis "behaves as though it were projecting that excitation outwards." But what does projection mean here when the so-called "endogenous" excitation has always already lain "outside" of the subject (even if not in the sense of a purely self-identical somatic factor)? In other words, one no longer knows whether Freud is describing anxiety or whether he repeats it in his description of it. No wonder that "'vertigo' occupies a prominent place in the group of symptoms of anxiety neurosis"!

I no longer have the time to put before you what I have here described as the vertiginous character of anxiety in Freud's later writings, especially in *Inhibitions, Symptoms and Anxiety.* Today I have to be content with the indication that an attentive reading of that text will show that anxiety does not so much represent itself as a "reaction" to a particular threat, but rather appears as the process in which the threat finds its own articulation to begin with, insofar as "threat" necessarily implies a given structure of time and place which can come into being only via anxiety.

I would like to represent this creation of time and place as an accomplishment that is specific to anxiety in a sort of narrative wherein anxious expectation, which is simultaneously remembrance, both stages and disguises itself. A specimen of that is "castration," which includes not only theory, but also history and anxiety. Instead of that I would like to close today with two related observations. The first consists in my contention that one of the most privileged scenes of reference in which Freudian thought plays itself out is represented by his very own texts and their readings, even if those are very special readings. Because if, as Lacan, as one of the very first people, has emphasized, Freud's discovery must be characterized as being marked by the movement of the signifier, this movement becomes accessible *through* and *as* a very specific manner of reading and writing. Even if this way of reading can take place anywhere, really, Freud's writings remain one of its most privileged scenes, and that is the case precisely because they not only describe the play of the signifier as object, but they also simultaneously, and maybe even precedingly, describe and reflect themselves within it. I will now give you one last example of this describing and reflecting: its source is the essay in which Freud responds to a criticism of his study of anxiety neurosis and consists of one single sentence in which Freud attempts to summarize the meaning of his earlier article: "Anxiety neurosis is created by everything which keeps somatic sexual tension away from the psychical sphere, which interferes with its being worked over psychically."[20]

This sentence, which is supposed to reflect unequivocally the meaning of Freud's examination of anxiety neurosis, is anything but unequivocal. For it also allows for "anxiety neurosis" to be read both as the subject of the sentence, and upside down, as "everything that keeps somatic sexual excitation separate from the psychic." The latter is surely the meaning Freud intended; but why should this conscious intention carry more authority and power in Freud's writing than it does in other such intentions by way of which Freud represents the limits of the conscious? And anyhow, Freud will later reverse cause and effect in his theory of anxiety anyway. What is articulated in this equivocation, however, is perhaps precisely the inadequacy involved in attempting to solve the problem of anxiety by some sort of causal relation; this is an insight that formulates itself implicitly here in this text as a kind of misrecognition. Consequently anxiety would in fact be a nodal point, but a nodal point that is unyielding to attempts to break through or resolve it because it really signals the inevitability and also the impossibility of such attempts at resolution. In order to indicate the direction Freud takes here, and to keep this short, I would maintain that this inevitable impossibility (in *Inhibitions, Symptoms and Anxiety*) culminates in the concept of "danger," of which I would not maintain, as does Lacan, that it is always in Freud's work "tied to the undefined concept of life threat,"[21] but rather that it is always connected with a rethinking of the constitutively split and ambivalent identity of the subject as it reveals itself in the structure of the ego. Danger, in Freud, finds its source in this ambivalence; it belongs to anxiety, which "reacts" to it and "signals" it but without thereby having to be placed sequentially after it (in order to have it follow the temporal logic of the conscious), as its mere effect. It is also for this reason that it is not only in anxiety that one sometimes experiences vertigo, but also during an attempt to arrive at a theoretical solution; it is almost impossible to avoid forming the assumption that this theory may be just one more instance in a list of anxiety equivalents. For the (re)solution or the articulation of this problem really constitutes a vertigo [here also in the secondary sense of "*Schwindel*" = swindle. —E. S.], at least according to the traditional economy of reason, of logic, which wishes to take symptoms back to their grounds, effects to their causes, signifiers to their signifieds. But anxiety mocks this wish and does so by seemingly allowing for it; because what anxiety seems to discover behind appearances is finally the undiscoverable, the unimaginable, what Freud calls "trauma" and what one could also define as the noneconomical origin of the psychic economy. Viewed from this perspective anxiety would represent in Freud's thought the subject's attempt to govern, to appropriate, economically the subject's uneconomical provenance, an attempt which is always more or less condemned to fail. Whether or not Lacan's attempt to explain anxiety in terms of its relationship to the Other/other (capitalized or not) in his 1962–63 seminars on anxiety also moves in that direction cannot yet be determined. I would like to give this to you to consider, however: that Lacan seems to want to locate and to discuss anxiety unequivocally, namely, as the uncertainty of the subject as to what sort of *objet petit a* it represents for the desire of the Other; and that Lacan sets up a "surmounting of anxiety" as something attainable through the self-naming of the Other as the Name-of-the-Father ("Il n'y a de surmontement de l'angoisse que quand l'Autre s'est nommé.")[22] And finally it seems to me that the aims that Lacan points to as the motives for such a "surmounting" show that precisely where Lacan seems to think that he is transcending Freud, he is not only repeating him, but he is actually falling behind him. Let's listen to Lacan's concluding words in his seminar on anxiety:

> I have already a number of times questioned you about what the analyst's desire would have to be so that in that place to which we want to take things, beyond the boundaries of anxiety, work is made possible. Certainly

the analyst would have to be the one who was in the position, no matter how little and no matter by what road, of bringing his desire back far enough into the *a* in order to provide a true guarantee to this question of the concept of anxiety.[23]

But whether anxiety can indeed be conceptualized, or more precisely, whether the question of the concept of anxiety really ever allows for such a "true guarantee"; whether or not the analyst's work can ever settle in a region that "lies beyond the boundaries of anxiety"; whether or not *any* work can play itself out in such a region, assuming, which I seriously doubt one has the right to do, that it is possible to know that there even is such a region—these are all questions which, according to my reading of Freud, have to remain without "true guarantees." And this brings me to my second concluding observation, which will take us back to the beginning. The fact that the reception of Lacan outside of France was effected first by literary scholars and only now, slowly, but increasingly, is beginning to interest also psychoanalysts, appears to me as a good break. For like literature, which is its object, literary theory itself as a discipline is vulnerable to the play of signifier and signified, even though, again, as a discipline, it often wishes to remain blind to this fact. It prefers to characterize its objects as the exclusive bearers of this play, just like Freud often attributes the unconscious to his patients without wishing to consider the necessary consequences (of his theory) for himself—or perhaps precisely in order to not have to consider them. The critic may often like to problematize the poet's intentions, but less often his own or those of his discipline. And yet literary criticism remains as closely tied to the play of language as is possible for any academic discipline that conceives of itself as a cognitive science. It is true, this "closeness" varies from nation to nation and is never free of contradictions. In this respect the possibilities that are opened up by the broadening dimensions of the reception of Lacan seem promising to me, provided that both analysts and literary theorists evaluate the respective situations in which they find themselves not only individually but also institutionally.

If one *is* willing to think about such things then Lacan's work can be enormously helpful. Because it, more than any other, has made us aware of the signifier's play with the signified and thereby also of the symbolic (and imaginary!) limits of one's own occupation. But I do not want to close without drawing attention to the danger that emerged within a certain strand of Lacan's reception as well, a danger which points back to the anxiety that these texts often provoke: the anxiety about not understanding something that seems to announce (present) itself as unquestionable authority, the anxiety concerning the *sujet supposé savoir*. The "danger" I see here is that this may involve that one forgets, precisely, to "presuppose," to "assume," and out of anxiety embraces one's "own" projection as truth in order to forget about those splits that determine all anxiety. In other words, the danger is that one may fall victim to the promise of reaching that realm of true guarantees where work without anxiety is possible. Nothing works better against this danger than the patient return to Freud's texts, a return which, especially in the German-speaking world, offers rich and probably inexhaustible possibilities, provided one is capable of renouncing guarantees and accepting some form of vertigo/swindle.

Notes

Paper given on February 18, 1982 at the Psychoanalytisches Seminar Zürich. [The German word for "vertigo" is *Schwindel*, which is a pun: it means both "vertigo" and swindle.—E. S.]

1. C. K. Ogden and I. Richards, *The Meaning of Meaning* (New York: Harcourt, Brace, 1946).

2. Ibid., 5: "Without the concept, [Saussure] says, the signifier is not a sign. The disadvantage of this statement consists, as we will see, in the fact that the process of interpretation is by definition included in the sign!" [Translation—E. S.]

3. Sigmund Freud, "The Economic Problem of Masochism," *Standard Edition, Volume 19* trans. James Strachey (London: The Hogarth Press), 160.

4. Samuel Weber, *Return to Freud: Jacques Lacan's Dislocation of Psychoanalysis*, trans. Michael Levine (Cambridge: Cambridge University Press, 1991), 65.

5. Cf. Samuel Weber, *Freud-Legende* (Olten: Walter, 1979), 85ff. English: *The Legend of Freud* (Stanford, CA: Stanford University Press, 2000).

6. Lacan means, I believe, nothing else by the *objet a*.

7. Sigmund Freud, *Introductory Lectures on Psycho-Analysis, Standard Edition, Volume 16*, 393.

8. Sigmund Freud, *Inhibitions, Symptoms and Anxiety, Standard Edition, Volume 20*, 132.

9. Sigmund Freud, "On the Grounds for Detaching a Particular Syndrome from Neurasthenia under the Description 'Anxiety Neurosis,'" *Standard Edition, Volume 3*, 90–115.

10. Ibid., *Standard Edition, Volume 3*, 91. It would be possible to cull from this something concerning the "arbitrariness of the sign," precisely in the agonistic sense of the use of the so-called *arbitraire du signe*: every sign is surely arbitrary when it is viewed in isolation, but the fact that there are in existence some constellations of signs but not others is not all that arbitrary after all; in

other words, there is no point which one could occupy and from which one could say that it is arbitrary—unless, of course, one were God. Rhetorically this agonistic moment corresponds to what I would call the "ambivalent imaginary structure of the Symbolic."

11. Ibid., 108.

12. Ibid., 115.

13. Ibid., 115.

14. Ibid., 94.

15. Ibid., 111.

16. Ibid., 95.

17. Ibid., 96.

18. Ibid., 93.

19. Ibid., 112.

20. Sigmund Freud, "A Reply to Criticisms of my Paper on Anxiety Neurosis," *Standard Edition, Volume 3*, 124.

21. Jacques Lacan, Seminar "L'angoisse," (unpubl. session of July 3, 1963).

22. "There is no overcoming of anxiety, if the Other has not named itself."

23. Jacques Lacan, Seminar "L'angoisse," (unpubl. session of July 3, 1963). [trans. E. S.]

16

From the Protective Shield against Stimuli to the Fantasm

A Reading of Chapter 4 of
Beyond the Pleasure Principle

HANS-DIETER GONDEK

I n chapter 5 of *Beyond the Pleasure Principle* we are introduced to the death drive by name. But already in chapter 4 of the same work Freud poses the question concerning death; he does so in the context of constructing the concept of the *protective shield against stimuli*, which generally is taken no more seriously than the "living vesicle" in relation to which it is developed. And yet this protective shield is endowed with a function that, as I will demonstrate, one comes across again in what Lacan was to introduce as the *fantasm*. And chapter 4 of *Beyond the Pleasure Principle* is worth reading for one other reason as well: in it Freud draws certain "philosophical consequences" from psychoanalysis and develops them—and this is what is most surprising about this gesture—by direct reference to one particular philosopher.

In addition, chapter 4 is a gathering point for all those metapsychological problems that had been left open. Once more Freud opens up the question of topography when he refers back to the "localization held by cerebral anatomy," which, with a royal gesture, he can apply to his argument, since he had already worked the problem out in his first book, *On Aphasia [Zur Auffassung der Aphasien[1]]*. This text has been forgotten by psychoanalytic orthodoxy and has never been republished, but it always provided Freud with a support whenever the organization of consciousness and memory were at stake. The branch of cerebral anatomy that deals with localization had identified the external cerebral cortex as the locus of consciousness: "What consciousness yields consists essentially of perceptions of excitations coming from the external world and of

221

feelings of pleasure and unpleasure which can only arise from within the mental apparatus; it is therefore possible to assign to the system Pcpt.-Cs. a position in space. It must lie on the borderline between outside and inside; it must be turned towards the external world and must envelop the other psychical systems.[2]

Turned towards and *enveloping*—a turning around and away that one will be quick to recognize as that of life toward but also against itself. Indisputably this particular topographical construct is merely a crude analogy that disregards the afferent and efferent pathways of excitation transmission. But topographical relations in Freud do not mimic anything ostensibly "natural" but are rather constructions sui generis. Freud never ceased working on that "thing" which he hoped, as he says already in his letters to Fliess, was really "a machine that shortly would function on its own."[3] In this sense the act of joining perception and consciousness together into one system is no more natural than is the separation of perception from consciousness—their forcing apart and distribution to two different "sides" of the psychical apparatus. In both cases what is at stake is a differential constructive description of functions, first for conscious perception, and then for the dream.

The topographical postulate as well as the principle "that becoming conscious and leaving behind a memory-trace are processes incompatible with each other within one and the same system"[4] establish the external conditions of each and every "living organism" which Freud schematizes "in its most simplified possible form as an undifferentiated vesicle of a substance that is susceptible to stimulation."[5] In this form it is the product of a turning-inside-out, of a retorsion, that allows the inside to travel to the outside and attain closure as a newly formed surface so that access to the inside, which had been opened up during this process, is again cut off (Freud refers to "embryology, in its capacity as a recapitulation of developmental history," in this context). The surface is restricted to being finitely stretched out, but it still continues to allow potentially infinite movements upon itself to occur insofar as they are not stopped by any external barrier.

At issue here is an exposition of consciousness, more specifically, of what makes consciousness possible. While memory supposedly rests on the retention of traces by the creation of paths, we may assume concerning the surface that is reserved for consciousness, that it is to remain free of all retention and to be permanently receptive; this is necessitated by "the exposed situation of the system Cs., immediately abutting as it does on the external world."[6] As "substrata" of memory, the paths function differentially by having to overcome resistances to transference. The system Cs. is spared that, so that "excitatory processes" in it "expire, as it were, in the phenomenon of becoming conscious."[7] One may, says Freud concerning the nature of this excitatory process, "form . . . [v]arious ideas . . . which cannot at present be verified. . . . ."[8] And concerning the vesicle, Freud can affirm the notion of it only if one "express[es] oneself as cautiously as possible on these points."[9] Freud limits himself to describing an economy of stimuli and their quantitative relations.

The living vesicle's attitude vis-à-vis "an external world charged with the most powerful energies"[10] is precarious—it requires a contrivance which Freud gives the name "protective shield against stimuli":

> It acquires the shield in this way: its outermost surface ceases to have the structure proper to living matter [in other words, whatever is alive must be an essentially pure and stimuli-receptive surface that virginally offers and gives itself—pure perception and pure consciousness at once— while memory is an instance that from the very beginning is marked by death.— H-D. G.], becomes to some degree inorganic and thenceforward functions as a special envelope or membrane resistant to stimuli. In consequence, the energies of the external world are able to pass into the next underlying layers, which have remained living, with only a fragment of their original intensity. . . . .[11]

For the sake of its "self"-protection, for the sake of its "self"-preservation as *life*, for the sake of its survival and sur-life *[Über-lebens]*, the organic substance hands parts of its "self" over to *death*, allows them to become inorganic, lets them die. In fact, it becomes it "self," in the sense of a "self" that belongs to self-preservation, no matter how primitive—only by giving up, sacrificing, parts of itself, by splitting, sharing, and distributing the self which it is in the process of becoming, handing one part over to death in order to preserve its other part as life. It becomes it"self" through "auto-tely," which is how Derrida refers to this dynamic in which death turns into the self-love of life and life turns into the self-love of death.[12] Death must be allowed onto this "virginal" surface on which consciousness can come into being in order that life may be better protected against death. Death protects against death, or better: it protects against its own premature and inessential appearance or occurrence. Death is introduced into life in order to preserve life, with the result that the detour toward death of the living organism is prolonged, and in order to prevent the short circuit of immediate death. All of this occurs—and this is no less true of the model of the "living vesicle" than it is of the explicit introduction of the death drive hypothesis—in order that "the organism shall follow its own path to death, and to ward off any possible ways of returning to inorganic existence other than those which are immanent in the organism itself"[13]; all of this happens in an "economy" of death, according to a law of "the proper" (*oikos, oikonomia*), through which life and death serve one another: "the proper" of life is the property of *its own* death, its *detour toward death.*[14]

With this subject of the living vesicle's topography, Freud has proleptically referred to the split between *soma* and *germ-plasma,* along the lines of which later on in the text (pp.81–94) he discusses the question of a potentially endless postponement of death for one part of the organism. The "virginality" of the surface that is untouched by paths and resistances has to be protected by a "special envelope or membrane." This membrane fulfills the double, diacritical function of screen and proportional reductor of stimuli—the function of a controlled permeability, in other words. This protection, of life and of species, is the *protective shield*:

> By its death, the outer layer has saved all the deeper ones from a similar fate unless, that is to say, stimuli reach it, which are so strong that they break through the protective shield. *Protection against* stimuli is an almost more important function for the living organism than *reception* of stimuli. The protective shield is supplied with its own store of energy and must above all endeavor to preserve the special modes of transformation of energy operating in it against the effects threatened by the enormous energies at work in the external world—effects which tend towards a leveling out of them and hence toward destruction.[15]

Freud is being proleptic in two ways here: not only does he refer to the "later" instance of the ego with this setup of a special reserve of energy,[16] but he also alludes to a second derivative method of protection against stimuli which will no longer depend on the death of living matter. But before doing so Freud takes a detour (and this in a text in which he exhorts himself and his readers ten times to "go a step further"). He describes the seat of the sense organs and their function ("[T]hey deal only with very small quantities of external stimulation and only take in samples of the external world. They may perhaps be compared with feelers which are all the time making tentative advances towards the external world and then drawing back from it"[17]), to then refer to Kant *ex abrupto*[18]:

> At this point I shall venture to touch for a moment upon a subject which would merit the most exhaustive treatment. As a result of certain psychoanalytic discoveries, we are today in a position to embark on a discussion of the Kantian theorem that time and space are "necessary forms of thought." We have learnt that unconscious mental processes are in themselves "timeless." This means in the first place that they are not ordered temporally, that time does not change them in any way and that the idea of time cannot be applied to them. These are negative characteristics which can only be clearly understood if a comparison is made with conscious mental processes. On the other hand, our abstract idea of time seems to be wholly derived from the method of working of the system Pcpt.-Cs. and to correspond to a perception on its own part of that method

of working. This mode of functioning may perhaps constitute another way of providing a shield against stimuli. I know that these remarks must sound very obscure, but I must limit myself to these hints.[19]

Even if one knows but little about Kant's theory of time, one will notice that Freud refers to Kant's pure forms of a priori intuition, space and time, as "forms of thought." This is due either to a mistake—this would be the most obvious assumption to make[20]—or to a different, idiosyncratic, analysis of time. It is impossible to gather from the statement and its context whether or not Freud had produced such an analysis. But that is irrelevant for now.

One can most certainly refer to Kant's conceptions of time and space as forms of thought: as those pure forms of intuition that must be thought as given so that something like a *unity* of *experience* can be thought. Kant's "Transcendental Aesthetic" contains only the assertion that the pure forms of the empirical order, time and space, must necessarily be imagined as *a priori given* so that there can be empirical knowledge; but, as is the case with their fundamental principle, it is necessary to join intuition and concept. Only at the end of *Transcendental Deduction of the Pure Conceptions of the Understanding*—with the assertion that the pure conceptions of the understanding, which are capable of bringing to the categories a priori understanding, as "principles of the possibility of experience," the objects of an intuition in general[21]—the *unity* of an intuition is *thought* as intuition, that is, as the *unity* of the representation of plurality which is combined into one intuition, in this case, the intuition of time. In order to conceptualize time and space, one must show that their unity too is due to an *a priori synthesis*, the same synthesis that makes possible the unity of an object. It is only because of this identity that it is possible to employ time as the form of that *inner sense*—indeed, of the spirit *[Gemüt]*—and thus of subjectivity, necessary for the description of objective relations. The goal of Kant's treatment of time is the "one time in which all different times must be located, not as coexistent but as in succession to one another"[22]—the time of pure succession, which makes it possible to conceive of time as a relation of time to begin with in that it functions as the latter's substratum.[23]

The "critique of pure reason," which was aimed at founding an objective determination of time, is incapable of doing justice to the *implicit phenomenology* of the experience of time as (self-)experience of thought, insofar as it is suggested by the concept of the inner sense and a localization of the pure forms of sensuousness in the spirit, because of its very teleology.[24] Admittedly, Kant does propose the notion of the mind's *auto-affection* ["the mode in which the mind is affected through its own activity" (Kant)—E. S.] through *time* as the form of the inner sense,[25] which Heidegger then appropriated in his reading of Kant and radicalized to the point of saying that the *self* is *time*, in the sense of Heidegger's ecstatic temporality.[26] But this notion is finally explained by Kant as the mind's relationship to itself. And so, at the very moment that Kant represents understanding as being capable of "making the representation of an object possible at all" "by *carrying* the time-order *over* into the appearances and their existence,"[27] he also loses sight of the fact that the a priori objectivity of objects is thereby determined by the event of *transference* itself, that is, by the *process/precession [Vorgang]* of a metaphor.[28] Even though Kant himself asserts the necessity of an image, of an external representation of time, he plays blind and deaf to the further implications of the genesis of this conception of time, especially to its linguistic and tropological character.

Freud's objection is directed precisely at linear causality and its pure temporality of succession. When Freud asserts that time produces no changes in unconscious processes, this is a statement about their indestructibility as it is described in the last sentence of *The Interpretation of Dreams*: "By picturing our wishes as fulfilled, dreams are after all leading us into the future. But this future, which the dreamer pictures as the present, has been molded by his indestructible wish into a perfect likeness of the past."[29] But what he is talking about is precisely the indestructibility of unconscious processes *in time*. The wish is indestructible because, as a simulacrum of the past, as its double, its repetition, it projects itself into the future and brings this future image into the staging of the dream by presenting it and making it present *[vergegenwärtigend]*. The wish emerges from the past *and* the future. Representing it as a present wish requires an *imaginary time*, an anticipatory time. But "in itself," the wish is radical discontinuity, that is, never present or even to be thought from the perspective of the present. The wish is indestructible because it is repetition; but the fact that it is repetition is brought to the fore only in deferment. It is not the past that rules over the wish and establishes it as repetition;[30] rather, the wish as the project of a *future perfect* is what makes access to its own past possible to begin with. [The future describes an action that will have been completed—and perfected—in the past.—E. S.] If there is a point of reference for the analysis of a dream, then it can surely be found only in the dream *narrative*, in the dream *interpretation* already contained in the latter, and in both of their *temporalities*. One can and must, if one is to take seriously Freud's references to a particular "working" time of the psychical apparatus, even assert that the past of the wish, the original, so to speak, of the simulacrum, is really only the constructed result of the wish in its projection and its narrative. Repetition is not preceded by an identity of what has been repeated as something to be repeated. The pastness of the wish as wish is always one that has come into being by deferment.[31]

The wish is a wish *as* wish-fulfillment; the wish is a presented *[vergegenwärtigt* = made present] *future* perfect—[the German] *Futurum II* or the *futur antérieur*, the tense form in French. Harald Weinrich describes the *Futurum II* from the point of view of "anticipatory information"—this suggests merely that information is given prematurely in terms of the action it expresses. Whether the prematurity is due to the action not yet having taken place or to the process having taken place unbeknownst to those concerned or is taking place just now—in all cases, confirmation does not yet exist, so that in each case the information is anticipatory and is necessarily characterized by a certain measure of uncertainty, even if later on it should emerge from additional information that the news given had been correct.[32]

The indestructibility of the wish in Freud is, then, its indestructibility *in time*. In which time? By no means in the time of pure succession—that much is clear. But also not in a grammatical, that is, the "modal"—time of linguistic theories of tense. For Freud's analysis does not determine the wish by the time of its fulfillment, by the "future perfect," but allows it to have retroactive presenting effects on its own past from the vantage point of this *Futurum II* in which it forms and formulates itself as something "perfected" (completed). Here too there must be a "substratum" of time that "grounds" this movement which (re)turns (to) and envelopes a "present" of the wisher, the dreamer. This time is the time of the psychical apparatus itself, the *modal time of its functioning,* which Freud circumscribes only inadequately and gropingly, even while intuiting its direction with his allusions to "a discontinuous or periodic temporality."[33] One must, of course, differentiate between the temporality of the dream and the temporality of waking.

"Amplitude,"[34] "period,"[35] and "rhythm"[36] are ciphers both for the admission of the problem and for the still insufficient suggestions for a solution. In "A Note Upon the 'Mystic Writing-Pad'" Freud relates the "method of working of the system *Pcpt.-Cs.*" to the concept of "discontinuity": a flow of innervation is periodically sent into the system *Pcpt.-Cs.* from the unconscious and then pulled back; the retrograde movement makes its appearance as " the periodic non-excitability of the perceptual system."[37] Accordingly, the "apperception" Freud talks about in relation to the psychical apparatus would have to be discontinuous and not the "abstract conception of time" which Freud regards as the result of this apperception. The task thus becomes more complicated: it is no longer just a matter of determining the temporality of the psychical apparatus, but also of explaining the genesis of the *appearance* of temporal continuity which, in opposition to the modal time of the psychical apparatus, presents itself as an image of time, as imaginary time. It is conceivable that a return to Kant is appropriate here: what Kant is concerned with in his analysis of time is to show that the subjective time of the "inner sense" falls together with the objective time of the possibility (of the objects) of knowledge. The fact that Freud makes no headway in this question is perhaps really a distant aftereffect of Kant's theoretical philosophy: Kant's primary reference to the "One Time" of succession and countability, which is really the aim of his demonstration, and which is used to cover up a phenomenology of time, forces Freud to let go of this particular conception of time in relation to time itself, so as to be able to conceive of the *dream* (in *The Interpretation of Dreams*), on the one hand, and *repetition* (in *Beyond the Pleasure Principle*), on the other. And yet, the thought of a radical *counterpresenting of the present* through the *process* and the *precedence* of the memory systems remains implicit and is not thought through to the end, especially in view of the consequences it would have for the temporality of the "subject of the unconscious."

It is only Lacan who will establish the connection between the time of the *futur antérieur* and the modal time of the unconscious and the transference. "I identify myself in language but only by losing myself as object within it. On the next page we are told that language is "a subtle body." What is realized in my story is not the completed past of what was, because it no longer is, nor is it the perfect of he who was in what I am, but the second future of what I will have been for what I am about to be."[38] As a characterization of a temporality constituted by constant deferment and displacement, this future perfect *[Futurum II]* should be conceptualized as a *mode*.[39] This irresolvable tension of a *futur antérieur*, understood to be modal, makes itself noticeable in the subject of the unconscious as the latter's inclination, and duty, toward repetition, as a repetition that strains to overcome a loss experienced as traumatic; but this repetition occurs in vain because the loss comes into being only and repeatedly in repetition itself and is, via the temporal modality of deferment, irreducibly bound to it. For the "It/d [it and id] was" signifies a radical temporal precedence (without being the past of a former present) with which no "I/ego" can catch up and which simultaneously represents and removes that self-reference that is supposed to be reined in linguistically by the "I (am)" and thetically by the "I (think)." This temporal precedence, and unbridgeable chasm, forces the I/ego-to-be precisely into the temporality of the *futur antérieur*.[40] *Where id/t was, there shall I be* also means, "Where *I* will have arrived, id/t has always already been." Before, and past. A bungled, missed encounter. Not a bungling and a missing that was ever at the disposal of the subject, but rather the bungling and missing that is insurmountable because of a temporal structure that forces the "I that thinks" to be forever late for the "I am": where the "I think" is supposedly allowed to grasp the "I am," it disengages the latter from it "self" and presupposes it *[setzt es voraus]* in its very act.[41] It does so in a deferred mode.

Descartes's *cogito* is possible as a citable and applicable philosophical *statement* only by transcending the temporality of its own *stating*. For what can be said about the sentence, "Cogito (ergo) sum," and even more so about its French variant, "Je pense, (donc) je suis" (I am placing *ergo* and *donc* in parentheses because the question of the consequence of the *cogito* should be bracketed here)—and this has not been acknowledged—is what H. Weinrich said about the tense structure of the *Futurum II*: "that the information is given prematurely in terms of the action correlated with it." The "I think" is premature if it wishes to be contemporaneous with the "I am," which, as *action*, it can, after all, only follow. What would be appropriate for the formulation of the cogito is the temporality of the *Futurum II*, or even that of the so-called *ne explétif*, that special negative particle that indicates the subjective coloring of apprehension or hope, of an inadequate counterreason or objection, in speech.

Kant had already made it clear that Descartes's statement of existence produces no consequences beyond this considered by Kant to be tautological self-affirmation in the *act* of thinking; it neither makes possible nor ensures perception of either the self or the world.[42] Lacan radicalizes this Kantian minimization of the relationship between *I think* and *I am* into a "*that* I am" (without any further determination of this my being-here) by positing the temporally contingent constitution of a discontinuous subject of the unconscious: structurally, the moment of grasping "oneself" always comes too late, always in deferment *[nachträglich]*, because the Being of the subject withdraws. Lacan talks about a "pulsative function" of the unconscious and about the scanned structure of its appearance and disappearing.[43] Descartes, in order to sew up this tear, bases the "I" on the deceptive identification of thinking and being. This, however, leads to the consequence that

> the cogito, in the harshest way possible, condemns the subject to having to think continuously in order to assure itself that it is; a peculiar situation in which the little amount of being that it manages to collect exhausts itself in its own thought, so that the cogito turns into an I think and I am not. But the formula now strives to demonstrate its own opposite: maybe I would be if I ceased thinking; perhaps one must in the end say: I think for fear of not being; the intimate relationship between the subject and negation can be perceived in this context in the so-called "*ne explétif*" . . . with which one refers both to the stating subject and the subject's disjunction from the subject of the statement.[44]

The primacy of the dream is the primacy of something that is situated *in between perception and consciousness*, which cannot be thought of as the past in terms of linear time, but rather which constitutes the paradox of a *lieu intemporel*, a "nontemporal locus," which will forever make reflexive self-assurance impossible.[45] What is possible is the repetition of a bungled, missed encounter; the repetition of what in repetition proves to be a trauma, as something real that takes place "as if by chance,"[46] that can be neither assimilated nor identified, even though it makes possible, through its return, the identification of the subject as one that desires. The place of this return is the fantasm, and Lacan determines one of its functions to be "the screen that conceals something quite primary, something determinant in the function of repetition."[47] Accordingly, the fantasm would be a sort of "screen" that covers and protects, even if it does so merely within the limits defined by its own domain; and insofar as, like any screen, it has an edge, reality can contour itself marginally against that edge.[48]

There emerges, then, a definite analogy between the fantasm and the protective shield against stimuli, which, at first, is limited to mere function. Curiosity as to whether or not this analogy will be confirmed, explained, and justified will now, after this "far-fetched speculation" (which has taken us into speculative philosophy), lead us back to continue reading the fourth chapter of *Beyond the Pleasure Principle.*

Especially conspicuous about the fantasm is what one could call its *imaginary* aspect: the fantasm presents what as a rule is a violent act of separation, of loss. That which is lost stands in a referential relationship to the *objet a.* But the fantasm has a symbolic aspect as well: in the fantasm the subject turns itself into the object for the Other; and vice versa, the Other becomes the object as the cause of the subject's desire. The substitute for the *objet a* may take on the function of a bait; above all, however, it functions as a *sacrifice* with which a defense against a(n) (imaginary) threat is attempted. The fantasm is *real,* to mention its third aspect as well, insofar as it is sustained on the subject's own body.[49]

In this sense the first concept of the protective shield against stimuli, the sacrifice of a portion of its surface on the part of the living organism, can already be described as a fantasmatic construction, since this sacrifice occurs for the sake of a defense against a danger threatening from outside, for the sake of diminishing something that pushes in from the outside. Freud shows this, of course, in a manner that places it far below the "complexity" of the fantasm because of its simplicity, which is due to the choice of model: the *living vesicle.* This changes, however, when, after his Kant parenthesis, Freud remembers the *inner boundary* of the system. For here protection against stimuli through the sacrifice of organic substance is out of the question:

> Towards the outside it is shielded against stimuli, and the amounts of excitation impinging on it have only a reduced effect. Towards the inside there can be no such shield; the excitations in the deeper layers extend into the system directly and in undiminished amount, in so far as certain of their characteristics give rise to feelings in the pleasure-unpleasure series.[50]

The fact that these feelings of pleasure-unpleasure are more commensurate with the system's mode of functioning, in terms of their quantity as amounts of excitation, compared to the amounts of excitation storming in from outside does not prevent them from becoming troublesome and dangerous as well. As soon as they bring about a too large "increase in unpleasure" the apparatus must defend itself. This occurs through a process which Freud will present as the prototype for projection and which consists in treating disturbing inner excitations "as though they were acting, not from the inside, but from the outside, so that it may be possible to bring the shield against stimuli into operation as a means of defence against them."[51] But Freud says nothing about the modalities, the *how* of this process. Should it consist of something other than a mere conjurer's trick, one would have to consider an actual externalizing, a real kicking out of the inner excitations in question: a tearing open of the vesicle, in other words, especially of its dividing and filtering membrane, followed by an immediate closing up again, and finally a cicatrization after the expulsion of the disturbance. Or, one would have to, topologically, construct a vesicle in such a way that its one and only protective shield would offer protection both against absolute exteriority *and* against that "second external world"[52] of unconscious psychical excitation. Lacan chose this second way in his topology constructions. Let's go on: no stimuli protection can deliver absolutely everything it promises. If it is perforated, the result is *trauma*: "There is no longer any possibility of preventing the mental apparatus from being flooded with large amounts of stimulus, and another problem arises instead—the problem of mastering the amounts of stimulus which have broken in and of binding them, in the psychical sense, so that they can then be disposed of."[53] The breaking in of foreign streams of excitation takes the shape of a special kind of unpleasure in the living vesicle, which, according to Freud, has no counterpart in the realm of pleasure. It was Lacan who opposed *jouissance*, enjoyment, even the experience of pain, to pleasure. As Jean Laplanche notes, there is in Freud a specific theory of pain which remains consistent from the "Project for a Scientific Psychology" up until *Inhibitions, Symptoms and Anxiety* and in which the phenomenon of pain is strictly separated from that of unpleasure:[54] while unpleasure requires no topographical framework in order to be determined, it is impossible to construct a theory of pain outside of a model of the body and its boundaries.[55] Flight or avoidance are impossible in the experience of pain. Freud even coins the concept of a "pseudoinstinct"[56] for the substratum of the experience of pain, this pseudoinstinct, which, like the drive, is a constantly pressing force with ultimately organ-damaging effects. The forces of pain, that is, the constant excitations that support it, must necessarily be bound. The "binding" of the forces that have invaded takes place in the form of an "'anticathexis' on a grand scale"[57] in the immediate area of the breach. "The reaction to pain replaces a materially firm boundary, constituted by the protective shield, by a boundary that is a sort of functional boundary created by the process of binding."[58] A price has to be paid for this: there occurs a pervasive impoverishment of energy in "all the other psychical systems . . . so that the remaining psychical functions are extensively paralyzed or reduced."[59, 60] Freud finds himself compelled to "reinstate the old, naive theory of shock," reconciled with the aspects of fright and the threat to life. In itself, shock is "the direct damage to the molecular structure or even to the histological structure of the elements of the nervous system"[61]— a mechanical invasion, that is; fright is a concurring cause, determined by the "lack of any preparedness for anxiety."[62] Preparedness for anxiety and "the hypercathexis of the receptive systems constitute the last line of defence of the shield against stimuli,"[63] a limited protection which is capable of arresting the forces of invasion only to a degree.

After all, preparedness for anxiety offers a sort of mobile and especially preparatory protective shield. Anxiety always preempts the invasion of the threatening outside, makes mobility possible in the simulated transgression and destruction of somatic boundaries and in this imaginary opening up of the free space of exteriority. And so anxiety, as a fantasmatic prolepsis of what effects anxiety, is itself the best defense against anxiety. Freud developed this idea, incrementally neglecting the fantasmatic aspect of anxiety, by developing it to the point where he distinguished between two forms of anxiety: to what he calls *anxiety as signal*, which is economically well tolerated, has its source in the ego and returns to it as a warning, he opposes a *neurotic anxiety*, whose source does not lie in the ego and which does not return to it, but rather hinders the ego from reacting adequately by developing an economically disproportionate anxiety.[64] What is lost in this distinction between a "good" and a "bad" anxiety, in this crude functionalization of anxiety, is the fact that anxiety can be a privileged site of truth for the subject. In his Seminar on anxiety, Lacan, on the other hand, goes so far as to say that anxiety is that "which does not deceive."[65] Anxiety grants a kind of certainty that the Cartesian *cogito* can never achieve: the certainty of the *objet a* in its approach *and* in its fading. The *objet a* does not hand itself over; the *objet a* does not exist; it is not of this world. The only possible way of "experiencing" it is in anxiety. It is the nonencounter with that because of which and by which anxiety exists, and in this sense it is its sign, without, however, allowing it to emerge. In this sense anxiety is closely tied to the fantasm, that opening up of an "other scene" in which the subject "encounters" its *objet a*, without ever being able to identify it, by separating itself off from it, as we said, rejecting and sacrificing it. The *objet a*, the product of a "self-mutilation" on part of the subject,[66] constitutes a sequel to the sacrificed living matter in the model of the "living vesicle" and its primitive protective-shield apparatus. Anxiety is the "perception of the desire of the Other"; it is tied to this desire insofar as the subject does not know *which objet a* it is for the Other.[67] But since, no matter in how masked a fashion, in the fantasm the *objet a* can be referenced in mediation on the part of anxiety, the fantasm turns into a site of recognition. According to Lacan, what we have here is the most enduring interrogation of Western philosophy.[68] It turns the body and its perceptions into the point of reference for the Real: it is not what consciousness verifies as real that is real, but rather real is what happens on and inside the body, whether consciousness, which, as such, always comes too late, is capable of even perceiving this occurrence or not. Real is what emerges in unconscious *jouissance:* on this side of perception and consciousness, where they are united; in between perception and consciousness where, topographically, they are separate. On this side of perception and consciousness *and* in between perception and consciousness, there lies the body. Anxiety is a bodily experience, the experience of the *objet a* at the moment of its severing *and* the experience of the desire of the Other which articulates itself around this severing. Anxiety is the experience of this severing cut with which the *objet a is* separated off from the body, lifted out, and marked, thereby taking on the function of shielding against stimulation by anticipating it, by informing on it and by pointing towards it anticipatorily. But it is not—and here Lacan draws consequences that differ from Freud's in *Inhibitions, Symptoms and Anxiety*—the ego to whom the signal is addressed; it is to the subject of the unconscious.

The decentering of consciousness, distinguished by sensation as the place where the Real occurs, is surely an essential moment in the critique of philosophy on the part of psychoanalysis. But this critique has been prepared for by philosophy itself. The heteronomy of the Real and of sensation as the only place in which the Real appears before and independently of perception and consciousness, as *appearance*, was formulated by Kant: "Reality, in the pure concept of understanding, is that which corresponds to a sensation in general; it is that, therefore, the concept of which in itself points to being (in time)."[69] There is as of yet no concept, and the postulate is made (and it is Kant who talks about *postulates*, of postulates of *empirical thought in itself*) that there are *perceptions*, "and, therefore, sensations of which we are conscious."[70] The function of transcendental apperception is postulated, and, "[i]t must be possible for the 'I think' to accompany all my representations."[71] With this function Kant formulates the epistemological necessity of a self-enclosed conceptual matrix of the possible that is capable of apprehending the *heteronomy* of the event of the Real and of sensation. Sensation plays "the role of origin, it is Being itself, reality."[72] Thus Kant already describes the Real in the same way in which Lacan formulates it: "The Real is the impossible. . . . " Or, to refer back to Weinrich's explanation of the *futur antérieur*: the "message" has always already "been given" even if it has not yet been confirmed. It is only the fact that the Real, as it is, is already capable of "arriving" and of manifesting itself in its effects somewhere, in the unconscious, that is, that Kant, because of the constitutional difference between *appearance* and the *thing in itself*, was not able to conceive. And yet, he laid the foundations for the thought: namely, by having fully brought the *I think* back into the finally ethical dimension of a postulate, of a demand that it *accompany* all of my representations, a demand that factually cannot always be satisfied, but which must be satisfied if one wishes to speak of cognition.[73]

Lacan, in contrast, makes it clear that it is still possible to speak of cognition when what evades *accompaniment* arrives in a place other than consciousness. For Lacan Kant's unconditional demand is nothing but a bare demand. A demand that always comes too *late: Where It[d] was, I [ego] shall become* is a response to Kant's demand for simultaneity, the *(simultaneous) temporality of accompaniment [Begleit(gleich)zeitigkeit]* of consciousness in the execution of the synthesis of perception. In terms of its own possibility, this response is based on the contradiction that Kant himself alludes to but does not develop (referred to above) between the deduction of an objective "One Time" and the *implicit phenomenology* of the subject's experience of time. Freud is quite correct when he says of his own exposition of Kant's theory of time and space, which he allows himself to "touch on" only "for a moment," that it really "would merit the most exhaustive treatment."[74] Time *is* time of interruption, of discontinuity. Time lies in between perception and consciousness, in between the *I think* and the *I am*, in between the Real and the possible (that which can be expected and demanded). And Lacan's analysis of the unconscious and its "experience" as radical discontinuity should be read as an intimate dialogue with Kant as well.[75]

Notes

Article first published in *RISS* 11 (1989).

1. Sigmund Freud, *Zur Auffassung der Aphasien* (Leipzig and Vienna, 1891). English: *On Aphasia: A Critical Study* (New York: International University Press, 1953). The conception of language and memory formulated in this "Critical Study" (the book's subtitle) already contains the main features of what in *Studies on Hysteria* is described as the functional mechanism of symptom formation and its therapeutic dissolution; this is then developed into a first theory of the psychical apparatus in "A Project for a Scientific Psychology" in 1895. Cf. also the studies of John Forrester, *Language and the Origins of Psychoanalysis* (London, 1980); and Johannes Fehr, *Das Unbewußte und die Struktur der Sprache: Studie zu Freuds frühen Schriften* (Zurich: Diss, 1987); as well as the first chapter of my book, *Angst—Einbildungskraft—Sprache: Ein verbindender Aufriß zwischen Freud—Kant—Lacan.* (Munich, 1989).

2. Sigmund Freud, *Auffassung*, 23. One should point out that Freud is here summarizing Meynert's "cortico-centric" theory of the structure of the brain, which, already in his text on aphasia, he had characterized as follows: "In his far-reaching explanation of anatomical relationships, Meynert asserts that the cortex is well-suited to grasp and to perceive all sensory perceptions given the exteriority of its location. In addition, he compares it to a compound protoplasmic organism which envelopes a body the parts of which it wants to assimilate by transforming itself into a cavity. The rest of the brain in its

entirety appears as the appendix and auxiliary organ to the cerebral cortex, the whole body as the armature of its feelers and tentacles which grant it the opportunity to take in the picture of the world and to act upon it" (Freud, *Zur Auffassung der Aphasien*, 47. English: *On Aphasia: A Critical Study*. New York: International University Press, 1953). With Meynert's death, the skull let go of its contents: it toppled over and granted Freud the opportunity of "a rare human pleasure: the opportunity to select from Meynert's library what suited me— somehow like a savage drinking mead from his enemy's skull" (Sigmund Freud, *The Complete Letters of Sigmund Freud to Wilhelm Fliess, 1887–1904*, trans. and ed. Jeffrey Moussaieff Masson [Cambridge, Mass: Belknap Press of Harvard University Press, 1985], 31–2 (letter of 7/12/1892).

3. Sigmund Freud, *Complete Letters*, 146, letter of 10/20/1895.

4. Sigmund Freud, *Beyond the Pleasure Principle, Standard Edition, Volume 28*, trans. James Strachey (London: The Hogarth Press), 24.

5. Ibid., 26.

6. Ibid., 26.

7. Ibid., 25.

8. Ibid., 26.

9. Ibid., 27.

10. Ibid., 27.

11. Ibid., 27.

12. In his minute reading of this Freudian text: "*Spéculer—sur 'Freud,'*" contained in *La carte postale, de Socrate à Freud et au-delà* (Paris, 1980), 382. [English version: Jacques Derrida, *The Post Card: From Socrates to Freud and Beyond*, trans. Alan Bass (Chicago: The University of Chicago Press, 1987), 287.]

13. Sigmund Freud, *Beyond the Pleasure Principle*, 39.

14. Jacques Derrida, 381. English: 286.

15. Sigmund Freud, *Beyond the Pleasure Principle*, 27.

16. Cf. ibid., 89 and also Sigmund Freud, "On Narcissism: An Introduction," *Standard Edition Volume 14*, 73–102.

17. Freud, *Beyond*, 28.

18. P.-L. Assoun, *Freud, la philosophie et les philosophes* (Paris, 1976), 159.

19. Ibid., 28.

20. Paul-Laurent Assoun reads Freud's statement about Kant's pure forms of perception a priori in this way, a mistake which, in his opinion, is the fault of the philosophers themselves: Schopenhauer (whom Assoun regards as the authority who permitted Freud access to Kant's philosophy), who misunderstands Kant, and Kant, who enables such misunderstanding through his ambiguity; cf. P.-L. Assoun, *Freud, la philosophie,*159–170. Nothing would be easier than to reprimand Freud for his objection to Kant because of the very form his objection takes (Freud doesn't quote, doesn't reconstruct, reduces Kant's elaborations of time and space to one sentence, is, it seems, terminologically imprecise. . . .) What one would lose thereby will at least be alluded to in this article.

21. Immanuel Kant, *Critique of Pure Reason,* B 159.

22. Ibid. A 188f./B 232; cf. also A 185F/B 228f.

23. Ibid., B 163.

24. Cf. Paul Ricoeur, *Temps et Récit III. Le temps raconté* (Paris, 1985), 74 f.

25. Immanuel Kant, *Critique of Pure Reason,* B 67 f.

26. Cf. Martin Heidegger, *Phänomenologische Interpretation von Kants Kritik der reinen Vernunft,* Vorlesung, Gesamtausgabe Band 25 (Frankfurt, 1977), 394.

27. Immanuel Kant, *Critique of Pure Reason,* A 199/B 244 f. (Author's emphasis).

28. Cf. Andrzej Warminski, "A Question of an Other Order: Deflections of the Straight Man," in *Diacritics* 9 (1979): 75.

29. Sigmund Freud, *The Interpretation of Dreams, Standard Edition,* Volume 5, 621.

30. Freud is not consistently as clear as he is in the above quotation. Even the immediate context of that quote appears to establish the *past* as the firm point of reference for the analysis of a dream and thereby to reduce this complex temporality to a linear one. Even the characterization of the *indestructibility* through "paths which have been laid down once and for all, which never fall into disuse and which, whenever an unconscious excitation recathects them, are always ready to conduct the excitatory process to discharge" (*The Interpretation of Dreams,* 580–1, footnote) seems to remain under the spell of an epistemology guided by linear temporality and causality.

31. In the passages of the *Critique of Pure Reason* that concern themselves with causality, Kant does come close to these questions, but what alone is at stake for him is resolving the *uncertainty* of the causal relation in terms of the

specification of a *cause* through the *certainty* of temporal succession (cf. A 203–204/B 248–249).

32. H. Weinrich, *Tempus. Besprochene und erzählte Welt* (Stuttgart, 1977), 63. [trans. E. S.]

33. Jacques Derrida, *Writing and Difference*, trans. Alan Bass (Chicago: The University of Chicago Press, 1978).

34. Sigmund Freud, *Beyond the Pleasure Principle*, 29.

35. Sigmund Freud, "A Project for a Scientific Psychology," *Standard Edition, Volume 1*, 295–343.

36. Sigmund Freud, "The Economic Problem of Masochism," *Standard Edition, Volume 19*, 160.

37. Sigmund Freud, "A Note Upon the 'Mystic Writing-Pad'" (1925), *Standard Edition, Volume 19*, 231. In "Negation" Freud will ascribe to the *ego* the capacity to periodically cathect the system *Pcpt.-Cs.* and, thus, to partake of the external stimuli (cf. Sigmund Freud, ibid. 237).

38. Jacques Lacan, *Écrits* (Paris, 1966), 299f. (*Author has modified the translation slightly—H.-D. G.*). English: *Écrits: A Selection*, trans. Alan Sheridan (New York: W. W. Norton, 1977).

39. Cf. M. Stingelin, "La théorie, elle aussi, brûle nos étapes," in *RISS* 6 (1987): 76, and also Samuel Weber, *Rückkehr zu Freud: Jacques Lacans Entstellung der Psychoanalyse*, (Frankfurt, 1978), 10 ff.

40. Cf. J.-C. Milner, *Les noms indistincts* (Paris, 1983), 20.

41. "*Pour penser, il faut être*," Descartes says in part 4, section 3, of his *Discours de la Méthode*. Cf. J.-L. Marion's important book, *Sur la théologie blanche de Descartes* (Paris, 1981). Marion describes the Cartesian *cogito* as an inherently paradoxical construction; for the sentence "Cogito ergo sum" is presented as a truth that discovers itself as a conclusion and therefore introduces a *logical anteriority*, but which is not by necessity identifiable with the *existential anteriority* of the aimed at demonstration, the certainty of *existence* (ibid., 372 ff.).

42. Cf., for example, Immanuel Kant, *Critique of Pure Reason*, A 355. Alain Juranville has shown that, despite his intended demonstration, Descartes's own argument leads to limiting the "I think" to the punctuality of the act of thinking; cf. *Lacan et la philosophie* (Paris, 1984), 144.

43. Cf. Jacques Lacan, *Seminar XI: The Four Fundamental Concepts of Psychoanalysis* (New York & London: W. W. Norton, 1981), 43.

44. Anonymous, *"Le clivage du sujet et son identification,"* in *Scilicet* 2/3 (1970), 108.

45. Cf. Jacques Lacan, *Seminar XI: Four Fundamental Concepts,* 54.

46. Ibid., 54.

47. Ibid., 60.

48. Cf. ibid., 108 f.

49. For the representation of these three aspects of the fantasm, cf. Alain Juranville, *Lacan et la philosophie,* 190 f., and also, in reference to the fantasm as sacrifice and bait, C. Calligaris, *Hypothèse sur le fantasme* (Paris, 1983), 29.

50. Sigmund Freud, *Beyond the Pleasure Principle,* 29.

51. Ibid., 29.

52. Sigmund Freud, *The Ego and the Id, Standard Edition, Volume 19,* 55.

53. Sigmund Freud, *Beyond the Pleasure Principle,* 29–30.

54. Cf. "Project for a Scientific Psychology," in *The Origins of Psychoanalysis:* "There is the question that pain has a specific quality aside from unpleasure."

55. Cf. J. Laplanche, *Problématiques I: L'angoisse* (Paris, 1980), 190.

56. Sigmund Freud, "Repression," *Standard Edition, Volume 14,* 146.

57. Sigmund Freud, *Beyond the Pleasure Principle,* 30.

58. Laplanche, *Problématiques I: L'angoisse,* 194.

59. Sigmund Freud, *Beyond the Pleasure Principle,* 30.

60. This model of trauma and its energetic and functional aftereffects corresponds to the principle of "functional disinvolution" developed by Hughlings Jackson, on which Freud based himself already in his *Aphasia* text of 1891 in order to explain that "as a whole," the linguistic apparatus reacts to disturbances "in a unanimous way; that is, it does not exhibit a sharply delineated deficit, but rather a general interference with its functioning.(Cf. *On Aphasia* [London & New York, 1953]).

61. Sigmund Freud, *Beyond the Pleasure Principle,* 31.

62. Ibid., 31.

63. Ibid., 31.

64. Cf. Sigmund Freud, *Inhibitions, Symptoms and Anxiety*. In my book (see note 1) I examine the conceptions of anxiety in the works of Freud, Lacan and Heidegger.

65. Jacques Lacan *Seminar X: L'angoisse* (unpubl., 12/19/1962; 3/6/1963, and 3/13/1963). [trans. E. S.]

66. Jacques Lacan, *Seminar XI: The Four Fundamental Concepts*, 62.

67. Jacques Lacan, *Séminaire X: L'angoisse* (7/3/1963). [trans. E. S.]

68. Ibid. (5/8/1963). [trans. E. S.]

69. Immanuel Kant, *Critique of Pure Reason*, A 142/B 182.

70. Ibid., A 225/B 272.

71. Ibid., B 131.

72. M. Henry, *Généalogie de la psychanalyse* (Paris: 1985), 130.

73. In my book I analyze the function and the "rhetorical structure" of the *I think* (cf. note 1).

74. Sigmund Freud, *Beyond the Pleasure Principle*, 28.

75. Lacan gives indication of this reference when he appreciates Kant's concept of *cause*; cf. *Seminar XI: The Four Fundamental Concepts*, 21.

17

Sacrifice and the Law

BERNARD BAAS

To subject the notion of sacrifice* to a general scrutiny may seem like a useless enterprise, since the term covers such a wide field and is implicated in investigations which in themselves do not guarantee that it is possible to tell whether or not a univocal determination is feasible or even whether it is possible to refer to any sort of systematic coherence. This difficulty is not accidental; I suggest that it is not simply the result of excessive range or of the excessive diversity of the objects and representations that one must consider when studying the vague rubric "sacrifice." On the contrary, this difficulty is an essential part of the question of sacrifice, because it is inherent in the ambiguity of the concept. Incidentally, one should note that this difficulty is the object of the preparatory thoughts in most theories of

---

*The term, "le sacrifice," here translated as "sacrifice," and in other contexts translated as the procedure of a "sacrifice to," is closely related to "le sacre," that is, "anointment," "crowning," "consecration"; "le sacré": the "saintly," the "sacral"; the adjective "sacré" means: "sacrificed," "sacred," "sacral," "consecrated," as well as "untouchable" in the juridical sense (it is often found in conjunction with "confounded"); the participle "sacrifié" has the same meanings, and it can also be translated as "offered up to"; the adjectival construction "sacrificielle" exists only in French [and English: "sacrificial"—E. S.] In German [and English] "la victime" is also rendered as "victim," which, however, is closer in meaning to "death toll," "casualty," "the dead"; but it also means "sacrificial victim," "object of ridicule," of "deception," or the "victim of hallucination"; in the religious context, it means the "victim," the "sacrificial victim."

Additionally, we find in the text the term "l'offrande," meaning "the offering," from the Latin "offerendous," "that which is to be offered in sacrifice" ("le sacré" has the same root); in some dictionaries we also find the word "sacrilège' in relation to "sacrifice." [Translation of German translators' note —E. S.]

241

sacrifice, including the sociological and ethnographic ones. Without straining things too much one could even say that every theory of sacrifice to begin with consists of removing anything from its field of investigation that would impede the construction of a uniform definition. And surely one cannot solve this difficulty by claiming, as does Marcel Détienne, that "the concept of *sacrifice* is a surpassed category of thought,"[1] because that would also mean that contemporary thought would have to demand of itself not to be conceptual.

If, on the contrary, we establish the *regulative* principle of our investigation to be to examine the possibilities of how one could construct a uniform concept of sacrifice, even if it were only a problematic uniformity, then a priori we should not be allowed to exclude even a single theory of sacrifice, nor should we arbitrarily limit the realm of thought that presents itself. Rather, we must examine the nature of the fascination that the concept of sacrifice has evoked in many modern thinkers, sociologists, philosophers and psychoanalysts. Because there *is* a fascination with sacrifice. And it is precisely this fascination that Lacan is concerned with in the passage I wish to use as a starting point for my reflections. But one could just as well say that all of my statements will amount to an attempt at furnishing a commentary on the enigmatic passage with which Lacan closes his Seminar on *The Four Fundamental Concepts of Psycho-analysis*:

> There is something profoundly masked in the critique of the history that we have experienced. This, re-enacting the most monstrous and supposedly superseded forms of the holocaust, is the drama of Nazism. I would hold that no meaning given to history, based on Hegeliano-Marxist premises, is capable of accounting for this resurgence—which only goes to show that the offering to obscure gods of an object of sacrifice is something to which few subjects can resist succumbing, as if under some monstrous spell.

> Ignorance, indifference, an averting of the eyes may explain beneath what veil this mystery still remains hidden. But for whoever is capable of turning a courageous gaze towards this phenomenon—and, once again, there are certainly few who do not succumb to the fascination of the sacrifice in itself—the sacrifice signifies that, in the object of our desires, we try to find evidence for the presence of the desire of this Other that I call here *the dark God*.[2]

Lacan then refers to Spinoza's *Amor Dei Intellectualis* as a unique exception insofar as this love corresponds to the unique but, according to Lacan, untenable position in which the philosopher's desire defines itself as being in a state of total affinity with divine attributes. He then continues,

Experience shows us that Kant is more true, and I have proved that his theory of consciousness, when he writes of practical reason, is sustained only by giving a specification of the moral law which, looked at more closely, is simply desire in its pure state, that very desire that culminates in the sacrifice, strictly speaking, of everything that is the object of love in one's human tenderness—I would say, not only in the rejection of the pathological object, but also in its sacrifice and murder. That is why I wrote *Kant avec Sade*.[3]

Undoubtedly, this passage is too dense, too crowded, for it to be possible to provide an explanatory paraphrase at first go. For the moment, I will limit myself to making a few observations.

The remark about sacrifice is introduced with an explicit reference to the extermination of the Jews, denoted here by the sacrifice-metaphor of the Holocaust. It is well known that this metaphor, in the double meaning in which it has been heard, used, and even exploited in certain media productions, has legitimately led the Jewish community to replace it with the word *Shoah*, an expression, which in the Hebrew tradition designates destruction, as far as this "destruction" evades all implications of sacrifice. But in Lacan's text the appearance of this metaphor frees it from any sort of foggily solemn or artificially compassionate intention. Its appearance enables one to recognize in a clear and twofold manner that Lacan thinks of the question of sacrifice in reference to the problems of identification. Indeed, this passage is on the one hand followed immediately by a reflection on the end/aim (*fin*) of analysis, a reflection which culminates in the idea of "overcoming the level of identification";[4] on the other hand, this reference to the extermination of the Jews is accompanied by a contestation of Hegelian and Marxist theories: that is, precisely the two philosophers who, each in his own way, defined the sense, direction, and progression of history as the result of identificatory processes. In other words, he suggests that the "drama" of modern history cannot be understood from the perspective of a theory that makes identification both the principle and the end, the aim, of history. According to Lacan, something else occurs beyond the logic of identification, something that makes it possible to understand the idea of sacrifice.

But before he proceeds to talk about the meaning, or, as he says, the "eternal sense," of sacrifice, Lacan insists on its irresistible attraction. In two separate places he comments on how rare those people, who are capable of "not succumb[ing] to the fascination of the sacrifice in itself," are. This fascination is not in itself the truth about sacrifice, but, on the contrary, it masks or "veils" the truth about sacrifice and thus, for Lacan, truth itself insofar as the latter exceeds the logic of identification. But when the "sacrifice in itself" is fascinating, then its truth is unbearable. This truth, for Lacan, is the truth of desire in its essential relation to the desire of the Other. I will return to this point below.

But first I want to point out that by saying this Lacan does not intend to limit the definition of sacrifice to whatever use it can serve in the analytic context. Because if at first sacrifice is approached as an "offering" to the gods, the continuation of the passage also clearly makes reference to the idea of the moral sacrifice in the sense in which Kant uses it in his practical philosophy. But then, says Lacan, it is no longer simply a matter of the trivial metaphor of sacrifice as renunciation; rather, what is really at stake is taking the metaphor literally, because the moral law would imply the "sacrifice" or "murder" of the pathological object, that is, of every sensual element, including that aspect of desire that falls under the category of what we commonly call sympathy or tenderness.

I will here conclude my observations regarding this passage and return to its main themes in their entirety below. For the moment I would like to establish that here we are dealing with an attempt at understanding sacrifice in a way that is not limited to the reality of those phenomena pertaining to sacrifice that are of interest to religious ethnology or anthropology. On the contrary, Lacan is really aiming at a general meaning of sacrifice, or better: he intends to bring back together into one single definition what many people, purely for their own intellectual comfort, wish to sever completely: ritual sacrifice and moral sacrifice.

Bringing these two uses of sacrifice under the same conceptual umbrella has clearly led to the formulations, but also the difficulties, of most sociological theories of sacrifice. Already in Tylor's theory[5] we find the idea that moral sacrifice is the result of a development whose point of origin had been the ritual religious sacrifice. Tylor summarizes its logic in the strict and economic formula, "*do ut des*" (I give, so that you give). We are dealing with evolutionism here, since moral renunciation would on the whole be the end, the telos, which is virtually contained in the archaic sacrifice insofar as this in a certain sense implies a material renunciation of the sacrificial object. Within an analogous evolutionistic logic, Hubert and Mauss attempted to show how the transition from "sacrifice *to* God" to the "sacrifice *of* God" was the result of a certain advance in disinterestedness. In the first case, the "sacrifice *to* God," sacrifice is a contractual process in which, according to the formulation of Hubert and Mauss, "disinterestedness is mixed with interest"[6*] and through which the sacrificer realizes an exchange with a god by identifying with the sacrificial

---

* "L'intérêt," in addition to interest, sympathetic interest, attentiveness, consideration, has also a passive connotation, that is, the stimulation or enticement, incentive, that something can produce; in addition, it refers also to interest in the sense of advantage, use, self-interest (to which the word "utilité" usually refers as well). The connotations of "l'intérêt" reach into the realm of monetary issues—all sorts of financial interests. One should point out in passing that Kant is the first philosopher to write in German who uses the concept of interest in the context of both theoretical and practical philosophy. He encountered this in the works of Rousseau and Hutcheson.

victim. The "identification" with the victim ("identification" is the term used by Hubert and Mauss) saves the sacrificer from having to lose himself completely, something to which he would have been condemned had he "put himself into the rite to the end."[7] To offer oneself "without return" is something that is impossible for the sacrificer to do. But for the god it is possible. And this is precisely what constitutes the second case, the "sacrifice *of* the God," which represents "the loftiest expression and the ideal limit of unconditional self-abnegation."[8] In both cases the human and profane order receives from the God a sort of "restorative" force,[9] about which Hubert and Mauss are really not very clear but which they explicitly relate to social functioning.[10] It was Durkheim who succeeded in clarifying this issue in his essay, *The Elementary Forms of Religious Life*,[11] where he explains that in every culture the social sense, the feeling of belonging to a community, implies what he calls the spirit of "renunciation," "self-overcoming," "detachment from the self," and therefore "suffering."[12] So ritual sacrifice links the spirit of renunciation to social communion. This enables Durkheim to reconcile within the same definition a working explanation that links ritualistic and moral forms of sacrifice with the idea of communion through sacrifice. In the meantime the theory of totemism has made its way to us; it too, from an evolutionistic perspective, makes it possible to establish a connection between the totemic meal, already described by Robertson Smith,[13] and the Eucharistic communion of the Christians. Thus, under this double aspect of the spirit of communion and the spirit of renunciation, Christianity is said to be in some way the truth of all primitive forms of sacrifice. Without forcing these issues too much, one could say that this is the viewpoint that both Cassirer[14] and Girard,[15] each in his own way, were to develop later on. This could be summarized in the following general formula: through renunciation, self-abnegation, and then forgiveness, the individual realizes his identification *with* the community and *as* a member of the community. Put differently, sacrificial destruction, whether it is violent or not, already implies the spirit of renunciation that defines moral sacrifice. This would be its meaning, a meaning that lay concealed within the primitive rituals but which became revealed in the Christian-modern form of sociality.

In order now to explain this ethnological and sociological tradition one can only approve of its very sharp critique in Marcel Détienne's study,[16] which opens the exposé of the research into *The Cuisine of Sacrifice in Greek Space*, edited by him and Jean-Pierre Vernant. Détienne and Vernant have incontestably earned the right to be recognized today as having emancipated religious sociology and ethnology from the profound influence which Hubert's and Mauss's theory had up until then exerted on it. Contemporary ethnologists, however, especially Luc de Heusch, in his work *Sacrifice in African Religions*,[17] are not ready to renounce all comparative studies of sacrifical systems under the pretense that (I quote the contribution by Jean-Louis Durand to the work compiled by Détienne and Vernant) the general concept of sacrifice is only "a lexical illusion" or "an ideological category of Judaeo-Christian reflection."[18] There are two observations to be made regarding the position of the new French Hellenistic School:

1. Its methodological principle consists in limiting the object of study simply to the "bloody-Greek-food-sacrifices"[19]—a translation of what the Greeks called the *thysia*[20]—as if this were an empirical given, something analogous to ethnological field work, and could be observed without the mediation of an established translinguistic vocabulary (in the name of what scientific procedure does one determine what is "illusory" in any given language?), and, above all, as if one could detach oneself from all modern conceptions in order to constitute it as an object. This endeavor consists essentially in supplying the correspondences between mythical elements, culinary practices, and social institutions in such a way that, instead of bringing to the surface the meaning of sacrifice, its explanation is finally led back to the repetition of the myth that underlies the organization of the sacrifices. Jean-Pierre Vernant's well-known study, "The Founding Myth of Sacrifice in Hesiod,"[21] is a typical example of this.

2. This position is dominated by the desire to distinguish itself from all modern theories of sacrifice which are guilty, *all guilty*, according to the merciless process of Marcel Détienne, of the *same* fault, which is to be attributed to what, incessantly and without any nuance whatsoever, is called "the Judaeo-Christian ideology"[22]: to have confused ritualistic and moral sacrifice and even to have wanted to confuse them. Nevertheless, two names—and they are not among the least—are missing in this list of the accused: Freud, on the one hand, and, more generally, psychoanalysis. In his own way, however, Freud is not an exception to the confusion that is being looked at here, since he explains the spirit of sacrifice and moral coercion, even in the shape of the Kantian form of the categorical imperative, as the manifestation of the cruelty of the superego, that is, as the effect of the Oedipus Complex,[23] so that, to sum all of this up as quickly as possible, the origin of moral sacrifice, the spirit of renunciation, is the archetypal form of all sacrifices: the original totemic meal following the patricide. This means that in his own way Freud does not succeed in evading the evolutionistic tendencies that characterize all previously mentioned theories of sacrifice. He too then could be accused both of propagating the mythical character of this type of universal history of sacrifice (which Lévi-Strauss did as well) and of accepting the hypothesis of totemism without reservation. But it would be very difficult to accuse him of having wanted to determine the Christian God of sacrifice and self-abnegation to be the *teleological* truth of primitive forms of sacrifice. It is therefore probably not a coincidence that Détienne shies away from mentioning Freud in his indictment.

It is also surely not a coincidence that he quietly ignores all of Georges Bataille's reflections on sacrifice. Because even if it is impossible to claim that all of his thoughts are based on one single theory of sacrifice, one can nevertheless recognize a red thread, a consistency in this context, whose principle it is to dissolve the assimilation of ritualistic and moral sacrifice; more: its principle is to develop an interpretation of ritualistic sacrifice which would specifically and essentially oppose it to moral sacrifice. But this is not the only thing that is at stake here. So when Bataille remains unmentioned precisely by those who claim to be leaving behind all reflections on the *concept* of sacrifice, that is, all philosophies of sacrifice, this is because Bataille does not shirk the difficulty of the question lying at the basis of the problem of sacrifice: the question of identification. It is precisely here that we find the explanation—I will develop it below—for why Bataille's thought secretly influences Lacan's.

Let me put all of this more precisely: to begin with, one can say, by simplifying things a bit, that Bataille's concept of sacrifice repels any interpretation that attempts to reduce it to an interest-based exchange, whatever this exchange may be. On the one hand, this goes for religious sacrifice, whenever what is meant by it is sacrifice of a commodity or a good to a god in order to gain divine favor in return, whether this gain be a plentiful harvest, a safe birth or even eternal salvation; on the other hand, it goes for moral sacrifice as the renunciation of a present gratification in the interest of something regarded as superior. In both cases, the sacrifice performs a *work*, as it implies a beneficent perspective. One can go as far as to say that sacrifice understood in this way falls, in a certain sense, under the category of investment, an investment, to be precise, which follows the calculation of combined interests. In this sense, sacrifice would be merely a "platitude" or even a "profanation": "A sacrifice which has its eye on a crude result like the fertility of the fields turns out to be a platitude in relation to the *divine*, to the *sacredness* which introduces religion into the game. . . . The works through which a Christian attempts to secure his salvation can then be understood as a profanation."[24] Put differently: sacrifice (the etymology of which is *sacra-facere*, doing sacred things or sacralizing things) loses all particularity as soon as one reduces it to a process of exchange, because it is difficult to see in what way one is then to distinguish the sacred from the profane. Because if the *profane* world necessarily obeys the servile order of the economy of trade, of profitable exchange, what would constitute the *sacred* and what would be the *divine* when sacrifice too is assimilated into interested, profitable exchange? Consequently, one cannot be satisfied with an economic conception of sacrifice. Incidentally, Plato had already shown this in the *Euthypron*,[25] when he heaps scorn on all forms of commercial exchange between gods and humans; the same thing drove Meister Eckhart (one of the mystics to whom Bataille paid so much attention) to say that every demand directed at God keeps the "merchants in the Temple."[26]

But Bataille is not content with pointing to the contradictory nature of this economic conception of sacrifice; he does not attempt to oppose a true meaning to it, because he recognizes that it is precisely the question of meaning that sacrifice brings into the arena. Indeed, if discourse, conceptual thought, can find meaning in sacrifice only when it understands it as profitable exchange, that is because "intelligence and human discursive thought have developed as a function of slavish work";[27] put differently, because the logic of meaning is nothing more than the logic of interest. Thus one must attempt to think of sacrifice within the context of what Bataille calls *sovereignty*, and from the start it must be understood negatively, as that which overcomes all interest and therefore every work. Without doubt, one can understand it *only* negatively, because "sacrifice is a *sovereign, autonomous* way of being only insofar as it is not represented by *significant* discourse. To the extent to which it is represented by discourse, what is *sovereign* is given in servile concepts. What is *sovereign* is by definition what does not *serve*."[28] If then what to the human being matters is "not to be merely a thing ("thing" is the term which in Bataille signals affiliation with the servile order of profitability) but to be in a *sovereign* manner,"[29] he must refer to his inner reality and expose himself to this inner truth by exposing it. Because sacrifice belongs to the movement by which the individual attempts to relate himself to himself, to his being and his identity, a movement which leads him to recognize himself as negativity, and thereby to place his own death so that it faces him and to place himself so that he faces his own death.

To formulate this also slightly differently, the meaning of sacrifice, strictly speaking, belongs to the realm of Hegelian negation. Bataille quotes the following passage from the preface to the *Phenomenology of Spirit:* "[The life of the mind] only wins to its truth when it finds itself utterly torn asunder. It is this mighty power, not by being a positive which turns away from the negative; . . . on the contrary, mind is this power only by looking the negative in the face, and dwelling with it."[30] But Hegel had not recognized that this laceration occurred in sacrifice insofar as terror and pleasure, fear and joy, coincide there. Indeed, for Hegel the prototype of the sacrificial human is less the sacrificer priest than the warrior hero. And this preference makes sacrifice tend toward the economic side, that is, the side of the spirit's own interest in its process of self-revelation and consequent realization. When the heroic death of the soldier is "objectively the real sacrifice of the personal Ego,"[31] then the identificatory process of the Spirit, in other words, of *history*, as we know, is in general the "altar" of all sacrifices.[32] Incidentally, dialectics itself is nothing other than the logic of negativity and hence the logic of sacrifice, but with the subtle difference, in the strong Hegelian sense of "difference," that *remaining contained* within it is what alone is the "positive" [instance] for the Spirit—namely, the gain of its progress in the direction of absolute identity. Dialectics is without reservation an economy of sacrifice. This can be seen in exemplary fashion in the section of the *Phenomenology of Spirit* dealing with "*Art-Religion*," or, more precisely, in the passage which refers to the meaning of sacrifice in cult.[33] Here Hegel defines sacrifice as a process in which the divine Being gives itself over to self-consciousness by surrendering pure essence, so that it makes itself become a single existing thing. In this process self-

consciousness elevates itself into Essence by renouncing the possession and pleasure of the sacrificed thing. On the side of self-consciousness, sacrifice is a "pure
abandon"; but it insinuates the gift coming from the divine substance because, as
Hegel says, "Essence (i.e. pure Being, divine substance) must have from the start
implicitly sacrificed *itself.*"[34] Abandon [*l'abandon*] versus gift, renunciation versus
renunciation: the dialectical sacrificial process is exchange regulated by the logic
of negativity, the "positive effectiveness" of which, however, as Hegel says, consists in allowing self-consciousness to become self-consciousness as essence. The
sacrificial process becomes conflated with the dialectical law of identification.

Understood thus, Hegel's theory is both very close to and very distant
from Bataille's thought. It is very close in the sense that for Bataille sacrificial
activity constitutes the individual's self-revelation vis-à-vis himself, his self-
consciousness and therefore identification, insofar as sacrifice (and drama and
representation on the whole) is subterfuge: the sacrificer dies himself by seeing
himself die *via identification* with the animal defeated by death.[35] At the same
time Hegel's thought is radically removed from Bataille's for three reasons: first,
because what Bataille terms "self-consciousness" as intimacy cannot be reduced
to what Hegel has in mind with the term "identification." Intimacy is not the
gratification of a consciousness which has access to its own identity; rather, it
surpasses all identificatory processes because it originates in a "joy vis-à-vis
death,"[36] or, as Bataille also puts it, in the "anguished joy,"[37] which in sacrifice
completes absolute laceration and opens up the door to sovereignty. Then,
because sovereignty is "the freedom of the moment, independent of a task that
will bring about perfection,"[38] not the product of a teleological process, but
"that which takes place in a fleeting, ungraspable manner,"[39] what is not programmed, so to speak, and lies outside of all intention. For this reason sacrifice
is essentially inactive and without reserve. "Sacrifice is the antithesis of production carried out with regard to the future; it is consumption/waste,* which is

---

*Bataille distinguishes very sharply (and also elaborates on this distinction) between "la
consummation"—(productive) consumption, that is, expenditure, use, what is required
for maintenance; this productive use is subordinated to the realm of production—and "la
consummation." The latter term is reserved for unproductive forms of consumption and
excludes all forms of consumption that serve as a means for production. In order to keep
this distinction clear, he often uses the phrase, "dépense improductive," which is to be
translated as "unproductive expenditure," as "waste," referring to an expenditure heavy
in losses," or as "devouring," that is, an offering that signifies destruction itself and that
is unreserved. To be noted is that the French language is perhaps the language richest
in expressions referring to different forms of use or waste—perhaps it was also France
that pushed feudalism to its limits. I will just list some of those that appear frequently
in Bataille's work: "la dilapidation," that is, "waste" in the strict sense; "le gaspillage,"
that is, "squandering"; "la dissipation," that is, "evaporation," "dispersion"; "la prodigalité,"
that is, a sort of addiction to wastage, as well as generosity.

interested only in the moment itself. In this sense it is gift and abandon; but that which is given cannot be an object of preservation for the one upon whom it is bestowed."[40] And finally, one must acknowledge, against Hegel (even if the concept is closest to him), the *delusion* (the French word *leurre* also means "lure")[41]—this is the word Bataille uses—the *delusion* involved in every identificatory process, for such a process is bound to miss the intimacy in which it originated. "How could man find or find himself again," Bataille asks, "when the act in which the investigation in some way engages him is precisely what removes him from himself?"[42] So one could say that Bataille's thought on sacrifice is a reflection on the end of sacrifice, which should be understood in its double sense: on the one hand, sacrifice is in itself an aim/end (*fin*), and to reduce it to the status of a means always goes back to robbing it of its own particularity by reintegrating it into the servile order of utilitarian acts;[43] on the other hand (but still, of course, related to the first point), sacrifice is the perfected, completed impossible thing for us; we can grasp it only within and through signifying discourse, that is, discourse that is always already servile.

Bataille's reflections, far from legitimizing the spirit of sacrifice, the moral order, by a theory of ritualistic sacrifice, define moral sacrifice, then, as what contradicts the truth of sacrifice and makes it unrecognizable. And in his *Theory of Religion* Bataille shows how historically the transition of the system of sacrifice into the military order led to a dislocation of the limits of the sacred and the profane and from there to the institution of morality as a universal order based on reason, an order about which Bataille specifies that it is the "order of things," that is, the profane order which serves utility.[44] This point can be found in the second part of *The Theory of Religion*, which bears the title, "Religion Within the Limits of Reason," a title which makes it clear that Bataille intends to respond to the Kantian understanding of the relationship between religion and morality—in order to break away from it. And indeed, in the fourth treatise of *Religion in den Grenzen der bloßen Vernunft* of Kant one finds a remark about sacrifice, a remark which Bataille doubtless finds unacceptable. Not far above that passage Kant had mentioned the sacrifices, the pompous festivities and the public games, through which human beings had attempted to gain the favor of the godhead; for Kant these are modes of behavior which belong to what he calls "religious delusion" in which human beings believe that they please God by exempting themselves from "the arduous and uninterrupted effort of affecting the innermost part of their [our] moral disposition."[45]* Kant then proceeds to clarify:

> [Yet sacrifices] (penances, castigations, pilgrimages, etc.) have always been regarded as more powerful, more likely to work on the favor of

---

*The term, "l'intention morale," is translated here ss "moral disposition" because it refers back to Kant. Ordinarily "intention" is to be translated as "intention," "plan," "purpose," or "will."

heaven, and more apt to remove sin, since they more forcefully serve to indicate unbounded (though not moral) subjection to the will of heaven. The more useless such self-inflicted torments are, the less aimed at the universal moral improvement of the human being, the holier they seem to be. For just because they have absolutely no use in the world and yet cost effort, they seem to be aimed solely at attesting devotion to God. . . . Visible here is the propensity to a form of conduct that has no moral value in itself. . . . Yet in our mind we attribute to this conduct the value of the end itself, or, what amounts to the same thing, we attribute to the mind's readiness to take on attitudes of dedication to God (called devotion) that value of these attitudes themselves. And this way of doing things is, therefore, a mere delusion of religion, which can assume all kinds of forms, in some appearing closer to the moral form than in others, yet in all not merely an unpremeditated deception but a maxim by which we attribute intrinsic value to the means rather than the end. And, because of this maxim, the delusion is equally absurd in all its forms, and, as a hidden inclination to deceit, equally to be condemned.[46]

Put differently, if sacrifices that are driven by interest belong to religious delusion, sacrifices that present themselves as disinterested and useless belong to a tendency to deceive. Religious delusion, as far as it is a "practical" delusion,[47] consists simply in desiring to attract divine favor to oneself, that is, to think of one's own interest, thereby neglecting one's moral convictions, which is here understood to be a *pure* conviction. On this premise one could think that the suppression of all interestedness in a ritualistic act (like the expiations or castigations which really are "useless within the world" and which supply no perceptible satisfaction, quite the opposite) bestows precisely the value of a purely moral conviction onto this act. Well, this is just an illusion. For such sacrifices not only do not contribute anything positive to the moral constitution, but they also allow that which is only a *means* to please the Godhead to pass as a disinterested *end*, that is, as an actual moral, and therefore sacred, act. Thus they are to be rejected for their tendency to deceive. One could formulate these condemnations equally well in the vocabulary of practical reason: the sacrifice that is motivated by interest, the sacrifice as exchange, is a delusion, or rather, it is *merely* a delusion, because, *without premeditation*, it assigns moral value to something which has none, namely to a mute (and unmotivated) action through a *hypothetical* imperative. On the other hand, seemingly disinterested religious sacrifices tend to deceive, are a trick, in other words; they attempt to allow an action which is actually subordinated to a *hypothetical* imperative to pass as an action which would be condemned by the categorical imperative. The tendency toward deception, in other words, consists in representing what is hypothetical as if it were categorical.

Kant wishes at all times to maintain the purity of moral conviction insofar as it belongs only to the categorical imperative, that is, the only constitution in which true disinterestedness is possible. Let us remember that the pure moral conviction is not that conviction which acts in view of the pleasure of an other, since that would mean making the will of the sensuous motive dependent on *pathological** love. No sort of sympathy and, in general, no sort of pathos could correspond to moral purity; on the contrary, it is only apathy—the absence of any sort of pathos—that could correspond to moral purity. But this also means that during the course of pursuing any sort of aim that is foreign to it, pure willpower, or in other words, pure practical reason, estranges itself into heteronomy and thus becomes servile in regard to sensuous tendencies, be it pathological love or self-love. Goodwill, insofar as it originates in pure respect for the law, can desire nothing but respect for the law, that is, its own law, the law of reason in its practical use; goodwill can desire nothing but itself, that is, its own autonomy.

"Autonomy" is also the term which Bataille uses to designate sovereignty,[48] insofar as it is understood as negative, as the absence of any sort of subjection to a foreign or external interest, that is, an interest in the service of [material] goods, of the "order of things." In an analogous fashion one could also compare Bataille's affirmation of the concept of "sovereignty" to the Kantian definition of the Highest Good insofar as this implies the idea of "a condition that is itself unconditional, that is, which is not subordinated to any other."[49] The essential thing here, however, is the persistence with which Kant shows that the interest of reason in its practical use applies only to pure reason; it is the interest in itself of the moral law, that is, both interest in itself and for itself of reason, so that moral action from the side of the empirical or the sensuous ego, from the side of the *pathological* ego, demands the most complete disinterestedness. It is for this reason that (in the passage which I quoted at the beginning) Lacan explains that the Kantian specification of the moral law amounts to the "sacrifice" of any sort of pathological object. And it is true what Jean-François Lyotard says in his study, "L'intérêt du sublime": "Kant does not have enough words to say what it is the spirit has to *sacrifice* in order to realize the moral law."[50] And Lyotard[51] shows that the sacrificial logic of this interest of rational law for itself concerns not only the sacrifice of the empirical ego which necessarily accom-

---

*Kant opposes "pathological" to "moral" or "practical." It is a "sense of pleasure founded on internal perception" (KpV) that serves the analysis of the "motive of pure practical reason" (ibid.). The first one, then, follows empirical principles, while moral pleasure is a priori founded on a pure principle.

panies moral action, but also, when it is a matter of explaining the interrelatedness of the faculties* within the sublime, the sacrifice of the power of imagination, or rather, the sacrifice of the freedom of the productive power of imagination when it places itself in the service of the moral law in order to lend it the use of its own sensuous representation.[52]

Consequently, the interest of the law implies the necessity of sacrifice. But this in no way means that one can use sacrifice as a means to elevate oneself to the level of the law. This is an essential restriction. To begin with, the restriction concerns religious sacrifices which certainly can at times represent some sort of aesthetic appearance of the sublime, but which are usually the result of a confused enthusiasm that can lead to fanaticism, to *Schwärmerei*, which always poses a threat to the purity of the moral law. In addition and above all, however, it concerns moral sacrifice which, in order to find access to morality, could not become the object of an interest for the empirical ego. Put differently, it would be completely contradictory if the ego were enabled to hope to achieve even the slightest positive satisfaction (such as self-satisfaction, self-love, pride, or even worse, happiness) in its fulfillment of the law, because that action which was to take place in accordance with the empirical ego's interest would lose its autonomy to the will.

What sort of action can the ego then *undertake* which would make it possible for it to elevate itself to the level of the law? That it can *undertake* any action to this end at all is out of the question. Be it for the sake of benefiting someone else that the subject sacrifices itself and thus subordinates its will to pathological motives, or be it that it sacrifices itself for the sake of its own self-satisfaction and thus subordinates its will to what Kant terms the "secret impulse of self-love,"[53]—in both cases the will loses its autonomy. Consequently, the empirical ego is unable to *undertake* any sacrifice at all, no matter how troublesome, because the simple fact of the undertaking transforms the sacrifice into a means toward an interest which is not the interest of the law, which, therefore, robs it of any value as disinterestedness and thus of any value as sacrifice. It is impossible to undertake moral sacrifice.

Of course Kant would not have supported any formulation of this sort. Still, the logic of moral disinterestedness in its relation to the purity of the law leads up to it. By the way, I am not the first one to have made this observation. I do wish to point out, however, that when one defines moral sacrifice as this kind of point of impossibility, one must at least recognize that there is a structural analogy here with what Bataille says about ritual sacrifice insofar as it is impossible to make it into a means *towards* gaining access to sovereignty without annulling it.

---

*The term, "Vermögen," in Kant is translated into French as "faculté," that is "faculty" in the Kantian sense, but also as "pouvoir": faculty, force, power.

Because, just as religious sacrifice originates in autonomous sovereignty (that is, in what Bataille also terms *"intimacy"*), without it being possible to pretend to be striving towards it *by means of* sacrifice, moral sacrifice emerges from the autonomous will (that is, what Kant also terms "the sacred"), again without it being possible to pretend to be striving towards it *by means of* sacrifice. Beyond all differences and all deviations existing between the thoughts of Kant and Bataille that could be legitimately pointed out, the same kind of logic dominates both of their interpretations of sacrifice. And I now wish to demonstrate that the same logic also dominates Lacan's reflections.

When Lacan, on the page I quoted earlier, speaks of "desire in its pure state" he does so in order to distinguish it from an articulated desire for an empirical object *(épithymène)*[*] and thus from a desire which is constituted within the signifying chain. The subject of desire, insofar as it is a subject only via alienation in the signifying chain, can give itself an object of desire only by crossing through the signifying net. This *alienation*, then, has a constitutive function for the subject. The dynamic of desire implies, however, that this desire is the result of lack. It would, however, be an illusion (a "myth"), according to Lacan, to assign a content of meaning to this lack—in other words, to designate it as something which results from the loss of an object which would have been the occasion for an original experience of satisfaction for the subject (we know that Freud equated this illusion with a temptation; this applies even more strongly to his descendants). Lack must therefore be conceived of as what it is: pure lack. Lacan calls this the Thing *(la Chose)*. Why the *Thing?* Precisely because lack is not a lost object. It can therefore not be referred to as the loss of an empirical object. Insofar as the subject is necessarily separated from what it lacks, this pure lack (the Thing) is, on the other hand, connected with what in experience emerges from that separation, that is, with what Lacan refers to as *objet a*, as far as it is specifically differentiated from the empirical object of desire. Indeed, the *objet a* cannot be identified with an empirical object even when, in experience, it is necessarily tied to empirical objects. This is the case with the breast and with excrement, which are not objects the subject had enjoyed and from which it had then been separated. For before separation there is neither subject nor object. It is *separation* that produces subject and object at the same time. *Alienation* and *separation* constitute the subject.

Accordingly, desire is always desire for an empirical object (epithymetic desire), because it necessarily passes through the signifying chain; but this desire, as far as it emerges from pure lack, from the Thing, is caused by what

---

[*]Epithymeo, thymos: to have a longing for something, to desire, wish; to epithymoun: longing, desire; epitinos: for something; epithymena: something longed for, as well as desire; epithymetes: lover, friend, student; epithymetos: desired, longed for, worthy of desire.

proceeds from pure lack—the *objet a*. That is why Lacan characterizes the *objet a* as the *object-cause-of-desire*. "Desire in its pure state" (this "pure" is to be interpreted in the strictest, in the most Kantian, manner) would be desire without an empirical object; in other words, desire which, without the mediation of the signifier, refers to that out of which it originates: pure lack, the Thing itself. Satisfaction of pure desire is what is called *jouissance*, which must be distinguished in a radical manner from pleasure, which is capable of producing an empirical object of desire (an epithymon). This *jouissance*, however, is strictly speaking impossible, because desire is incapable of detaching itself from the signifying chain within which it constitutes itself. There is only an indication, a kind of small leftover, of this *jouissance*, of what within desire belongs to pure lack—the *objet a*, in other words. For this reason Lacan says of this *objet a*, object-cause-of-desire, that it is an "excess [or supplementary] *jouissance*," an expression which I am not sure has always been understood in its full ambiguity: certainly "excess enjoyment" (*plus-de-jouir*) signifies a supplementary enjoyment within desire; but it is also necessary to hear something akin to "there is *no more jouissance*" (*il n'y a plus de jouir*) as an indication of the radical impossibility of desire. This shows that, essentially tied in with the subject's desire, within desire as far as it is aimed at an empirical object, there is the will to *jouissance* which Lacan refers to as the Will of the Other or the desire of the Other in order to illustrate the split within the subject. To say of the subject's desire that it is caused by the *objet a* also means that it is dominated by the Will to *jouissance*, to impossible enjoyment. Surreptitiously but also radically, the subject's desire is subjected to the law of *jouissance*, the law which comes to him from the Other.

The point of all of these definitions is to allow us to understand why, in reference to sacrifice, Lacan invokes Kant and Sade. Without rehashing my commentary on Lacan's text, "Lacan With Sade," which was printed elsewhere (see note 60), I will simply repeat this: in Sade's fantasm, in the terms in which Lacan defines it, the separation of the subject does "not require being joined in a single body."[54] For this reason the "calculatedness" of the Sadian subject in satisfying the law of the Other (the Will to *jouissance*) consists in reducing itself to being merely an executive agent of the law, the object-cause-of-desire (the *objet a*), by delivering the effects of this subjection to the law to the sacrificial victim. The act of sacrifice is supposed to allow the subject to identify with the law. But this calculatedness is also a deception, as Lacan shows when he comments on the end of *Philosophy in the Bedroom*: despite everything, *jouissance* remains prohibited to the subject. Analogously, the Kantian subject, in order to satisfy the rational moral law, can only impose all those sacrifices upon his empirical ego, which the latter would have to bear should the law be fulfilled. For this reason, then, Lacan is able to say that Sade is the truth of Kant,[55] because in both cases subjection to the law demands the sacrifice of the pathological object—indeed, "everything that is the object of love in one's human tenderness."

According to the same logic one could also speak of a *calculatedness* concerning consciousness within the act of sacrifice as it is understood by Bataille, because he refers to sacrifice as a subterfuge in which the sacrificer identifies with his sacrificial victim and sees himself die in the death of his victim. But this subterfuge is also a "deception" as soon as one purports to be using this sacrifice as a means to finding access to sovereignty. It is easy to see that Lacan has remembered Bataille's lesson well.

If, then, the law demands sacrifice, one can in no case use sacrifice to elevate oneself to the level of the law. That which demands sacrifice is also that at which sacrifice is aimed: the sacred; in other words, sovereignty, *jouissance*. And yet, sacrifice allows access to neither the sacred nor to sovereignty or *jouissance*. Sacrifice originates in the sacred but it does not allow access to the sacred because what is legislated for humans is the empirical order over and above the interest of sensuousness and of self-love (what Kant calls "the simply evil"). Sacrifice originates in sovereignty, but it does not allow access to sovereignty because for humans the empirical order is ruled by utility and servility (what Bataille calls "the order of things"). Sacrifice originates in *jouissance*, but it does not allow access to *jouissance*, because what is legislated for humans is the empirical order of desire through the necessary mediation of the signifier (what Lacan calls "alienation").

Even if all desire aims at empirical objects (the epithymenes), even if this desire is always interwoven within the chain of signifying identifications, it always takes place within what lies beyond the level of identifications and thus really forms the cause of its desire: this is the other side of desire, the desire of the Other, the will to impossible enjoyment. The object-cause-of-desire, the *objet a*, is then always bound up in the chain of signifying identifications, but it itself is not an element in this chain; it is, if one can put it this way, intimately excluded in this signifying chain; it is, as Lacan says, "extimate." And for this reason the subject can come to terms with the truth of its own subjective separation in analysis only under the condition of this "transgression of the level of identification" of which Lacan speaks and concerning which one imagines that the analysand has to pay for it with an excess of renunciation (*de plus d'un renoncement*), with more than renunciation (*de plus que d'un renoncement*). For the couch (*le divan*, the couch, is practically homophonous with *le divin*, the divine) is the altar of many sacrifices for sure.

But let us leave clinical issues behind and return to the definition suggested by Lacan in order to attempt to clarify it: "[S]acrifice signifies that, in the object of our desires, we try to find evidence for the presence of the desire of this Other that I call here *the dark God*." The trace, the evidence, of the desire of the Other, that is, of the will to *jouissance*, can only be the *extimate* object, the object-cause-of-desire. For sacrifice is *calculatedness, subterfuge* of this sort, in which the subject's separation seeks to represent itself in the duality of the sacrificer and the sacrificed. I do not mean to say thereby that this *calculatedness* of sacrifice is to be related back to the *calculatedness* of the Sadian fantasm. Because in the Sadian fantasm it is the tormentor, the executioner, who takes up the position of the object-cause-of-desire. In sacrifice, by contrast, we must acknowledge that this position of the object-cause-of-desire belongs to the sacrificed. The sacrificer offers to the God what is his, which *becomes* him *[ihm zukommt]*, to be understood as what *comes back [zurückkommt]* to him; what, in other words, had come from him originally: the object-cause-of-desire, what in desire comes from the will of the Other. In order to disavow the reality of pure lack, whence his desire originates—in other words, in order to disavow his own subjective splitting—the sacrificer transfers onto the god the law which makes him a desiring subject and which demands the sacrifice. This point is confirmed by another statement of Lacan's, which I quote from his text, "Science and Truth": "Let us say that a religious person leaves responsibility for the cause to God, but thereby bars his own access to truth. Thus he is led to place the cause of his desire in God's hands, and that is the true object of his sacrifice."[56]

Handing over to God the cause of one's desire means leaving to God what is our gift from God. Surrender versus gift: Lacan's comment is valuable also as an illuminating reiteration of Hegel's interpretation of sacrifice; though with the subtle difference that here Lacan, like Bataille, comments on the "deceptiveness" of sacrifice. His definition of sacrifice makes a strong and subtle point, namely that what is purely and simply at stake is some sort of attempt to find evidence for the presence of the desire of the Other. The calculatedness of sacrifice does not allow the sacrificer access to *jouissance*; nevertheless, it allows him to proceed to *the limit* of *jouissance*. It is within this dimension that sacrifice could be understood in terms of a logic of the sublime; the sublime approaches *jouissance as much as it possibly can*—it touches *on the limit* of impossible enjoyment. And this is precisely what distinguishes the act of sacrifice from the Sadian fantasm. Because, if in Sade fear occurs entirely on the side of the sacrificial victim, in sacrifice, by contrast—and Bataille saw this very clearly—fear occurs on the side of the sacrificer; it is the moment of that "anguished joy," which, however, is *only a moment*, a limited point.[57]

Consequently, sacrifice constitutes access to the border of this impossible Thing that demands the sacred, sovereignty, and *jouissance*. This impossible Thing which, in human experience, orders a sacrifice is, for human experience, simultaneously its *source*, its limit, and its menace. First, it is its *source*, because the sacred, which would characterize an absolutely autonomous and thereby good will, is the total fulfillment of the moral law, that is, the way it has been defined by Kant: the law of the rational universality of noncontradictoriness, which is postulated as its given rule by every human legislature as well as, in general, by all forms of reciprocity in interpersonal relations; it is its source in that every form of exchange fundamentally emerges from the principle of nonproductive expenditure, and therefore also from sacrificial annihilation; it is its source because every desire emerges from the desire of the Other, from the will to *jouissance*. This impossible Thing is also the *limit* of human experience, because it is impossible to procure the sacred for oneself by miming an interest-free sacrifice; because one is really just distancing oneself from the sacred when one attempts to use sacrifice in order to gain access to sovereignty; because desire cannot lead to *jouissance*. This impossible Thing that sacrifice demands is finally the *menace* to human experience, because the sacred would annihilate all sympathy, because sovereignty would annihilate all exchange, because *jouissance* would annihilate all desire.

The use of sacrifice consists in getting as close as possible to what is simultaneously the source of, and limit and menace to, human experience. Sacrifice lends the sacrificed object the status of the extimate, and, therefore, within human experience, the present object, which, however, is always connected to what transgresses this experience. The logic of sacrifice is the logic of excess, the logic of extimacy.

But it is important not to deceive oneself about the meaning of this determination. My intention is not, hereby, to define the universal truth of every sacrifice. I only wish to point to the common element in all of these theories of sacrifice without going into the other ways in which they differ or may even be opposite. Put differently, I do not intend to lay out a "model" of sacrifice the way Hubert and Mauss did[58]; I merely observe that the majority of the theories of sacrifice, and especially the most developed ones (in particular the sociological and ethnological theories—I will presently demonstrate this), emerge from the same model, which I have here designated as the logic of extimacy. Also, I wish to remind the reader of what I have attempted to demonstrate in another essay[59]: that Lacan's logic of extimacy, that is, the logic of the *objet a*, as the mediating element between pure lack and the empirical order, corresponds exactly to Kant's logic of the transcendental model insofar as it is a mediating element which founds the synthesis of the a priori and empirical reality. Without playing with words too much, I would like to suggest for this reason that the model of sacrifice is precisely the sacrifice of the model, the sacrifice of an object of experience that has been given the status of an extimate object.

This logic of extimacy, as far at it is possible for us to trace it in Kant's, Bataille's, and Lacan's reflections on sacrifice, also appears in sociological theories of sacrifice, even if there it certainly never presents itself as such. It is not surprising to find it in the works of Hubert and Mauss, as they are, in part, inspired by Bataille's reflections. In correspondence with the etymological meaning of sacrifice as consecration and transformation, Hubert and Mauss describe the sacrificial procedure as the act by way of which "the profane enters into the relation with divinity. . . . But . . . it approximates it only by keeping a distance. . . . When religious forces are the principle itself of the life forces in themselves, then they are of a nature which makes contact with them very dangerous for the profane. . . . Thus the sacrificer can approach them only with the utmost caution. . . . Were he to enter the ritual without reservation he would come upon death, not life. The sacrificial object stands in for him."[60] The sacrificial object is therefore an extimate object: it is what it is only via the divine element which lies within it and which excludes it from the profane order in which it nevertheless remains inscribed. The only thing left to do, then, is to hand over to the God that part of the sacrifice that is his due: "The spirit which is within [the object], the divine principle which it now contains, is allowed to enter his body, and through this last tie it is connected to the world of profane things. Death will free it, because in this way the transformation, the consecration, is made to be definitive and irrevocable."[61]

The same logic of extimacy, even if in a completely different way, is at work in René Girard's conception of sacrifice: the sacrifice that is made, as a substitute for the representative sacrifice* (of the *pharmakos*), can satisfy the function Girard ascribes to it—to be simultaneously what assures the community of the blessing by the sacred *and* what keeps the sacred at a distance from the community—only because it holds this strange position of being inscribed in the social network while simultaneously not really being a part of it,[62] as was the case with the representative sacrifice. The sacred sacrifice makes concrete the relation of the community to the sacred order, which is also the order of violence, from which the community emerges, but which at the same time menaces it. The object of sacrifice is then the extimate object of and in the Symbolic order which constitutes the communal bond.

In contrast to the central place which Girard accords to violence in all sacrificial acts without making any distinctions at all, Luc de Heusch, in his reflections accompanying his studies of the ritual of the sacrifice of the king in certain African societies, demonstrates that the essence of sacrifice is not violence; rather, he assigns blame to what he calls "the world of the elsewhere"[63] (that is, we could say, the Other world, the world of the Other). From this world of the elsewhere emerges the power of the sacred king who embodies the community as "body-territory."[64] The sacrifice of the king constitutes the response to a sacrificial guilt that "belongs to the social order as if it constituted its regulating mechanism."[65] Luc de Heusch makes no bones about his interest in Bataille's *Theory of Religion*. For this reason he makes the point, reiterating Bataille's formulation, that "sacrificing is not murdering but surrendering (*abandonner*) and giving. . . . Sacrificing, to begin with, means being cunning

---

*The term, "victim émissaire," is translated as "substitute victim"; "l'émissaire" also means "ambassador," "secret messenger," "emissary." What is lost is the allusion to "le bouc émissaire": "the scapegoat," and, the realm of anatomy, the site of discharge (of a gland).

vis-à-vis death."[66] Elsewhere, Luc de Heusch says, "When one sacrifices, one does so in order to fill a gap, to expiate guilt, . . . to set the symbolic order back in motion."[67] The object of sacrifice, the king himself, is, because of his double appearance, from then on destined for the empirical social order and the world of the elsewhere, whereby the sacrifice creates both communication *and* rupture. His status is that of the extimate object, and Luc de Heusch's following statement confirms this: "All myths of consecrated kingship, like the rites, define a place of power which lies outside of society, a place that is both external and internal to society, a paradoxical place. It is external, because the king is no longer part of society; he is outside of the clan, he no longer has either mother or father. This is one of the functions of royal incest: to allow him symbolically to rupture his relations to the classical law, the law of exogamy (much more at stake than the law of the father is the law of the group). On the other hand, he is also at the heart of this social structure, which, symbolically, he leaves precisely at the moment of his installation, for he is the representative of the social order. *He is simultaneously outside of the law and the guarantor of the law.*"[68]

In their studies of *The Sacrificial Kitchen in Greek Space*, Vernant, Détienne, and Durand similarly demonstrate that the body of the proffered sacrificial victim describes the topology of the social space. The dissection of the sacrificial body mimics that topology which subdivides the space of the gods, the space of humans, and, among the latter, the space of the priests. Jean-Pierre Vernant shows that the sacrificial act reiterates what, according to the myth recounted by Hesiod, originally occurred in Mékonè, when Prometheus deceived and offended the gods by having them choose that part which had been formed by fat and bones, thereby retaining for humans the other part, the one consisting of the flesh and the intestines. At least in this point Vernant's thesis could be shown to correspond largely with Freud's observation, which I quote from *Totem and Taboo:* "The importance which is everywhere, without exception, ascribed to sacrifice lies in the fact that it offers satisfaction to the father for the outrage inflicted on him in the same act in which that deed is commemorated."[69] But it is necessary to go further and inquire about the status which the dissection of the sacrificial victim gives to that part (of itself) designated for humans but that is nevertheless prohibited to them: that is, the intestines, as far as they are "those parts saturated with blood whose product they are."[70] Jean-Louis Durand's work demonstrates that the intestines, of which he himself says that they constitute "the center of *desire* and of *anxiety*,"[71] represent this atopical place, because, on the one hand, they are the empirical object present in the human realm, but on the other, they contain the blood, and the moment of the blood's spurt "belongs to the gods."[72] For this reason the ceremonial moment of the cutting of the throat and the splashing of the blood are generally not represented in Greek sacrificial iconography; and this nonrepresentation, says J.-L. Durand, "simultaneously reveals and conceals the moment of truth: the animals'

blood lies outside of the human realm."[73] Put differently, by reflecting the splitting of the social-symbolic order, the dissection of the sacrificial body seeks to
grasp the intimate object which, in this symbolic realm, is already on the outside. Consequently, in the sacrificial kitchen the sacrificial object is also the
extimate object. Jean-Pierre Vernant formulates this sacrificial logic of extimacy
(it should be understood that he doesn't designate it such) as follows: "No more
contact with the gods that, through the sacrifice, is not also the transformation,
the consecration of an unbreachable barrier between mortals and immortals."[74]
For this reason the intestines belong to the priests, while the other participants
in the sacrifice are entitled only to the fleshy parts (in Greece, too, it is only
the priests who, if I may put it this way, have communions of both types*). The
act of devouring the intestines places the priests in that atopical position, which,
within the symbolic realm of the community, is that of the extimate object.

All of this should enable us to take our inquiry even further. Because, if
the sacrificed body corresponds perfectly to the social body, and if, within this
body, the entire symbolic order is organized around a point which is itself
excluded from it, is organized around this center of the Symbolic, which transgresses the Symbolic, what then would be the equivalent in the social body, in
the empirical order of the city, to this extimate object? Put differently, we must
also ask what the logic of extimacy could be in the political order; we would
have to attempt to develop a theory of the political *Thing*. I will not get into
this here, but I will make an observation that is connected to the question of
sacrifice. In his study of the sacrificial kitchen of the Greeks, Détienne makes
the point that the communal sacrifice takes place "in the center (of the city),
the *house* of the city (*le méson* de la Cité),†" which is formed by the realm of
the *hestia* (foyer, hearth, home),‡ where the sacrificial altar used to be built.[75] In
The Anthropology of Ancient Greece, Louis Gernet says of this *hestia* that it was
a "very general institution," even a "universal"[76] one, and he makes the point

---

*In Catholic terminology: offering communion and receiving it; going to communion;
in Protestant terminology: to partake of the Lord's supper, but also to feel intimately
united and as One; to feel a spiritual communion and to share something (feelings, for
example) in a very profound way.

†The expression "le méson de la Cité": a play on words; it is homophonous with "la
maison," the house; the prefix "me-" means "mid-" in the spatial as well as temporal sense;
in other words, it can be used in constructions like "mid-city," "mid[dle]-tone," and so on.

‡"Hestia" (Greek) is the hearth, and by extension, the house, home, dwelling; the
family; the altar, the shrine; the center, the main point.
  Hesta, Vesta: the goddess of the hearth. Aristotle tells the story of Heraclitus behind
the kitchen oven (Hestesan); he plays with these meanings when he requests his visitors
to enter, as there are gods in this space too.

that it usually was circular in shape, thereby marking the central point around which the order of the city was organized. It is not surprising that the sacrificial act occurs precisely in this atopical realm of the city, in this place extimate to politics, that is the *hestia*. This place, which is simultaneously internal and external to the communal realm, is what in old German was called *das Ding*.[77] The concept of the *Thing*, which Lacan translates as *la Chose*, represents the cardinal point of the early Freud's reflections in the *Project for a Scientific Psychology*.[78] This is why I just spoke of a political *Thing*, which is how I designate the extimate point which organizes the political field, while it is simultaneously external to it. We have gotten to know some of this *Thing's* forms of presentation in our contemporary experience: it is, for example, the large circle which, by keeping the extimate space in the heart of the republic separate and inaccessible, consecrates the supposed sacrifice of the so-called unknown soldier, that is, of the anonymous soldier, the one who is established as lying beyond any kind of identification; or an even more trivial example would be the empty space which recently the famous "Corbeille" had marked off, and around which all of the businesses of small-trade servility were settled . . .

I will not go any further. Before I end, I must return to what constituted the basis for Lacan's remark about sacrifice: the annihilation of the Jews. It is clear by now what makes it legitimate for Lacan to declare that every philosophy which understands the end, the aim, of history to be the fulfillment of a process of identification is incapable of rendering justice to what has occurred "at the end"; rather, every philosophy that does that ought to recognize there that fact that it disavows. Because sacrifice is precisely the monstrous result which the logic of identification secretly carries within itself. The result, but not the final aim: no process of identification can, in this senseless point of final solution, lead to anything but to its catastrophic encounter with the law which demands of it the blind and useless fulfillment of sacrifice. Hannah Arendt has shown in what way, within the political order, Nazism followed this unfulfillable logic of identification, up to the horror that was the Shoah.[79] Others have tried to demonstrate the necessity with which the Jews became the victims of this sacrifice. I myself would be more careful.[80] But what is certain is that, in view of a political logic, which makes the State the concrete realization of identity in itself and for itself of the community, that individual [that is, the Jew], whose God is present only by way of his absence or his distance, necessarily appears to be scandalous.

It is the God of Abraham. When Abraham decided to carry out the sacrifice of the one who was his own blood, this occurred, according to Genesis, in order to obey the *voice* of God. It is impossible to imagine with what sort of *scream* Isaac's *throat* quaked, when, as we're used to seeing in so many representations of it, the sacrificial knife came down upon it . . . The impossible sacrifice did not take place. The God distanced himself. What remains is only the *voice*, that extimate object: it is the scream, lamenting and terrifying, which, when the sound is allowed to appear, the ram's horn, the shofar, intones. And it is this anguished and anxiety-provoking scream of the shofar that resounds again on the Day of Remembrance, or, to be more exact, at that moment when being silent is the only way of remembering those who died. For nothing.

Notes

First published in *Les Temps Modernes* (August/September, 1990).

1. Marcel Détienne and J.-P. Vernant (with contributions by J.-L. Durand, F. Hartog, and J. Svenbro), *La cuisine du sacrifice en pays grec* (N.R.F., 1979), 34.

2. Jacques Lacan, *The Four Fundamental Concepts of Psycho-Analysis*, ed. Jacques-Alain Miller and trans. Alan Sheridan (New York: W. W. Norton, 1981), 274–275.

3. Ibid., 275–276.

4. Armand Zaloszyc has demonstrated the significance of this idea for a general understanding of Lacan's discourse in this Seminar. Cf. Bernard Baas and A. Zaloszyc, *Descartes et les fondements de la psychanalyse* (Navarin-Osiris, 1988), 41–57.

5. E. B. Tylor, *Primitive Culture* (New York: Harper, 1958).

6. H. Hubert and M. Mauss, "Essai sur la nature et la fonction du sacrifice" (1899), in M. Mauss, *Oeuvres*, part 1 (éd. De Minuit), 305. [translation E. S.]

7. Ibid., 303.

8. Ibid., 305.

9. Ibid., 269.

10. Cf. Ibid., 306–307.

11. Emil Durkheim, *Les formes élémentaires de la vie religieuse* (Paris, 1912).

12. Ibid., 451 (cited in Détienne, 29). [trans. E. S.]

13. Robertson Smith, *Religion of Semites* (London, 1889).

14. Ernst Cassirer, *The Philosophy of Symbolic Forms* (New Haven: Yale University Press, 1953–1996).

15. René Girard, *Violence of the Sacred* (Baltimore: Johns Hopkins University Press, 1977).

16. Marcel Détienne, "Pratiques culinaires et esprit de sacrifice," in *La cuisine*, 7–35. [trans. E. S.]

17. Luc De Heusch, *Le sacrifice dans les religions africaines* (N.R.F., 1986). Cf. note 45–46. [trans. E. S.]

18. J.-L. Durand, "Bêtes grecques (Propositions pour une topologie des corps à manger)" in *La cuisine*, 136. [trans. E. S.] (This essay appears also in the text cited in note 1.)

19. Ibid.

20. *Thysia:* sacrificing, the act of sacrificing, to be engaged in sacrificing; the sacrifice, to prepare the sacrificial ritual, to carry out the sacrificial ritual; the sacrificial animal; in the New Testament: the sacrificial offering.

21. J.-P. Vernant, "A table des hommes (Mythe de fondation du sacrifice chez Hésiode)," in *La cuisine*, 37–132. [trans. E. S.]

22. Cf. especially Détienne, "Pratiques" 35 fn. 1: the criticism is directed at René Girard.

23. Sigmund Freud, "The Ego and the Id," *Standard Edition, Volume 19*, trans. James Strachey (London: The Hogarth Press) 54–5.

24. Georges Bataille, *La part maudite* (Minuit-coll. Points, 1967), 169–170. [trans. E. S.]

25. Plato, *Eutyphron*, 14 d. Sqq. The reference is to section 17, thesis 4: "Piety is knowing about the gift and request to the gods," as well as section 18, "Piety as exchange between gods and humans."

26. Cited by L. Cognet, *Introduction aux mystiques rhénoflamands* (Desclée, 1968), 97–101. [trans. E. S.].

27. Georges Bataille, "Hegel, la mort et le sacrifice," in *Deucalion* 5 (Éd. de la Bacconière, 1955), 40. [trans. E. S.]

28. Ibid.

29. Georges Bataille, *La part maudite*, 181. [trans. E. S.]

30. Quoted in Georges Bataille, "Hegel, la mort et le sacrifice," 26, 32.

31. Ibid., 36 (end of footnote 1 on p. 35).

32. Cf. G. W. F. Hegel, *Reason in History*, trans. Robert S. Hartman (New York: Boobs-Merrill, 1953), 25, 27: "To this end [freedom] all the sacrifices have been offered on the vast altar of the earth throughout the long lapse of ages. . . . But in contemplating history as the slaughter-bench at which the happiness of peoples, the wisdom of states, and the virtue of individuals have been sacrificed, a question necessarily arises: To what principles, to what final purpose, have these monstrous sacrifices been offered?"

33. G. W. F. Hegel, *The Phenomenology Mind*, trans. J. B. Baillie (New York: Harper Row Publishers, 1967), 720–724.

34. Ibid., 722.

35. Georges Bataille, "Hegel, la mort et le sacrifice," 33. [trans. E. S.]

36. Georges Bataille, *Essais de sociologie. Oeuvres completes* (Paris: Gallimard, 1970), 242. [trans. E. S.]

37. Georges Bataille, "Hegel, la mort et le sacrifice," 39.

38. Georges Bataille, *La part maudite*, 246, fn.8.

39. Georges Bataille, "Hegel, la mort et le sacrifice," 33.

40. Georges Bataille, *Théorie de la religion* (N.R.F.-coll. TEL, 1973), 66–67. [trans. E. S.]

41. Georges Bataille, *La part maudite*, 247.

42. Ibid., 181.

43. Georges Bataille, "Hegel, la mort et le sacrifice," 41.

44. Georges Bataille, *Théorie de la religion*, 87–97.

45. Immanuel Kant, *Religion Within the Boundaries of Mere Reason, and Other Writings*, ed. Allen Wood and George di Giovanni (Cambridge, 1998), 165.

46. Ibid., 165–66.

47. Cf. ibid., 196.

48. Cf., for example, Georges Bataille, "Hegel, la mort et le sacrifice," 40.

49. Immanuel Kant, *Kritik der praktischen Vernunft* (Suhrkamp Taschenbuch Wissenschaft, 1974), 127.

50. J.-F. Lyotard, "L'intérêt du sublime," in *Du Sublime* (Belin, 1988), 163.

51. Cf. ibid., 174–175.

52. Cf. Immanuel Kant, *Kritik der Urteilskraft* (Allgemeine Anmerkung zur Exposition der ästhetischen reflektierenden Urteile), (Meiner), 113ff.

53. Cf. Immanuel Kant, *Foundations of the Metaphysics of Morals in Philosophical Writings*, ed. Ernst Behler Geerman Library, vol. 13 (New York: Coninuum, 1986), 74.

54. Jacques Lacan, "Kant with Sade" in *October* 51 (winter 1989): 66.

55. Ibid., 55.

56. Jacques Lacan, "La science et la vérité," *Écrits*, p. 872. English: Lacan, "Science and Truth," trans. Bruce Fink, *Newsletter of the Freudian Field* 3, nos. 1&2 (spring/fall 1989): 20.

Let us clarify, however, that the deception involved in this kind of procedure of "handing over" never appears more explicitly than in what, according to him is, "the single trait which is common to all religions: . . . that the good which is sacrificed . . . is precisely the thing that religion undertakes to recupereate." Cf. Jacques Lacan, *The Seminar of Jacques Lacan: Book VII: The Ethics of Psychoanalysis* (New York: W. W. Norton, 1992), 322. This reappropriation is made manifest in what Lacan calls the "priest's feast behind the altar" (ibid., 372), and also in "religious heroism," that is, in that sort of self-satisfaction which must accompany the sufferings of the saints and martyrs. This strange observation of Lacan's makes it possible to connect to all of this the information M. Détienne provides us with regarding the devouring of the intestines of the Greek sacrifices, which was limited to the priests, the intestines which were saturated with what is most divine: blood (cf. ibid., 72). But then, according to this logic, one would similarly have to look into the reappropriation of the bodies of the sacrifices in the camps on the part of the Nazis for very obvious economic motives (hair, gold teeth, and so on). One is also led to remember what Bataille says about the turning of consummation (devouring, wasting) around into consumption (consumption, demand), when the waste, the excess (of riches) itself becomes the object of appropriation (*La part maudite*, 118). And finally, one would have to juxtapose all of this with Derrida's observation in his commentary on Bataille's text on Hegel and sacrifice: "The consumption of the excess of energy by a determined class is not the destructive consuming of meaning, but the significative reappropriation of a surplus value within the space of restricted economy. From this point of view, sovereignty is absolutely revolutionary." Derrida, Jacques, "From Restricted to General Economy: A Hegelianism Without Reserve," in *Writing and Difference*, trans, intro., and notes Alan Bass (Chicago: University of Chicago Press, 1978), 337, n. 33. The question remains: is not every "revolutionary" program—as program—necessarily condemned to its reappropriation in and through the teleological order of interests, whatever they may be? Clearly, sovereignty as program does not evade "deception." Poorer than even Kant was, without illusions, this forces us to repeat the question with which his *Critique* left him: What can we hope for?

57. One can be precise about the frequency with which this definition of sacrifice or sovereignty occurs in Bataille's discourse: "What takes place occurs in one sense (which is at least intent on occurring, or which occurs in a fleeting, ungraspable way)" ("Hegel, la mort et le sacrifice," 32–33); "sovereignty, which is freedom in the instant" (*La part maudite*, 246, note 8); "sacrifice . . . is the devouring which holds interest only for the instant itself" (*Théorie de la religion*, 66), and so on. [trans. E. S.]

58. Hubert & Mauss, 212 ff.

59. Bernard Baas, "Le desir pur (a propos de "Kant avec Sade" de Lacan)," in *Ornicar?* 43 (1987): 56–91. [German version: *"Das reine Begehren,"* in *Wo Es War* 7/8 (Hora Verlag, Vienna)]

60. Hubert & Mauss, 303.

61. Ibid., 233.

62. Cf. René Girard, all of chapter 1.

63. Luc De Heusch, 327.

64. Ibid.

65. Ibid., 313.

66. Ibid., 329.

67. Luc De Heusch, "Le roi sacrifié (A Conversation with Luc de Heusch)," in *Quarto (Revue de l'E.C.F. en Belgique)* 30 (1988): 55. [trans. E. S.]

68. Ibid., 53 (author's emphasis).

69. Sigmund Freud, *Totem and Taboo, Standard Edition, Volume 13*, 15.

70. Marcel Détienne, "Pratiques," 20.

71. J.-L. Durand, 146 (author's emphasis).

72. Ibid., 139.

73. Ibid., 138. One will note, even if with a smile, that this formulation of truth as "revelation-distortion" is indebted in its entirety to Heidegger, who is not cited; the same has occurred recently in the work of Détienne, who owes just as much to Heidegger. (Cf. Marcel Détienne, *Les maitres de vérité dans la Grece archaique* [éd. Maspero, 1967]).

74. J-P. Vernant, 146 (author's emphasis).

75. Marcel Détienne, "Pratiques," 25.

76. L. Gernet, *Anthropologie de la Grece antique* (éd. Maspéro, 1968), 384. [trans. E.S.]

77. I owe this information to the noteworthy (but unfortunately not yet published) investigations of Ferdinand Scherer on the origin of the Lacanian "Thing."

78. Cf. Sigmund Freud, "Project for a Scientific Psychology," *Standard Edition, Volume 1*.

79. Cf. Hannah Arendt, *Elements and Origins of Total Domination* (New York, 1955).

80. Indeed, it seems to me that when one designates "the Jews" as the ones who have been consecrated to take upon their shoulders the forgetting of the law or the distancing from the origin, or as the prototypical figure of abandonment,—or, to put it differently, as the ones who (by their very existence) embody for others the radical impossibility of presence or of identity, who are in some ways the referent of their [the others'] hopelessness or anxiety—then one runs the risk of formulating the preliminary statement of a process whose last word would be (and has already been): now they must pay for all of this. It is impossible to repeat (no matter in what sort of modern theoretical version) the myth of chosenness without running the risk of repeating what has always accompanied it. And, to be perfectly frank, I fail to see what is courageous about these types of intellectual strategies which consist in playing "the Jews" off against the Greeks in order to more easily liquidate the Christians. The urgency of thought must not be satisfied with any kind of sacrificial logic.

18

Freud and Democracy

PETER WIDMER

"Psychoanalysis and Democracy": as they stand face to face these are two concepts, two fields, which at first glance do not seem to have much to do with each other. Psychoanalysis is something private; its recognitions emerge from the conversations between analyst and analysand, which are subjected to certain regulations. Even when it is possible to transfer psychoanalytic recognitions onto social groups or society on the whole, they still seem to contrast strongly with the realm of politics, which by definition concerns itself with the public realm. In addition, their interests are very different: psychoanalysis is interested in the revelation of unconscious relationships, in proving the determined nature of symptoms, inhibitions, and fantasms; it attempts to prove its points via singular elements, to open proof up to experience through singularities. Politics, on the other hand, is oriented toward the organization and government of social issues, around struggles concerning power and distribution, behind which the even more fundamental issues of, say, the idea of the good life—today one would say, the happiness regarding the grouping of social subjects, or even the happiness of their totality—are discernible. One could easily go on forever with this dichotomizing, by saying, for example, that psychoanalysis works within its so-called setting—that is, with transference, interpretation, the fundamental rule, a system of remuneration, and so on—while in the field of politics the construction of such rules and regulations would be absurd. It is only with irony that one can still speak of an eight hundred kilometers-long couch between Basel and Hamburg!

But it is impossible to remain within such sterile dichotomies. The private sphere in which psychoanalysis is most effective is structured legally, and there can be no public sphere without the private. Even the conscious is not simply the rigid opposite of the unconscious; rather, the world of the conscious, of the predictable, repeatable, of what can be calculated, is structured by the unconscious, by the signifier, as Lacan says, whose existence we surmise only through its effects. And what about the respective interests of psychoanalysis and politics? Are they really so fundamentally different as it seems at first glance? When we think of the original idea behind politics which consisted in getting to the bottom of those things that can constitute the good life for human beings within society, to carry them out and to guarantee them, is it still possible then to keep psychoanalysis out of this idea of the good life? But what sort of relationship does this idea of the good life have to truth, which is what psychoanalysis is concerned with?

There is a concept which plays a leading role, especially in the late Lacan, in terms of his conception of psychoanalysis, and which implies a *rapprochement* to politics: *la jouissance*, usually translated as "enjoyment." One need only think of typical everyday talk about pleasure to see that it is there that one discovers the proximity of psychoanalysis. Isn't it people who are incapable of experiencing pleasure who come into analysis? Perhaps they do so because they can find no joy in anything, because they are suspicious of all pleasure, or because, overcome by pleasure, they are still not capable of experiencing any? In any case, pleasure is a far-reaching topic in politics. Maybe I am particularly intimate with these relationships because I come from a country that is also referred to as a "Confederation" [Pun is not directly translatable; *Genossenschaft*—sharing the same verb stem with *geniessen*—can be loosely translated as "a society come together through pleasure."—E. S.]. A confederation without socialism, founded on an agreement—founded on the word—a brotherly agreement, one might add.

This brings me to Freud. But now I do not want to attempt to identify these confederate brothers who rebelled against the Austrian masters with the descendants of the horde of brothers as they were described by Freud in *Totem and Taboo*; doing so would tie my discussion too closely to Switzerland, even if realized or failed assassinations of tyrants have attained a constitutive significance in other countries as well. Rather, I would like to explore the relationships—the compatibilities and incompatibilities, the mutual foundations and exclusions—between Freudian psychoanalysis and democracy. Throughout my discussion I will remain within the framework of Freud's work; examination of the relationships between the work of Lacan and democracy will be the content of a later work.

Freud's Social-Theoretical Works and Their Relationship to Democracy

It is a well known fact that there are a great many works in which Freud took society as a whole to task; the most famous of these texts are *Civilization and Its Discontents*, *Totem and Taboo*, and *Group Psychology and the Analysis of the Ego*. But one must also include works like "Thoughts for the Time on War and

Death"; [. . .]; *The Future of an Illusion*, "Why War?," *The Man Moses and the Monotheistic Religion*; and finally even early works like "My Views on the Part Played by Sexuality in the Aetiology of the Neuroses," or "'Civilized' Sexual Morality and Modern Nervous Illness," which are concerned with social issues, as are, in a wider sense, all of the works that deal with religion.

When Freud addresses questions that have to do with sociality, he typically posits a single person at the head of a particular grouping, be it the primal father in *Totem and Taboo*, Moses for the Jews, Christ for the Christians, a general for the soldiers, a father for the children. This does not imply, at least not within Freud's argument, that democracy is therefore unthinkable or illusory. When Freud speaks of democracy explicitly he is referring to the equal rights that the members of a group would receive through the agency of a leading figure.[1] Democracy, then, does not apply to everyone—there is always one exception, and one could even say that this exceptional figure is of central significance in Freud's discussions of democracy. When everyone is subject to democratic law, then there must be, or there must have been, the one who issued the law; in other words, the one who holds a predemocratic, prelegal position. Freud thought to have found the most wonderful example of such a social, democratic bond in the Catholic Church, a bond which is also embodied in the army.[2]

A first thesis would then go as follows: *The existence of a democratic organization assumes that there is an exception, which is what constitutes democratic law.*

In order to underline the extraordinary nature of this statement one must add that this One, this exception, is not subjected to a vote by those he leads; he does not become a leader in the way in which, for example, a president becomes president of his country; rather, this One either himself engenders the law to begin with, or, insofar as he is already present within a constitutive hierarchy or in a social association already in existence, he is appointed to such a position from above, the way an officer is appointed by his general. Thus, it is naturally the founding figures of human history that are most interesting: Abraham, Moses, Christ. They take their places within the succession to the nameless primal father. It would be closer to the truth to say of these figures that they chose their people rather than that their people chose them. To make this observation does not necessarily mean excluding a dialectical moment, the struggle for recognition, to which even the God of the Old Testament has to submit.

Is it really possible to position all of these founding figures in one continuous line, beginning with the primal father? The primal father in *Totem and Taboo* lacks the divine charge by which the founders of religions felt themselves to have been hailed; Freud's description of this mythological figure makes him sound more like an orangutan than a person.[3] If he nevertheless stands at the origin of culture that is because through his unrestricted possession of women he embodies a No, a No to his descendants' sexual desires, which is equivalent to a barrier to incest (one can really only speak of an incest *prohibition* proper when the barrier has become linguistic—even to speak of a "barrier to incest" is problematic; in any case, it refers to a concept that is projected into the past). It is in this sense that Freud can put this guy up there with the founders of religions. The difference in their respective positions—that the first embodies a barrier through his bodily strength, while the strength of the founders of religions was spiritual—is irrelevant in view of the motive for murder, which was the elimination of the required renunciations and privations.

What does all of this have to do with our topic, "Psychoanalysis and Democracy"? Let us recall the first thesis, according to which in Freud's argument the existence of democracy is based on the presence of an exception. An association then turns out to be the more democratic the more egalitarian its father figure is in his treatment of his subjects, that is, the more equitably he distributes rights among them. But this picture of power really doesn't correspond to our own conception of democracy, which goes out from the premise that a social association is democratic only when everyone, without exception, is subject to the law, when there is legal equality, that is. From this perspective, *in a strictly structural sense, true democracy was introduced with the slaying of the primal father*. It was at this point in time that the exception was eliminated and, for a moment, at least, everyone was equal. One could qualify this moment even further: immediately after the killing, there resulted a lawless condition, a club law, the same for everyone. Freud describes the subsequent events for us as follows: because of their remorse and consideration for one another the brothers neither committed incest nor fought over who was to succeed the killed father.[4] Out of the dead and devoured father emerged the corpus of the law, valid for everyone. It is here, in other words, in the act of killing the tyrant, that the origin of democracy is to be found, that democracy whose law is nurtured by guilt, remorse, and homosexual connectedness. From this moment on the descendants formed an egalitarian society, a society that was *free*—that is, free of the primal father—, *equal* in so far as they made sure that no one of them would take over the place of the dead father, and *brotherly*. True democracy, in other words, replaced a tyranny where it had not been the case that everyone was equal. We can thus formulate a second thesis which modifies and qualifies the first one: *the exception of the One who has privileges, an exception which is constitutive of democracy, falls away when his power transforms into the law for All*. This second thesis is in part based on Freud's conception of what occurred in human prehistory, and, on the other hand, it points to a certain consequence resulting from this, a consequence as far as democracy is concerned, which Freud did however not make explicit. I will return shortly to the probable reasons for this omission.

Democracy, from this egalitarian perspective, assumes an ambiguous guise: it is closely associated with the intention to abolish the demands for renunciation and limitation, even sublimation on the whole. It verges, then, on being barbaric and uncivilized; it is a vulgar mass society, it even furthers the biologization of human beings. But on the other hand, it is also the result of the law, that is, of the internalization of the primal father's threatening gesture, which has become the origin of the law, the No which can be articulated linguistically and which is made effective within everyone, without exception. In this way democracy becomes both the guardian of the first law, which is valid for all, and the carrier for a culture which has been wrested from the state of nature.

In other words, things turned out differently from what the horde of brothers had expected: instead of universal liberation of the instincts, what emerged was a social bond based on remorse for the murder, on the belated discovery of love of the father, on mutual consideration, and renunciation. A power, whose existence the brothers had never even suspected in their dark intentions, established itself. Freud does not represent this outcome as a liberation from the drives but rather as a precarious condition which repeatedly led to revamped versions of leader figures who inevitably had to be killed as well. Put differently, egalitarian democracy could not maintain itself; again and again someone who wanted to be the exception enforced his authority, whereupon the murder principle, which Freud saw most impressively embodied in the tragic hero Oedipus, asserted itself. In addition, Freud assumed that aggression is directed not only at the one exception, and that it asserts itself not only intergenerationally but intragenerationally as well. He makes this clear in *Civilization and Its Discontents* when he represents the foreigner as worthy of hate, as someone undeserving of love,[5] or when in general he viewed human relationships, even close familial ones, as resting on a foundation of hatred. He believed that the commandment against killing was a reaction to an archaic death wish.[6]

In terms of vindicating the existence of democracy this is not inconsequential; on the contrary: the presence of such murderous aggressive tendencies would seem to make a demand for agencies of power which would restrain this destructive potential. "Human life in common is only made possible when a majority comes together which is stronger than any separate individual and which remains united against all separate individuals. The power of this community is then set up as 'right' in opposition to the power of the individual, which is condemned as 'brute force.' This replacement of the power of the individual by the power of a community constitutes the decisive step of civilization."[7] These pillars of right and morality are wrested away from their instinctual basis, which, Freud assumed, maintained itself throughout the course of human history. It is most probably in this murderous destructive drive, which is active intragenerationally as well, that one must look for the reason why Freud did not even consider developing his conception of an equality between the brothers; this, no doubt, would have seemed much too good to be true to him and would not have made much sense within the context of this basic murderous impulse.

As far as the history of the brother hordes after the slaying of the tyrant is concerned, very likely the brothers, perhaps later generations as well, dropped their original consideration for one another which had been the basis for the social bond, and entered into relationships of rivalry with one another—rivalry concerning succession to the position of the primal father, concerning women, power and influence, or all of this at once. In the interest of social coexistence and the security of individual life, there came into being powers which were to set a limit to intragenerational *aggression,* powers which were themselves endowed with an aggressive potential. It is here that the condition of being a threat to itself, which characterizes every society, originates. Thus we can formulate a third thesis: *The existence of a society that is based on equal rights is constantly threatened by a tendency toward aggressiveness which is effective also intragenerationally.*

In his late work Freud conceives of destructiveness and aggression as outwardly oriented manifestations of the death drive, which actually works silently and is turned inward and, together with Eros, is one of the two basic drives.[8] In *Totem and Taboo* Freud still traces the first murder back to factors like oppression and envy; the mutual consideration of the brothers for one another had to do with potential rivalry, the emergence of which was checked by the law. Beginning with *Beyond the Pleasure Principle* these same phenomena are represented as forms of expression of a death drive turned towards the outside world. Put differently, rivalry, envy, and other factors have turned into factors that unleash the death drive; the cause for their emergence lies not within them but rather in the necessity of turning lethal forces towards the outside. Surely, such a conception must have ramifications for how one evaluates the possibility of democracy.

Another observation is forced upon us: in Freud's conception, right is something secondary; his primary point of reference is a preexisting as well as prelegal instinctual basis.[9] The legal system represents a mighty reaction formation which has been constructed over archaic instinctual wishes, a consequence of the experiences of humanity. Freud says in this context that with this whole construction of culture human beings had exchanged a piece of possible satisfaction for a piece of security.[10] On the one hand, this legal system is codified; on the other, it has to be appropriated by the members of a society. This appropriation, which Freud designates in part as sublimation, in part as reaction formation, occurs by robbing the instinctual energies of some of their resources, which are then used to counter the archaic instincts. This process occurs with the assistance of psychic instances—ideals, for example, and the construction of a conscience. Since their constitution presupposes the existence of an archaic instinctual basis, the position of culture in general and law in particular is an especially fragile one.

When one regards Freud's arguments, as I have presented them so far, from a distance, one must ask oneself how human beings have survived at all.

Wouldn't the ineradicable powers of destruction, together with the suffering that civilization brings, have driven people to kill each other? Which life-conserving factors does Freud believe to have made the difference? Freud asks himself this question and, as far as he is concerned, there is only one answer: they are the constraints that are imposed upon people; they are imposed on a "resisting majority" by a minority.[11] The minority has been successful in taking possession of the means of power and coercion. Freud's conclusion is as follows: "[I]t does not even seem certain that if coercion were to cease the majority of human beings would be prepared to undertake to perform the work necessary for acquiring new wealth."[12] As a result coercions are not final causes; rather, they are themselves consequences of a striving for power, which, in turn, is based on envisioned and hoped for pleasure, the kind of pleasure that the primal father had embodied. In the context of our question regarding democracy this means nothing other than that this state of affairs must result in a profound skepticism regarding the possibility of the very existence of democracy: if human beings were not constrained by coercions imposed on them by a minority, they would not only be too murderous to exist in a society based on equal rights, but they would be too lazy as well. Thus, a fourth thesis would go as follows: *The average laziness of humankind makes the maintenance of civilization on a democratic level impossible.* This thesis results from the first one; it throws light on it by explaining why Freud speaks of the "heroes of civilization" and why he can conceive of democracy only when it is something that single individuals force upon a majority.

According to Freud, the ongoing conflict between minorities and majorities, between exercising and suffering at the hands of power, has undergone a number of transformations during the course of human history. Of course it hasn't escaped his observation that the nature of the coercive powers has changed. He writes, "It is not true that the human mind has undergone no development since the earliest times and that, in contrast to the advances of science and technology, it is the same to-day as it was in the beginning of history. We can point out one of these mental advances at once. It is in keeping with the course of human development that external coercion gradually becomes internalized; for a special mental agency, man's super-ego, takes it over and includes it among its commandments."[13]

Freud's statement creates more questions than answers. Why does external coercion get transformed into internal coercion over the course of history? Is there some sort of reason at work here? Freud mentions the superego, which he conceives of as the "heir of the Oedipus Complex."[14] This too is a statement that just provokes more questions, such as: how is it that the formation of a conscience becomes intrapsychically sedimented? One can observe this happening in children, but observation is not explanation. By asking questions of this sort we are pushing up against the limits of Freudian psychoanalysis. He does not want psychoanalysis to be a *Weltanschauung*, and he is skeptical not only of all philosophy but of religion as well. This is especially apparent when he represents psychoanalysis as a "method of research, an impartial instrument, like the infinitesimal calculus, as it were."[15] His refusal is at least in part motivated by his apprehensions concerning the practice of psychoanalysis: were there within psychoanalysis a unified concept or explanatory matrix of the sort that religion has to offer, the result, according to Freud, would be a dangerous flattening out of psychoanalytic treatment. Any ideological perspective of this sort would come to function as a means to avoid coming face-to-face with those destructive forces that are a part of everyone; instead of articulating, and thereby recognizing, these forces, they would be passed over; instead of reaching the generality by way of the traversal of the particular, the particular would be subordinated to an already established generality. Freud feared and despised nothing so much as the lullabies about the "good person" or the impulse to take for granted our ultimate preservation within a higher context of meaning. If there is such a thing as reason, according to Freud it can be experienced only by traversing the subjective element—by sublimation. Sublimation presupposes an instinctual base; culture is wrested from it: "Where id was, I shall become."

So let us be careful, then, even if that does not mean that we should stop asking questions.

Eros, as the counterdrive to Thanatos, seems most suitable for spurring on the development of civilization as it is described by Freud. Doesn't the movement of gathering disparate material up into larger unities constitute the principle of progress? But, like the death drive, Eros also bears death within itself.[16] If all elements become unified, the differences which are the basis for life, fall away. Life is propped up solely by the mixture of Eros and Thanatos; but how is progress in cultural development supposed to result from the mixture of two antagonistic forces? This dualism is not itself subordinated to history and historical transformation; rather, it was just as active in the primal horde as it is in our society today. Accepting this instinctual dualism, then, does not lead to an understanding of the forces that sustain life. Freud was aware of this difficulty and tried to construct an anthropological theory: primal human beings did not yet experience a limitation to their drives; for this reason they were in constant danger of being themselves killed. So what would have been more reasonable than exchanging a piece of instinctual freedom for a piece of security and to construct a *law* which would protect the life of the separate individual by the threat of punishing all transgressions?[17] One can speak here of a *reemergence of the law*; it absorbs the aggressions and rivalries which had posed a threat to equality by guiding them into sublimated channels and by binding them in contractual thought. A fifth thesis would then go as follows: *With the establishment of the right to enter into contracts which applied to all, a form was created for the conflicts which had previously been ended by violent means, a form which simul-*

taneously demanded a work of mourning: renunciation, that is, on the part of the physically more powerful human beings to enforce their own interests.

A next step consisted in declaring this law to be holy in order to safeguard its effectiveness; for this reason instances with allegedly superior powers were introduced which were assumed to side with rights and agreements—in the name of the gods, or, later, in the name of God the Almighty.

A subsequent step was concerned with overcoming the privations experienced by humans. In *Civilization and Its Discontents* Freud calls the human being a prosthetic God.[18] In doing so he makes it apparent that the idea of God apparently functions as the telos of human history. But Freud does not regard this telos as something objective, in the sense of a divine power independent of human beings; rather, he traces this idea back to anthropological factors. He continues to insist on seeing psychoanalysis as a form of natural history. His argumentation forces one to recall Feuerbach who, as is well known, thought of the idea of God as a human projection. For Freud the figure of the primal father, once again, is strategically decisive because it allows him to trace the origin of the idea of God back to a mythologically conceived event in natural history from which the human telos—Being, as well as God—emerged. It is nature that creates life, and in nature both drives, Eros and Thanatos, work together. Freud rejects the religious notion founded on a transcendental principle which itself is not natural. He regards this as a stupefying power, a bulwark against the acceptance of the fact that human suffering is insurmountable, an instance that makes those human beings who believe in it compliant, trusting in authority, and easily seduced. He believes that the reason for the emergence of the gods lay in their threefold task: "[to] exorcise the terrors of nature, . . . [to] reconcile men to the cruelty of Fate, particularly as it is shown in death, and . . . [to] compensate them for the suffering and privations which a civilized life in common has imposed on them."[19] Religion is a higher power only in appearance; it is the unrecognized work of human beings themselves who at some point in the past wanted to guard their laws and their civilization against human destructiveness, which, however, had the opposite result: religion became independent and transformed itself into an inhibitor of culture insofar as god-fearing human beings no longer recognized their own power and reason, but attributed them to God.[20]

According to Freud, there is no transcendent power which binds Eros and Thanatos or, indeed, guides them into culturally favorable channels, or toward sublimation; rather, it is the necessities of life, *ananke*, which drive humans to defend themselves, to construct a civilization which extracts power from the noxious aspects of the drives; for *ananke* is also the source of reason. Freud regarded the dawn of the scientific era as having arrived; it was to surmount superstition and illusion and base itself on rationality.

It is difficult for me to draw consequences from all of this for an estimation of the possibility of democracy. Implicit in taking the side of the scientific era is an affirmation of democracy rather than its rejection, for an essential aspect of science is that no one is excluded from it a priori. On the other hand, Freud was enough of a realist to see that the social upheavals induced by science require a lot of time to become fully entrenched. After all, he himself postulated the necessity of a nonreligious education in order to counteract the stupefaction by religion that he had "agnosticated." If he nevertheless remained skeptical vis-à-vis the projection of beautiful models of society, it was because he recognized that the human basis in the drives repeatedly tears through the thin veneer of civilization, leading to the outbreak of wars and barbarism, which, Freud actually hoped, could be prevented by the intellectual exertions of single individuals rather than by a democratic and rational society. On the other hand, human laziness, which he assumed to be present, and the true expression of the silent and unobserved workings of the death drive, feeds his skepticism regarding the possibility of a model of a society that is not split up into a leader and the people he leads.

When Freud discusses leaders or authorities he distinguishes between those who are useful to civilization and those who are concerned only with their own power. In his work "Why War?"[21] he categorizes the former as "an upper stratum of men with independent minds, not open to intimidation and eager in the pursuit of truth, whose business it would be to give direction to the dependent masses" while he locates the culturally inhibiting forces in transgressions on the part of the powers of state and in the church's prohibition of freedom of thought. But such a subdivision between good and bad authorities is too simple, for Freud knows well that intentions certainly do not always correspond to results. Were one nevertheless to hold on to this distinction, it would in any case not accord with the criterion of "force/forcelessness." In this same work Freud refers to wars that had contributed to "the transformation of force into law";[22] the French kings' desire for increase, for instance, is supposed to have created a peaceful, unified, and blossoming France.[23] He does not, however, derive from this a justification for force, and certainly not for war, but hopes rather, in the end, for the victory of reason even if everyone is not equally endowed with it: "Of course, the ideal condition would be a community of people who have subjected their instinctual lives to the dictatorship of reason. Nothing else could provoke so complete and capable of resistance a unification of people—even with the renunciation of all emotional ties amongst them. But this is most probably a utopian hope."[24]

Before shifting the focus of my inquiry into Freud's work to the practice of psychoanalytic treatment, I would like to say one more word about the possible gender specificity of the statements I have referred to and discussed: aren't Freud's statements *very male-oriented?* Where are the women? The primal figure in *Totem and Taboo* is not a woman, nor does Freud say anything about the daughters; it also seems that Freud sees only the role of men in the development of civilization! Of course, one may read Freud naturalistically, in which case there is no doubt that women have no place at all in civilization. Freud himself says in reference to two of the pillars of civilization, the church and the military, "In the great artificial groups, the Church and the army, there is no room for woman as a sexual object. The love relation between men and women remains outside of this organization."[25] On the other hand, one of Freud's major accomplishments is to have distinguished between a logical and a biological level. Gender and belonging to one of the genders—these were by no means the same thing for Freud! Even if one has reservations about the emergence of a phallic phase, one must nevertheless admit that Freud never derived psychical phenomena immediately from physical ones, but rather that for him knowledge, fantasms, and infantile sexual theories were of very decisive significance.[26] This comes down to saying nothing less than that on the psychic level femininity and masculinity are not what they are on the physical one. A woman could, therefore, not even be a woman if she were not also a man, and a man could not be a man were he not also a woman. When, in reading Freud, one then gets the impression that civilization is masculine, it does not immediately follow that women are excluded from it a priori. On the other hand, one must admit that Freud paid very little attention to these problems when discussing social relationships; we will see that on the level of psychoanalytic treatment women's speech was of paramount significance to Freud, to psychoanalysis and to Western culture, significant in a way that has certainly not been diminished today.

Freud's Insights into Democracy within the Context of Psychoanalytic Treatment

At this point I would like to move away from Freud's work in cultural theory and focus my inquiry on the realm of psychoanalytic practice and treatment. Is there any relationship to speak of between democracy and psychoanalysis in this arena? For one thing, we are dealing here with a relationship between only two people, and for another, it is really not possible to speak of equality between analyst and analysand! However, the two-person relationship unfolds in a *legal framework* without which psychoanalysis would not be possible. It is remarkable that psychoanalysis exists above all in Western societies and that it does *not* thrive in places governed by religious or totalitarian powers. Consequently, subjectivity and its legal moorings must be of decisive significance—otherwise the premises for psychoanalysis are missing. It seems, in other words, that the Western democracies contribute something to psychoanalysis; is the opposite true as well?

Freud determined the capacity to work and to feel pleasure to be the aims of psychoanalytic treatment. Can one deduce from this that he was really talking about adapting to society? If we think of the development of the so-called psychoanalytic technique which spans from hypnosis, through suggestion, all the way to free association, and if we ask ourselves what the reasons were for this transformation, the first thing that we would be led to would be Freud's conviction that the patient ought to be respected: that he should not be the object of the analyst's prejudices but rather that his speech, his ideas, and everything unpredictable that may introduce itself should be heeded. In this sense Freud's hysterics contributed enormously to the Freudian theory of psychoanalysis. This weighting toward the side of subjectivity and of the articulation of what suddenly occurs to the analysand, this partisanship, which is communicated to the analysand in the so-called fundamental rule, could be observed already during Freud's student years. When he was introduced to Bernheim's experiments with hypnosis in Nancy he became indignant with his teacher when one of his patients proved not to be compliant. "The man certainly had a right to employ counter-suggestions when he was being made to subject himself to suggestions," he said, and continued, "Later my resistance took the shape of a rejection of the idea that suggestion, which explained everything, should itself not be subjected to explanation."[27] And when he himself later still urged his female patients to have sudden ideas when he pressed his hand against their foreheads, he listened quietly to one of his patients' protests and a short time later drew the necessary conclusion by simply renouncing this method even if that led to an increased occurrence of resistances.[28]

This respect for the other, for his or her speech, indeed this allowance for the emergence of what had previously been suppressed, kept secret, this rendering testimony to a *truth*, even if it cannot be spoken immediately and once and for all—isn't this where we see Freud's contribution to democracy, even if the founder of psychoanalysis never did formulate this explicitly? Psychoanalytic method corresponds with a democracy in which everyone can speak in his or her own name without external pressure. "Everyone"—this also implies free access and, consequently, justice, at least in the formal sense. This dimension surely has consequences on the subjective level; all one has to do is think of the sibling rivalry that appears in analyses which is directed at the other analysands. But one could also say that the repression of disagreeable thoughts and facts on the intrapsychic level corresponds to a dictatorship, a censorship unworthy of any democracy. But where there is no democracy vis-à-vis the "inside," where speech is not free, there can be no democracy in the relationship to the "outer," to the other. Lies and untruth tarnish the relationship to one's fellow human beings just as they do the assessment of oneself. A sixth thesis would go, then, as follows: *The analyst's allowance for the emergence of the analysand's subjectivity and respect for it is a democratic occurrence.*

Obviously what is at stake in these statements is what I call the mental, even subjective, dimension of democracy as opposed to its structural dimension. Freud recognized the *significance of speech* early on; as we all know, it was already

Bertha von Pappenheim, alias Anna O., who referred to the analytic process as a "talking cure." By "speech" one may mean many different things: calculated, scheming, unrestrained, uncontrolled speech, speech that evades conscious intention, and much else besides. What sort of speech is at stake in analytic treatment and what are its relationships to the question of democracy? Regarding this question there is, once again, in Freud an ambiguity, which is expressed in the motto of psychoanalysis, "Where id was, I shall become." It can be understood to mean that the "I" must go to the place of the id, must engage with it, in order to take into itself what comes from it. But one can also see in it the Zuydersee model: the I is to be strengthened at the cost of the id; it is to dry the id out as much as possible, to civilize it, to bring it into its service. It is not very helpful to consult Freud's contributions to the technique of psychoanalysis to understand which reading corresponds more closely to his intentions; it is clear, though, that Freud is interested in *psychic truth*, and he assumes regarding this truth that it is to begin with a shed, averted, repressed, or denied truth, and that it requires work to bring it to light. But where is this truth located? In the id or in the ego, or possibly even in the superego? The confusion even increases when one starts wondering about what the ego's characteristics are, characteristics which are hardly homogeneous, and which actually point to the fact that in the ego two functions intersect, an imagistic one and a reasonable one, or, if we also include the criteria of the conscious and the unconscious, we can say this: it is not only the id that appears to be unconscious in quality, but Freud identifies parts of the ego as being unconscious as well; even the highest human qualities could be unconscious.[29] One time he even writes about the voice of the intellect that it is soft[30]—isn't one forced to think then that the unconscious is much closer to what in the history of thought has commonly been called *reason?* On the other hand, isn't the speaking ego the deceived, the fooled ego, as one can deduce from the simplest examples from *The Psychopathology of Everyday Life?*[31] In these examples something else often breaks in, something the speaker had allegedly not meant to say; thus, for example, *Vorschein* ["appearance," in the sense of "something made its appearance then"—E. S.] becomes *Vorschwein* [*Schwein* = pig], and what one had meant to say evades one, as Freud's own "*Signorelli*" example makes clear.

The truth comes knocking where one does not expect it. Could this in any way *not* have consequences for democracy? The counterquestion would be: with what justification do I assume that that which occurs in psychoanalysis can be transposed onto the political level? There is in any case no psychoanalytic claim that would demand this! Freud, however, never regarded analysis as a space where one would be spared the demands of social life. Its aims would be absurd if they were not to be applied outside of the analytic space. The assumption that something could be effective *first* within analysis and *then* outside of it has to be put in question even in Freud's own terms. At one point it is an event that takes place within the analytic treatment that attracts the attention of analyst and analysand; then it is the memory of a significant situation outside of the analytic room, or even a memory of something that occurred a long time before the analysis even began that demands to be articulated and heard. In each case what is at stake is a truth that occasionally surprises both speaker and listener; it is this truth that at privileged moments takes command and delivers the speaker. Hasn't Freud, with his method of listening, given us an instrument that can be applied also outside of the analytic space, in the realm of the politicians, for example? Even if it were not to result in an express agreement which would oblige the speaker to approach the truth as closely as possible, it would bring *the truth in public places, in politics,* into play. This by no means implies that it is always immediately and intentionally possible to articulate it. It is precisely its missing, its not reaching, its pending nature, that is so important for democracy; why otherwise should one debate, why have a parliament, when from the beginning all had already been established, if there were nothing but harmony? It is at this point that analytic experience and political theory intersect. For instance, Freud showed in his cultural writings what the consequences are of a mistaken theory;[32] one could draw an analogy between symptoms on the individual level and symptoms on the social level; put differently: the signs of repression correspond to scapegoats. Haven't we experienced such examples in the recent past, examples that demonstrate what happens when the foundation of a society cannot bear examining its own truth? What was lost from sight if not precisely the subjective factor? And aren't we also in a dilemma because we sense that capitalism and ecology are perhaps not very compatible, are perhaps completely incompatible, without there being a viable alternative on the horizon, an alternative which would allow us to perceive the conflict in all of its complexity?

Let us return to analytic practice. At stake is the subjective dimension that manifests itself in speech, in the discovery of truth. This independence is not something the analyst has invented; rather, he takes it for granted in his work. It would be contradictory to want to lead someone toward independence; that would simply mean being obedient vis-à-vis the analyst, an adaption to a demand addressed to him. The situation of the analysand, that is, being in the position of an object, would then be dissolved only in appearance. Nevertheless, Freud found himself at this point confronting a disagreeable experience which put in question even his best intentions: he was forced to establish the effectiveness of a negative transference,[33] or, put differently, the refusal to affirm one's own existence, to take *responsibility* for it. Whoever believes that people want nothing better than to validate their own independence will have to accept being called naive; ever since the Freud of the middle phase it has become necessary to contradict that conception. Freud had to recognize that the defenses against being expected to be autonomous are tough. And this is the case not only in the negative transference; the positive transference does not imply mutual recognition between analyst and analysand either. Nothing seems more difficult and laborious than to affirm one's own existence, to take over the decision-making process regarding oneself, to take responsibility for oneself, to accept the fact that one is alone. On the other side, it seems that many advantages are to be gained from taking up an accusatory position. Under these conditions it becomes possible to delegate one's own guilt, and to strengthen one's own narcissism. Another way of getting out of having to affirm one's own existence consists in contriving oneself for another, or in making the other serviceable in terms of one's own wishes.

In essence, Freud saw two reasons for the development of such difficulties: one he associates with hysteria and thus principally, but not only, with the female gender; the other he associates with obsessional neurosis, and thus principally, though again not exclusively, with the male gender. In terms of hysteria he speaks of a "psychic gap,"[34] a metaphor for the fact that something always remains unfulfilled, that there is a general dissatisfaction that characterizes the hysteric. This—and this is especially important in terms of its connection with democracy—also concerns relations to other people; *hysterics have a hard time with democracy, as they are always looking* for the master whose protectorate they want to claim. As far as obsessional neurosis is concerned, Freud talks about *jouissance,*[35] about a resulting repression with powerful reaction formations. One possible development of this is excessive shyness, or even impotence. These observations become intelligible only when one considers that Freud will interpret all of these phenomena against the foil of the Oedipus complex. Here the father plays a central role, since it is he who, on the one hand, threatens castration, and, on the other, is the ideal emulated by his descendants. In terms of the connection of all of this to the question that concerns us, the question of democracy, one must say that *the obsessive compulsive has trouble with the authorities:* either he struggles against them as a consequence of his father-hatred, or he becomes passively submissive and thereby gives up his independence and his masculinity, while the hysterics remain fixated on the authorities and thereby spare themselves the testing of their capacity to be alone. Let's formulate another thesis: *Neurotics are characterized by the fact that they have a disturbed relation to democracy. Each and every neurosis can be investigated in terms of the extent to which it implies a distortion of democratic life.*

Perhaps one could say with Freud that maybe even more important than the theory which underlies the analytic cure is the transferential event, which regularly occurs within it. Surely one can say here too that it would never even be noted if it weren't for theory, but it stands out so much for every analyst that it precedes in importance all other metapsychological structures, indeed, that it is what makes possible their very construction. It is in the relationship of the analysand to the analyst that what is most decisive in the analysis occurs and it is precisely here that one can best locate the relationship to politics. Regularly the analyst observes that his person is given special importance, even that external details, such as his clothing, the ways in which he decorates his office, even the way he clears his throat, are assigned special meaning. Freud was far from considering such behavior mad, or, of course, from condemning it. On the contrary, he used these transferential events for his insights into psychic events and thereby to forge interpretations. The intention of these interpretations is to confront the analysand with the psychic truth that had not been accessible to him before. This was possible only because Freud did not confront the analysand with a norm regarded by the patient as external to himself, but instead made it possible for this psychic reality to be articulated. Both analyst and analysand thereby found out that they were deeply involved in this struggle for truth. By standing fast against the transference Freud made it possible for the analysand to recognize and to experience to what extent he had needed the Other for himself, or the extent to which he had been ready to offer himself up to the Other. This impossibility of satisfying the drives by way of the analyst never had any other meaning than returning to the patient his own disposal of himself, leading him back to an independence which—and this is important—had always already been assumed by the analyst to be something always already posited, even if not yet accepted. In addition, through his independence the analysand was to be freed of his asociality, which Freud thought was a consequence of neurosis.[36]

The analytic cure in Freud's sense—that is, the setting with all of its agreements and duties—can certainly not be declared to be democratic. Analysis is not simply a conversation under symmetrical conditions. Nevertheless, the sense of the analytic cure can be made to coalesce with the idea of democracy, since it appeals to sublimation and thereby opens up the possibility for the analysand not to be unknowingly and unprotectedly offered up to his symptoms and fantasms.

If what is at stake in the analytic cure is really knowledge and experience, it is nevertheless an acquisition of another, nontraditional, sort of knowledge. Freud says more than once that it is impossible to overcome skepticism regarding the insights of psychoanalysis with verbal arguments and persuasion. For this reason he gave the experience of the transference, the testing of this phenomenon—or rather, testing *through* this phenomenon—a completely different sort of weight. This also says something about his estimate concerning the dissemination of psychoanalysis. Even under externally democratic conditions, that is, in the absence of censorship or other sorts of prohibitions of publication, psychoanalysis is not as easily transmitted as are scientific discoveries. Nevertheless Freud never renounced conducting sociotheoretical analyses. But he is always very careful when this leads to suggesting ideas for reform. It was his skepticism regarding the validity of purely rational arguments that led him to this prudence. Freud knew that one could not order progress; if that were not so, psychoanalysis would be located in the traditional realm of transmitted doctrine, where there is never a shortage of leaders and led—or better, leaders and seduced; he set his stakes on the articulation of what would undo the resistance to looking into the abyss. The question crops up whether Freud was perhaps basing himself on a form of reason that was conceptually not really anchored in his metapsychological structure. There is talk at one point about the God Logos: "Our God, *Logos*, will fulfill whichever of these wishes nature outside us allows, but he will do it very gradually, only in the unforeseeable future, and for a new generation of men."[37] But if one remembers that Freud conceives of everything that has to do with religion as the product of the human confrontation with nature, even the Logos, at least in the way in which Freud talks about it, appears to be an invention of the *anthropos*, who, in turn, was brought forth by natural history.

Notes

A partially expanded, partially abridged version of a paper entitled *Psychoanalyse und Demokratie*, Dec. 3, 1994, given in Hamburg, upon the invitation by the Lehrhaus der Psychoanalyse.

1. See Sigmund Freud, *Group Psychology and the Analysis of the Ego*, *Standard Edition*, *Volume 18*, trans. James Strachey (London: The Hogarth Press), 93–4.

2. Ibid., 95.

3. Sigmund Freud, *Totem and Taboo*, *Standard Edition*, *Volume 13*, 140–1.

4. Ibid., 144.

5. Sigmund Freud, *Civilization and Its Discontents*, *Standard Edition*, *Volume 21*, 109–110.

6. Sigmund Freud, *The Future of an Illusion*, *Standard Edition*, *Volume 21*, 42, and *Civilization*, 128.

7. Sigmund Freud, *Civilization*, 46–47.

8. Cf. Sigmund Freud, *Beyond the Pleasure Principle*, *Standard Edition*, *Volume 18*, 53–54, 63.

9. Sigmund Freud, *The Future of an Illusion*, 10–11.

10. Sigmund Freud, *Civilization*, 114–115.

11. Sigmund Freud, *The Future of an Illusion*, 6.

12. Ibid., 7.

13. Ibid., 11.

14. Ibid., 11.

15. Ibid., 36.

16. Cf. especially chapters 5 and 6 of *Beyond the Pleasure Principle*.

17. Sigmund Freud, *The Future of an Illusion*, 40.

18. Sigmund Freud, *Civilization*, 43.

19. Sigmund Freud, *The Future of an Illusion*, 18.

20. Ibid., 41.

21. Sigmund Freud, "Why War?" *Standard Edition*, Volume 22, 195–215.

22. Ibid., 207.

23. Ibid., 207.

24. Ibid., 213.

25. Sigmund Freud, *Group Psychology and the Analysis of the Ego*, 141.

26. Cf. e.g. Sigmund Freud, "The Infantile Genital Organization," *Standard Edition*, *Volume 19*, 141; or "Some Psychical Consequences of the Anatomical Distinction between the Sexes," *Standard Edition*, *Volume 19*, 248.

27. Sigmund Freud, *Group Psychology and the Analysis of the Ego*, 88–89.

28. Cf. the case history of Emmy von N . . . , in Josef Breuer & Sigmund Freud, *Studies on Hysteria*, *Standard Edition*, *Volume 19*, 101–2.

29. Sigmund Freud, *The Ego and the Id*, *Standard Edition*, *Volume 19*, 27.

30. Sigmund Freud, *The Future of an Illusion*, 53.

31. Sigmund Freud, *The Psychopathology of Everyday Life*, *Standard Edition*, *Volume 6*, 2.

32. He referred to communism, for instance, as an "untenable illusion"; cf. *The Future of an Illusion* or *Civilization and Its Discontents*.

33. Cf. e.g., Freud, "The Dynamics of Transference" *Standard Edition*, *Volume 12*, 104–105, 147, and *An Outline of Psycho-Analysis* *Standard Edition*, *Volume 23*, 176.

34. Sigmund Freud, *Extracts from the Fliess Papers*, *Standard Edition*, *Volume 1*, 228.

35. Sigmund Freud, *Letters of Sigmund Freud to Wilhelm Fliess 1987–1904*, ed. & trans. Jeffrey Moussaieff Masson (Cambridge, Mass.: Harvard University Press, 1985), 223 (letter Dec. 6, 1896).

36. Sigmund Freud, *Group Psychology and the Analysis of the Ego*, 142.

37. Sigmund Freud, *The Future of an Illusion*, 54.

19

The Lacanian Thing

ALAIN JURANVILLE

The Thing: this is the proper concern of philosophy. Philosophy is in fact in search of absolute knowledge (*connaissance absolue*). The desire that drives it must then be subsumed under the term "the Thing," just as in everyday language one speaks of a thing (or an object: *la chose*). A thing is first of all what is present in the perception of what lies outside of the self, what is encountered in the Real. But one would not speak of a "thing" were one not to assume a consistency, a unity, a "truth," in what one encounters in the Real. By striving to speak an absolute truth, which it first perceives outside of itself, philosophy searches for a "Thing"—truth, the truth of the Thing, the site where it, philosophy, situates the Highest Good (*le Souverain Bien*).

Can knowledge of the Thing be attained? Is there even such a thing as the Thing? As far as empiricism is concerned, the Thing is an illusion. For Kant the only possible object of human knowledge is the phenomenon; the Thing forever remains something that is "in itself," unknowable, and that can be postulated only by practical reason. How does psychoanalysis think of these issues, and, more specifically, how does Lacan think of them?

Lacan introduces the Thing in his Seminar on *The Ethics of Psychoanalysis*; the Thing is the Seminar's heart. He says there that it is an essential term as far as Freudian thought is concerned; he says that for analysts it responds so much to the inner necessity of their experience, that the only living place within psychoanalytic theory (the time period concerned is 1959–60), the Kleinian School, had made its impact solely by having pushed the Thing into the foreground in the shape of the mythical body of the mother, the object of primal aggression, for which one [the infant] later attempts, in different ways, to make restitution.

How must one speak of the Thing in psychoanalysis? First of all, as the illusion of an absolute truth. A real illusion, doubtless, the point of an effacement, which is decisive for the constitution of human desire as partial truth. Nevertheless, still an illusion. For this reason Lacan says that Freud's decisive step, the one he took on the level of the pleasure principle, consisted in showing us that there is no Highest Good, that the Highest Good, which is the Thing, which is the mother, which is the object of incest, is a prohibited thing (*bien interdit*), and that there is no other Good. But subsequently, Lacan's thought was to be turned up a notch by the dialectic of analytic discourse, which he was to develop with ever-increasing rigor. To "posit" the Thing in discourse, even as an absolute, impossible truth, means accepting a truth separate from the partial one of desire, and thus to take up once again, even if in a different manner, the problem of the Thing.

But is it possible for analytic discourse to continue speaking of the Thing even after it has emerged that there is no such thing as pure truth? After the *Ethics* Lacan hardly ever mentions the term again except by way of allusion. The hypothesis I will offer is that there are reasons for this silence, reasons that are related to analytic discourse itself. Lacan's teaching nourishes the antinomy that constitutes it. On the one hand, analytic discourse must assume the existence of a total truth which emerges from what the discourse itself essentially is; the idea of the total truth of the Thing does not cease approaching psychoanalysis as a demand, not only on the level of theory, but also directly in order to shed light on practice and clinic. On the other hand, analytic discourse must not speak this idea of total truth, must, indeed, even exclude it if it doesn't want to risk losing its faculty as act. Only philosophical discourse is capable of dissolving this antinomy—but only by appealing to psychoanalysis. Otherwise nothing would connect total truth—which philosophical discourse wishes to unfold—to the Real; instead, it would simply hover as a mere possibility of reconciliation.

I will attempt, then, to speak about the "Thing" philosophically, which is how we understand it in Lacan's teaching. Placed into my title in this sense, it first functions as a promise. Lacan said jokingly that for Descartes—who marched off against the truth of the Thing with the step of a conqueror, aware of the danger that he might encounter nothing but an expanse of emptiness—he said that for Descartes "people were clothes taking a walk (*pro-mènade*). Clothes—they promise the maenad when they are taken off." Clothing, here, is the name, the Thing. The maenad (we will see whether or not it appears): that would be the encounter with the Thing.

I will suggest three levels on which the encounter with the Thing occurs, and one could say that within each of the three periods which J.-A. Miller distinguished in Lacan's teaching, Lacan emphasized the development of one of these levels:

1. the Thing as absolute, mythical object of desire
2. the Thing as woman
3. the Thing as analytic discourse

The Logic of Psychoanalysis:
The Thing as the Absolute, Mythical Object of Desire

For analytic discourse the Thing appears first as the absolute, mythical object of desire, the "object impossible to reach," as Lacan says, "forever lost for the search and for desire." Analytic discourse, in fact, distinguishes itself by its hypothesis of the unconscious, and its first dimension is a *logical* one. The unconscious cannot be grounded empirically, only logically. Lacan understands it from the vantage point of language, as the signifier on this side of any appearance of the signified, as the signifier that in the act of speaking allows the signified to emerge. This emergence determines an ontological, but merely partial, truth. But this partial nature of truth must be perceived in time. Initially truth is believed to be absolute. Hence the Thing's location at the heart of the unconscious, and hence the fact that the encounter with the Thing is essentially a missed encounter. The reality of the unconscious then takes on the appearance of sexual reality in lieu of another, truer, one.

Let us briefly clarify the extent to which the hypothesis of the unconscious leads to the affirmation of an ontological truth, and what that truth might be.

In order to establish the unconscious Lacan dispenses with any empirical evidence, which would contradict the very notion of the unconscious, and bases himself on the interpretation of language, which had been suggested to him by contemporary structuralist linguistics, in which linguistic terms achieve value only as a result of their difference. What structuralist linguistics says concerning the signifier, which also applies to the signified—pure symbolic difference— meshes exactly with what Freud says of unconscious ideas and of the processes that articulate them.

But Lacan goes beyond this conception of linguistics that juxtaposes signifier and signified in parallel fashion. In order to think the unconscious, one must, on the one hand, assume that the order of the signified (the world as the domain of consciousness) distinguishes itself from the domain of the signifier by its organizing principle. The difference concerns temporality: on one side, the imaginary time of anticipation and of mastery, and, on the other, the real time of unpredictable emergence. On one side the world, on the other the Real. On the other hand, one must assume that the signified is constructed, derivative, illusory in its essence, even if it pretends to be sufficient. Lacan here comes face to face with contemporary thought, especially with Heidegger, who questions, as he says, the traditional, "metaphysical" conception of the relationship between being and time and understands time positively.

Subsequently, for Lacan the unconscious is the "discourse of the Other," of the absolutely *Other* who speaks in every other and who interferes as the third term in every intersubjective relationship, and to whose law the human subject must submit as soon as he or she enters speech. Like Heidegger's Being, the Other erects the world. It is a pure signifying game that brings forth the signified. That of which every human subject is advised, his or her "destiny," is desire and lack, and the fact that there is something which signifies, but that a signifier signifies not in itself, but only from the "perspective" of another signifier. This is an ontological truth, but a partial one.

One cannot stop at this term of the Other, however. The interpretation of the unconscious through the signifier leads to a "truth" that is different from that of Heidegger's Being, the significant act which brings forth the signified. On this side of the emergence of the signified, there is, according to Lacan, a temporal articulation of the pure signifier, which is already desire, but not yet desire as the law. The proof of negativity has not yet taken place there. What from the viewpoint of the signifier emerges as something significant appears as the site of absolute significance. It is the Thing; it is what speaks and that first generates the proof that there is only partial truth when it, the Thing, arrives as a subject (Lacan says that it is "the true, even if not the good, subject, the subject of desire") by establishing, in the metaphorical act of speech, the Other of the Law, to which it submits.

For psychoanalysis it is not the Other who takes precedence, but rather this (missed) encounter with the Thing. That is what Lacan is aiming at when, in *The Four Fundamental Concepts of Psycho-Analysis*, he engages the Aristotelian terms *tuché* and *automaton:* "For what we have in the discovery of psychoanalysis is an encounter, an essential encounter," he says, "an appointment to which we are always called with a real that eludes us. . . . [The *tuché*] [w]e have translated . . . as *the encounter with the real.* The real is beyond the *automaton,* the return . . . of the signs. . . . The real is that which always lies behind the automaton, and it is quite obvious, throughout Freud's research, that it is this that is the object of his concern."[1] There is an essential difference between *automaton* and *tuché,* between the blind insistence of the symbolic Other and the impossible encounter with the Real. When Lacan is able to say that the Real eludes us, which Real is he talking about? On the one hand, one misses the Real in its meaning as non-sense, because something comes to stand in its place: the Symbolic, the "signifier." But one wants it, one wants this Real, because one had once thought it to be absolutely desirable, and significant in itself. The signifier has a double aspect: the incidental aspect, where it confuses itself with the Symbolic, and its principal aspect, where it appears in its significance and allows for the creation of an illusion of truth which will, however, be effaced. In this sense the encounter with the Real is the encounter with the Thing. When Lacan says that "the Thing is that which, coming from the real, suffers at the hands of signifiers," one must emphasize that the Real is at first thought to be true and that the signifier is posited as being significant; the Thing's Passion unveils itself and undergoes its sufferance only within time.

The Thing, then, divides itself, or better, makes its split or even its spreading, its quadripartite elements *(é-cart-élément)*, felt, since this split is realized in accordance with the quadripartite structure of desire, as Lacan has elaborated it in so many schemas, and which is nothing else but the structure of the metaphor of the Father.

First there is the *object*, what remains of the Thing when significance has been effaced and it is no longer desirable. The internal cavity formed within the "subject" is experienced by the subject as though it, the cavity, had found its own missing, severed counterpart in this leftover. This is one of the functions of what Lacan calls the *objet a*. The relationship to this object is no longer based on desire, but on drive, where time is essentially reversible and repeatable. At the base of this drive, which is tied to the object, when, with any kind of reerection of desire, all that is encountered is emptiness—proof of the lack of any object—we find the death drive.

Then there is the signifier of the Thing as desiring *subject*, a subject identified in the world. This is the stroke made "Thing," also referred to by Lacan as the "single stroke"—the structure or the sensible schema—conceived of first as signifier and established as such by desire (hence the expression "single stroke"; the signifier posited as significant is single), which then, however, appears significant only through the operation of an other and not in itself (hence the subsequent final determination as S_2, as "binary" signifier).

The third term is the signifier, which remains such and which guarantees the maintenance of desire. This is the *signifier of the Other*, the Name-of-the-Father.

Finally, there is the phallic meaning, the significance of the *phallus*. In order to maintain (and prop up) desire in spite of the absence of the absolute object, the law of castration demands the relinquishing of the drive and of the object, which then, as effaced object, becomes the signifier.

This "quadripartite term" assembles the whole significance of the Thing's spreading out, and the proof of its significance is *jouissance*, enjoyment mixed with suffering, what remains of enjoyment in face of the impossibility of absolute *jouissance*, of the Highest Good. Above all, it appears in the sexual act; Lacan reminds us that psychoanalysis makes this the central site for any sort of fulfilling joy: in this unique moment, he says, a being can stand in the place, simultaneously dead and alive, of the Thing for another being.

Let us list a few examples of this encounter with the Thing, which in fact and in truth is the encounter with S_2, which, however, carries the value of the true signifier (S_1). Lacan also designates S_2 by the term *Vorstellungsrepräsentanz*, which to him means "stand-in" *[tenant-lieu]* for representation, which, on the one hand, belongs to the world, to the realm of representation, but which is also and to begin with a signifier, more precisely, the signifier of the *jouissance* of the mother.

For the Wolf Man the encounter with the Thing is the V of the mother's legs in the primal scene, an identificatory stroke with the mother as a desiring one, which the Wolf Man seemed to have extracted from the primal scene but which he ceaselessly encountered in the maternal desire. The encounter with this signifying stroke is the encounter with the Thing for him every time: for example, when he suddenly notices the butterfly spreading its wings.

Or, also, the two dreams which Lacan, still in the same session of *The Four Fundamental Concepts of Psycho-Analysis*, mentions. One of them is a dream of Lacan's. The other one is a dream from *The Interpretation of Dreams*, the dream of *"Father, can't you see I'm burning?"* In both cases we witness a perceptual phenomenon taking place in reality which is admitted into the dream, soon to be followed by awakening. Lacan asks, *"What is it that wakes the sleeper?"* Is it, as one might easily be led to believe, what has been perceived, the noise or the brightness of the fire? Or isn't it rather what is "most real," which the dream has allowed the dreamer to reach? "There is more reality in this message than there is in the noise, isn't there?" says Lacan. Why more reality? Because the dream, by hallucinating, opens up access to the most real, which was the "loss expressed in an image at the most cruel point of the object," the dead child, the Thing in its moment of non-sense and of horror; hallucination of the Thing in its illusory plenitude, a signifier taken in its pure significance (here, of the message, "Father, can't you see I'm burning?"). But in the dream, and insofar as in it the desire to sleep finds realization, this signifier does not ordinarily efface itself; the most real is not encountered.

And finally what Lacan calls "peace of the evening" in his Seminar on *The Psychoses*. He does so in the context of examining hallucinations. Lacan refers to those experiences one can have in certain places when evening is falling and which, thick with affective significance, can be summarized in this expression, "peace of the evening." Only speaking beings who are capable of coining such expressions can experience it, he says. But then there are two possibilities: either "we . . . have formulated this expression before uttering it"—that is, it belongs to our world, and that is what I was trying to get at with my reference to imaginary time—or "it takes us by surprise or interrupts us, calming the movement of agitation that dwelled within us"—and, in this case, we no longer know whether this articulation, "peace of the evening," comes from inside or outside; this is the hallucinatory emergence of the Thing, an instant of real time. "We have now come to the limit," says Lacan, "at which discourse, if it opens onto anything beyond meaning, opens onto the signifier in the real."

The Ethics of Psychoanalysis: The Thing as Woman

The Thing then appears as woman (and the analyst is put in this place). Because analytic discourse does not express only unconscious desire. It also appeals to another sort of relationship with desire, aside from the neurotic one; this is the *ethical* dimension of psychoanalysis, according to which a pure truth could be found in sublimation, through writing. This is an essentially finite possibility, however. There is always a sublimation to be accomplished that one cannot accomplish. Sexual difference represents this limitation. Woman is the one who has accomplished this finite sublimation. She is the Thing, no longer as myth, but as reality. But "the other *jouissance*" which she knows, which is not mixed up with suffering and is in this sense pure, cannot be derived from phallic *jouissance*. Total truth remains an illusion for analytic discourse.

Let us attempt to show to what degree there is such a thing as an essentially ethical nature of psychoanalysis and to what sort of truth it leads.

What stands in the way of an ethics of psychoanalysis is that even if the instance of the law cannot be led back to anything, the relation to the law is nevertheless described as working in accordance with the pleasure principle, especially where the Law appears in its most demanding, even cruelest, shape. The whole analysis of the superego implies this. The struggle against pleasure, fundamental to any kind of ethics, is, then, according to this view, carried out in the name of another pleasure and not as a consequence of deliverance from the pleasure principle. Psychoanalysis finds its final determination in the Oedipus complex and in the relation to the Law, which is depicted as the relation to what is prohibited. Psychoanalysis remains, still according to this description, in the realm of therapy—a subtle pleasure technique.

This is where the central novelty of the Lacanian position, if not in relation to Freud, then nevertheless to the letter of Freud, is situated. It consists of a reference to a *Beyond the Oedipus*, and it can be summarized by a formula used in the *Ethics*: namely that *it is more comfortable to suffer the prohibition than it is to take castration upon oneself.* In the "Mythe individuel du nevrosé"[2] Lacan announced, "The entire schema of the Oedipus is to be criticized," and further, "The Oedipus complex is Freud's dream. Like all other dreams, it has to be interpreted." Freud knew very well that the Oedipus and the superego were of neurotic stamp; but he thought that they were constitutive of human desire and in this sense could not be overcome. For Lacan the Oedipus can be overcome; it is the subject himself who surrenders himself to neurosis in order to veil the horror of the Thing; in order to prop up between himself and the Thing the image of the full-blown love/hate of the rival, and finally, in order to believe that the Highest Good remains out of reach because of the rival who keeps it all to himself. Human desire is not oedipal and incestuous desire. It is incestuous and prohibited only in order to repress the deeper desire, the desire for the Thing, which is not the father's woman. It is better to hate than it is to love and to step into the field of the Thing with determination; it is better in desire to reproach the other with one's present sufferings and to flee from desire, which nevertheless remains indestructible. The ethics of psychoanalysis call for another choice: to surrender oneself to castration, to overcome hatred, guilt, and fear. This is the choice Oedipus makes—the Oedipus of the tragedy who, as Lacan often said, does not have an Oedipus complex. This is the choice that the patient in analysis must make.

This leads one to a decisive reconsideration of Lacan's first theory, which one may call the "symbolic Oedipus." According to this theory, the law of language is the law of prohibition (hence formulas like, "Enjoyment is forbidden to anyone who speaks") since, after all, the law of language is the law of castration. Furthermore, according to this theory, the original object, the Thing, becomes desirable by way of the prohibition ("The law which prohibits the mother forces one to desire her"); desire is imposed from the outside on a being, a subject-to-be, which had previously been characterized by need; it is the Other who posits the Thing; the sign precedes the signifier; the Imaginary is what exists initially, and it is then crossed [and thwarted] by the Symbolic. All of these statements must be put into question again if one is to pay close attention to the rigorous nature of Lacan's analysis as well as to the ethical dimension that he underlines in his psychoanalysis.

What does this ethics of psychoanalysis call for? What sort of relation to desire and to the Thing does it ask for? I have in this context suggested the term "sublimation," which to me seems to fall directly in line with Lacan's thought. Like neurosis (and I have developed these elements for psychosis and for the perversions as well), sublimation is characterized by a process and by a phenomenon. Instead of repression there is negation *(dénégation)*. In the place of the symptom there is *writing*, which alone is capable of opening up the possibility for what Lacan has called "true speech" or "full speech." In writing the emerging unconscious signifier is posited as being in itself both significant and nonsignificant—this is the failure of negation: "That is not it." Not to accept unconscious desire (into a world, into discourse), not to integrate it, but to leave it be by crossing it out. This is the letter *(la lettre)*.

Writing has a double relation to the Thing. Lacan says of sublimation that it is "the raising of the object to the dignity of the Thing." On the one hand, elevated to the "impossible" dignity of the Thing, the object, made into the letter and the emergence of the signifier, is at the same time posited as not significant in itself: it establishes the absence of the Thing. On the other hand, the Thing reappears to some extent in writing. Even if the letter is not significant in itself (and also does not create that illusion) it is still significant in relation to the point from which one writes; it is posited as being significant. It is here that the process of accomplishment, to which one is led by writing, originates: also to draw this other signifier on the page from whose point the letter was posited. Another letter. Until the articulation of letters is such that one can add nothing more. If writing has achieved its consistency, first that of the basic four-point structure of desire, then the object has most probably attained the dignity of the Thing, whose structure it has even if it is not the forever lost, original Thing. Writing is, then, work, writing that "speaks," because the point from which one writes, from which the letter is posited as significant, is the point of the Other to whom the word refers.

The Thing has now to be examined in a new way. Through writing, in sublimation, it is possible to arrive at a truth other than the truth of desire. When the letter attains its consistency, nonsignificance, which constantly characterizes the verbal signifier, sets itself down in speech and in its phallic enjoyment, and the structure of the letter preserves only that in which it is significant. The truth which it possesses is therefore pure, as pure as the *jouissance* which one experiences within it. Such a pure *jouissance* of the verbal signifier had doubtlessly already been present in the position of the signifier of the Other, of the Name-of-the-Father as signifier, in metaphorical speech, but it is habitually confused with the phallic enjoyment of the symptom. It is necessary for there to be sublimation in order for this *jouissance,* which is "constitutive of the speaking being," to be set free; this *jouissance* is nothing other than the unconscious in its truth, the unconscious as Thing and no longer as Other, symbolic Other, unknown knowledge *(savoir insu).* "The Unconscious," says Lacan, "is that the subject enjoys when speaking and that it wants to know nothing besides, to know nothing at all."

In place of a mythical, absolute *jouissance,* the Thing, by way of the *jouissance* that is set free in sublimation, takes on reality and shape: that of *woman.* In what sense woman? Lacan lays out the difference between the sexes by beginning with logical considerations; this he does by asking himself what writing can do. The discovery of the unconscious erupts into writing (into scientific writing, to be precise) and imposes limits upon it. There is a truth that cannot be known, that no writing can record. Writing the limits of scientific writing leads Lacan to the "formulae of sexualization." By taking up Aristotle's famous logical square, Lacan retains for the first two fundamental propositions the formulation of symbolic logic: $\forall x.f(x)$ and $\exists x.f(X)$. For the last two he introduces the so far unmentioned and, "for science," impossible ones: $\bar{\forall}x.f(x)$ and $\bar{\exists}x.f(x)$ (which is where he locates both of von Gödel's theorems about the incompleteness of arithmetic). The first two formulae demonstrate the process of writing; the first indicates the place of the Other, the point from which one writes, the other indicates the place of the subject, the vehicle of writing. The last two characterize accomplished sublimation: the one indicates completed writing, writing that speaks, what emerges in writing, without allowing its articulation in a written relation, in a law (this is the function of Lacan's "not-completely" *[pas-tout]*); the other indicates that speech which I wish to call pure speech and which lies outside of all sublimation, what is forever rejected, foreclosed from writing. Identification with the first two is proper for man; identification with the latter two is proper for woman. Woman is the one who has sublimated, or who is in no need to do so; man is the one who must sublimate. By sublimating, the speaking being, *homme* (which it had been), gets to the place of his part of woman, without this part of "woman" ever having to present itself as "whole." The difference between the sexes marks the finite character of sublimation for the human being: as woman it does not move in the direction of more sublimation, and as man it tends in that direction without, however, ever reaching it.

Woman is the Thing. As pure speech she is the otherworldly Thing; in the illusory splendor of her absolute *jouissance* and her impossible sufficiency she is the virgin. As writing that speaks, she is the Thing of the missed encounter and of phallic *jouissance*, but simultaneously with this pure *jouissance* she is the mother. Because pure *jouissance* is made real only through sublimation, where phallic *jouissance* is left in the condition of its non-sense, the sexual encounter with the woman is for the man what in one formula is called "the hour of truth."

The analyst comes to inhabit this place of the female Thing. He arrives there through his discourse that pronounces unconscious desire and finite sublimation (or also: the "sexual nonrelation," the establishment of the irreducible lack in the encounter between the sexes). In the fundamental fourfold field, which has been analyzed from the perspective of being, analytic discourse takes up a specific position (I will not go into the details of discourse theory here); it supports the assertion that truth exists only in its partiality, that absolute knowledge is a mirage, and that truth appears in real time and evades governance by any form of knowledge.

There are two consequences to be drawn from this: on the one hand, through the sublimation which is accomplished within it, analytic discourse allows for the truth of desire to arrive at and find its place in the other, where the question (the subject) is embodied, which is also the case with the analyst himself (in his interpretive speech); it is this truth which, according to Lacan, analytic discourse produces: S_1, the master signifier. On the other hand, the analyst rejects the idealization of the transference in his affirmation of a merely finite sublimation; he offers himself as the site of nonsignificance, as a storage place for *jouissance* insofar as it is of a sexual, "phallic," nature; this is the analyst as *objet a*. In him pure *jouissance* emerges, then, as separate from phallic enjoyment. At that point he is the Thing, and if analytic discourse can speak the unconscious without denying it through this act, that is because at the moment that the analyst says the unconscious and communicates the illusion of an absolute knowledge, he experiences, at least for himself, the actual truth of the unconscious as pure *jouissance*.

Then the analyst is no longer, as he was in Lacan's first theory, the Other, the site where the word of the analysand's desire is stored, the Other of knowledge, where the analysand must discover his destiny. The analysand is to let go of the analyst as the Thing, to renounce neurotic idealization, to step into the fundamental fantasm the object of which the analyst embodies, and to traverse it, because any perverse result is inadmissible in analysis. The analyst is not simply an object, but rather an "object to which desire attaches itself and to whom knowledge is imputed": $\frac{a}{S_2}$ in Lacan's schema, that is, the Thing. And it is only by the analysand seeing in the analyst the Thing that he can turn him into the Other, that he can recover the knowledge of truth which he had imputed to the analyst in the transference. Here the strict conception of the unconscious parts ways with all Heideggerianism.

The Politics of Psychoanalysis: The Thing as Analytic Discourse

Finally, I wish to show that the Thing is analytic discourse itself. For analytic discourse must establish itself in a social world that at first forecloses it. To that extent its deepest dimension is *political*. Because through its arrival it questions the traditional world and the sacrificial violence that characterizes that world, analytic discourse inaugurates history. However, it can establish itself against the "discourse of the master," which dominates traditional society, only through its truth, through the consistency of its meaning. The political act that is constituted by the rise of analytic discourse calls for a total, if not infinite, sublimation. Pure *jouissance* then becomes absolute and ready to ceaselessly effect its own effacement and the test of non-sense. For the human being destined for finite sublimation analytic discourse is the Thing in its total truth, the first form of the Highest Good.

To what extent is it possible to speak of a "politics of psychoanalysis"? And to what extent does it lead to the idea of a total sublimation?

It may seem that there is nothing political about psychoanalysis. As theory, it is no more political than any other science. As practice it does aim for liberation, albeit a personal one. And, finally, as discourse it takes no position against the violence and injustice of that or the other organization within the social world. If psychoanalysis is political in its very essence, that is because it intervenes in the social world solely because of its arrival as discourse: by questioning the principle of the traditional world as well as what brings about the sacrificial violence that characterizes it: namely the rapport of fascination. It also does so by in effect inaugurating new forms of sublimation vis-à-vis the sacrificial system, which in turn delimits them. In other words, it leads into a new social world in which less violence is committed.

Let me be more precise. The traditional social world presents itself as a harmonious, unbroken whole in which everything has its place, and where human forms of behavior are predetermined by tradition. But if for psychoanalysis this order, as a collective mode of being, presupposes sublimation, then the illusion of having achieved a totality, which is projected by this order, can be propped up only by way of sacrificial violence.

In his Seminar on anxiety Lacan observes that Lévi-Strauss's very pertinent structural analyses of primitive societies pass in silence over the passionate
element—violence—that is essential within them. Sacrifice perpetuates the
fundamental rapport of fascination. On the one hand, there is he who has
entered sublimation and gives his desire. On the other hand, there is the one
who is fascinated, who in the face of this desire and in order to ward of the
horror of lack which desire brings with it, offers himself up as object. By exercising sacrificial violence, the "master," he who had sublimated and now renounces all increase in sublimation, sanctions the illusory complementarity
which is brought into play by the fascinated one and which is that of the
fantasm, according to which the subject desires and has an object. One can
then find this fantasm in all of the hierarchies that characterize the traditional
world: in age groups, genders, and various social groups. Those who offer their
desire, or who are in the position to offer it, and who function as fetishes
(through their speech, their gestures, their habits, their insignia) are answered
by those who offer themselves up as objects or who are in the position of
objects, and who play the role of waste products.

How can we now characterize traditional sublimation? On the one hand,
through the symbolic thought that is unfolded there, "mythological discourse"
becomes the site of real knowledge. In the literal [buchstäblichen] formalization
of modes of behavior and of knowledge the partial truth of desire becomes
writing. Symbolic thought is in this sense a "putting-to-work of the paternal
metaphor." On the other hand, however, the investigation of lack, which desire
and metaphor imply, is erased when the metaphor is transformed into analogy.
The illusion of completeness, to which fascination is attached, finds its most
elevated form in the affirmation of the idea that "there is a sexual relation," that
it is the play of a male principle and a female principle that constitutes the
unity of the world. "Metaphor shows only that—the sexual relation," Lacan says
finally. This is the double aspect of traditional sublimation which is brought to
light by the mode of initiation of its transmission: one undergoes a sort of
encounter with the truth of sexuality as death, but one also arrives at "knowledge about *jouissance*," within which sexuality guarantees cosmic unity.

In opposition to the traditional world, analytic discourse, characterized by
not falling prey to the "fascination of sacrifice," as Lacan says, questions the
illusory character of this "whole world" where everything has been given a
meaning. It reinforces the irreducibility of the proof of non-sense, the *Real*. In
this way it intervenes politically: "[I]t is at this juncture of the real that the
political element breaks through and where the psychoanalyst would find his
place were he capable of doing so" [trans.—E. S.], we read in "*Radiophonie*."
Lacan has no other aim than to say the Real: "Will I be successful in telling you
that which one could call the tip of the real?" he asks at the end of one of the
seminar sessions in *Le Sinthome*. "For the moment one must say that Freud did

only sensible things *(du sensé)* and that robs me of all hope." But then again, how can one affirm the Real if not through and within sense? Analytic discourse rejects the illusoriness of sense as the exclusive consistency of the world, without rejecting either sense on the whole or consistency, for that matter. In fact, analytic discourse requires absolute consistency. This is what Lacan is getting at when he appeals to a sense effect in the face of the fascination effect of mythological discourse, and says, "The sense effect demanded by analytic discourse is not imaginary. It has to be that it is real." For mythological discourse does not lack all consistency; it contains the partial truth of desire, elevated to the level of writing through sublimation. The fascination effect comes into play when this sublimation is considered to be sufficient, when partial truth is considered to be total truth. Analytic discourse thinks of partial truth as merely partial, and this is made possible only by reference to the idea of a total truth, through deduction, that is, the source of which is a possible total truth. The deduction allows it to appear as a real truth. The transition from fascination effect to sense effect is identical with the transition from an apparent, absolute consistency, supported by a real and partial consistency, to a real and absolute consistency.

In other words, psychoanalysis leads to the affirmation of a total sublimation, to an absolutely consistent writing. This is what Lacan meant to suggest when he introduced the *Borromean knot*, about which I will only say that what it shows is no longer a partial truth, but an absolute one; that it no longer shows the fourfold structure of desire, but rather the threefold structure, through which all thought, whether it be religious or philosophical, determines Being: there the Symbolic (desire) is articulated with the Real on the one hand and with the Imaginary on the other. Every element, as well as the whole, is made real through its existence, symbolic through the articulation of differential elements, and, by the fact that these elements stick together, are inseparable and consistent, each and every element is also imaginary.

So what about the Thing? There is a total truth, a *jouissance* that has become absolute, that appears in the Real—it is the *jouissance* of the knot itself—the total truth of the Thing; but it does not cease in effecting its own effacement by generating the Symbolic from within itself—the partial truth of desire, the gap; and, when it allows itself to be reinstated as absolute *jouissance* through the work of sublimation, it nevertheless always allows the Highest Good, which it represents, to slip away from human beings, to remain external to them, even where it is attained. Total sublimation is a finite possibility for humans: they cannot become "all sublimation." In fact, because of the fact that humans are never successful at taking possession of it completely, the Highest Good remains in the Real as Thing, and is always lacking for humans who exist and are forever destined for "radical evil."

So what it this Thing, then, which no longer has anything mythical about it, and which, according to the concept by which I referred to it at the start, appears in all its reality? It is analytic discourse itself, as a historical Thing. Absolute consistency, as we have seen: it is not the Highest Good in its freedom, but rather the first form in which it can give itself to human beings marked by finite sublimation. Through this truth it introduces a break with the traditional world and begins history (and here one must note that, of course, psychoanalysis does not appear in history entirely as itself, that the detraditionalization of the social world has to have been accomplished for the historical Thing in itself to appear—this is what is specific to the epoch we have entered). But analytic discourse determines the truth, which it announces and embodies, to be a truth that is always lacking for human beings in the world. Analytic discourse inscribes evil into the history into which it leads, inscribes it as something that cannot be overcome, and it imposes on history the irreducibility of non-sense. It is for this reason that Lacan can say, "If there are things that belong to history, then these things are of the order of psychoanalysis. What is called history is the history of epidemics. The Roman Empire, for instance, is an epidemic. Christianity is an epidemic. Psychoanalysis is also an epidemic." Freud himself, when he set foot on American soil, said, "I'm bringing them the plague." And Lacan too writes apropos his Borromean knot, "It is the order which I have explored basing myself on my experience that has led me to this hellish trinity. I want to play no card here that is not Freudian . . ." (by having, he means to say, introduced the dimension of an absolute consistency). "Flectere si nequeo Superos, Acheronta movebo" [If I cannot bend the Higher Powers, I will move the Infernal Regions] (indeed, it hands human beings over to the hellish gods, to the possibility of extermination, for example, through a nuclear weapon which Lacan also presents as the Thing, one of the products of the impossible demand for infinite sublimation).

By having thus, from the point of view of psychoanalysis, established psychoanalysis itself as the Thing, in its total truth as a historical Thing, I do not believe I have played a card that is not Lacanian. Lacan unceasingly asked himself the question about the essence of psychoanalysis. For him it is the Real ("as surprising as this may seem, I say that psychoanalysis, i.e. that which opens up a procedure/process as the field of experience, is reality"), and it is simultaneously necessary that it be consistent: "I am still occupied with interrogating psychoanalysis about the manner in which it functions," he says in one of his last seminars. "How can it be that it still holds its ground? And that it constitutes a practice that is sometimes even effective?" Psychoanalysis is, then, for psychoanalysis itself as well as for all discourses that appear in the historical world, the Thing. And with this Thing it can only make its cause, do its thing. But it runs up against the contradiction of having to say total truth as such within a discourse that excludes that. Hence the contradictory style (*dédit*) which characterizes Lacan's relation to the "Thing."

It is up to philosophy to say the Thing. It can do so through its relation to the historical Thing, which, as a social symptom, lends an actual presence to philosophy's own question. And it must do so in order to justify the historical world and the absolute freedom which the world houses. In the contemporary world psychoanalysis itself is the Thing—to an overwhelming extent it is Lacan's "discourse" that is the Thing. The latter is, in fact, the "Lacanian Thing."

What does philosophy do, then? It pronounces absolute truth as such. In reference to the fundamental trinity, which Lacan recovered in the Borromean knot, philosophical thought, throughout its history, is characterized by having seen in that fundamental trinity the three "ecstasies" that constitute time and by having seen them as the unity that thinks consistency. "Metaphysics" conceives of absolute truth as being situated outside of time, and Heidegger thinks of it as time itself, as a significant [or signifying] act that brings forth the signified. I have attempted to show in my reading of Lacan that the unconscious leads one to think of time in an even more positive way—to think of it in the pure signifier.

Of course I will not develop these issues here, but I would like to point to their clinical significance, especially in terms of the transference and the analytic relation in psychosis. The transference in psychosis can only be understood as a transference onto the Thing in its absolute *jouissance*. There is no other kind of love, because the psychotic by no means suffers castration, the breaking of desire. He seems then, in order to enable himself to bear the Real of desire, to demand of the analyst that he accomplish the paternal act of [pro]creation (to speak in theological terms), that he effect the production of the Symbolic from the point of origin of the Real, that he generate a signifier from within himself, a "new signifier," and that he himself suffer the process of becoming a subject without being able to accuse anyone else of this. In the signifier of desire, as it generally functions, in the "Name-of-the-Father," it is in fact always possible to accuse someone of succumbing to desire (the father . . .). In his last session on *"L'insu que sait de l'une-bévue s'aile à mourre"* ["One Knew that It Was a Mistaken Moon on the Wings of Love"] Lacan insists on the significance that the invention of a signifier would have, as all of our signifiers are always already derived. To invent a signifier would mean recreating (rebegetting) the world from an older point, which lies on the other side of the differential nature of language (where the "unconscious experiences of a people" are contained), on the side of pure speech. This is what a psychotic like the author of "Schizo and Languages"[3] attempts to do; he does so by allowing languages to communicate, but he is incapable of "saving" himself. It is necessary that the invention come from others.

This is the point to which Lacan has led us: to introduce at the far limits of rigorous discourse the demand for a new signifier that has no sense. "A new signifier," he says, "the kind that would have no sense whatsoever, perhaps it is that that could help us find access to what I, in my clumsy movements, call the Real. . . . A signifier which, contrary to what is customary, would have an effect. It is certain that all of this is characterized by extremity. If I have arrived here through psychoanalysis then that is not without significance." At last, and because his discourse is the Thing itself, Lacan brings forth this signifier himself—for instance, when at the end of his Seminar "Dissolution" (1979–1980) he says of the "subject, which is subordinated to knowing": "It is the evening caller, or better, it is that kind of sign that is drawn on the door by angels' hands. More certain in its existence of not being ontological, and coming perhaps from a place—one knows not Yah-where"[5] (*"et àvenir d'on ne sait Zou"*).[4]

Notes

The German translation of this piece was based on the version of a paper first published as "La Chose lacanienne" in the journal *L'Artichaut* 3 (June, 1986): 19–39.

1. Jacques Lacan, *The Four Fundamental Concepts of Psycho-Analysis*, ed. J.-A. Miller and trans. Alan Sheridan. (New York: W. W. Norton, 1977), 53–54.

2. In *Ornicar?* 17/18 (1979), 289–307. German: *Der Wunderblock* 5/6 (1980): 50–68. [trans. E. S.]

3. L. Wolfson, *Le schizo et les langues* (Paris: Gallimard, 1970).

4. [i.e., "Yahweh." Lacan's pun is difficult to reproduce in English or German: "und nicht von einem Ort kommen mögend, man weiss nicht wo-Herr."—E. S.]

Contributors

Coeditors

Richard Feldstein is Professor of English at Rhode Island College and the editor (with Kate Mele) of *Literature and Psychology: A Journal of Psychoanalytic and Cultural Criticism*. He is the author of *Political Correctness: A Response from the Cultural Left* (Minneapolis: University of Minnesota Press, 1997) and co-editor (with Bruce Fink and Maire Jaanus) of *Reading Seminars I and II: Lacan's Return to Freud* (New York: State University of New York Press, 1996), *Reading Seminar XI: Lacan's Four Fundamental Concepts* (New York: State University of New York Press, 1995), *Feminism and Psychoanalysis* (Ithaca: Cornell University Press, 1989) and of numerous other volumes. He is currently writing *Specular Colonialism* with Daniel Scott.

Maire Jaanus is Professor of English at Barnard College, Columbia University. She is the author of *Georg Trakl* (New York: Columbia University Press, 1974), *Literature and Negation* (New York: Columbia University Press, 1979; Rept., 1988), *She: A Novel* (New York: Doubleday, 1984), and co-editor (with Richard Feldstein and Bruce Fink) of *Reading Seminars I and II: Lacan's Return to Freud* (New York: State University of New York Press, 1996) and *Reading Seminar XI: Lacan's Four Fundamental Concepts* (New York: State University of New York Press, 1995). She has also published numerous articles.

Elizabeth Stewart, translator, is Assistant Professor of English at Yeshiva University, New York. She has published on Nietzsche and Derrida and presented numerous papers on Freud, Lacan, Benjamin, Kafka, Benn, science fiction and cyberpunk, and the films of Lars Von Trier.

Contributors

Bernard Baas teaches philosophy at the University of Strasbourg. His publications include *Le désir pur. Parcours philosophiques dans les parages de J. Lacan* (Louvain: VRIN, 1992); *Descartes et les fondements de la psychanalyse* (with Armand Zaloszyc) (Paris, 1988); "La loi et le sacrifice," *Les Temps modernes*, (Aug./Sept. 1990); "Das Opfer und das Gesetz," *RISS* 21, (1992).

Rudolf Bernet is Professor of Philosophy at the University of Leuven, Belgium, Director of the Husserl Archive, and editor of Edmund Husserl's Collected Works and the series *Phaenomenologica*. He is also a practicing psychoanalyst and translator. His publications include *Edmund Husserl. Darstellung seines Denkens* (with Iso Kern and Eduard Marbach) (Hamburg, Meiner, 1989); *An Introduction to Husserlian Phenomenology* (Evanston: Northwestern University Press, 1993); *La vie du sujet* (Paris 1994), and many articles that have appeared in *RISS*, *Fragmente*, *Phänomenologische Forschungen*, *Études Phénoménologiques*, *Revue philosophique*, *Lch louvain*, and *Tijdschrift voor filosofie*.

Raymond Borens, co-editor of *RISS* since 1998, is a practicing psychoanalyst and psychiatrist, member and training analyst of the Swiss Psychoanalytic Association; editor of *Wunde Körper Wunde* (*Wounded Bodies: On Psychoanalytic Psychosomatics*); author of many articles in German and French on various psychoanalytic topics. He performs supervisions in Swiss and German Psychiatric and Psychosomatic Institutions.

Johannes Fehr wrote his dissertation on *Das Unbewusste und die Struktur der Sprache: Studien zu Freuds frühen Schriften.* (Zürich: Diss., 1987). In 1997 he wrote his *Habilitationsschrift* (a dissertation written for formal admission as an academic lecturer) on *Ferdinand de Saussure. Linguistik und Semiologie* (Frankfurt a.M.: Suhrkamp, 1997). He is Lecturer at the University of Zurich and Associate Director of the Collegium Helveticum.

Hans-Dieter Gondek teaches philosophy at the University of Bremen. He is a translator of Derrida, Foucault, Lacan, Merleau-Ponty, and Ricoeur. He has published *Angst? Einbildungskraft? Sprache: Ein verbindender Aufriss zwischen Freud—Kant—Lacan* (Munich: Boer, 1990), many articles in *RISS*, *Fragmente*, *Parabel*, *texte*, and *Philosophische Rundschau*. He has edited Jacques Derrida's *Vergessen wir nicht — die Psychoanalyse?* (Frankfurt: Suhrkamp, 1998) and *Jacques Lacan—Wege zu seinem Werk* (Stuttgart: Klett-Cotta, 2001).

Lucien Israël was Professor of Psychiatry at the University of Strasbourg and a practicing psychoanalyst. He was a member of the *École freudienne* and the author of many books. His *L'hystérique, le sexe et le médecin* appeared in German translation under the title *Die unerhörte Botschaft der Hysterie* (Munich: Reinhardt, 2001). Israël died in 1996.

Alain Juranville is a psychoanalyst and Maître de conférences at the University of Rennes where he teaches Philosophy. He has published *Lacan et la philosophie* (Paris Universitaires de France, 1984), which has been translated into German, Japanese, Portuguese and Spanish; *Der psychoanalytische Diskurs nach Lacan* (RISS-Verlag, Zürich 1994), and many articles in France. In 2000 he published a three-volume work: *La philosophie comme savoir de l'existence:* vol. I: *L'altérité,* vol. 1, *Le jeu,* vol. 2, and *L'inconscient,* vol. 3 (Paris: Press Universitaires de France, 2000). Further volumes of the enterprise will follow.

Anne Juranville is Professor of Clinical Psychopathology at the University of Nice (France), author of *La femme et la mélancholie* (Paris: Press Universitaires de France, 1993) (Spanish translation published by Nueva Vision, Buenos Aires), and *Figures de la possession. Actualité psychanalytique du démoniaque* (Presses Universitaires de Grenoble, 2000).

Christian Kläui, co-editor of *RISS* since 1998, is a practicing psychiatrist and psychoanalyst in Basel, Switzerland, and the author of theoretical and clinical articles on psychoanalysis.

Sebastian Leikert is Doctor of Psychoanalysis and a practicing psychoanalyst in Karlsruhe. Among his publications are "Das Objekt des Geniessens in der Musik," *RISS*, "Johann Sebastian Bach: Einschreibung des Vaternames im Wohltemperierten Klavier," *Psyche* (1996), and "Orpheusmythos und Symbolisierung des primären Verlusts: Genetische und Linguistische Aspekte der Musikerfahrung," *Psyche* 2001.

Monique David-Ménard is a practicing psychoanalyst and teaches philosophy at the University of Paris. She has published *L'hystérique entre Freud et Lacan* (Paris: Editions Universitaires, 1983); in English *Hysteria from Freud to Lacan: Body and Language in Psychoanalysis* (Ithaca: Cornell University Press, 1989); *La folie dans la raison pure/ Kant, lecteur de Swedenborg* (Paris: Vrin, 1990); and articles in *RISS* and *Die Philosophin*.

André Michels is a practicing psychiatrist and psychoanalyst in Luxembourg and Paris, co-editor of the journal *apertura* (until 1994) and of *Jahrbuch für klinische Psychoanalyse* (Tübingen: Diskord, 1998–2002) 4 volumes published, and editor of the collection of essays, *Actualité de l'hystérie* (Paris: Erès, 2002). He has also authored many articles.

August Ruhs is Doctor of Medicine, a psychiatrist, a teaching psychoanalyst, and Professor and deputy director at the Clinic of Depth Psychology and Psychotherapy at the University of Vienna. He is a founding member of the *Neue Wiener Gruppe/Lacan Schule* and co-editor of *texte. psychoanalyse. ästhetik. kulturkritik* (Vienna: Passagen Verlag).

Joachim Saalfrank is a psychologist and has published a number of articles in *RISS*.

Regula Schindler is a practicing psychoanalyst and was co-editor of *RISS* until 1993. She has published many articles in a wide array of journals.

Dieter Sträuli was co-editor of *RISS* until 1993, and is an Associate Professor in the Psychology Department at the University of Zurich.

Samuel Weber is Avalon Foundation Professor of Humanities at Northwestern University and has worked as a dramaturgist in theater and opera. His publications include: *Rückkehr zu Freud: Jacques Lacans Entstellung der Psychoanalyse* (Berlin, 1978; in English *Return to Freud: Jacques Lacan's Dislocation of Psychoanalysis* [Cambridge: Cambridge University Press, 1991]); *The Legend of Freud* (2nd edition, Stanford: Stanford University Press, 2000); *Institution and Interpretation*, (Stanford: Stanford University Press, 1987); and *Unwrapping Balzac*, (Toronto: University of Toronto Press, 1979).

Elisabeth Widmer is a practicing child psychoanalyst and author of numerous articles. She translated Françoise Dolto's *L'image inconscient du corps* (*Das unbewußte Körperbild* [Berlin: Quadriga, 1987]).

Peter Widmer is a practicing psychoanalyst and founder and publisher of *RISS*. He has taught as a Visiting Professor at the University of Innsbruck and the University of Kyoto. He is the author of *Subversion des Begehrens: Jacques Lacan oder die zweite Revolution der Psychoanalyse* (Frankfurt am Main: Fischer, 1990); *Die Lust am Verbotenen und die Notwendigkeit Grenzen zu überschreiten* (Zurich: Kreuz Verlag 1991), and many articles in *Psyche, texte*, and *RISS*. Together with André Michels, August Ruhs, Regula Schindler, and Elisabeth Widmer, he participated in the 1993 founding of the *Assoziation für die Freudsche Analyse* (of which Christian Kläui has in the meantime also become a member). Peter and Elisabeth Widmer also participated in the 1997 founding of the *Lacan Seminar Zürich* (also joined, in the meantime, by Regula Schindler).

Index

222; knowledgeable, 56; organization of, 221; perception and, 222, 229, 233, 234; protection against death, 223; as repression of the unconscious, 56; theory of, 243
Conservatism, 128
Construction, 128
Countertransference, 142
Cratylus (Plato), 133
Creativity, 114; melancholia and, 136
Critique of Pure Reason (Kant), 236n31
Crucifixion: as negation, 6
Cry of the angel, 5, 13, 14, 17
Cubism, 130, 192
The Cuisine of Sacrifice in Greek Space (Détienne), 245, 260
Cultural: denial, 60; identity, 86; law, 6; revolution, 60; ritualization, 85
Culture: construction of, 274; digital, 51; global, 51; images of, 82; Judeo-Christian, 34; neurosis and, 30; origin of, 19, 20, 33, 132, 260, 270, 271; sexual relations and, 60

Dada, 3, 176
Dada (journal), 175
Dali, Salvador, 6, 28
Dance, 91
Danger, 217, 232
David-Ménard, Monique, 1, 128, 147–57
Death: desire and, 127, 134; drive, 127, 128, 132, 134, 138, 197, 200, 201, 206, 221, 274, 276; postponement of, 224; preservation of life and, 223; as protection against death, 223; real, 22; self-love of life and, 223; symbolic, 22–23; wish, 273
Death wish, 19; articulated by analysands, 25; directed at imaginary aspects of father, 25; Freud on, 24
Deception, 256
Defense mechanisms: in pedophilia, 29
Delirium: phases in, 191–92
Delusion: religious, 250, 251
"Demand and Wish" (Israel), 129, 175–87
Democracy: aggression in, 274; egalitarian, 273; establishment of laws in, 276, 277; exception to, 271, 272, 273; Freud and, 269–85; hysteria and, 200; laziness of humankind and, 275; neurosis and, 200; origin of, 200; privileges of the One in, 272; psychoanalysis and, 200, 269–85; rivalry and, 274; skepticism over existence

of, 275; slaying of the primal father and, 272
Democracy (RISS), 2
Denial, 86; perversion and, 142
Dependence, 54
Depersonalization: body image and, 80–81; disturbance of, 95
Depression, 131–43; aggression in, 137; desire to evade desire in, 140; exhaustion, 140; gender and, 140; hysteria and, 140; identity in, 140; narcissistic misrecognition and, 143; neurotic, 140; non-psychotic, 127; nostalgia in, 128; obsession compulsion and, 140; persistence of, 142; reactive, 140; relinquishment of desire in, 127; uncritical diagnosis of, 140; women and, 128
Derrida, Jacques, 55, 87, 199, 205, 223; Of *Grammatology*, 205; on woman, 79
Derrida/Lacan (RISS), 2
Descartes, René, 29, 125n58, 203, 228, 229, 290
Desire: analyst as cause of, 42; as anonymous process, 56; anxiety of, 49; appearance and, 92; based on insurmountable split, 24, 50, 92; become-figure, 7; cause of, 108; condition for, 91; for death, 127, 134; defined by signifying cut, 91; demand and, 92; dependency on desire of the Other, 62; depression and, 127, 140, 141; for desire, 92; directed at a lack, 24, 50, 92; directed at objects other than the mother, 19, 20; as dissatisfied desire, 93; drive-backed, 20; emerging, 81; epithymetic, 254; for forbidden object, 160; guarantor of, 39; human, 295; hysterical, 91; identificatory, 7, 38; incestuous, 110, 295; for knowledge, 134; as lack, 59; maternal, 25, 30, 31, 163, 164, 169; mobile nature of, 49; of the mother, 102; movement of, 59; neurotic, 91; nonsymmetrical types, 81; objects of, 39, 87; original subject of, 55–56; origin of, 12; of the Other, 87, 103, 122n5, 217, 233, 243, 258; perversion and, 86, 88; phallic, 60, 141; phallus as symbolic articulation of, 55; to possess the life of another, 24; power of, 65; as principle aimed at a lack, 38; prohibited, 93; pure, 7, 243, 254; realization of, 38; regulation of, 92; representative object of, 59; resulting from experience of lack, 23; searching for object, 23; sexual,

of, 104; as total love object, 61; wish to remain with, 182

the Mother (RISS), 2

Mourning, 3; authenticity and, 82; language and, 135; in melancholia, 88, 139; by parents, 23; sublimation and, 135

"Mourning and Melancholia" (Freud), 131

Murder: demand for possession and, 24; of father, 19; motive for, 24; real, 24, 25; symbolic, 20, 24, 26, 50

Music: "blue note" in, 14; cadenzas in, 15; concealed meanings in, 9; cultural association with Germany, 5; development of, 13; experienced in bodily Real, 17n3; instrumental, 15; *jouissance in,* 9–17; opposition of note and pause in, 16; perversion and, 9, 12; psychoanalysis and, 9; score in, 10, 17n3; signifier in, 10

Music (RISS), 2

"My Views on the Part Played by Sexuality in the Aetiology of the Neuroses" (Freud), 271

Nabokov, Vladimir, 38, 39

Name-of-the-Father, 107, 217; closing from its position in the signifier, 113; foreclosure of, 51, 83, 129, 180, 181, 194; identification with, 61, 113; metaphorical function of, 90; position in the Symbolic, 113; the Real and, 103, 113, 114; saving, 110; as signifier, 297; turned object, 86

Narcissism, 131, 132, 138, 143; ego and, 56; Freud and, 45; incest prohibition and, 164; melancholia and, 127; perversion and, 90; phallic, 82; primary, 19, 26; secondary, 164; strengthening, 283

Narcissus, 116

Narrative: mythical, 133

Nature: laws of, 5; as tragic, 5

Necrophilia, 7

Negation, 296

Negation deliria, 80

"Negation" (Freud), 86

Nessus shirt, 75

Neurasthenia, 212, 213, 214

Neurosis: anxiety, 211, 212, 213, 214, 216; constitutive, 79–80; culture and, 30; disturbed body image in, 97n5; fatherward, 113, 115; gender and, 283; making one's self into subject in, 93; obsessive, 61; prohibition of *jouissance in,* 13; relation to democracy in, 200, 283; role of object in, 11

Nietzsche, Friedrich, 8, 90; art and, 8; *The Gay Science,* 45; understanding of relationship between truth and aesthetics, 46; on woman, 79

Noah's cloak, 109

Object: bad part, 134; cause-of-desire, 256, 257; of desire, 39; of the drive, 11; essence as failure, 134; extimate, 199; forbidden, 134, 160; good, 134; of identification, 38; inner, 83; loss of the thing in, 88; lost, 11, 132, 134, 135; as most variable aspect of the drive, 141; pathological, 199; in relation to death drive, 134; representation by memory trace, 11; role in neurosis, 11; sexual, 29; substitution and, 134; voice as, 17; wish, 185

Objectivism, 64; pornographic, 64; scientific, 64, 66

"The Object of *Jouissance* in Music" (Leikert), 5, 9–17

Object (RISS), 2

Objet a, 83, 87, 92, 107, 108, 200, 230, 232, 233, 255, 293; as element of fantasm, 16; logic of, 199, 258; nature of, 16; as object of *jouissance,* 11; as voice, 5

Objet petit a, 89, 217

Objet sonore, 14

Obsession compulsion, 283; depression and, 140; fabrication of an impossible in, 93; nonrelationship with signifier, 108

Obsession (RISS), 2

Odysseus, 38

Oedipus, 32, 33, 132, 273; guilt and, 32, 33; symbolic, 296

Oedipus complex, 135, 275, 283, 295; as constructed perverse structure, 20, 21; critiques of, 19, 20; desires of the child in, 32; directed at the father, 24–25; dominance of the masculine in, 21; female, 21; first to commit unnatural act, 19; foundations for structure of, 11; Freud and, 19; generational conflict and, 21; incest prohibition and, 132; loss inherent in, 19, 20, 33, 132; origin in descendant generation, 21; parental hatred for children in, 5; phylogenesis and, 19; as protective screen for the Real, 134; resolution of, 165; rivalry in, 26; role of parental desire in, 21; sexual identity and, 55; sexualization of, 21; as symptom, 117